DATE DUE

Pitt Latin American Series

CUBA

After the Cold War

Carmelo Mesa-Lago

Editor

UNIVERSITY OF PITTSBURGH PRESS

PITTSBURGH AND LONDON

Published by the University of Pittsburgh Press, Pittsburgh, Pa., 15260
Copyright © 1993, University of Pittsburgh Press
All rights reserved
Manufactured in the United States of America
Printed on acid-free paper

Library of Congress Cataloging-in-Publication Data

Cuba after the Cold War / Carmelo Mesa-Lago, editor.
   p.   cm. — (Pitt Latin American series)
   Includes bibliographical references.
   ISBN 0-8229-3749-2(alk. paper). — ISBN 0-8229-5503-2 (pbk. : alk.
paper)
   1. Cuba—Economic policy.   2. Cuba—Economic conditions—1959–
3. Cuba—Politics and government—1959–   I. Mesa-Lago, Carmelo,
1934–   II. Series.
HC 152.5.C797   1993
338.97291′009′049—dc20   92-50847
                                                                                        CIP

A CIP catalogue record for this book is available from the British Library.
Eurospan, London

For Shirley A. Kregar,
who has done so much for Latin American Studies
at the University of Pittsburgh,
in her twenty-fifth year of service.

CONTENTS

ACKNOWLEDGMENTS

THE RESEARCH, international conference, and publication of this book were made possible by a generous grant from the Andrew W. Mellon Foundation in 1991–92, thus continuing the financial support awarded in 1979 and 1984 to the Center for Latin American Studies (CLAS) at the University of Pittsburgh. The center supported the project in each of several facets. Special thanks to the CLAS staff: Former Director Mitchell A. Seligson for his leadership of the entire project; Secretary to the Director Linda Ireland who organized the international conference and provided administrative support for the project; Assistant Director Shirley A. Kregar who coordinated production of the manuscript with the University of Pittsburgh Press; Lillian Thomas who did a first editing of the manuscript, with final editing done by Jane Flanders at the University of Pittsburgh Press; Associate Director John Frechione who designed the conference brochure and took care of many other aspects of the project; administrator Lynn Young for handling all the finances; Nichole Parker, Ivonne Martínez, and Connie Acosta for clerical assistance; and Latin American Librarian Eduardo Lozano, the builder of the Cuban collection at Pitt that was so useful for the researchers.

The four chapters by Carmelo Mesa-Lago and the overall editing work were partly carried out during a sabbatical leave from the University of Pittsburgh, grants awarded by the Howard Heinz Endowment and the Alexander von Humboldt Stiftung, and sojourns at the Instituto Universitario Ortega y Gasset (Madrid) and Max-Planck-Institut für Ausländisches und Internationales Sozialrecht (Munich). None of these institutions is responsible for the contents of this volume; each author is solely responsible for opinions and statements in his or her chapter.

CUBA

After the Cold War

1

Introduction: Cuba, the Last Communist Warrior

◆ ◆ ◆

CARMELO MESA-LAGO

An Island Where Orthodoxy Survives

COMMUNIST REGIMES have collapsed all over Europe, and those few that still remain in Asia and Africa are busy implementing or studying market-oriented economic reforms. The Soviet Union has disappeared, Marxism-Leninism is universally in crisis, and the cold war era has ended. Cuba is the only country left in the world (with the possible exception of North Korea) with both an orthodox Communist regime and a socialist Command economy. Furthermore, since the mid-1980s, President Fidel Castro has introduced antimarket reforms and, in the 1990s, has become virtually the last defender of orthodox Marxism-Leninism. The Fourth Congress of the Cuban Communist party, held in October 1991, rejected market-oriented reforms and party pluralism, while minor concessions granted by the congress (such as direct election of members of the National Assembly and more opening to foreign investment) have not significantly changed the politico-economic nature of the regime. Since 1990, Castro's speeches always end with the motto ''Socialism or death.'' Some observers believe that he has developed a bunker mentality and, in the spirit of Numancia, is willing to sacrifice the entire country defending the revolution and Communism.

Cuba's stand is even more remarkable if one considers that it was for three decades the socialist nation most dependent on trade and aid from the Soviet Union and the Council for Mutual Economic Assistance

(CMEA). Not only has such economic support entirely ceased, but also trade with the former USSR has declined by at least one-half, while aid and trade with Eastern Europe have virtually vanished. In addition, the United States (now the only superpower) has tightened the thirty-year-old embargo against the island and has intensified its pressure on other countries to cut their trade with Cuba. Finally, many former governments that were Cuba's allies in Latin America and the Caribbean are no longer in power, and the extreme Left is in disarray throughout the region. And yet, contrary to expectation, the fall of the East European dominos did not reach Cuba; its orthodox regime has so far survived in the post-cold war era, despite Cuba's increasing isolation and appalling economic deterioration.

This book deals with the crucial issues and questions raised above. The introduction describes the disintegration of the socialist camp and the ensuing conflicts between Cuba, on the one hand, and the USSR and East European countries on the other. The remaining chapters elaborate on the causes of the downfall of the Soviet bloc nations, the impact of their fall on Cuba, and the implications of these historic changes for Latin America.

Disintegration of the Socialist Camp and Increasing Conflicts with Cuba

Castro and the End of European Communism

After the introduction of perestroika and glasnost, the Soviet Union and Cuba slowly moved apart. In 1986–88, Castro did not directly criticize the Soviet reforms but chastised the "errors" Committed by Cuban planners in 1976–85 by "mechanically copying" the timid pre-Gorbachev economic reform because it attempted to use capitalist economic laws and categories (such as profit) to build socialism, led to a decline in the Communist party's role, and promoted corruption and crime—thus weakening the people's willingness to defend the revolution at home and socialism abroad. In 1986, Castro launched an economic counter reform (the Rectification Process) that set Cuba against the worldwide socialist current of market reform (see chapter 5). He also noted that the dramatic improvement in USSR-U.S. relations had resulted in peace among the two superpowers, but that the United States' war against small socialist countries such as his own continued. During

Gorbachev's visit to Havana in April 1989, Castro validated his own choice of models, stating that he respected the reforms taking place in Eastern Europe, even the building of capitalism. But he also warned that those reforms were flawed and eventually would be rectified, as was happening in Cuba.[1] The dramatic changes that took place in Eastern Europe and the USSR in 1989–90 prompted Castro to make a stronger, more direct criticism of the reforms. At first he excluded the USSR from this critique but it often happened that the Soviet leaders eventually joined Eastern Europe in some of the measures previously criticized by Castro. On other occasions, he obliquely criticized a step taken by the Soviet government without naming that country.[2]

According to Castro, the socialist camp had disintegrated both politically and economically, and a rapid transition was taking place, characterized by the following features: (1) criticism of Marxism-Leninism, slander against socialism, and growing antiCommunist feelings ("It is disgusting to see how many people, even in the USSR itself, are engaged in denying and destroying . . . the Soviet history and Lenin's role"); (2) elimination of the constitutional article that guaranteed the leading role of the Communist party (Castro said that the USSR was an exception just a few days before the Soviet party followed suit); (3) toleration of plural parties and representative democracy, dropping the name "Communist" from the party, and removing that party from power; (4) reintroduction of private property, a market economy, and capitalism ("U.S. presidential advisors and other experts are programming capitalist development in Eastern European countries. . . . Imperialism is urging these countries to become recipients of its surplus capital . . . and to join [them] in plundering the Third World"); (5) promotion, inside the USSR, of a media campaign against economic aid and preferential trade with Cuba ("Some publications [are] calling for an end to fair and equitable trade relations . . . to begin practicing unequal trade by selling its products to us at even higher prices and buying ours at even lower prices, just as the U.S. does with other Third World countries . . . in short they want the USSR to join the U.S. blockade against Cuba"); and (6) also in the USSR, increasing conflict among nationalities, strikes, and states moving to independence, which could lead to "a great civil war in the Soviet Union" or that country's total collapse.

Confronting these trends, Castro stressed the principles enshrined in Cuban socialism: (1) continuation of Marxism-Leninism ("When others are . . . removing Lenin's name from streets and parks and destroying statues of Marx, Lenin and Engels, we continue to build them here''); (2) ratification of the constitutional principle of the Communist party's monopoly on power and rejection—as capitalist deviations—of a multiparty system and opposition within the National Assembly (''We will never renounce the glorious title of socialists and Communists . . . we see the party ruling indefinitely''); (3) rejection of market-oriented reforms (''Nowadays the advocates of capitalist reforms are called progressive [while] the defenders of Marxism-Leninism . . . [and] of Communism are called rigid. Long live rigidity!''); and (4) rejection of private ownership of the means of production by individuals, cooperatives, or groups (''There can be no other concept of socialism than the people [the state] being the owner of the means of production.'' In line with these principles, free peasant markets were abolished in Cuba, small private manufacturing activities were banned, private home construction and exchanges were restricted, and self-employment was curtailed. The gap between the USSR and Cuba thus widened.[3]

According to Castro, speaking in 1989 and 1990, the dramatic changes occurring in Eastern Europe and the USSR posed sinister political and economic threats for Cuba. ''The biggest problem is the euphoria of the imperialists . . . [who argue that] if socialism disintegrated, the Cuban revolution would disappear. This reasoning increases the aggressiveness and hostility of the U.S. towards us.'' A second problem was the ''extremely serious lack of supplies,'' the worst case being fuel, since the USSR might curtail or even cut off oil supplies; in addition, due to strikes and disruption of production in the USSR, materials and equipment could be delayed or not arrive at all. A possible scenario could be a total blockade imposed by the United States: ''Not a single liter of gasoline, not an ounce of food, not a single bullet would enter the country.''

Worst-case scenarios envisioned by Castro were ''a war of attrition . . . and, finally . . . an invasion of our country.'' If the described trends continue, ''the world would move from bipolarity toward unipolarity under U.S. control,'' thereby increasing the probability of U.S. aggression against Cuba. Finally, Castro believed that the United States, together with other developed nations, was pressuring the USSR (and attaching conditions for aid to that country) to end its economic and military assistance to Cuba. Except for a total U.S. blockade or invasion of

Cuba, all Castro's fears materialized in the early 1990s (see chapters 3 and 5).

"Reactionaries and imperialists believe"—said Castro—"that we won't be able to overcome these difficulties . . . even some friends are already mourning us as if we were dead already and others believe that the revolution may collapse [as in other socialist countries]." But he staunchly rejected that outcome:

> For the last ten years we have been strengthening our defenses . . . and getting ready. . . . If fate were to decree that one day we would be among the last bastions of socialism, we would defend this bulwark until the last drop of our blood. . . . Our challenge has no parallel in history . . . we are confronting an imperialist system at the height of its power . . . if the USSR were to disappear, we would still go on defending socialism. . . . Perhaps one day we will have to apply the concepts of the War of All the People to ensure the survival of the revolution. . . . Socialism or death!

As this book goes to press, most of Castro's predictions have come true.

Soviet and East European Criticism of Cuba

Until 1987, the Soviet press and specialized journals praised Cuban achievements but, from the beginning of that year, there was increasing criticism of Cuba in publications such as *Moscow News, New Times, Sputnik, Literaturnaya Gazeta, Pravda, Izvestia,* and *Komsomolskaya Pravda,* as well as in the TV newscast "Vremya."[4] (Members of the Soviet Parliament and academia also were skeptical.) Critics pointed to persistent flaws in the Cuban economy such as a slowdown in development, poor labor productivity, a third of the enterprises operating at a loss, sugar monoculture and export concentration, low yields in agriculture and in the sugar industry, extensive food rationing, and a severe housing shortage. Advances in social services were still praised, but some critics began to notice that some of those services (for example, health care) were better than those in the USSR, which was partly footing the bill. Soviet critics saw the costs of Cuba's projected social improvements as contrary to common sense and economically unfeasible. And Cuba's expenditures in defense (and deployment of troops abroad) were chastised as excessive, not clearly justified, and costly in terms of development.

The Rectification Process was seen as an idealistic error long ago corrected in socialist countries because economic mechanisms (such as profit) are absolutely necessary, while moral incentives cannot work in the long run—excessive egalitarianism dampens initiative. Cuba was portrayed as an impoverished police state that follows ideological dogmas and administrative economic models—at best mimicking those of Brezhnev's era, at worst a remnant of Stalinism. In view of Cuba's flaws, Soviet critics judged Castro's attacks against economic reform in socialist countries to be ill-founded.

A second focus of criticism was the cost and misuse of Soviet economic aid. The Cuban debt, first unveiled in the Soviet Parliament in 1989 and later in the news media, was considered excessive, and the result of overly generous terms—low interest rates, long amortization periods, and several postponements of principal and interest. Soviet largesse was also noted in preferential prices paid for Cuban sugar and nickel as well as charging low prices for Soviet oil. Additionally, shipping services were subsidized, and the USSR paid hard currency to Cuba for the oil committed for delivery but not consumed by the island. As Cole Blasier found in conversations with Muscovites in 1991 (described in chapter 3), such generosity was increasingly conspicuous in the midst of growing scarcities in the USSR. Furthermore, Soviet aid was said to be used inefficiently by Cuba because of flawed planning, delays in installing imported equipment, poor labor discipline, and underused Soviet technical personnel. Last but not least, the Soviets regarded Cuban exports as deficient; for example, sugar exports had been lower than planned for several years.

A University of Miami seminar in the spring of 1990 brought together U.S. scholars, Cuban-American politicians, and a team of Soviet congressmen, government advisors, journalists, and scholars. Some of the U.S. participants exhorted the Soviets to end economic aid to Cuba and to promote democratic change in that country. Sergio Mikoyan (son of Anastas Mikoyan and an expert on Latin America) said, "Like all countries in the world, [Cuba] should hold democratic elections and allow political opposition parties." Giorgi Arbatov (an advisor to Gorbachev) suggested that Cuba was no longer a priority for the USSR, that "many things are at stake domestically," and that "empires are very expensive and yield few benefits." He added that Soviet aid, often excessive and generously granted, had been wasted by inefficient bureaucratic administrations. Soon after this meeting, the Cuban Ministry of Foreign Relations widely distributed a statement—attributed to its Soviet counterpart—denying that the Soviet team was trying to establish ties with the Cuban exile Community in Miami and declaring that Soviet-Cuban ties were as solid as ever.[5]

Castro's reactions to the above criticism—until the downfall of Soviet Communism in 1991—were mostly cautious and moderate: "There are people in the USSR—not in the government, not in the Party, but in the media and the parliament—who favor suppressing the type of economic relations that exists between the USSR and Cuba. . . . We didn't hesitate to stop the circulation of certain Soviet publications [*Moscow News, New Times, Sputnik*] that are full of poison against the USSR itself and socialism. . . . Imperialism, reactionary forces and the counter-revolution are responsible for that tone."[6]

The Cuban press also featured supportive Comments by sympathetic Soviet experts[7] and, even more prominently, by government and military authorities. These included an interview with Leonid I. Abalkin, vice chairman of the USSR Council of Ministers, on the importance of Cuban exports to the USSR; a statement by Egor Ligachov, Politburo member and leading orthodox ideologist, in favor of international solidarity and strengthening links between the two countries; a rejection by Valentin Falin, chief of the CPSU's International Section, and by Aleksandr S. Dzasokov, president of the Soviet Parliament's International Department, of pressure from congressional groups seeking to cut economic aid to Cuba; and the declaration by Gen. M. A. Moiseev, Commander of the Soviet armed forces, on a visit to Havana that Soviet ties with Cuba were strong and would continue that way. The latter prompted the following response from Gen. Ulises Rosales, chief of Cuba's General Army Staff: "We have embraced the Soviet generals just as in the best times; . . . we confront the same problems and every day our friendship deepens."[8] Havana lobbied intensively to have well-known Soviet authorities visit Cuba to see for themselves that the USSR was not giving something for nothing. When Gorbachev moved away from the forces of reform toward orthodoxy, Castro became more daring in his criticism of those who opposed him in the USSR; hence at the end of 1990, he depicted them as "a group of mercenaries and miserable CIA sellouts."[9]

Cuba adopted a cautiously neutral position during the attempted coup in the USSR in 1991; its failure led to the elimination not only of those Soviet leaders who supported aid and strong ties with Cuba but also of sympathetic institutions such as the KGB and the Soviet Communist party. Soviet aid stopped at the end of 1991, and open criticism of the USSR (and later the CIS) was unleashed in Cuba thereafter (see chapters 3 and 5).

In mid-1989, as a result of the changes in Eastern Europe, the Hungarian, Czechoslovakian, and Polish news media also began to criticize Cuba. The official publication of the Hungarian Patriotic People's Front expressed doubts that Castro had no foreknowledge of the drug dealings of the executed Gen. Arnaldo Ochoa and suggested that he was a victim of a power struggle; in addition, it reported increasing discontent in the midst of an "economy in ruins." A caustic response from Havana prompted the Hungarians to trace a parallel between the democratization of their country, which had led to journalistic freedom, and the lack of liberty in Cuba, where even Soviet publications were banned. Next, the Hungarian government's official newspaper analyzed the negative consequences of the Rectification Process (shortages, expanding rationing, and "paralysis of creative economic thought") as well as other problems such as trials, drugs, and exiles which "are not sources of pride in the Latin American bastion of 'real socialism.' " Finally, it noted that Cubans could be ideological radicals because they were "eating others' bread and building socialism at the expense of another country." In late 1990, a Hungarian journalist was deported for reporting that two Iraqi oil tankers had unloaded in Havana harbor in violation of the UN embargo.[10]

Castro's support of the Soviet invasion of Czechoslovakia could not be forgotten. This hostility was aggravated in 1990 when a correspondent from Radio Prague was deported because of a report he filed on the crisis in Cuba. Soon after, a cameraman from Czech television was beaten, handcuffed, and taken to a police station; eventually he was freed with an apology from the Ministry of Foreign Relations. In the same year, President Vaclav Havel met with Cuban exiles and condemned the imprisonment of dissidents in Cuba; a serious incident occurred when several Cubans took asylum in the Czech embassy in Havana; and Czechoslovakia ceased to represent Cuban interests in Washington.

Castro's antipathy for the Solidarity movement, unveiled as early as the 1981 military coup in Poland, was exacerbated when Lech Walesa received the exiled Cuban poet and human rights activist Armando Valladares as a "freedom fighter" in Warsaw. The climax occurred in March 1990 when Czechoslovakia and Poland sponsored a UN resolution criticizing Cuba's violations of human rights; the resolution was approved with votes from Bulgaria and Hungary (the USSR voted against it), an action called treason by Castro and by Cuba's party newspaper.[11] East European countries were accused of being "used in the worldwide campaign against socialism carried out by the United States" and of abandoning political principles in the quest for economic profit.[12]

The death of the CMEA in 1991 and the downfall of Communist leaders in virtually all Eastern European countries led to a termination of all economic aid to Cuba and the near disappearance of trade with the island. The Soviet and East European news media widely criticized Cuba's Fourth Party Congress because it did not allow the presence of foreign journalists, did not approve any serious resolutions, rejected all attempts to change the island's orthodox economic model and introduce private initiative and, hence, "signed the condemnation" of the Cuban regime.[13] By 1992 Castro claimed that Eastern Europe and the former USSR had joined the United States in the embargo against Cuba (see chapters 2 and 5).

The Research Project and the Scope of the Book

This book represents a multidisciplinary and multiregional approach. The project began in 1990 with the organizaiton of a research team of internationally known economists and political scientists, experts on Cuba, Eastern Europe, the USSR, and Latin America. Scholars conducted field research in fifteen countries (including formal surveys and informal interviews) and worked with hundreds of printed materials, transcripts of TV and radio newscasts, and unpublished documents. The research team met twice to coordinate their various projects. Draft papers were thoroughly reviewed by authorities in their fields and presented at two international conferences before final revisions that updated their research as late as April 1992.[14]

Ronald H. Linden in chapter 2 asks whether the recent economic transitions in Eastern Europe are relevant to Cuba, identifying common economic and political features among the Soviet-dominated East European countries before the 1989–90 revolutions, describing how these revolutions erupted, and noting relevant differences. Among the underlying factors contributing to change, Linden discusses the lack of the regimes' political legitimacy; forced land collectivization and other measures that fueled the opposition: the rise of a more aggressive younger generation; a deteriorating economy; and the influence of Western Europe as a countermodel. "Proximate factors" of change were the emergence of a domestic opposition and mass politics; the contagion factor or domino effect; Soviet acquiescence and even support for change; military inertia; and a history of past rebellion. Linden's speculations about the impact of the downfall of East European socialism on Cuba lay the groundwork for chapter 10.

In chapter 3, Cole Blasier studies the end of the thirty-year Soviet-Cuban politico-economic partnership and the delicate triangulated relationship linking the USSR, Cuba, and the United States. He describes how the Soviet-Cuban tie first emerged and the debate between "conservatives" and "refomists" about its continuation arising from the dispute in the USSR about the nature of its own politico-economic system. Gorbachev's foreign policy shift from confrontation toward cooperation with the United States also induced a withdrawal from intervention in Latin America and Africa—changes that eliminated major common interests between Cuba and the USSR and threatened Castro's regime. Blasier looks at possible future relations that might protect what is left of Soviet interest and influence in Cuba.

Chapter 4, by Jorge I. Domínguez, analyzes what factors made Cuba receptive to external ideas (mostly from the socialist world) between the early 1960s and the mid-1980s: severity of state crises, leadership unity, good Soviet-Cuban relations, and the influence of economists on policy. When those factors were absent, there was a closing to external ideas. The concepts of glasnost and perestroika enjoyed a modest receptivity in Cuba until 1987 (through subtle techniques), but that small zone of freedom disappeared by 1989. Castro was responsible for that closing and he has imposed new techniques of control and repression.

In chapter 5 Carmelo Mesa-Lago studies the domestic and external changes that affected the Cuban economy between 1986 and 1992: the antimarket Rectification Process (RP) and other recentralization measures and their drawbacks; the termination of the Cuban-Soviet economic relationship; and the virtual disappearance of economic relations with Eastern European countries. He describes the adjustment policies made necessary by these events and assesses the overall economic and social effects of the crisis.

In chapter 6 Mesa-Lago evaluates Cuba's current policies to confront the crisis and the possibility of a market-oriented reform. He assesses the difficulty of expanding trade with other countries, of diversifying the economy away from sugar with nontraditional exports and tourism, of attracting foreign capital and finding new sources of energy to compensate for the massive cut in oil supplies. He analyzes the output targets of the crucial Food Program, finding them unrealistic, as even Castro now admits. He foresees continuous gradual economic deterioration and increasing discontent among the people.

Chapter 7, by Mitchell A. Seligson, studies Cuba in relation to Central America—in the 1980s a major focus for superpower rivalry in the hemisphere. However, with the end of the cold war and less threat of Cuban intervention in the region, trade relations could develop between Cuba and Central America. Crucial issues are what Central Americans think of Cuba, the United States, and other nations, and how they balance the perceived threat of communism against the potential benefits of market relations with Cuba. Seligson's chapter answers these questions by describing the results of a survey of 4,000 respondents in the Central American countries and Panama.

In chapter 8, Silvia Borzutzky and Aldo Vacs evaluate the impact of the collapse of the Soviet bloc and the Cuban crisis on Southern Cone communist and socialist parties, after more than a decade or more of military repression. All leftist parties in the region have suffered blows to their morale. Socialists have adapted variously by renouncing strict Marxism-Leninism and armed struggle and by supporting pluralist democracy and a market economy. Communist parties—more severely affected, losing financial support from the USSR—have typically split into reformist and orthodox factions. Borzutzky and Vacs discuss Castro's former influence on the Latin American Left based on his charisma, successful social policies, and defiance of the United States with Soviet support in a bipolar world; now, however, both Castro and Cuba are criticized by Latin America's socialists and reformed communists. But the region's economic crisis continues to stir discontent, so there is perhaps still a role for the Left to play—or, in its absence—for a new brand of unpredictable nationalism.

Cuba's potential strategy for a transition to a market economy is addressed in chapter 9 by Jan Svejnar and Jorge Pérez-López. Whereas

Cuba's system resembles those of many centrally planned economies—whose moves toward a market economy are detailed in the chapter—it has unique features that could either make the transition more difficult or facilitate it. The authors describe the serious obstacles to stabilizing the Cuban economy: a budget deficit, state subsidies, monetary overhang, and debt per capita—all possibly the highest within the defunct CMEA. Overwhelming dependence on sugar, very small trade with market economies, and no membership in international financial organizations are barriers to the reinsertion of Cuba in the world market. Privatization is obstructed by a very high degree of collectivization. Substantial labor redundancy, poor economic incentives, and an extensive welfare system are other problems. In the task of securing external assistance to modernize Cuba's infrastructure and attract foreign investment, however, the Cuban community abroad could be an asset.

Recapitulating previous chapters and going beyond them, Carmelo Mesa-Lago and Horst Fabian conclude by asking whether the factors that led to the downfall of socialism in Eastern Europe and the USSR are present in Cuba and describing various politico-economic scenarios for the island's possible transformation. They find that most of the factors of change are not present in Cuba except for grave economic deterioration. But Cuba's loss of a socialist community has been ideologically, politically, and economically devastating, and the current strategy seems incapable of turning the economy around. Mesa-Lago and Fabian describe five possible future scenarios, the first four under Castro, and the last without him: (1) continuation of the status quo, (2) growing militarization and repression without economic change, (3) a shift to a Chinese-Vietnamese model of political authoritarianism and market socialism, (4) democratization and market-oriented economic reform, and (5) breakdown of the regime.

Although no chapter specifically focuses on the United States, several chapters discuss the U.S. role in Cuba and the consequences of the collapse of socialism for the United States in Latin America. Blasier analyzes the triangular USSR-Cuba-U.S. relation, how it evolved under the revolution, and how it changed after Gorbachev's reforms and the collapse of socialism. Mesa-Lago deals with the United States' pressures on the Soviet Union to cut aid to Cuba, as well as tightening its embargo and the possibilities for changing that situation. Seligson studies how Central America became the focal point of cold war foreign policy, how the situation has changed, and Central American perceptions of Cuba and the United States. Borzutzky and Vacs examine Soviet and U.S. policies in South America and the dramatic changes introduced by the Gorbachev's new thinking in foreign affairs. Finally, Fabian and Mesa-Lago review the potential U.S. role in the future of Cuba.

NOTES

1. For a detailed analysis of these events and sources, see Carmelo Mesa-Lago, "Cuba's Economic Counter-Reform *(Rectificación)*: Causes, Policies and Effects," *Journal of Communist Studies* 5, no. 4 (December 1989): 99–104.

2. The remaining analysis and quotes in this chapter are based on the following speeches by Fidel Castro: "Speech at the 36th Anniversary of the Attack on the Moncada Garrison," *Granma Weekly Review* (hereafter *GWR*) 6 August 1989, pp. 3–4; "Speech on the 30th Anniversary of the Disappearance of Camilo Cienfuegos," *GWR*, 12 November 1989, pp. 2–4; "Speech at the Opening of Construction Material Complex," *GWR*, 19 November 1989, pp. 2–3; "Speech at National Funeral Services for Internationalist Fighters," *GWR*, 17 December 1989, pp. 2–3; "Fidel at the Award Ceremony," *GWR*, 31 December 1989, pp. 2–3; "Speech at the Closing Session of the 16th Congress of the CTC," *GWR*, 11 February 1990, pp. 2–4; "Discurso en la Clausura del V Congreso de la FMC," *Granma (Suplemento Especial)*, 10 March 1990, p. 5; "Speech at the Main Rally for the 37th Anniversary of the Assault on Moncada," *GWR*, 5 August 1990, pp. 3–5; and "Discurso en la Clausura del Congreso de la FEU," *Granma (Suplemento Especial)*, 31 December 1990, pp. 1–8.

3. For a comparison of Soviet and Cuban economic and political models at the end of 1990, see Carmelo Mesa-Lago, "On Rectifying Errors of a Courteous Dissenter," *Cuban Studies* 20 (1990): 87–108.

4. Vladislav Chirkov, "How Are Things, Compañeros?" and "An Uphill Task," *New Times*, 1 January 1987, pp. 18–19; ibid., 17 August 1987, p. 16; A. Mosieev, "Much Remains To Be Done: A Comment from CMEA Headquarters," *Pravda*, August 1987, p. 4; Andrei Kozyrev, "Confidence and the Balance of Interests," *International Affairs* 11 (November 1988): 3–12; *Izvestia*, 2 March 1990; *Vremya* (TV), 8 October 1987, 6 March 1990; Viktor Pyatigorski, "An Oil Drum Plus a Strong Box Stuffed with Dollars: More About Soviet Trade with Cuba," *Moscow News* 19 (20–27 May 1990): 12; Vladimir A. Orlov, "Being True to Principles or Principles Being True: Slogans and Reality in Today's Cuba," *Moscow News* 10 (18–25 March 1990): 12; *Pravda*, 8 April 1990; "Cuban Economic Trade Balance Problems," *Literaturnaya Gazeta* 16 (18 April 1990): 14; A. Kamorin, "What Are the Causes?" *Izvestia*, 31 August 1990, p. 5; and A. Novikov, "Turn Out the Lights," *Konsomolskaya Pravda*, 1 September 1990, p. 3. Possibly the most daring criticism has been on Castro's private life and wasteful means: A. Novikov ("Wives, Villas, Guards and Other Details: From Fidel's Personal Life," *Komsomolskaya Pravda*, 18 October 1990, p. 3) reported thirty-two houses at his disposal and 9,700 guards responsible for his personal security.

5. *El Nuevo Herald,* 27 May 1990, pp. 1A, 6A; 28 May 1990, pp. 1A, 6A, 1B; 3 June 1990, p. 3A. Both the *Herald* and *Time* magazine published a photo of Yuri Pavlov (Latin America expert at the Soviet Ministry of Foreign Relations) engaged in conversation with the leader of the Cuban American National Foundation, Jorge Mas Canosa. In 1990, both Rolando Bonachea (head of Radio Martí) and Heberto Padilla (renowned exiled Cuban Poet) visited Moscow.

6. Carlos Rafael Rodríguez, "A Difficult but Steady Ascent," *New Times,* 9 October 1987, p. 16; Castro, "Speech at the National Funeral"; "Speech at the Closing Session of the 16th Congress," p. 3.

7. Bogomolov, "Tackling the Problems of Growth," *New Times,* 21 September 1987, pp. 14–15; V. Venediktov, "Azúcar, naranjas y una cucharada de hiel," *Bohemia* 27 (6 July 1990): 62–63.

8. L. I. Abalkin, *Sovetskaya Rossiya,* 5 May 1990, p. 5; "Entra el XXVIII Congreso del PCUS en la segunda mitad de sus trabajos," *Granma,* 7 July 1990, p. 8; "Commitments between Cuba and the USSR Remain Valid," *GWR,* 21 October 1990, p. 1.

9. "Fidel Closing Speech at 8th Regular Session of National Assembly of People's Power," *GWR,* 13 January 1991, p. 2.

10. Gabor Nagy, "The General and Drugs," *Magyar Nemzet,* 18 July 1989, p. 2; Tibor Varkonyi, "The Granma Phenomenon," ibid., 14 August 1989, p. 2; Victor Palfi, *Magyar Hirlap,* August 1989; Csaba Nagy, *Nepszabadsag,* 13 November 1990.

11. *GWR,* 18 November 1989, p. 9; 21 January 1990, p. 9; 11 February 1990, p. 11; "Shameful Decision at UN Human Rights Commission," 18 March 1990, p. 4; Castro, "Speech at the Closing Session of 5th Congress of the FMC," *GWR,* 18 March 1990, pp. 8, 12.

12. "Trafficking in Slander," *GWR,* 13 August 1989, p. 11; "Hungarian Journalists Join AntiCuba Campaign: Shameful Path," *GWR,* 27 August 1989, p. 8; *GWR,* 22 October 1989, p. 9; "The Transfiguration of a Correspondent," *GWR,* 21 January 1990, p. 9.

13. For a summary of criticism published by *Pravda, Konsomolskaya Pravda, Moscow News,* and *Nezavisimaya Gazeta,* see *Miami Herald,* 18 October 1991.

14. Preliminary papers were completed in winter 1991 and reviewed by Ivan T. Berend (history, Hungary), Rodolfo Cerdas (political science, Costa Rica), Pedro Monreal (international relations, Cuba), Jorge Pérez-López (economics, U.S.), José Luis Rodríguez (economics, Cuba), Sergei V. Tagor (international relations, Russia), and Aldo Vacs (political science, Argentina). Papers were presented at the "Cuba in the Post Cold War Era" conference held at the University of Pittsburgh in April 1992.

The entire team then moved to Washington, D.C., where a second conference—more focused on policy—immediately followed at the Woodrow Wilson Center, coordinated by Joseph Tulchin, director of the Latin American Program. Susan Eckstein (sociology), Richard Fagen (political science), and Wayne Smith (political science), all U.S. scholars, provided commentaries. The two groups of commentators were selected to provide contrasting points of view, some of which were incorporated into the papers—in some cases meriting coauthorship.

2

Analogies and the Loss of Community: Cuba and East Europe in the 1990s

❖ ❖ ❖

Ronald H. Linden

In my view, Cuba, too, sooner or later will be affected in one form or another by what is historically inevitable, i.e., that the totalitarian systems of the communist type are at least being transformed into something else or disintegrating, that more democratic conditions are being formed.

—Vaclav Havel

THE REVOLUTIONS OF 1989 in East Europe removed from the ranks of the world socialist camp six states in six months. Within another year, two more European socialist countries, Yugoslavia and Albania, were transformed. Elsewhere other highly centralized Soviet-style socialist regimes came under pressure or were removed. Cuba now finds itself, if not totally alone, at least with substantially fewer comrades, in all senses of the word, than it had at the beginning of 1989. This chapter considers a key part of Cuba's external environment, how it has changed, and how these changes have affected and may continue to affect Cuba. This chapter is not a study of Cuba, but of developments in East Europe and, by extension, the impact of these developments on Cuba.

This impact has two dimensions. First, changes in East Europe have a possible analog effect on potential developments in Cuba; that is, they may provide both an inspiration and a model to those in Cuba who hope for similar changes in their homeland and to a regime eager to prevent just such a change. Second, whether or not the analogy holds, Cuba as an international actor has unquestionably suffered a loss of community. The removal from the socialist ranks of six, then eight, middle-sized European communist regimes robbed Cuba of both a critical reference group for its own political and economic system and a body of allies whose ideological, political, and material support could usually be counted on.

I will first sketch briefly the situation in East Europe before the revolutions of 1989, then describe and analyze the events of 1989 and their immediate aftermath. Those familiar with the Cuban situation may decide to what extent the revolutionary dynamics in East Europe are comparable to possibilities in Cuba. I will explore the changes in East Europe's international relations, focusing particularly on how they have affected the region's relations with Cuba. My discussion will cover primarily political changes, as economic ties are discussed in chapter 5.

East Europe Before the Revolutions

The establishment of communist power in East Europe after World War II produced states with certain common features, though (as with any description of East Europe) there were differences. Domestically, a central feature of all of the states was the political dominance of the communist party. The party exercised a monopoly of political power; legislatures were compliant; and party members filled responsible positions throughout the government and the economy according to the system known as the *nomenklatura*. Public opposition outside the party, ipso facto illegitimate, typically took the form of underground politics. Internal opposition, for the most part kept from public view, took the form of debates and struggles over policy and power. The official political culture stressed the inevitability of socialist victory and the ever improving lot of the workers and peasants in whose name the party governed. The regimes strove to maintain both political and ideological control by dominating the sources of information and debate.[1]

Party control in Eastern Europe, as in the Soviet Union, extended also to the economy, where the informing Marxist ideology emphasized the necessity of developing an industrial base as the precursor to socialism and communism. Thus, between 1950 and 1960 the East European Six averaged 5.6 percent annual growth in GNP per capita, with growth in industry favored over agriculture.[2] At the same time, the ideological bias against private property in general and against the peasantry in particular led to rapid collectivization. This proceeded with varying degrees of success, but in most cases produced rapid urbanization.

The communist parties of the region sought political and economic dominance due both to their ideology and old-fashioned power politics. They recognized that their control had weak roots, as in most of the countries there had been no strong indigenous support for radical socialism before the upheaval sparked by World War II. In some, strong opposition came from institutions and groups linked to previous regimes— for example the Catholic church in Poland.

Finally, the communists' political control was required by the power and desires of the Soviet Union, to which most of these regimes owed their existence. The Soviet Union wanted the East European states not simply to be aware of but to comply with its security interests in Europe. The region would provide allies—which the USSR had never had before World War II—and would strengthen its ideological profile by replicating Soviet-style socialism. From Moscow's point of view, these needs could be achieved only if control of the East European countries were assured by the communist parties—in particular those in which the Soviet Union held predominant influence.

Thus East European party leaders found themselves in a dilemma. They needed to reassure Moscow that they were in control while trying to preserve that control with a mixture of repression and conciliation at home. They needed to serve both powerful foreign and potentially dangerous domestic constituencies.[3] Because of this double bind, party leaders sometimes pictured themselves as willing to take strong reform measures, yet forced to move slowly because of presumed or real Soviet hostility to such reform.[4] The disappearance of this rationale during the time of Mikhail Gorbachev proved how fragile this method of holding power was.

Before 1989, the international politics and economics of East European states were also dominated by Soviet concerns. The region validated the position of the Soviet Union as a world power; assured it a major role in determining the future of Germany and of Europe; was expected to help protect the USSR in the event of physical attack from the West; and helped to satisfy the needs of the Soviet economy.[5]

Soviet dominance of the region was carried out through bilateral means—direct representations, visits, and agreements. This system was supplemented and legitimated by multilateral institutions intended to broaden the structure of Soviet influence and to counter nominally similar institutions that had arisen in the West. The Warsaw Pact, formed in 1955 in response to West Germany's entry into NATO, was designed to legitimize the USSR's military presence Eastern Europe—and, in the case of Czechoslovakia in 1968, its actions—while ensuring full coordination and subservience to the Soviet Union of the region's combined militaries in the event of war. The pact also advanced various Soviet foreign policy initiatives over the years.[6]

The Council for Mutual Economic Assistance (CMEA) was founded in 1949. In the early 1960s, Nikita Khrushchev sought to strengthen the organization's ability to direct and coordinate the economic plans of its members in response to the vigor of the European Economic Community and the rising political challenge from China. While the CMEA never achieved the status of a multilateral economic community, it further isolated East Europe from the world economy. Trade among the CMEA members was conducted essentially on a barter basis using an artifact known as the "transferable ruble." None of the countries' currencies was convertible even among other CMEA members, nor was there any method by which one country could settle its yearly deficit with another. New, poorer, members such as Cuba were added in 1972, and various attempts to "strengthen cooperation" within the organization were launched, but with few results.[7]

But it was bilateral Soviet economic dominance that most significantly isolated the states from the world economy. The East European economies, like that of the USSR itself, were driven not by demands or opportunities of an internal or external market, but by the exigencies of the Soviet supply system. The USSR was the largest single supplier and importer of goods produced in each of the East European states, controlling a share of trade ranging from 20 percent to nearly 60 percent as late as 1989. In the supply of energy and raw materials, Soviet dominance was even more pronounced, except for Romania, which was able until the mid-1980s largely to avoid dependence on Soviet supply. Some East European states—for example, Poland and Romania—cultivated some ties with the West or with developing countries. And economic ties did not always work to the USSR's advantage, as supplying energy to East Europe at less than world prices in return for overpriced manufactured goods constituted a substantial subsidy.[8]

Because the USSR possessed most of the energy sources of the region, the CMEA states—and even those only associated with them such as Yugoslavia—depended on a steady supply of Soviet natural resources. These were supplied at "friendship" prices which, though adjusted, still typically lagged behind world prices. This fact, plus the widespread (if erroneous) Western perception of a Soviet "umbrella" over the growing East European debt, allowed the states of East Europe to avoid painful adjustments forced by the global energy trade on more vulnerable market economies.[9]

Critical to East Europe's post-1989 attempts to enter the global economy, the USSR also dominated the region's export sales. The industrial structure of the East European states was geared toward supplying the Soviet Union, an undemanding and seemingly inexhaustible market. As a result, suppliers were held to less rigorous production standards than a global market would have imposed. The need to keep East Europe linked to the Soviet economy had political origins. Satisfying the Soviet market kept the regional hegemon satisfied, for the most part, and East European laborers employed. But there were economic consequences. The needs of the Soviet economy were not comparable to those of the West. Feeding the eastern "market" kept East European industry less competitive—a fact that was not crucial until interaction with the West increased, first in particular countries and industries, then all at once in the wake of the revolutions of 1989.

In international politics the East European states, except for Yugoslavia, Albania, and sometimes Romania, tended to support the Soviet Union and its initiatives. Bulgaria and the German Democratic Republic (GDR) were most ardent in endorsing the perspective of the "socialist commonwealth." Hungary, too, was loyal on foreign policy issues, in an almost explicit attempt to retain greater freedom for its domestic economic reforms begun in 1968. Poland was most active in pursuing economic ties with the West, but demonstrated strict solidarity on the international political front, fiercely attacking the Prague Spring reforms in 1968, for example, and then joining in the Soviet invasion of Czechoslovakia to crush them. Romania also began actively seeking Western trade and political support in the 1960s and over the next two decades pursued a foreign policy that was often at variance with Moscow's on several key issues, such as relations with China and arms control. In

1968 Romania condemned Soviet pressure on Czechoslovakia and did not join in the invasion of that country.[10] While East European countries differed in their international political behavior, and these differences grew between Brezhnev's time and Gorbachev's, until 1989 there were limits to how far they could go. Of the East European Six, not even Romania withdrew from the Warsaw Pact, for example.

The East European states were also active outside Europe. None approached the visibility of Yugoslavia, a founding member of the Non-aligned Movement, but some—for example, Romania—were active in pushing trade and diplomatic ties. Some, such as East Germany, did so partly to establish their own bona fides and partly to make themselves indispensable to Soviet foreign policy.[11] In international forums and through bilateral ties, including trade, most of the East European states demonstrated firm ties to Arab countries, to Angola, Ethiopia under Mengistu, and to Fidel Castro's Cuba.[12]

The Revolutions of 1989 and 1990

1989: The Year of the Fall

The revolutions of 1989 in East Europe began in the Soviet Union, notably with Mikhail Gorbachev's push to alter some fundamental features of Soviet-style socialism, including communist party dominance of the political system and central control of the economy.[13] Gorbachev's moves signaled that the bureaucratism and smothering state control of the economy could be dramatically cut back in East Europe, and if this occurred the new Moscow leadership would be less likely to become alarmed or to contemplate intervention. Still, until 1989 there was no clear evidence that Gorbachev would not ultimately back away from reform, as Khrushchev had done in Hungary in 1956, or that he had definitely parted company from the so-called Brezhnev Doctrine by which the Soviet Union arrogated to itself the right to intervene to protect socialism throughout the region.[14] The events of 1989 provided that evidence conclusively.

The end of communism in East Europe began in the country where communism had always been a forced fit—Poland. Strikes in 1988 and early 1989 forced the Polish Communist party to agree to "round-table" talks with the Solidarity labor movement. Partially free elections followed, with a majority of seats in the lower house of Parliament guaranteed to the Communists, but open contests stipulated for a new upper chamber. But even this arrangement could not keep the party's rule intact. When the Peasant and Democratic parties defected from formal alliance in August, the Communist party lost its numerical majority. President Wojech Jaruzelski—himself barely reelected as part of another arrangement—was obliged to accede to the creation of the first noncommunist government in East Europe since the 1940s.

The Soviet Union's acceptance of Tadeusz Mazowiecki, a prominent Catholic intellectual and Solidarity advisor, as prime minister signified the end of the Brezhnev Doctrine in East Europe. Within four months, regimes that had ruled in the region for more than forty years were overthrown.

In Hungary, which had undertaken economic reform long before its neighbors, the Communist party initiated its own process of reform. In February 1989 independent political parties were sanctioned, and fortifications on the Austrian border were dismantled soon after. When in September 1989 the Hungarian government announced it would not honor its agreement with East Germany to prevent illegal flights to the West, the stream of emigrants became a flood and sparked demonstrations inside the GDR itself. Unlike the Hungarian party, the East German party resisted reform to the last. Street demonstrations began and grew to huge proportions—nearly 100,000 people marched in Leipzig—and without Soviet backing for the use of force, Erich Honecker was forced to yield both his party leadership and soon after, control of the society and the country. Borders were opened, including the Berlin Wall on the night of November 9; the East German party made two more changes of leadership, round-table talks began, and elections were scheduled for spring of 1990.

The Czechoslovak regime faced similar pressure and tried repression briefly before it too yielded. Soon the wave of change swept over Bulgaria, regarded as the most orthodox of the East European states, with a leadership having the longest tenure (thirty-five years). Only in Romania was political change accompanied by widespread violence. Nicolae Ceausescu had repeatedly rejected Gorbachev's political and economic reforms and felt no need to secure popular compliance through economic payoffs, preferring instead to use the security apparatus. When the dam of public tolerance finally broke unexpectedly, Ceausescu had to be violently driven from power. His execution on Christmas Day punctuated the end of his rule and the collapse of fanatic resistance on the part of Romanian security forces.[15]

The Changes of 1990

In all of the states that experienced revolutions in 1989 (except, ironically, for Poland), national legislative elections were held in 1990. The elections showed overwhelming support for center-right political parties in Hungary, Czechoslovakia, and East Germany, and strong if not total rejection of the communist parties in these states. Coalitions were formed, and in Hungary and the GDR conservative prime ministers were appointed. The former communist prime minister of Czechoslovakia, Marian Calfa, kept his job, in part because of the immense moral power brought to the government by the new president, Vaclav Havel. In Bulgaria and Romania the elections produced new mandates for renamed communist parties. In Poland the deal arranged between the Communist party and Solidarity in 1989 that had left Wojech Jaruzelski the presidency was not changed until late 1990 when Lech Walesa was elected president. National legislative elections were not held until October 1991.[16]

In attempting to deal with a faltering economy, only Poland opted for a rapid "shock therapy" approach, freeing prices, ending subsidies, and making its currency internationally convertible on January 1, 1990. Other states proceeded more slowly. In Hungary, Czechoslovakia, and Romania, the governments tried partial freeing of prices accompanied by partial compensation and campaigns to prepare the public for more increases. It was not until mid-1991 that the prices of most goods were free of control in these countries. For the GDR, the die was cast by the elections, which showed overwhelming support for rapid economic and political union with the Federal Republic of Germany. Economic union began on July 1, 1990, with the joining of the two countries' currencies—at rates extremely favorable to the East Germans—and political union was sanctified on October 9, less than a year after the wall was opened.

The revolutions of 1989 did eventually have an impact on Albania as well, despite that country's best attempts to deny their validity and restrict their impact. Pressure from reformers grew on party leader and state president Ramiz Alia. In spring 1990, the first steps toward economic reform were taken, accompanied by changes in the country's legal system and institutions expanding civil liberties and protection of rights for the country's 3.2 million people.

But the effect of the changes in East Europe and the small steps taken in Albania served only to stimulate rather than calm that society's long-repressed demands. In July 1990, nearly 5,000 people took refuge among Tirana's embassies, demanding the right to leave. Student demonstrations pressed the regime throughout the country in December, and the country's economic situation—already the worst in Europe—became desperate. At the end of 1990, the Albanian Communist party abandoned its monopoly of power, as its East European counterparts had done a year earlier. In 1991, the renamed, reshuffled, and reformed Communist party won a two-thirds majority (largely because of the rural vote), and Alia was reelected president by the new legislature. Shortly after, a coalition government was formed, followed by new elections and the first noncommunist government since World War II.[17]

Prelude to an Analogy: The Dynamics of the East European Revolutions

When considering the possible parallels between the revolutions in East Europe and the situation in Cuba, one should ask: What were the key aspects of the revolutionary dynamic that produced these far-reaching changes in Europe? Are they present in Cuba? How does the situation there compare to the prerevolutionary situation in East Europe?

Underlying Factors

First, at the social level, the East European communist regimes lacked fundamental political legitimacy. With the exception of Yugoslavia, all of the governments of East Europe were created by communist parties that had little or no political position in their states, few members before World War II (except for Czechoslovakia, where the party was legal), and an unknown indigenous leadership. None could point to interwar leaders of political stature, and although the communist political philosophy had some followers in Czechoslovakia and in Bulgaria, in none was there a tradition of communists in government. The communists' accession to power after the war was accomplished by electoral manipulation, intimidation, and Soviet pressure rather than by a genuine electoral mandate.[18]

Thus the communist regimes installed in the region were seen by the population as alien, imposed by outside force. Moreover, that outside force, the Soviet Union, had been despised, feared, and in some cases battled against in much of the region. Indeed, one-third of Poland and parts of Romania had been occupied by Stalin after the Molotov-Ribbentrop pact of 1939, and several other territorial adjustments were made after World War II to ensure for the USSR new borders with Czechoslovakia and Hungary.

To those sources of hostility was added the domination of the "Muscovite" wing of most party leaderships—that is, those who had spent the war in the USSR, as opposed to fighting in their home country. Alleged "nationalist" communists such as Wladislaw Gomulka in Poland were purged, and key offices were often staffed with Soviet personnel—until 1956 the Polish defense minister was a Soviet general. National prerogatives on economic development were subordinated to those of the Soviet Union. In 1948 resistance to this interference was a key factor contributing to Yugoslavia's break with the new Soviet "bloc." The USSR's suppression of the Hungarian revolution in 1956, a similar action in Czechoslovakia in 1968, pressure on Poland during the 1980–1981 Solidarity period, and the presence of Soviet troops in many parts of the region all served to remind the population that even the communist leadership of their country was not theirs.

Second, the new regimes that took over were regimes of mobilization. They were leaders of the "revolution," even if the revolution needed a little help from the Soviet Union. Their programs called for rapid transformation of their countries through forced industrialization and collectivization, applied more or less thoroughly throughout the region. The result was tremendous social upheaval. Industrialization and collectivization were two sides of the funnel into which were poured dispossessed peasants from the land to emerge as part of the new proletariat in the cities. While many supported and profited from this process, and living standards improved as modernization came to the countryside, a large class of dispossessed, political and economic enemies of the communist regimes, was created. In a sense these regimes were right to fear their opponents as "enemies of the revolution," because as private property disappeared, as land was appropriated, and the church was suppressed, these regimes did create enemies. And many of those who opposed what happened in East Europe when communism was put into high gear in the 1950s were still around in 1989.

But even more significant than this generation was its offspring. Moshe Lewin writes of the Soviet Union that those who made Gorbachev's changes necessary, even inevitable, were not the dispossessed peasants. They were too busy literally fighting for survival in the cities after being uprooted from their former lives by the communist program. But their descendants, by now confirmed city dwellers whose basic level of material satisfaction had been assured and who no longer feared for their very survival, began to want more than their fathers and mothers had. Because of their exposure to urban life, this generation began to know more of what other people elsewhere had, and they pressured the party into the political and economic changes necessary to make possible material improvements in their lives. They created, in Lewin's words, "the Gorbachev phenomenon." Because the party needed these people's knowledge and expertise in an increasingly complex and technical world, it yielded.[19]

In Eastern Europe this young urban generation is certainly in evidence. While the proportion of the population between the ages of fifteen and thirty-nine was virtually the same in 1985 as it was in 1950, urbanization had increased substantially. For example, in Hungary 55.5 percent of population lived in rural villages in 1949; by 1988 only 40.9 percent did. By 1985, 78 percent of those living in the Czech lands and 72 percent of those in Slovakia lived in urban areas. Partly this was the result of collectivization. But in Poland, a country that retained an extensive network of noncollectivized farms, the rural population stayed constant while the urban population nearly tripled.[20] The new generation was less fearful; they had not experienced the war or Stalinism or even the repression after the invasion of Czechoslovakia. Writing on the "new working class" in Poland, Seweryn Bialer describes it as "more self-assured and willing to take risks . . . more activist . . . [and] better able to compare their own conditions with those of workers in the West or in more developed East European countries."[21]

While not all of the younger workers were as exposed to external influence as those in Poland, the description of this generation applies more or less throughout the region. When faced with the difficulties brought on by the collapse of East European economies, the intransigence of the old regimes, and the opportunity presented by Gorbachev, the new urban generation was less patient than their parents and more willing to take to the streets. In Czechoslovakia, Bulgaria, and East Germany, huge demonstrations, mostly of young people, forced the regime's hand and revealed their essential weakness. In Romania it was the young who challenged Ceausescu in the streets and, in disproportionate numbers, died to make the revolution. In Romania, as in these other countries, it was a "revolution of the children."

A critical factor behind the challenges that led to the 1989 revolutions was the disintegrating economic situation of the East European states. Lacking in legitimacy, these regimes could not create what David Easton calls "diffuse support" for themselves—that is, generalized support for the political and economic system based on its values and authority.[22] Thus the communist regimes had been obliged to retain power through three basic techniques: (1) repression of political opponents and control of possible bases of social or political opposition; (2) implicit and sometimes explicit cooperation with the Soviet Union for help in repressing social and political opposition (that is, the threat of Soviet intervention); and (3) economic payoffs, especially to key sectors of society. The first two were commonly used during the 1950s and 1960s, and the third was practiced in one form or another by most of the East European regimes after the crushing of the Prague Spring of 1968 and the fall of Wladislaw Gomulka in Poland in 1970. Both events, as well as intermittent labor pressure on the Polish regime, had economic roots.[23]

During the 1970s and 1980s the East European regimes clearly struggled to maintain and improve the standard of living in order to avoid the pressure that had built up in Czechoslovakia and Poland. In the latter case, the regime of Eduard Gierek began to borrow substantial sums from the West in an attempt both to improve the domestic economy rapidly and to provide more consumer goods. Hungary began economic reform in 1968. Although progress was uneven, it had advanced more than any other nation in East Europe by the time of the revolutions. Even in Ceausescu's Romania, life improved, by most measures, at least in the 1970s.

This strategy of achieving "output support" ran into problems with the economic decline of the 1980s.[24] Years of distorted investment patterns, delayed reforms, and the limits of "mobilization economies" produced sputtering stagnation. (See table 2.1.) Globally, the two oil shocks of the 1970s simultaneously curtailed the West's lending largesse and, even more critically, the ability of Western industrialized nations to import goods from the East. Hence almost all the East European states found it more difficult to repay their loans. In addition, their own economies were belatedly affected by the oil shocks and most were slow to adjust to price increases and uncertainties of supply.[25] Altogether, by the mid-1980s the communist regimes could no longer afford their end of the "social contract."

Moreover, the economic situation in the Soviet Union—the region's chief supplier and market—also worsened. Economic growth continued to decline, and Soviet oil production and supply began to slide. Pressure for reform of the individual economies and of the CMEA began to be generated from—instead of fought by—the USSR.[26] Added to this was pressure for reform coming from the West. By the end of the decade, debt to the West approached $100 billion (or $842 per capita for the East European Six) and the price of new loans, when available, was reform. At the same time, Western investment was available to aid recovery, but only when conditions at least promised to be favorable.

As their own situation grew worse, the people of East Europe became increasingly aware of the failure of their own regimes to provide an acceptable level of prosperity, even by their own standards. More critical, they were increasingly aware of the political freedom and economic health of Western Europe. For the people of East Europe, in general, the Soviet Union was clearly *not* the model, despite years of party-fed propaganda. Most looked to West Europe, more than to the United States, as indicating where they should be and where they would have been if their present and future not been distorted by the dictates of imposed regimes. Contacts, trade, and information flows increased as by-products of these regimes' attempts to purchase or borrow a better economic situation from the West, and awareness of this important counter model grew. Poles in particular traveled extensively in Europe both before and after the imposition of martial law, were in constant touch with a 12 million-strong diaspora, and were most exposed to Western media. For all East European states, Western media became more accessible as the decade ended; the jamming of Radio Free Europe, for example, had stopped by 1988.

The significance of the counter model was seen in the revolutions of 1989, when throughout the region the cry was for a "return to Europe."

TABLE 2.1
East European Economies and Living Standards
(rates of growth)

	Gross National Product				Standard of Living[b]			
	1970–1975	1975–1980	1980–1985	1985–1990[a]	1970–1975	1975–1980	1980–1985	1985–1990
Bulgaria	4.5	1.2	0.9	-1.0	4.2	1.6	2.2	2.8[c]
Czechoslovakia	3.4	2.2	1.4	0.8	3.1	1.6	1.8	1.6
GDR	3.5	2.4	1.7	1.8	4.6	2.0	1.4	2.3[c]
Hungary	3.4	2.3	0.9	-0.1	3.5	2.6	0.5	0.3
Poland	6.6	0.9	1.2	-1.1	5.5	2.0	0.5	0.9
Romania	6.2	2.8	0.6	-3.4	5.0	4.6	-0.4	4.4[c]
Average	4.6	2.0	1.1	-1.0	4.3	2.4	1.4	0.9[d]

a. For GDR, 1986–1987 only.
b. Calculated from indices of constant values of private and social consumption using 1970 = 100.
c. 1985–1987 only.
d. Average of Czechoslovakia, Hungary, and Poland only.

Sources: GNP: For GDR, Thad Alton et al., "Economic Growth in Eastern Europe 1970 and 1975–1987," *Research Project on National Income in East Central Europe.* Occasional paper no. 100 (New York: L. W. International Financial Research, Inc., 1988), p. 27. For others, Alton et al., "Economic Growth in Eastern Europe 1975–1990," *Research Project on National Income in East Central Europe.* Occasional Paper no. 115 (New York: L. W. International Financial Research, Inc., 1988), pp. 30–31.

Standard of Living: Alton et al., "Money Income of Population and Standard of Living in Eastern Europe 1970–1987," *Research Project on National Income in East Central Europe.* Occasional Paper no. 103 (New York: L. W. International Financial Research, Inc., 1988), p. 13; Alton et al., "Money Income of the Population and Standard of Living in Eastern Europe, Selected Countries, 1970–1990," *Research Project on National Income in East Central Europe,* Occasional Paper no. 118 (New York: L. W. International Financial Research, Inc., 1988), p. 10.

This applied to both domestic politics and economics. Key opposition leaders, soon to become government leaders, and their groups' programs, indicated they wanted to be a "normal" country. In Bulgaria one reform group from within the ruling party even called itself "the Bulgarian Road to Europe."

Proximate Factors

The existence of an alternative was another part of the dynamic of revolution in Eastern Europe. In most, but not all, of the states there were institutions, groups, or people who represented this alternative. In Poland the Catholic church acted as social conscience, the one center of social activity essentially outside the control of the Communist party. By virtue of its very presence, the church eroded the party's monopoly over the lives of its citizens. The church's singular position was weakened in the 1980s with the rise of Solidarity, which challenged the regime politically more directly and, unlike the church, did so at the workplace. In 1989 those eager for change in Poland looked to this nationwide organization as an alternative despite its official suppression. Solidarity's anticommunist credentials and national legitimacy were unchallengeable. Even more than the church, which after all had coexisted with the regime for thirty-five years, Solidarity and its politically aware and savvy leadership were ready and able to take up power in 1989.

Other states in East Europe did not have such a bold or broad organization, did not have the experience of Poland's repeated challenges to the regime or the luxury of an opposition church. Still, there were moral beacons that were ready when events presented the opportunity to take on the role of revolutionary. In Czechoslovakia this role was played by the human rights activists of Charter 77 and especially by Vaclav Havel, an outspoken playwright whose works were banned in his own country and who had been arrested many times for his dissidence, most recently in January 1989. Havel, even more than Aleksander Dubcek, represented a clean break with the past. He was an outspoken conscience of the revolution who could take Czechoslovakia into Europe, which he proceeded immediately to try to do.

For citizens of the GDR, West Germany provided the alternative, a rich, powerful and *German* demonstration of where the country and society could be without the communist party. The Lutheran church in East Germany had also become active in supporting opposition figures and occasionally challenging the regime, but during the extraordinary events of 1989 its influence and stature were rapidly eclipsed by the strong popular drive to take East Germany into West Germany.[27]

Such an alternative or competing power center did not exist in all cases. There was no such strong institution or individual in Hungary or Bulgaria, though there were opposition figures, and there was virtually no public opposition in Ceausescu's Romania. There were vigorous reform activists within the party in Hungary, and some reforms had eased repression before 1989. Here broader, if less dramatic, political and intellectual opposition combined with the nation's economic deterioration to form the basis for the challenge to the regime.

The opposition was less well established in Bulgaria, indicated by the fact that the challenge that provided the catalyst for the 1989 revolution was mounted by small, ecologically oriented parties that took advantage of the large media presence in Bulgaria in the fall of 1989 covering an ecology conference sponsored by the Conference on Security and Cooperation in Europe (CSCE). A dissident intellectual, Zhelju Zhelev, became president after repeated attempts to elect a socialist failed, but that was not until mid-1990, and he was not a figure of Havel's stature. Nor was there a Bulgarian opposition with the history and strength of Charter 77 or Solidarity. Finally, in Romania the successive "rotation of cadres" and repression of worker demonstrations in 1977 and 1987 and intellectual dissidents such as Doina Cornia and Paul Goma left the country virtually devoid of an opposition base. Not even a "forum" organization was formed at the time of the Romanian revolution of 1989.

Thus while one could not say that the existence of an opposition center was a critical factor in making the revolutions of 1989, in some cases a domestic alternative played a vital role in facilitating the transfer of power. Moreover, in almost all cases, we can see the presence of a broad opposition forum that during the revolutionary process acted as an umbrella organization for disparate groups ready to challenge the regime. Most were formed in the heat of the revolutions themselves: Czechoslovakia's Civic Forum was formed in November 1989; the GDR's Neues Forum in September. Most presented broad programs calling for rapid and fundamental change in their countries. In Poland, Solidarity played this role, and it too included various strains of opposition.

These organizations took advantage of two related phenomena in East European politics. First, 1989 saw the emergence of public opposition to the regime. There had always been opposition movements and groups, despite the regimes' best attempts to suppress them, but such opposition was usually driven underground. Views were spread through thousands of *samizdat* (or self-published) publications in Poland, for example, or in church-protected meetings in East Germany, or by Western publicity given to opposition groups like Charter 77 in Czechoslovakia.[28] In 1989 for the first time the regimes did not have the ability to call for Soviet help. Hence, opposition groups were able to propagate their views publicly, knowing they would have to face only domestic police and security. When challenges and demonstrations multiplied, forum-type organizations channeled disparate strains of opposition toward one goal: breaking the party's monopoly of political power. Thus the focus on demands for round-table political talks, elections, and abandoning the party's constitutionally sanctioned "leading role." In some cases, as with Vaclav Havel, the opposition was able to offer specific alternative individuals for symbolic but important changes.

Second, the forum organizations were both a cause and a result of the awakening of mass politics, which was crucial to the success of the revolution. While certain groups, such as young people or labor, were the spearheads of the revolutions, the events of 1989 brought the mass public into political involvement, in a way which the communist governments had prevented for four decades. Under communism, popular participation was encouraged, but in a prescribed and carefully circumscribed manner and always in ways that supported the regime's goals. "Voluntary" associations, mass meetings, party membership, and elections with 99 percent positive returns were examples of such "mobilized" participation. Even socioeconomic modernization failed to broaden signficantly the regime's base of participatory support.[29] In contrast, political activity in 1989 was broad, spontaneous, and directed not just against certain of the regimes' policies but their very form. The reappearance of public politics was seen in mass demonstrations. Hundreds of thousands of people in Liepzig and Berlin, in Prague and Sofia, demanded changes. Hundreds spontaneously swarmed over the opened border in Berlin on the night of November 9; 700,000 people visited the West two days later, and within days 4 million visas had been issued. While most returned home, the demonstration of what people wanted was unmistakable. During the fall of 1989 each of the regimes, especially those of the GDR, Bulgaria, and Czechoslovakia, faced the choice of acquiescing to the mass opposition or using physical violence on a large scale to try to hold on without Soviet backing. Fortunately, none chose the latter.

Before the elections of 1990, hundreds of political parties and groups were born, thousands of new media outlets emerged, especially in the print media, as public expression of opinion was once again possible. Even where the communist party was retained (though in a different form), Romania and Bulgaria, genuine political involvement—voting and campaigning, strikes, meetings, and written expression—emerged on an unprecedented scale.

These two factors, the rise of umbrella organizations and their ability to channel mass public involvement in challenging the regimes, are crucial to explaining the occurrence and success of the 1989 revolutions. But they alone cannot account for the nature and scope of these revolutions. There had been broad public opposition before, as in Poland in 1980, or Hungary in 1956. There had also been difficult economic times before, such as during the years of adjustment after Stalinist industrialization in the 1950s. Such times had even produced a change of regime, such as in Poland in 1970 or 1980, but not the overthrow of the governing political and economic order. This occurred in 1989 because of two additional factors, both external: the fact that pressure on all the ruling regimes of East European nations occurred almost simultaneously, and the acquiescence of the regional hegemon, the Soviet Union.

The totality of the revolutions of East Europe in 1989 was partly the result of "contagion." If times were bad in Poland, where the year's precipitating events really began, they were also bad elsewhere. Economic systems were fundamentally similar across the region: a state-directed economy; a preference in investment toward heavy industry to the detriment of agriculture and consumer goods; a predominance of Soviet-determined supply and demand in international trade. Also similar were the results of forty years of this system: inadequate housing, too few consumer goods, and a broadening gap between the regimes' pronouncements and day-to-day reality. Finally, the regimes were also determed to limit political choices, reinforced by the constitutional sanction of the communist party's "leading role." Then, when the Polish party was forced by labor upheaval to accept a noncommunist, Solidarity-chosen prime minister, and when the USSR made no move to prevent it, the signal both to regimes and to opposition forces elsewhere in the region was clear.

Seeing what had happened in Poland when the party was weak and opposed to reform, the Hungarian party tried desperately to reorganize its leadership and its program, to no avail.[30] Here too a "round-table" was formed and elections had to be promised by the party if it hoped to retain any influence, a hope that proved illusory. The challenge to the East German regime came in the form of public demands for lifting travel restrictions and quickly became overwhelming.[31] It was at this point— October—that Gorbachev came to East Germany and gave his unmistakable signal that time was running out on the Honecker regime. Events in what was long considered the most restrictive of the East European regimes sparked similar demands in nearby Czechoslovakia and even in more distant Bulgaria. Aware from foreign broadcasts of events unfolding elsewhere in East Europe and then right next door in Bulgaria, the Romanian people finally yet unexpectedly challenged Ceausescu, a challenge that led to his removal and death.

This kind of contagion had never occurred before; never had so much happened all at once. East European and Soviet leaders had been able to isolate developments in Hungary in 1956, for example, and in Czechoslovakia in 1968, though there were limited reactions in other countries. During those and other challenges, tighter media control, especially the absence of foreign coverage, a less experienced and organized opposition, the absence of broad organizations able to take advantage of the situation, and ultimately the hovering Soviet presence had stemmed the tide of revolution. In 1989, these factors were all changed, and most important the last.

During the time of its hegemony over Eastern Europe, the Soviet Union had through speech and action established the limits of acceptable behavior.[32] Such control was justified both on grounds of protecting the revolution and socialism in these countries and, privately, on geopolitical security grounds.[33] Mikhail Gorbachev and those around him gave indications that a wider range of reform would be tolerated and even encouraged in East Europe. However, until the acceptance of a Solidarity government in Poland, there remained the possibility that the USSR would still enforce the Brezhnev Doctrine. But when Gorbachev backed up his words with inaction, it proved a lightning bolt that brought to revolutionary life the many elements that needed only a spark to bring them alive. This particular combination had never come together before and when it did, East European communism was undone.

Other Factors

By way of completing the analysis of developments in East Europe it is worth exploring momentarily the role of other factors which one might expect to have made a difference in the provoking or preventing of the revolutions of 1989.

First, degree of Communist party vigor and unity seems not to have mattered in the run-up to the revolutions. None of the parties were able to prevent the revolutions or preserve their rule as it had been before. The Polish party was decimated and dispirited by years of quasi-military rule and its abject failure to govern the country, but the Romanian, East German, and Bulgarian parties were united and under the firm control of the party leadership. The Hungarian party had many strong reform-minded leaders as well as hard-liners, while the Czech party had purged most reform-minded elements. At the time of the public challenge, none of these parties—whatever its degree of cohesion—was able to withstand pressure to fundamentally change its position atop the political system. However, the Romanian and Bulgarian parties, which were able to maintain a degree of unity *after* the revolutions—and even, in the Bulgarian case, after some reform elements emerged— fared better in the elections of 1990. The ability to act as a coherent force during the electoral campaign, especially in the countryside, was critical to their continued rule. In contrast, the Hungarian party split into orthodox and more social democratic wings and was thrashed at the polls.

Second, the role of the armed forces should be considered. Although Soviet forces were considered to be the ultimate protectors of the East European regimes, local armed forces, including regular army, security police, or special police, had also been used to ensure and preserve regime tenure. In Romania the ubiquitous Securitate (security force) was virtually a state within a state and was dedicated to preserving Ceausescu's rule over both the society and the party. In Poland the Zomos, or militarized riot police, were often the martial law regime's special instruments for attacking public demonstrations.

In 1989, with the Soviet Union no longer the chief enforcer, local armed forces were key to the course of revolutionary developments. In every case except one, military and paramilitary forces stood aside when the final crunch came. Police were in evidence in Czechoslovakia, Bulgaria, and the GDR. In Czechoslovakia, violent repression on the night of November 17, 1989, only broadened revolutionary sentiment.

East German leaders apparently went to the brink of using force but decided, like the Bulgarians, that with the whole world watching, with similar developments occurring throughout the region, and with the ultimate savior in Moscow no longer available, force would not work.[34] Only in Romania was Ceaucescu's personal army, the Securitate, called on to try to preserve his rule, and they nearly succeeded in doing so. The tide turned only after the army sided with the revolution and the execution of Ceausescu and his wife denied his fanatical supporters their chance to achieve a restoration.

Could the armed forces, if used vigorously and forcefully, have prevented the revolutions? Possibly, in an isolated case. They had done so in Poland with the imposition of martial law in 1981. But, as noted, the events of 1989 were not isolated. Party leaders and the armed forces willing to use violence would have to have done so knowing it would firmly isolate their country from developments elsewhere in Europe and, moreover, would have to be done without Soviet backing. While the violent repression of dissidents in China's Tianamen Square indicates that authorities can retain power through brute force in individual cases, in East Europe the decision not to use the armed forces in all cases but one guaranteed the communists rapid and total defeat.

Two other factors that played only insignificant roles in the revolutions themselves nevertheless affected the course of the governments that emerged afterward. First, the degree of homogeneity of the population seems to have neither accelerated nor retarded the revolutions. Unlike the situation in 1968, for example, the Czechoslovak opposition was able to remain united under the umbrella of the Civic Forum and its Slovak sister organization, the Public Against Violence, long enough to topple the regime. Initially, Romania's National Salvation Front contained elements from both the Hungarian and Romanian communities and the Front government moved to address some of the major grievances of the Hungarian minority. Later, in both Romania and Czechoslovakia, and to an extent in Bulgaria, the ethnic minority presented key issues that directly affected the policies—and in the Czechoslovakian case—the structure of the ensuing government. But at the time of the revolution neither the homogeneity nor the heterogeneity of the population was a determining factor.

Second, whether or not a nation had a history of rebellion offers a tantalizing subject for comparison. Regime change came first in Poland, which had the longest and most consistent history of political opposition, yet change was most thorough, in the sense of the party's complete electoral defeat, where challenges to the regime had failed: the GDR (in 1953), Hungary (in 1956) and Czechoslovakia (in 1968). And regime change was least thorough in those two states that had experienced communist rule since World War II without a significant social or political uprising against the regime—Romania and Bulgaria. This suggests that the lack of an experience of rebellion can be a limiting factor even if a regime change is forced, as it was in both of these cases, and even if an umbrella organization is formed to challenge the regime and force political accommodation, as it was in Bulgaria. This factor is related to the presence (or absence) of an opposition center or force with the moral authority or political savvy to challenge the regime. As noted, there was no such opposition in Romania or Bulgaria, and along with a lack of past rebellions, this may explain the retention of power—albeit through elections—by the communist party's successor, the Bulgarian Socialist party and Romania's National Salvation Front.

The Effect of the Changes in East Europe on Cuba's International Relations

The Loss of Community

The most significant impact of the revolutions in East Europe on Cuba is the loss of community or reference group. Since securing the revolution and gaining firm Soviet support, Fidel Castro and Cuba have defined themselves unequivocally as part of the world's socialist camp. This has meant close if not always identical association with Soviet foreign policy positions and actions and strong opposition to the industrialized Western states on most issues.

In this Cuba had been joined by the East European Six. Though not a member of the Warsaw Pact, Cuba could nevertheless count on this organization and its members to support its foreign policy initiatives. This ranged from rhetorical support to involvement in and backing for movements and governments Cuba supported among developing countries, especially in Africa.[35] Cuba was a member of CMEA, having joined in 1972 and participated in various forms of bi- and multilateral cooperative efforts mediated by that organization.[36] As a less-developed member of CMEA, Cuba was entitled to various forms of special treatment, subsidies, and guaranteed purchases.[37] (See chapter 5.)

Following the East European revolutions, both organizations rapidly attenuated and died. Very soon after the revolutions, even before the new governments were elected, the East European states indicated their preference for a revamped CMEA trade system, one that would facilitate rather than obstruct trade. The new system would be based on world prices and hard currency and would help the East European states emerge from the Soviet-dominated zone.

The move to reform or replace CMEA did not have as a major aim excluding or isolating Cuba. But the consequences of reform certainly pointed in that direction. To begin with, the reform was perceived as designed to facilitate contact between reforming—soon to be market-based—economies. Thus by definition only those states moving toward a market economy would be a part of the new cooperation. Cuba, firmly rejecting this movement, would not be part of this reform. The Cuban delegate to the Forty-fifth CMEA Session in Sofia stated this explicitly. Carlos Rafael Rodríguez, vice president of the State Council and of the Council of Ministers, said he did "not deem it necessary that the council [CMEA] should renounce already established principles." He warned against introducing market elements and eroding "the decisive role of state ownership."[38]

The reform of CMEA also threatened relations with Cuba because changes were clearly aimed at improving relations among the more developed members only.[39] While some European CMEA members, notably Bulgaria and Romania, were less forceful in their demands for reform—arguing for a transition period, for example[40]—none favored preserving multilateral support for less-developed members such as Cuba and Vietnam. In fact, Hungary proposed that cooperation proceed most quickly among an "inner circle" of central European states that were farther along the road to reform.[41] Poland, too, backed "economic cooperation of a strictly regional character" and Hungary's Prime Minister Jozsef Antall commented at the closing CMEA session that "the more remote countries of the dissolved Comecon would necessarily play a smaller role in Hungary's relations."[42]

Throughout 1990, momentum gathered either to radically reform CMEA or, more likely, eliminate it. The three Central European states pushed hard for abolishing CMEA with its mandated "privilege" for less-developed members.[43] Even Bulgaria and Romania, less ardent reformers, came around to the idea of excluding non-European former

CMEA members.[44] In the end, when CMEA died in June 1991, only vague talk of some kind of continuing forum was heard, but with a European membership. A plea was added at the meeting that served as the funeral for the organization to extend preferential treatment for the non-European CMEA countries now set adrift.[45]

The death of CMEA, and in particular Cuba's exclusion from even the possibility of membership in a follow-on organization, reflected the most fundamental change in foreign policy orientation brought about by the revolutions in East Europe. Everywhere the cry was for a "return to Europe." In concrete terms this meant a desire on the part of the new leaders, and—extrapolating from election returns—of the population, to reorient the states of East Europe toward West Europe. In practical terms this meant several things. First, as indicated above, it meant breaking ties to Soviet-dominated multilateral organizations. Further, most states moved to become associated with or, if they could, to join West European organizations. In October 1990, Hungary was formally admitted to the Council of Europe, the first East European state to gain this status; Czechoslovakia joined in February 1991, Poland in November, and Bulgaria in May 1992. Some leaders voiced a willingness to join NATO or become associated with it in concrete ways; most joined its legislative assembly and hosted NATO Security General Manfred Woerner in their capitals. NATO was in some instances forced to cool the ardor of its suitors.[46]

Similar eagerness was displayed with regard to the European Community (EC), with which Poland, Czechoslovakia, and Hungary began negotiating "association agreements" in 1990. These were initialed in November 1991. This involvement was supplemented by a substantial aid and assistance program facilitated by the Group of Twenty-four, by the EC, bilaterally and by increased involvement of Western financial institutions such as the IMF, the World Bank, and the new European Bank for Reconstruction and Development (EBRD). Finally, the shift of trade from East to West was dramatic.[47]

What this meant for East Europe was a move away from what had been its reference group—East Europe, the Warsaw Pact, the CMEA, and the Soviet Union—toward a new one, toward a European identity. While this proceeded more slowly than some of the states would have liked—and more slowly for some, such as Bulgaria and Romania, than others—the shift was unmistakable. Left behind were the norms of behavior, the canons and cant of the "socialist commonwealth," including relations with Cuba. As Prime Minister Jozsef Antall's statement about "remote" countries indicates, the foreign policies of the new East European states focused more on their neighborhood, on perceived security concerns now that the frozen system that had provided security for four decades was no more. Given the fluid situation in Yugoslavia and the former Soviet Union and the extremely difficult economic situation that most of the newly democratic states now find themselves in, it is clear that security is not automatically assured by democracy. With a wide range of foreign policy options available without compulsion from the metropolis, the new leaders of East Europe find themselves facing "backyard" issues.[48]

But the new regimes are eager to expand their ties with Europe for another reason. Most have undertaken enormously difficult economic transitions, causing substantial economic dislocation and pain at home. These regimes are unable to promise better or even good times right away, and there is a limit to public tolerance. In contrast, foreign policy offers a way for new states to gain some popularity fairly "cheaply." By taking actions they know will be popular, they can build up some credit with an impatient and exhausted population. Steps to "normalize" their foreign relations by embracing European organizations and values serve this goal. Reestablishing broken relations with states previously on the Soviet-dictated taboo list is another; these include Israel, South Africa, and Chile, with all of whom the East European states resumed relations after the revolution. Breaking or reducing ties to Soviet-determined "revolutionary" regimes like Cuba is also part of this shift. Foreign policy actions that demonstrate the regimes' new distance from the Soviet Union and their new independence are likely to be popular. It was not surprising, for example, that in 1991, upon his return from a Latin American trip (that did not include Cuba) and facing his government's first parliamentary elections, Poland's foreign minister, Krzystof Skubiszewski, took pains to point out that Cuba would "no longer enjoy priority as it did under the communist regime. . . . Moreover, the Polish government [was] deeply concerned over the human rights problem in that country."[49]

This is not to suggest that the shift to policies that ignored or criticized Cuba were only cynical attempts to build popularity. Philosophically the new regimes in East Central Europe are in fact right-of-center, antisocialist regimes. The direction of developments in Poland, Hungary, and Czechoslovakia—not to speak of East Germany—is decidedly opposite that to which Castro is committed. People like Arpad Goncz, Tadeusz Mazowiecki, and Vaclav Havel are poles apart from the political and economic orientation of Fidel Castro.

The Emergence of Controversial Issues

In the first months of his presidency, Czechoslovakia's Vaclav Havel was extremely active. Through visits, statements, and actions he demonstrated a desire to move quickly and decisively to restore Czechoslovakia's place in Europe and the world. Czechoslovakia resumed relations with Israel and the Vatican, announced plans to end the export of plastic explosives (linked to terrorist acts), and in an action that angered the Chinese, invited the Dalai Lama to Prague.[50] Early in 1990 Czechoslovak-Cuban relations were described as suffering from "deformations," and the Prague government pledged to change the "ideological character" of these relations.[51]

Havel's actions soon brought him into conflict with Cuba on issues of civil and political rights. In March, Czechoslovakia, along with Bulgaria, Hungary, and Poland, voted to support a U.S.-sponsored resolution at the United Nations Human Rights Commission that chided Cuba for not cooperating with its investigation into the human rights situation there.[52] Cuba's deputy foreign minister José Viera called this action "an unfriendly step."[53] Blaming "a conspiracy of lies at the international level," Castro blasted Poland and Czechoslovakia for co-sponsoring the resolution and Hungary and Bulgaria for voting for it. Of the latter two he said, "They have fallen on the lap of the Yankee empire."[54] The Czechoslovak response pointed out that "democratic changes that take place in Czechoslovakia demand that [its] foreign policy also promote the respect and observance of human and civic rights."[55]

Havel continued to call Cuba to account. In June he sent Castro a letter condemning the sentencing of seven human rights activists, calling the action "another step by your country toward the darkest past."[56] In reply, Castro said that Havel's letter revealed his "absolute ignorance of problems in our country" and said the imprisoned people were tools of North American imperialism "which you [Havel] are so pleased to support."[57]

Throughout 1990 Havel took every opportunity to restate his view. In August, in the first visit of a Czechoslovak head of state to Latin America, he visited Mexico and the new noncommunist government of Nicaragua, and in a stopover in Miami he took a swipe at Castro. Noting that Czechoslovakia wanted people in Cuba to achieve their basic rights in a peaceful way and to have freedom and democracy, Havel said, "If this arouses Fidel Castro's anger, there is nothing that can be done about it."[58] Havel met with Cuban opposition figures in December and in June 1991 with Armando Valladares, a dissident Cuban poet who had spent more than twenty years in jail in Cuba and who became the permanent U.S. representative to the Human Rights Commission.[59]

Cuba's relations deteriorated more sharply with Czechoslovakia than with any of the other East European states in part because of Havel's clear desire to establish his and his country's new views on world affairs. But they were also harmed by the events of summer 1990 at the Czechoslovak mission in Cuba and by Czechoslovakia's decision to cease representing Cuban interests in the United States. In July twelve Cubans took refuge in the Czechoslovak embassy in Havana and demanded political asylum. The Czechoslovak government requested that they be allowed to leave Cuba, but the Cuban government denied they were political dissidents. The incident was settled after some irritated exchanges.[60] The Cuban government assured Prague that the people would be investigated and allowed to return home.

During and after this incident, Deputy Foreign Minister Vojtech Vagner said that his country would continue to represent Cuban interests in Washington, as it had since 1977.[61] But pressure grew from human rights organizations and the U.S. Congress.[62] Czechoslovakia "reassessed" its position over the summer.[63] The decision to stop representing Cuba was announced in December—a break attributed to "fundamental changes" in their countries' relations, especially differences on issues of human rights. And it was leaked that despite the apparently amicable settling of the embassy incident, the Czechoslovaks' presumption that this was a Cuban provocation evidently contributed to their decision.[64] Castro denounced the action as "repugnant opportunism" and called Havel a "vulgar agent of imperialism."[65]

While human rights and representation issues made Czechoslovak-Cuban relations the worst among former allies,[66] economic issues began almost immediately to burden Cuba's ties to all East European states. Trade between Cuba and East Europe dropped sharply (see chapter 5), and Cuba's failure to meet its contracts led to substantial growth in its debt to East Europe and to useless trade surpluses for the East Europeans. Negotiations produced interim agreements with a few governments, but in August 1990 Hungary suspended trade over Cuba's failure to fulfill its contracts. By 1991 Cuba's debt to Hungary had reached 160 million rubles.[67] In mid-1990 Czechoslovakia said it was carrying a surplus of 70 million rubles and a total Cuban debt of 350 million rubles. In June 1990 delivery of Czechoslovak goods was suspended.[68] (In contrast, in October Czechoslovakia forgave Nicaragua $20 million in interest it owed on its $150 million debt and then forgave another $25 million and signed a repayment agreement in February 1991.)[69] Overall Cuban debt to East Europe was estimated by mid-1990 to exceed 9,900 million rubles ($1.5 billion).[70]

For his part, Castro criticized Hungary, Czechoslovakia, and Bulgaria for sending low-quality goods and failing to supply spare parts, a charge rejected by the East European partners.[71] And, despite denials, it is possible that Cuban exports were cut off as a result of these countries' support for UN action on human rights abuses in Cuba. At the same time, Cuba withdrew its students from Hungary and Czechoslovakia and began to repatriate some 5,300 workers, who had in the past stayed in Czechoslovakia for up to four years.[72]

Changed Media Environment

The change to democratic systems produced another kind of tension between the East European states and Cuba. With the dismantling of communist power, control over the media dissipated. This was especially true in the print media, where outlets proliferated, but it affected radio and television as well. Subjects that had heretofore been treated only according to the approved line were now open to objective, even critical treatment. Foreign policy issues were not exempt; for example, there were critical discussions of CMEA, of the situation in other countries, and of the previous regimes' foreign policies. In January 1990 the Czechoslovak daily *Lidova Demokracie* wrote very critically of the previous regime's foreign aid practices and in particular singled out Cuba's special treatment. The "squandering of our national income," the journal wrote, included buying Cuban sugar at 30 percent above world prices and then reselling it at a great loss.[73] Changes in the media and emerging pluralism also allowed for public lobbying on foreign policy. For example, in July 1990 a conference in Prague entitled "Democracy by Peaceful Path" called on democratic countries to "isolate the Cuban government economically, politically, and diplomatically."[74]

In January 1990 a correspondent for Prague Radio, Michal Cermak, filed a very critical report about the situation in Cuba, including the rigors of rationing and food shortages. Calling the situation "a calm before a storm, but of the Romanian type," he concluded, "It does not look as if a gentle revolution is going to take place here."[75] Three days later, Cermak was expelled from Cuba, eliciting sharp protest from the Czechoslovak government.[76] Similarly, in November 1990 a Hungarian journalist lost his accreditation after he reported seeing an Iraqi oil tanker leaving Havana in violation of UN sanctions. After this incident, a foreign policy commentator for Radio Budapest described Hungarian-Cuban relations as "almost cold."[77]

Of course, the open media environment in East Europe meant that alternative views on Cuban relations could also be heard. Supporters of previous regimes, or of their successors still in power, could wave the banner of "fraternal alliance." The army paper in Bulgaria wrote in May 1990 that the Cubans had "achieved a considerable social justice," that "no one is starving or destitute [in Cuba]," that the rationing system was due to the U.S. economic blockade, and that standards for health care in Cuba were those "we in Bulgaria could only dream about." The article denied that it was time for Castro to step down and declared that Bulgarian-Cuban economic relations were "to no one's disadvantage."[78] The new pluralism in East European countries meant that organizations which for ideological or other reasons wished to pursue transatlantic relations could do so—a situation that has left Cuba some ties to the region. In Hungary, for example, the new Socialist Workers' party, the orthodox successor to the previous ruling party, established contact with the Cuban party, and Laszlo Udvarhelyi, a party central committee secretary, visited Havana in November 1990. In his view, "The MSZMP and the Cuban communist party are united by our consistent representation of a communal society model."[79] Such sentiments, like the institutions that voice them, are in the distinct minority, especially in Central Europe, and are countered in most of the region by a strong public and official desire to break with past practices and policies.

Though Cuba's ties have attenuated with the East European Six since the revolutions, they have not disappeared. During the summer of 1990, Romania and Cuba exchanged visits of their foreign trade ministers and conducted apparently useful talks.[80] In Czechoslovakia the Cuban government sought to outflank the central government by exploring ties with the Slovak National Council, one of the country's two regional legislatures.[81] But overall there can be no doubt that all of the former CMEA states of East Europe, even those whose regimes represent less of a break than others, have begun to broaden and shift their foreign policy attention out of the narrow shaft to which they had been confined by Soviet hegemony.

The Loss of the Orthodox

Cuba has suffered defections from its general international support group, the socialist states. But the revolutions of 1989 also removed Cuba's most important reference group, the orthodox communist states. Hungary had already begun economic reform in the late sixties, and the Polish government was obliged to coexist uneasily with opposition forces such as Solidarity, the Catholic church, and private farmers. But Czechoslovakia, East Germany, and Romania entered the Gorbachev period with their political forces set firmly against reform, though for different reasons.

The Czechoslovak regime's obsession with rooting out and destroying any vestiges of the reform socialism that had spawned the Prague Spring and its relative success in cultivating an implicit social contract with its population put it squarely in the orthodox camp, resisting Gorbachev's push for reform. The GDR also feared the political consequences of reform and, further, claimed that reform was not necessary, as the East German economy was the most productive in the region. In Romania and Albania Cuba found its most ardent ideological kin. Romania's rejection of Gorbachev's reforms derived primarily from the political view and control of its undisputed leader, Nicolae Ceausescu. The force of the second oil shock (1979), magnified because of the Ceausescu regime's unwillingness to respond to it, jolted the Romanian economy. Furthermore, policies instituted in the mid-eighties—such as the ill-advised drive to pay off the country's debt before the end of the decade—stripped Romania of all exportable items, cut critical imports (especially from the West) and produced an economy that was dead in the water by the end of the decade. But Ceausescu rejected both Soviet-style perestroika and glasnost. In 1987, speaking of Gorbachev's early moves to sanction small-scale private enterprise, Ceausescu said: "In no way can one speak of improving socialism by looking back, by speaking of the so-called market socialism, of free enterprise, and all this by invoking objectives. There cannot be improvement of socialism through the so-called development of the small private property. Capitalist property, big or small, is still capitalist property."[82]

In Ceausescu Fidel Castro had a kindred spirit. When Cuba's foreign minister visited Romania in November 1989, Ceausescu clearly aligned himself with the Cuban view of the most recent developments. The press reported:

> President Nicolae Ceausescu stressed the necessity of strengthening the collaboration and solidarity of the socialist countries of the progressive forces everywhere in the struggle against imperialism . . . and [its] attempts to destabilize the situation in the socialist countries . . . to promote its policy of domination and oppression, of interference in domestic affairs and violation of the peoples' independence and sovereignty . . . confidence was expressed that the progressive forces, the socialist states, the peoples would be able to curb and eventually bar those antisocialist tendencies and actions aimed against the peoples' independence, to ensure the triumph of the struggle for the development and consolidation of socialism.[83]

Cuba's relations with Bulgaria were also warm, especially after 1987 when party leader Todor Zhivkov's apparent urge to transcend the reforms of Gorbachev and move even faster was undermined by Gorbachev himself. From that point on, the Bulgarian regime, which had made some significant economic chagnes earlier in the decade, offered only lip service to reform. When Jorge Valdes, Cuban Politburo member and party secretary, visited Sofia in October 1989, Bulgarian leaders gushed about "the friendly relations and cooperation between the two parties, between Bulgaria and Cuba, relations which are developing on the basis of Marxism-Leninism and international solidarity" and explicitly asserted that the smaller socialist states should not be pushed in directions they did not want to take: "The processes of fundamental renewal of socialism should be further enhanced by taking into consideration the specific conditions of each party and country."[84] Thus among the Soviet Union's allies Cuba could count on strong support for its position on reform from at least four. The loss of these states, not just to reform, but to revolution, dramatically reduced the number of Cuba's conservative spiritual allies.

But the revolutions also deprived Cuba of states that had been allies in more substantial ways. Apart from economic ties, Cuba, Czechoslovakia, and especially East Germany shared support for revolutionary movements around the world. Often these states cooperated to support such movements with more than just words and in doing so acted as agents in support of the Soviet foreign policy goal of undermining Western influence wherever possible. Between 1976 and 1990, Czechoslovakia provided military training to more than 3,000 experts from socialist and "progressive" states around the world. Among this number were some thirty Cubans.[85] Czechoslovakia also served as a main conduit for supplies, weapons, and military equipment—its own and from East Germany—to governments and movements in Africa for which Cuba supplied the troops.[86]

East Germany's involvement in Africa predates Cuba's by more than a decade and, at least initially, served East German as well as Soviet foreign policy goals. Chief among these was the desire to counter the influence of the rival Federal Republic and, perhaps even more important, secure international recognition from the newly independent states.[87] Normalization of inter-German relations, including mutual recognition, coincided with the collapse of Portuguese colonialism in Africa, and the GDR's role shifted to offering substantial diplomatic and material support for the Soviet-backed revolutionary movements fighting for power in Angola (the Popular Movement for the Liberation of Angola, MPLA) and Mozambique (Liberation Front of Mozambique, FRELIMO). The GDR provided technical equipment, training, and military advice. This meshed with the logistical and arms support of the Soviet Union and the manpower provided by Cuba.

The same division of labor also applied to support for liberation groups in Rhodesia (Zimbabwe) and Southwest Africa (Namibia) and for Ethiopia in its struggles with Somalia and its own Eritrean rebels.[88] By 1978, East German and Cuban troops were together in seven different African countries, when some 21,000 Cubans were in Angola and 17,000 in Ethiopia. Though the number of Cubans dropped in the eighties, the two countries still cooperated throughout the continent and as late as 1988 were together in Angola, Ethiopia, and Mozambique.[89]

While there is little evidence of extensive use of East German combat troops directly, East German technical and training support was critical to the achievement of power by groups supported by Cuba and the USSR, and afterward to the defense of their position against domestic challenges.[90] One observer labeled the GDR an "invaluable adjunct of Soviet foreign policy" toward Africa.[91] By supplying the advisors, the funds, the training, and the material, East Germany covertly complemented the more public and direct involvement of Cuban troops. In Angola, for example, cooperation with Cuban forces was crucial to the success of the MPLA in 1975. One observer noted; "It took the combined efforts of Soviet generals, Cuban soldiers, and East German military advisors to provide the MPLA leader with a secure position of power."[92]

After the establishment of regimes in these African states, East German involvement continued, embracing essential economic and technical aid as well as provision of security advisors.[93] When the revolution occurred in East Germany and, even more significant, when it took the course it did leading to the rapid absorption of the GDR by West Germany, Cuba lost a valuable ally in its own most spectacular realm of foreign policy exertion. At the same time, Soviet foreign policy shifts, changes in South Africa's position, a political agreement in Angola, and a shift away from socialism in Africa put an end to the need and support for an extensive Cuban presence in Africa.

Albania: The Last Comrade

Finally, Cuba was robbed of its last comrade in Europe when the tide of change swept Albania too. Tirana had shared Castro's hostility to reform and to developments in East Europe and the Soviet Union. In January 1990 the party's official organ stated bluntly, "The prescriptions of the capitalist road, of perestroika and bourgeois reform are unacceptable to our people and party."[94] Repression against possible challenges increased.[95] In December 1989, the government news agency quoted Castro extensively on his insistence that "Cuba will not abandon its revolutionary principles" and on his characterization of the "grave wound of capitalism" that the East European states were bringing on themselves.[96]

In November Isidoro Malmierca made the first visit of a Cuban foreign minister to Albania, met with Prime Minister Adil Carnacai and with Ramiz Alia. The latter insisted at this time that the Albanian people had "bound their life to socialism," and agreements on economic, industrial, technical and cultural cooperation were signed.[97] Over the course of the next year, no fewer than five other delegations from Albania visited Cuba, including a return visit by the foreign minister who during his stay held a "warm and friendly talk" with Castro.[98] During the summer of 1990, when people stormed various embassies in Tirana, those who came to the Cuban embassy were handed over to police—an action that likely provoked a bomb attack on the embassy.

But the changes being forced in the country's domestic governance and economic policy had their external consequences. Albania's move to align its internal order at least with East Europe and in the direction of West Europe was accompanied by renewed diplomatic activity designed to bring the country back to the European and world community after years of shrill hostility. In mid-1990 the government announced its intention to join the Conference on Security and Cooperation in Europe. Ramiz Alia visited the UN to offer a new, less ideological foreign policy, and within a year the country had eliminated virtually all the diplomatic barriers and black holes it had held to for so long. Ties were established with the European Community, the Vatican, the United States, the Soviet Union, and Israel. Albania joined the IMF and World Bank and initiated substantial cooperation—spurred by the country's miserable situation and continuing exodus of refugees—with Italy, Greece, and Germany.[99]

For Albania, as for the other East European states that had experienced dramatic changes, a new government, a new economy, and a new democracy meant a new international orientation, one more suited to the country's needs. The Albanian Communist party cut to the heart of the matter and could have been speaking for all the East European states:

> Today's Europe is not the same as yesterday's in many ways. The great changes taking place on the continent create new movements and relations that cannot be understood by *a priori* schemes. There is a well-known saying: "Foreign policy cannot be based on the ideas of the past."[100]

Conclusion: Cuba and the East European Revolutions

Recent events in East Europe affect Cuba in two major ways, one more than the other. First, the newly democratizing states have sought to reorient their foreign policies, to change the pattern of their bilateral and multilateral affiliations, and in several cases to articulate new principles of foreign policy, such as a concern for human rights, and to act on them. In this respect, the loss to Cuba has been indisputable and widespread. Cuba is now more isolated than ever internationally, and unless patterns of change are reversed in East Europe or Cuba itself changes, this isolation will continue.

Less certain is whether the events of East Europe's annus mirabilis will soon be Cuba's fate. East Europe might prove an inspiration or a model of how state-dominated socialist systems can be challenged and their leadership overthrown, even where state power appears to be all-pervasive. After all, the East European states and Cuba shared several key characteristics: the communist party's dominance of politics; subordination of the executive organs of the government, the judiciary, and often the party's own rank and file; control of the media; party control over the allocation of resources; and restriction of market-oriented economic activity to a minor role. Most East European states were more developed and industrialized than Cuba and less dependent on one commodity for international returns. Most were also more involved in the noncommunist global economy. But, like Cuba, virtually all depended heavily on the Soviet Union to supply raw materials and purchase their exports.

In East Europe, Soviet-style socialism was thrown out—history was, in Marxist terms, reversed—because of a unique combination of factors, some new, others of longer standing. Undermining the regimes' position over the years and from within was their lack of popular legitimacy. Also contributing to their collapse was the failure of the regimes to deliver economically combined with the emergence of a younger, more aggressive, more impatient, and less fearful urban generation. At the same time, the presence of increasingly well-known and flourishing counter models, such as Germany and Western Europe, chipped away at both passivity and tacit support, especially among the young.

While crucial, these corrosive aspects of the situation were of long standing and might be standing still were it not for a combination of proximate factors: the existence of an alternative opposition force within the nation, either moral or political; the emergence of mass politics and the appearance and effectiveness of an umbrella group to channel that force into a challenge to the regime; the lack of response from the armed and security forces; and the nearly simultaneous nature of the challenge throughout the region. Finally, galvanizing all and bringing the mix to critical mass was the push for reform in the Soviet Union and its abandonment of intervention in East Europe as a way of protecting the regimes it had put in power.

Others will have to judge which of these factors are present or would be important in the Cuban case. The East European regimes' lack of legitimacy, for example, made them continuously vulnerable to domestic challenges, challenges ultimately blocked by the Soviet Union. Once the possibility of that force of last resort was removed, the likelihood increased of another challenge and of a challenge succeeding. By the same token, if the East European regimes had been able over the years to head off or mollify social discontent, had been able to provide some approximation of the prosperity available elsewhere in Europe, such challenges might not have occurred or succeeded. Do these same equations apply in Cuba? Has the Soviet Union been the ultimate guarantor of the Communist party's position, and does its removal as backstop threaten the Cuban regime? Can it rely on some other kind of support, such as popular legitimacy or economic satisfaction? Or must it rely on repression and a constantly invoked foreign threat to ensure public compliance? If so, how much longer will these devices work?

Questions like this were asked in the East European case but, if truth be told, all analysts missed their mark. No one predicted the events of 1989 either in timing, scope, or breadth. To be fair, observers lacked a template. Most pointed to the regimes' lack of legitimacy or the economic decline, and of course all noted the importance of the Soviet guarantee. But the significance of the other factors vis-à-vis the regime was usually dismissed or ignored largely because such a momentous change had never been carried through before. Thus no one thought to ask: What if it all comes together at once?

Now that it has, one can begin to ask why and how it happened and consider the comparability of the situation to other situations, as observers. In doing so, some factors will be cast out as not applicable. But observers of Cuba should be sure to add in, as a possible force contributing to change, the very fact that these revolutions in East Europe did occur. History *was* "reversed" and in systems very much like Cuba's. Thus those who would push for such changes now know it can be done and those who observe and analyze the possibility of such changes should be cognizant of the power of such thinking.

NOTES

I would like to gratefully acknowledge the insightful comments and suggestions on this paper by Ivan Berend, Jorge Domínguez, and Carmelo Mesa-Lago and the research assistance of Ben DeDominicis and Andrew Stein.

1. For discussions of East Europe before the events of 1989, see Teresa Rakowska-Harmstone, ed., *Communism in Eastern Europe* (Bloomington: Indiana University Press, 1984); J. F. Brown, *Eastern Europe and Communist Rule* (Durham: Duke University Press, 1988); and Joseph Rothschild, *Return to Diversity: A Political History of East Central Europe since World War II* (New York: Oxford University Press, 1989).

2. From data in Robert W. Campbell, *The Socialist Economies in Transition* (Bloomington: Indiana University Press, 1991), p. 132. See also M. C. Kaser, ed., *The Economic History of Eastern Europe 1919–1975*, vol. 3 (Oxford: Clarendon Press, 1986).

3. See Ronald H. Linden, "The Security Bind in East Europe," *International Studies Quarterly* 26, no. 2 (June 1982): 155–89.

4. See the discussion in H. Gordon Skilling, *Czechoslovakia's Interrupted Revolution* (Princeton: Princeton University Press, 1970), pp. 272–79.

5. It is estimated that between 1945 and 1966 the Soviet Union removed from East Europe in various ways roughly the same amount of resources ($14 billion) that the United States provided to Western Europe under the Marshall Plan. Paul Marer, "Has Eastern Europe Become a Liability to the Soviet Union? The Economic Aspect," in *The International Politics of Eastern Europe*, ed. Charles Gati (New York: Praeger, 1976), p. 65.

6. See Ronald H. Linden, *Bear and Foxes: The International Relations of the East European States* (Boulder: East European Quarterly and Columbia University Press, 1979), pp. 53–176.

7. William V. Wallace and Robert A. Clarke, *Comecon, Trade and the West* (London: Frances Pinter, 1986); Zbigniew Fallenbuchl, "The Council for Mutual Economic Assistance and Eastern Europe," *International Journal* 43, no. 1 (Winter 1987–88): 106–26.

8. Michael Marrese and Jan Vanous, *Soviet Subsidization of Trade with Eastern Europe: A Soviet Perspective* (Berkeley: University of California Institute of International Studies, 1983). The Marrese-Vanous calculations are not accepted uncritically by other analysts. For a review of the debate, see Charles Gati, *The Bloc That Failed* (Bloomington: Indiana University Press, 1990), pp. 119–24.

9. Egon Neuberger, Richard Portes, and Laura D. Tyson, "The Impact of International Economic Disturbances on the Soviet Union and Eastern Europe: A Survey," Joint Economic Committee, *East European Economic Assessment*, pt. 2, "Regional Assessment," 97th Congress, 1st session (Washington, D.C., 1981), pp. 128–47; Laura D. Tyson, "The Debt Crisis and Adjustment Responses in Eastern Europe: A Comparative Perspective," *International Organization* 40, no. 2 (Spring 1986): 239–85.

10. Linden, *Bear and Foxes*, pp. 173–203.

11. Michael Sodaro, "The GDR and the Third World: Supplicant and Surrogate," in *Eastern Europe and the Third World*, ed. Michael Radu (New York: Praeger, 1981), pp. 106–41.

12. Michael Radu, *Eastern Europe and the Third World* (New York: Praeger, 1981).

13. See, inter alia, Stephen White, *Gorbachev in Power* (Cambridge: Cambridge University Press, 1990).

14. For the authoritative Soviet statement laying out this "doctrine," see *Pravda*, 26 September 1968, p. 4. For a discussion of indications of changed Soviet thinking on East Europe before the 1989 revolutions, see Gati, *The Bloc That Failed*, pp. 161–69.

15. For a review of developments during 1989, see Radio Free Europe Research, "1989: Year of Upheaval," *Report on Eastern Europe* 1, no. 1 (5 January 1990).

16. On the 1990 elections in East Europe, see Radio Free Europe, "Toward Democracy in Eastern Europe," *Report on Eastern Europe* 1, no. 28 (13 July 1990).

17. For a review of Albanian developments in 1990–91, see Louis Zanga, "Mixed Fortunes as the New Year Begins," *Report on Eastern Europe* 2, no. 3 (10 January 1991): 1–5; and Louis Zanga, "Albania: Between Democracy and Chaos," *RFE/RL Research Report* 1, no. 1 (3 January 1992): 74–77.

18. On the communist accession to power, see Thomas T. Hammond, *The Anatomy of Communist Takeovers* (New Haven: Yale University Press, 1975), esp. pp. 310–432; Rothschild, *Return to Diversity*, pp. 76–124.

19. Moshe Lewin, *The Gorbachev Phenomenon*, exp. ed. (Berkeley: University of California Press, 1991).

20. Joseph Toth, "Depopulation of Rural Areas in Hungary," in *The Processes of Depopulation of Rural Areas in Central and Eastern Europe*, ed. Andrzej Stasiak and Wlodzimierz Mirowski (Warsaw: Institute of Geography and Spatial Organization, 1989), p. 238; Zdenek Rysavy, "Depopulation of the Rural Settlements in Czechoslovakia, 1969–2040," ibid., pp. 202, 206; Andrzej Stasiak, "Problems of Depopulation of Rural Areas in Poland After 1950," ibid., p. 14.

21. Severyn Bialer, "Poland and the Soviet Imperium," *Foreign Affairs* 59, no. 3 (1981): 527.

22. David Easton, *A Systems Analysis of Political Life* (New York: John Wiley, 1965), pp. 267–310.

23. On Czechoslovakia, see Skilling, *Czechoslovakia's Interrupted Revolution*, pp. 57–62. On Poland, see David Kemme, "The Polish Crisis: An Economic Overview," in *Polish Politics: Edge of the Abyss*, ed. Jack Bielasiak and Maurice Simon (New York: Praeger, 1984), pp. 29–55.

24. Easton, *A Systems Analysis*, pp. 343–468.

25. Ellen Comisso and Laura D. Tyson, eds., *Power, Purpose, and Collective Choice: Economic Strategy in Socialist States* (Ithaca: Cornell University Press, 1986).

26. For example, Yuri Shiriaev, director of the CMEA Institute of International Economic Research, said in 1987: "However perfect CMEA might become, we cannot expect to be successful if conditions are not created in each country for enterprises and branch agencies to consider participation in the integration as being in their own interest. This will require the creation of suitable incentives within [the] national economic mechanism." *Magyar Hirlap*, 21 February 1987 [*Foreign Broadcast Information Service*, [hereafter FBIS], 6 March 1987, p. BB3].

27. See Robert F. Goeckel, *The Lutheran Church and the East German State* (Ithaca: Cornell University Press, 1990).

28. For a review of pre-1989 opposition, see Janusz Bugajski and Maxine Pollack, *East European Fault Lines: Dissent, Opposition and Soviet Activism* (Boulder: Westview, 1989).

29. See the discussion in Donald E. Schulz and Jan S. Adams, eds., *Political Participation in Communist Systems* (New York: Pergamon, 1981).

30. Gyorgy Szoboszlai, "Elections and Political System Change in Hungary and Czechoslovakia," in *Demokratikus Atemenetek* (Budapest: Magyar Politikatudomanyi Tarsasag, 1991), pp. 202–11.

31. See the poignant essay by Jens Reich, "Reflections on becoming an East German dissident, on losing the Wall and a country," in *Spring in Winter: The 1989 Revolutions,* ed. Gwyn Prins (Manchester and New York: Manchester University Press and St. Martin's, 1990), pp. 65–98.

32. See the discussion in Ronald H. Linden, "Premises and Practices of Soviet Policy in Southeastern Europe," in *Problems of Balkan Security,* ed. Paul Shoup (Washington, D.C.: Wilson Center, 1990), pp. 235–50.

33. Cf. the letter of five Warsaw Pact members sent to the Czechoslovak party in 1968 (MTI Domestic Service, 17 July 1968 [Foreign Broadcast Information Service, 18 July 1968, pp. A1–A5]) and the discussion in Zdenek Mlynar, *Nightfrost in Prague* (New York: Karz, 1980).

34. On this point, see J. F. Brown, *Surge to Freedom: The End of Communist Rule in Eastern Europe* (Durham: Duke University Press, 1991), p. 146.

35. On Soviet and East European ties with developing countries, see Brigitte N. Schulz and William Woltansen, eds., *The Soviet Bloc and the Third World* (Boulder: Westview, 1989); Roger E. Kanet, ed., *The Soviet Union, Eastern Europe and the Third World* (Cambridge: Cambridge University Press, 1981); and Radu, *Eastern Europe and the Third World.*

36. Julio Diaz, "Kuba V Sotsialisticheskoi ekonomicheskoi integratsii" ["Cuba in Socialist Integration"], in K. I. Mikul'skovo, *CEV—Novyi etap sotrudinchestva* [CMEA—new stage of collaboration] (Moscow: Ekonomika, 1986), pp. 220–39.

37. Marie Lavigne, "The Impact of Reforms in Eastern Europe on Trade and Economic Cooperation with Developing Countries Members of the CMEA and Other Socialist or 'Socialist Oriented' Countries." Study prepared for the Committee for Development Planning. DIESA, United Nations, June, 1991, pp. 31–38.

38. BTA in English, 9 January 1990 [FBIS, 10 January 1990, p. 9].

39. See Hungarian Prime Minister Miklos Nemeth's speech, for example; BTA in English, 9 January 1990 [FBIS, 10 January 1990, p. 4].

40. See the statement at the CMEA session by Romania's prime minister, Petre Roman, Rompres in English, 10 January 1990 [FBIS, 11 January 1990, p. 1]; and the statement by the Bulgarian prime minister, Georgi Antanasov at the same meeting, BTA in English, 9 January 1990 [FBIS, 10 January 1990, p. 9].

41. Budapest MTI in English, 10 January 1990 [FBIS, 11 January 1990, p. 1].

42. MTI in English, 28 June 1991 [FBIS, 2 July 1991, p. 14]; see the Polish Council of Ministers' Statement, PAP in English, 26 February 1991 [FBIS, 28 February 1991, p. 19].

43. See for example the interview with Hungarian deputy Prime Minster Peter Medgyessy, *Magyar Hirlap,* 30 January 1990 [FBIS, 9 February 1990, p. 1].

44. See BTA in English, 11 March 1991 [FBIS, 13 March 1991]; Rompres in English, 21 March 1991 [FBIS, 26 March 1991, p. 49].

45. MTI in English, 28 June 1991 [FBIS, 10 July 1991, p. 1]. Hungary did extend preferential treatment to Cuba as well as Mongolia and Vietnam when it began to impose import duties on goods from CMEA countries. MTI in English, 27 December 1990 [FBIS, 31 December 1990, p. 31].

46. See, for example, the NATO reaction to Bulgarian expressions of interest in membership, Reuters, 27 November 1990.

47. For a review, see Ronald H. Linden, "The New International Political Economy of East Europe," *Studies in Comparative Communism* 25, no. 1 (March 1992): 10, 20.

48. See the article by Jiri Dienstbier, foreign minister of the Czech and Slovak Federal Republic, "Central Europe's Security," *Foreign Policy,* no. 83 (Summer 1991): 119–27.

49. PAP in English, 14 August 1991 [FBIS, 15 August 1991, p. 33].

50. Jiri Pehe, "Vaclav Havel's First Two Months in Office," *Report on Eastern Europe* 1, no. 11 (16 March 1990): 11–15.

51. Ibid., p. 14.

52. For a text of the resolution (no. 1990/48), see Commission on Human Rights, *Report on the Forty-sixth Session* (29 January–9 March 1990) (New York: United Nations, Economic and Social Council Official Records, 1990), supplement no. 2, p. 109.

53. MTI, 8 March 1990 [FBIS, 9 March 1990, p. 55].

54. "Speech by Fidel Castro at the closing session of the Fifth Congress of the Federation of Cuban Women," Havana Domestic Radio and TV, 7 March 1990 [FBIS, 8 March 1990], pp. 3–4.

55. Prague D.S., 20 March 1990 [FBIS, 21 March 1990, p. 15]. For a similar Bulgarian response, see BTA in English, 9 March 1990 [FBIS, 12 March 1990, p. 2].

56. Prague D. S., 22 June 1990 [FBIS, 25 June 1990, p. 9].

57. CTK in English, 29 June 1990 [FBIS, 2 July 1990, p. 3].

58. CTK in English, 16 August 1990 [FBIS, 17 August 1990, p. 6].

59. CTK in English, 6 December 1990 [FBIS, 11 December 1990. p. 17]; CTK in English, 18 June 1991 [FBIS, 20 June 1991], p. 17]. During his trip Valladares was accompanied by several Cuban-American businessmen.

60. At one point, Czechoslovakia suggested that the occupation might be the act of provocateurs. CTK in English, 18 July 1990 [FBIS, 19 July 1990, p. 13]. The next week Czechoslovakia rejected a Cuban charge that it had staged the whole incident. Bratislava D.S., 30 July 1990 [FBIS, 31 July 1990, p. 11].

61. Reuters, 15 and 17 July 1990; Czechoslovak D.S., 18 July 1990; *Mlada Fronta,* 19 July 1990 [FBIS, 23 July 1990, p. 28].

62. During a visit by Havel advisor Saša Vondra later in the summer, 68 congressmen sent a letter to Havel suggesting that the continued representing of Cuban interests implied tacit agreement with Castro's policies. *Lidova Demokracie,* 28 July 1990 [FBIS, 31 July 1990, p. 11]; see also *Los Angeles Times,* 20 December 1990.

63. Prague D. S., 2 August 1990 [FBIS, 3 August 1990, p. 8].

64. CTK, 18 December 1990 [FBIS, 19 December 1990, p. 24]. In February 1991 it was announced that Switzerland would take over the representation of Cuban interests in Washington.

65. Reuters, 21 December 1990.

66. In September 1990, Cuba reduced the provision of aviation fuel for Czechoslovak Airlines, and in response the airline suspended flights to the island. *Rude Pravo,* 25 September 1990 [FBIS, 2 October 1990, p. 16]. In November the two countries clashed at the UN over decolonization policy (RFE correspondents' report [New York] 23 November 1990], and in June 1991 Czechoslovakia announced it would not sell tanks either to Cuba or to North Korea. *Lidove Noviny,* 13 January 1991 [FBIS, 17 June 1991, p. 16].

67. MTI, 5 February 1991.

68. Prague D.S., 3 June 1990 [FBIS, 5 June 1990, p. 13]; *Lidova Demokracie,* 4 June 1990 [FBIS, 14 June 1990, p. 17]; Tanjug in English, 23 June 1990 [FBIS, 26 June 1990, p. 10].

69. CTK, 17, 18 and 19 February 1991.

70. AFP, 13 June 1990.

71. During his speech to the women's congress, Castro complained about Bulgarian forklifts: "They are such worthless things and have so many problems that we are the only ones who buy them." Hungarian "junk buses," he said, "fill the city with smog. They poison everybody." "Speech by Fidel Castro at the closing session of the Fifth Congress of the Federation of Cuban Women," p. 15. See also BTA in English, 16 March 1990 [FBIS, 19 March 1990 p. 8]; *Rude Pravo,* 16 March 1990 [FBIS, 23 March 1990, p. 28].

72. MTI, 12 June 1990; CTK in English, 13 June 1990 [FBIS, 14 June 1990, p. 43]; AFP in English, 27 March 1990 [FBIS, 28 March 1990, p. 17].

73. *Lidova Demokracie,* 24 January 1990 [FBIS, 26 January 1990, pp. 24–25].

74. Prague D.S., 7 July 1990 [FBIS, 9 July 1990, p. 49].

75. Prague D.S., 8 January 1990 [FBIS, 10 January 1990, p. 28–29].

76. Prague D.S., 11 January [FBIS, 12 January 1990, p. 18]; and Prague D.S., 12 January [FBIS, 16 January 1990, p. 32]. In their own riposte Cuban television in June 1991 broadcast a program highly critical of Havel and his government, drawing yet another protest from Prague. CTK in English, 17 June 1991 [FBIS, 18 June 1991, p. 12].

77. Reuters, 20 November 1990; Radio Budapest, 20 November 1990. For other examples, see chapter 5.

78. *Narodna Armiya,* 17 May 1990 [FBIS, 25 May 1990, pp. 5–6].

79. *Nepszadbadsag,* 6 November 1990 [FBIS, 14 November 1990, p. 26].

80. Rompres in English, 11 June 1990 [FBIS, 12 June 1990, p. 54; ibid., 20 July 1990.

81. Bratislava D.S., 20 August 1990 [FBIS, 22 August 1990, p. 18].

82. Agerpress, 26 January 1987 [*Summary of World Broadcasts,* 26 January 1987, p. EE/8477/B/9].

83. Agerpress in English, November 14, 1989 [FBIS, 21 November 1989, p. 79]. In addition to this visit and that of Jorge Valdes to Bulgaria in the fall of 1989, a Cuban army delegation visited East Germany; the minister for economic cooperation visited East Germany and Czechoslovakia, and the minister of culture visited Czechoslovakia.

84. Sofia D.S., 2 October 1989 [FBIS, 6 October 1989, p. 15]. For the Bulgarian government's warm assessment of Cuban relations just before the end of the Zhivkov regime, see *Otchestven Front,* 20 October 1989 [FBIS, 25 October 1989, p. 7].

85. CTK in English, 8 February 1991.

86. Czechoslovakia's role as an arms provider and expediter declined after the Prague Spring of 1968 as the Soviet Union began direct supply and utilized East Germany more. See Vratislav Pechota, "Czechoslovakia and the Third World," in *Eastern Europe and the Third World*, ed. Radu, pp. 83–85; and Jiri Valenta and Shannon Butler, "East German Security Policies in Africa," in ibid., pp. 146–47.

87. Sodaro, "The GDR and the Third World."

88. Gareth M. Winrow, *The Foreign Policy of the GDR in Africa* (Cambridge: Cambridge University Press, 1990), pp. 130–32.

89. Ibid., p. 133.

90. Gareth Winrow concludes that there is "no hard evidence" proving that East German combat troops were used in Africa. However, "tripartite" cooperation between the USSR, Cuba, and East Germany is evident in East Germany's offer in 1982 to send troops to Angola so that Cuban troops could be dispatched to Mozambique.

91. John M. Starrels, "East Germany Marxist Mission in Africa," in *Hearings before the Subcommittee on Security and Terrorism*, U. S. Senate, Committee on the Judiciary (Washington, D.C.: Government Printing Office, 1982), p. 786. See his discussion in ibid., pp. 134–44.

92. Henning von Lowis, "Das politische und militarische Engagement der Deutschen Demokratischen Republic in Schwarzafrica," *Beltrage zur Konfliktforschung* (January, 1978), p. 40, quoted in ibid., p. 809.

93. Winrow, *The Foreign Policy*, pp. 137–51.

94. Reuters, 11 January 1990.

95. See reports in *Los Angeles Times*, 10 January 1990; *The Guardian*, 28 December 1989.

96. ATA in English, 13 December 1989 [FBIS, 14 December 1989, p. 5].

97. See coverage by Tirana Domestic Service, 8–11 November 1989; ATA, 10 November 1989 [FBIS, 16 November 1989, pp. 2–7].

98. ATA, 13 December 1990 [FBIS, 18 December 1990, p. 4].

99. Incidents of mass flight occurred to Greece in December 1990 (5,000) and in January 1991 (10,000), and by boat to Italy in March (20,000) and in August 1991 (22,000).

100. *Zeri i Popullit*, 5 May 1990, quoted in Louis Zanga, "Albania's New Path," *Report on Eastern Europe* 1, no. 24 (15 June 1990): 4. It is worth noting that when the Albanian foreign minister, Reis Malile, visited Cuba (noted above), he also visited Mexico and Argentina.

3

The End of the Soviet-Cuban Partnership

◇ ◇ ◇

COLE BLASIER

CUBA'S REMARKABLE thirty-year partnership with the Soviet Union came to an end in 1991 not primarily because of changes in Cuba or the United States, but because of internal developments in the Soviet Union. The Soviet Union was Cuba's and Fidel Castro's lifeline, and Moscow regarded Cuba as one of its post–World War II political triumphs. Both sides had often pledged eternal loyalty to one another. To understand why and how this seemingly unbreakable partnership ended, we need to examine the connection between bilateral relations and Soviet domestic policy.

The End of Political Partnership

The Soviet Union and Cuba were not allies in the strict military sense, but rather partners. Soviet leaders were always aware that Cuba, even backed up by Soviet contingents, was not defensible against the United States. Nor was the USSR ever known to have believed the Castro regime to be worth the cost of a military encounter with the United States in the nuclear age.

Unlike the East European countries, Cuba was never a satellite of Moscow. Most East European leaders were instruments of the Soviet Communist party and remained in easy reach of Soviet military forces. Castro came to power as the military leader of his own revolution, joined up with Moscow only later, and jealously guarded his power thereafter. Cuba was theoretically within the reach of the Soviet military, but the Soviet military, although influential, never controlled Cuba.

Soviet leaders from Khrushchev to Gorbachev took pains not to make a formal commitment to defend Cuba. To deter foreign attack, they often gave the impression that the USSR stood firmly behind Cuba militarily, when in fact this was mainly bluster. In the early years and especially before the missile crisis, Castro may have hoped that he could count on Soviet military support if attacked. When he finally realized the limitations of the USSR's commitment, he accepted the Soviet refusal to form a military alliance or admit Cuba to the Warsaw Pact and publicly recognized that his regime would ultimately have to defend itself.

Cuba's proximity to the United States and its revolutionary anti-imperialist regime were the major reasons why the Soviets went to Cuba. The USSR maintained its transworld relationship with Cuba at great cost, especially in freight and communications. Soviet aid to Cuba may have been greater than to any other country, and by 1990 Cuba had the largest debt to the USSR of all socialist and nonsocialist countries.

The two governments collaborated not only between themselves, but also worked together closely in world affairs. Their policies were often sufficiently convergent as to make Castro a kind of spokesman and political ally on policy issues in the nonaligned movement, in the United Nations, and elsewhere. In Africa, Castro served as a paladin in Soviet-sponsored military operations.[1]

Despite the genuine closeness of the relationship and seeming harmony, the partnership had an Achilles' heel: Castro's extreme dependence on the USSR. Soviet authorities have always had the power to bring the Cuban economy to a screeching halt simply by cutting off oil deliveries. The Cuban armed forces depended on the USSR for spare parts for most of their military hardware, inventories of which the Soviet military has typically limited. Such dependence also applied to most raw materials, food, and manufactured goods. Castro was always painfully aware of this fact, especially after the USSR cut off oil supplies in 1968. This insoluble contradiction, his frustration over his ultimate vulnerability, and the demeaning nature of his dependence often made him a stubborn and contentious partner.

The Soviet-Cuban partnership was, nonetheless, remarkably durable because it served common interests, as perceived by both parties. For the USSR it was an element in its global strategy in the cold war rivalry with the United States.[2] The tie with Cuba made it possible to bring Soviet military power to the U.S. doorstep as a strategic counter to the many

U.S. military installations near Soviet borders, and it provided better political-strategic access to Latin America and the Caribbean. For Castro, the USSR represented an economic pipeline, and the Sovietization of Cuban institutions and foreign policy also served his long-term purpose of political survival. The Soviet Union provided a one-party political model that institutionalized and helped to preserve his personal and centralized dominance of Cuba.

Until Mikhail Gorbachev, conflicts between the two governments were resolved or papered over. Castro's political elimination of Soviet-sponsored old-guard communists, whom he viewed as a nuisance or potential political threat, was disconcerting for the Brezhnev leadership. Soviet leaders concluded that they had little choice but to go along with the man who led the revolution and controlled Cuba.

The Soviets, always less optimistic than Castro about the prospects for revolution in Latin America, did not want to see hard-earned communist cadres decimated by ill-fated revolts. Soviet ties were with the communist old guard, Castro's were with younger radical nationalists. Caught between competing factions on the Left, Moscow strategists maneuvered as best they could in the region, compromising with or tolerating recalcitrant forces. In any case, Cuba's revolutionary ardor was dashed by the absence of popular support or by successful repression of revolutionary initiatives in other Latin American nations.

Perceived Soviet and Cuban interests were not identical even where their convergence was greatest, as was the case in policy toward the United States.[3] While Cuba served Soviet interests in its superpower rivalry, Moscow did not want Cuba to interfere with the cooperative aspects of the USSR-U.S. relationship. This was particularly relevant with respect to detente under the Nixon administration and arms control issues generally. Moscow usually succeeded in balancing water on both shoulders, Castro's sensitivities notwithstanding.

Castro's only alternative would have been rapprochement with the United States. Yet he probably feared that if that took place, Cuban society would necessarily open up in unpredictable and uncontrollable ways that would ultimately challenge his monopoly of power.

One must ask: given all these problems, why did the USSR hang on so long in Cuba, and at such great material cost? Knowing the political-strategic value of its Cuban prize, official Moscow did not want to let Cuba go as long as the Soviet-U.S. strategic rivalry continued. While kept from the Soviet people, the huge cost of Soviet aid was not a domestic political problem. Cuba served the purposes of Soviet leaders, as long as the cold war and the international communist movement continued. When both collapsed, Cuba lost much of its value to the USSR.

The Soviet Apparat

Most of the major issues in Soviet relations with Cuba are well known and have been treated elsewhere.[4] Little attention has been paid, however, to where and by whom that policy was made—that is, to the Politburo, the Secretariat, and its departments. Soviet officials used to refer to this apparat simply as the Central Committee. Whatever coherence Soviet policy had—requiring the coordination of all government departments, the republics, and other agencies—was achieved by this apparat, Cuba's ultimate Soviet partner. But with the breakup of the Soviet Union, Cuba had to deal with an unwieldy array of powers: a dozen independent states, their many ministries, and a proliferation of foreign trade organizations.

Official Soviet views on Cuba have not been monolithic over the years, although censorship and the prohibition against airing internal disputes make that argument difficult to prove. Yet—to oversimplify—one sees in the leadership opposing groups, one relatively flexible, another more rigid. In the former group was Anastas Mikoyan, Khrushchev's closest collaborator, who was instrumental in establishing the relationship after visiting Cuba in 1960 in connection with an offical trip to Mexico. Soon after, Khrushchev met Castro at a meeting at the United Nations and liked him. In fact, the personal compatibility of the two leaders, bordering on that of father and son, established a good foundation for close relationships later.[5]

Meanwhile, arrangements favorable to incorporating Cuba into the socialist bloc were established in Moscow. Yuri Andropov was appointed head of the Secretariat's Socialist Countries Department in 1957; Khrushchev and Mikoyan had been impressed by his performance as Soviet ambassador during the Hungarian revolution, especially his capacity to understand more than one side of the conflict. When Castro declared Cuba socialist in April 1961, Cuba fell under Andropov's charge. But when Andropov was selected to head the KGB in 1967, his authority over Cuban policy faded.

After Khrushchev's removal in 1964, Mikhail Suslov, one of the most senior members of the Politburo famous for his dogmatism and orthodoxy, took over supervision of Cuban policy. He exerted a strong influence until his death in early 1982. When Brezhnev followed him in November, Yuri Andropov succeeded him as general secretary until 1983. Vitali I. Vorotnikov, once "exiled" to Cuba as the Soviet ambassador (1979–1982), joined the Politburo while Andropov was in charge and remained in influential positions for several years.[6]

Shortly after Gorbachev came to power in 1985, he got rid of aging officials in the CPSU secretariat and brought in Anatoli Dobrynin, former ambassador to the United States, to head the International Department. This department, which had originated as a kind of headquarters for world revolution, was now led by a classic diplomat and former social lion of the Washington diplomatic community. Gorbachev also reassigned foreign policy responsibilities among Politburo members, adding Eduard Shevardnadze, Aleksandr N. Iakolev, and later Evgeni Primakov to the Politburo. Meanwhile, the CPSU was rapidly losing power to the government and was eventually dissolved.

Officials who were most influential in shaping Soviet policy toward Cuba probably were Nikita Khrushchev, Anastas Mikoyan, Yuri Andropov, and Mikhail Gorbachev. Khrushchev and Mikoyan established the link; Andropov was associated with Cuba for twenty-five years in the Secretariat, in the KGB, and as general secretary; and Gorbachev ended Cuba's privileged treatment.

The heads of the Socialist Countries Department, except Andropov, appear not to have been innovators. Most were trained as engineers, had little foreign experience as young men, and, with a few exceptions, gained whatever analytical and diplomatic skills they possessed on the job. Vorotnikov, for example, had no major foreign experience before he went to Cuba as ambassador in 1979. (He later joined the Politburo and served as chairman of the RSFSR Council of Ministers.) Most of their careers were made in party management posts.

Cuba was only one of many socialist countries with which Soviet officials were concerned, but was a kind of favorite in the family. Some individuals not in the chain of party command probably exerted considerable influence on policy. One was Nikolai Leonov, a KGB official and admired associate of Yuri Andropov, who met Raúl Castro on his way to

Mexico in 1953.[7] This chance encounter led to a wide acquaintance among the 26 of July Movement and close personal ties with the Castro regime. He accompanied leading Soviet figures on visits to Cuba and served as interpreter for Castro, Mikoyan, Khrushchev, and Brezhnev, among others.[8]

Oleg T. Darusenkov, who headed the Cuban sector of the Socialist Countries Department for many years and edited several publications on Cuba, was later appointed Soviet ambassador to Mexico. Sergo A. Mikoyan, a leading Soviet specialist on Cuba, visited the island with his father in 1960 and followed Cuban developments as editor of the journal *Latinskaia Amerika*. Although not in the chain of command, Mikoyan was one of the most knowledgeable observers of Soviet policy toward Cuba.[9]

The magnitude of Soviet aid to Cuba for thirty years suggests that Castro must have been remarkably adept at dealing with the Soviet apparat, even though his massive dependence on the USSR must have been intimidating. If (as Soviet observers believe) he had a "hot line" to the top leadership, he must have been tempted to use it often. But if he had done so, as a pleader or supplicant, he would surely have lost much of his authority. Marshaling his limited credits with Moscow, he probably had subordinates deal routinely through the secretariat, government agencies, and after 1972 through the Cuban-Soviet Joint Commission.

An important element in Castro's success in extracting many billions of rubles from the USSR was his psychological manipulation of the relationship. Somehow he got the Soviets to feel indebted to him. From time to time Castro had fits of temper to chasten his benefactors, as with his refusal to attend General Secretary Chernenko's funeral. Castro was the hero; the Soviets were his bankers. Since he was the "victim" of the United States, he deserved their help. The Soviets had to prove the self-abnegation of socialism in contrast to the greed of capitalism. Castro somehow managed to get the USSR to come to Cuba, not Cuba to the USSR.

Soviet-Cuban Divergence: National Liberation Movements

In the stream of history, few partnerships have been more integrated, stronger, or more durable than that of the USSR and Cuba. It is hard to say whether the extreme dependence of the junior partner was a strengthening factor or a liability. What drew them together was less ideology than perceived state interests. The central tie was shared hostility to the United States: for Castro the United States was the one foreign power ultimately capable of overthrowing him, and one that had tried to do so; for the USSR, the other superpower was an antagonist in a life-and-death struggle between socialism and capitalism.

Always more threatened than Moscow and bearing the scars of Cuba's former encounters with the United States, Castro was more stridently and bitterly anti-American. But Moscow welcomed an enemy of the United States who could make such persuasive arguments against U.S. imperialism in the Third World. At the same time, Brezhnev and other Soviet leaders, pursuing détente and arms control, were able to distance themselves from Castro's extremist statements. Differences were matters of degree.

Another major tie was support for national liberation movements. Soviet backing for social revolution in the Third World went back to the Bolshevik revolution and the founding of the Communist International.[10] The aim of promoting bourgeois uprisings as a transitional step, and of socialist regimes later, was a fixed Soviet objective. Castro was more impatient than that, and there were disagreements about when and how to use force. Arguments within the leading circles in the USSR and in Cuba, and between the two, were not about the ultimate objective, but how to get there.

Castro's more radical policies were designed to help him survive in the face of what he viewed as U.S. hostility. His long-term strategy was to support the establishment of a network of radical nationalist or socialist regimes in Latin America. He did this by backing revolutionary movements, communist parties, and governments sympathetic to his cause, such as the Sandinistas in Nicaragua and the Allende government in Chile. Moscow did not oppose armed landings and revolts in principle, but was against them when prospects of success and holding on after the seizure of power were poor. In view of its international position, Moscow also preferred to provide military and other support to recognized governments such as the Sandinistas and the Cubans, rather than guerrilla movements in places like El Salvador and Bolivia. In the end, this strategy was vindicated; virtually all of Castro's paramilitary interventions failed.

In the late 1980s Gorbachev and Eduard Shevernadze, his close ally, revised the official line on the class struggle to serve foreign policy objectives vis-à-vis the West, but this revision gutted the theoretical base for the national liberation effort. Emphasizing reconciliation rather than confrontation, the new leaders, shorn of opponents like Yegor Ligachev, delinked the class struggle from international relations.[11] While the class struggle had lost resonance in the USSR (presumably class differences had been largely overcome), Castro continued to stress the issue, especially in the Third World. His leadership of the class struggle in Cuba helped to justify his long tenure in office.

Castro even more strongly resisted the implications of Gorbachev's view: that socialist nations should make some kind of enduring peace with the capitalist powers, particularly the United States, and together seek to resolve "regional" conflicts. In espousing collaboration with capitalism in the Third World, Gorbachev's policy struck at the heart of national liberation strategy. Castro's revolutionary legitimacy rested on his anti-imperialism. Now Gorbachev sought cooperation with the United States, whose hostility to Cuba has been a rationale for Soviet aid.

Glasnost and perestroika dealt a severe blow not only to Castro's political model and Cuba's economy, but also to his reliance on Soviet backing for his strategy for regional security. Under Gorbachev the USSR has ceased active support for such movements and ceased to lead the communist parties in Latin America. This major development took place with barely a peep from either Moscow or Washington. Until the coup attempt of 1991, Moscow found this political retreat an embarrassment; Washington welcomed its benefits but, for tactical reasons, has been grudging in giving credit.

Moscow has folded up most of its organizational ties with communist parties in the Western Hemisphere. The *World Marxist Review,* a pale echo of earlier international communist organs, ceased to publish in Prague in 1990. When Gorbachev shifted power from the party to the government, the International Department of the CPSU became more of an observer than a political operator. Soviet sponsorship of many international communist activities came to an end. (Indeed, the communist parties in Latin America have never had lasting success, and their future prospects were dim.) For the Soviet Union, leading the international communist movement proved costly in terms of time and money, while yielding little. And support for communist parties has hurt the USSR with respect to democratic governments in Latin America, in the United States, and elsewhere.

The ossification of Cuban socialism, the invasion of Grenada, the electoral defeat of the Sandinistas, the overthrow of Noriega in Panama, the pact between the guerrillas and the government in El Salvador, the dimmed prospects of the revolutionary Left in Latin America, and the spread of democratic governments in that region and elsewhere were massive blows to the morale of the communist parties. Torn by faction-alism, the communist movement had already entered one of its politically weakest periods. Gorbachev's revolution was not the straw, but the load that broke the camel's back. His resignation as general secretary of the party, the seizure of its properties and the sealing of its records, and its separation from government functions ended any remaining pretense that the USSR could dominate foreign lands. Communism is in even sharper retreat at the center than on the Latin American periphery.

Soviet colleagues have expressed to me their personal sympathy for the Latin American communists, but explicitly state that their downfall was politically and economically inevitable, and probably deserved. The communist parties in Latin America have never led a successful revolu-tion, and lost to competitors like Castro in Cuba and the Sandinistas in Nicaragua. Nor does any have a large political base today. The Soviet Union has cut off most or all financial support and political leadership. The political model advocated by Latin American communists for sev-eral generations has been repudiated almost everywhere, including Mos-cow. Once held together by Moscow's support, most communist parties are now badly divided. (See chapter 8).

Many Latin American communist leaders are totally confused, trying to understand the changes in the Soviet Union, unable to find direction, even to stay afloat in a sea of change. Many are old and will be unable to adapt to new circumstances. When asked which groups would take charge of the Left and capitalize on the issues that have characterized revolutionary contests in the past—exploitation and foreign domina-tion—a Soviet colleague specializing in national liberation movements replied that the twentieth century was the age of revolutions; the twenty-first will have other themes.

The collapse of the international communist movement in Latin America has deprived Castro of political leverage. He always aspired to lead it and occasionally did so, sometimes to Moscow's displeasure. The diminished stature of communist parties further reduces their prospects for gaining power and ending Castro's isolation as the only socialist nation in the hemisphere. If he ever hoped for a growing community of socialist nations in the Western Hemisphere that could counter U.S. dominance during his lifetime, such hopes must be totally dashed.

The USSR and Cuba withdrew from Ethiopia and Angola relatively early in the Gorbachev period. On December 22, 1988, Angola, Cuba, and South Africa signed an agreement in New York providing for the independence of Namibia. At the same time, Angola and Cuba agreed on a phased withdrawal of Cuban troops from Angola, the last of which left in 1991. The USSR and the United States facilitated both agreements, to which Angola, Cuba, and South Africa were the main parties. The Soviets supported this settlement primarily because of the immense political and economic costs of continued involvement.[12]

The rationale for Cuba's intervention in Africa, apart from fulfilling the leadership's commitment to national liberation movements, was that it served as a political-strategic payoff for Soviet economic aid. But when the Soviet Union had no more aid to offer and collapsed, so did the rationale. Whatever pluses these operations had in establishing Cuba as an international player—and they had many—Cuba had little to show at home for the sacrifice of lives and money when the troops returned.[13]

In sum, Gorbachev's policies threatened Castro's political system and the Cuban economy, favored Soviet reconciliation with Castro's main enemy, the United States, and gutted Soviet support for Castro's principal allies, the national liberation movements.

Reformists versus Conservatives

In the late 1980s Cuba became the focus of an internal Soviet debate on two related issues. The first, a political one, was whether the personalistic, totalitarian regime of Fidel Castro was a suitable partner for the USSR as it underwent rapid democratization under glasnost and perestroika. The other issue, economic in character, was whether the USSR should continue to provide large amounts of aid, or any aid at all, to Cuba.

The two issues were related, since supporters of the old Soviet regime tended to favor aid, while critics were opposed. As a result, these Cuban issues became closely linked to the larger national debate over the character of the Soviet regime or that of its successor. To oversimplify, conservatives, who wanted a neo-Stalinist system, tended to accept Cuba; reformists, who wanted free markets and a democratic orientation, rejected the Castro regime. Soviet policy toward Cuba depended on the outcome of the larger political question.

There was lively discussion of these issues in the USSR between the time of Gorbachev's visit to Havana in 1989 and the failed coup two years later. Official policy sought to protect the Soviet political investment in Cuba, although it was becoming clear that Cuba was less important to the USSR than vice versa. Views on the Cuban question changed as Soviet conditions changed. Whereas leaders on both sides once invoked their common adherence to Marxism-Leninism as a reason for continued collaboration, Castro (despite his claims) always seemed motivated more by pragmatic than theoretical considerations, particularly because of Cuba's need for Soviet aid. As for the Soviets, Marxism-Leninism was a useful weapon for maintaining oligarchic control.

When it first became clear that aid would have to be reduced, many in the Soviet Union sought to minimize the cuts, feeling that the USSR, as a model and a patron, bore a responsibility toward Cuba. But as the social revolution in the USSR gained momentum, there was less and less support for aiding Cuba.

It was glasnost that broke the harmony. Cuba's and the USSR's domestic and foreign policies diverged after Gorbachev came to power. His policy of glasnost threatened the status quo in both countries, where public criticism of official policy had not been permitted. Gorbachev was not answerable for the past policies he criticized; but Castro could not escape responsibility for most of what happpened in Cuba after 1959. The USSR was now open—and Cuba still closed—to publications criticizing their socialist systems.

Opening up the Soviet Union to criticism of public policy, and ultimately of the system itself, threatened Castro. He feared, probably correctly, that glasnost in Cuba would endanger his political dominance, as ultimately happened to leaders in the USSR. He even found it necessary to prevent the distribution in Cuba of certain Soviet periodicals critical of himself—a clear indication of his vulnerability.

The central issue of the debate was Soviet aid to Cuba. It was particularly conservatives, notably Soviet intelligence and military people with close ties to the Cuban elite for more than a generation, who favored continued support.[14] Some of their views on aid, however, were shaped more by their attachment to the old Soviet system than fondness for Cuba. They saw no important place for themselves in the new order, while under the old they knew what they could expect and how they would come out. Soviet citizens sent to Cuba had enjoyed better compensation, easier access to hard currency, and a respite from Soviet central authority. Proud of the USSR's status as a superpower and deeply disillusioned by the morass in which it now found itself, conservatives saw strong ties with Cuba as a sign of the viability of the old system.

The reformists, who reflected a wide and shifting spectrum of Soviet opinion, and who included managers, professionals, academics, and artists, favored decentralization and privatization. Restructuring the economy meant democratization. By the spring of 1991, they had grown impatient with Gorbachev's domestic policies, indecisiveness, and dependence on conservatives; with some exceptions, they solidly backed the policies of Boris Yeltsin, who had already (in May 1990) come out in favor of "substantial reduction of assistance to other countries."[15] For ideological, political, and economic reasons, reformists urged a reexamination of Soviet relations with Cuba.

Unlike conservatives, reformists believed that the Castro regime— personalist, totalitarian, and politically repressive—was precisely the sort of government the USSR should not support.[16] They asked what permanent Soviet interests had been advanced over the long history of the USSR-Cuban relationship. Some anticipated major changes in Cuba.[17] Not only had they no desire to save Cuban socialism, they doubted that fresh infusions of Soviet assistance could save it anyway. They believed that the authoritarian model was a failure in both the USSR and in Cuba.[18] Moreover, resources were desperately needed at home and would be better spent there. In any case, they ultimately won the day because the Soviet economy was no longer able to support Cuba.

In April 1991, I asked Soviet citizens in Moscow about aid to Cuba in discussions with taxi drivers, students, shoppers, workers, housewives, and others on the street. All knew about Cuba and Soviet assistance. No one supported it: nine out of ten of my interviewees opposed aid to Cuba, and others were evasive. They gave generally similar reasons: "We don't have the aid to give," "We can't afford it," "They live better than we do," "The aid is needed more here than there," and "Why should we give to a dictatorship like Castro's?" Most expressed their opposition with vehemence, going beyond the Cuban issue to complain of current Soviet living conditions. Soviet observers whose judgment I respect said that giving aid to Cuba was generally unpopular throughout the USSR.

Military Ties

The Soviet Union's main strategic purpose in Cuba was to establish a military presence in the Americas as a part of a global strategy without provoking direct armed conflict with the United States. Troops in Cuba served as a symbolic counter to U.S. forces near Soviet borders and added to the USSR's superpower credentials. Soviet military and intelligence forces, and especially Cuba's electronic listening station at Lourdes, provided a new perspective on the United States. Finally, Soviet forces in Cuba were regarded as a deterrent against U.S. attack, however unlikely it might be in the near future.

To establish this presence, the USSR sent military advisors, a military detachment, and arms and equipment to Cuba. In 1990 the International Institute for Strategic Studies in London estimated that there were 7,700 Soviet and military personnel stationed in Cuba.[19] The advisors were primarily concerned with the receipt and efficient use of military assistance. The military brigade—a kind of counterpart to U.S. troops in West Berlin—was a trip wire for, or a deterrent against, possible U.S. attack. On some occasions its mission was described publicly as training Cuban forces. In addition, Soviet aircraft made frequent visits to Cuba, and there had been twenty-seven naval visits by 1988.[20] Although the USSR did not own permanent military bases there, Cuba offered Soviet military forces many of the same services as those provided by bases: resupply, repair, and rest and recreation.

The extent of Soviet aid in the form of military supplies and equipment is difficult to estimate, but it amounted to many billions of rubles. Most assume that military assistance was provided free because Cuba lacked the capacity to pay. Almost all of Cuba's modern military equipment since 1960 came from the USSR. Table 3.1 describes the volume of Soviet military hardware and personnel in Cuba. Note that much of this equipment serves defensive rather than offensive purposes.

From Cuba's perspective, Gorbachev's innovations in Soviet diplomacy had a negative impact on military relations. Soviet-U.S. accommodation, for example, was a thorn in Castro's side. The Soviet-Yugoslav Statement of Principles of March 19, 1988, also laid to rest the Brezhnev Doctrine that claimed the right to intervene militarily to protect socialism from imperialism. Soviet leaders implemented the March 1988 declaration by refusing to send military forces to protect the socialist governments of Eastern Europe. (See chapter 2.) These

TABLE 3.1
Soviet Military Assistance to Cuba

SELECTED SOVIET MILITARY HARDWARE IN CUBA, 1990

Army	Main battle tanks	1,100
	Light Tanks	60
	Armored fighting vehicles	650
Navy	Submarines	3
	Frigates	3
	Patrol and coastal combatants	56
Air Force	Fighters, ground attack	156
	Fighters	199
	Transport aircraft	82
	Attack helicopters	46
	Transport helicopters	123
	Surface-to-air missile sites	200
	Training craft	89

SOVIET MILITARY PERSONNEL IN CUBA, 1990

Military advisors	2,800
Military detachment (brigade)	2,800
Electronic technicians (Lourdes)	2,100

Source: International Institute of Strategic Studies, *The Military Balance 1990–1991* (London: IISS, 1990), pp. 192-93.

developments were explicit confirmation of what Castro had long known, that he could not expect Soviet forces to protect him from internal revolt or foreign attack.

Nevertheless, until 1991 leading Soviet military and intelligence officers associated with Cuba tended to support military assistance to the island. They had invested heavily and personally in Cuba's military prowess, the Cuban tie was a source of continuing prestige and perquisites, and the Soviet military did not wish to lose a strategic place in the USSR's global strategy. Even those who opposed further heavy expenditures in Cuba recognized a moral obligation not to let an ally down, especially one that owed its present fate in no small part to the USSR. Yet Soviet policy wavered beteewn 1988 and the summer of 1991, when Soviet-Cuban military relations were transformed and with them the nature of the bilateral relationship.

The End of Economic Partnership

The first Soviet commitments to Cuba in the summer of 1960 seemed limited and manageable. The USSR agreed to buy the sugar the Eisenhower administration spurned, supply the oil foreign companies refused to refine, and furnish weapons long embargoed by the United States. Although severe U.S. trade sanctions were imminent, Moscow probably did not fully realize that sugar, oil, and arms were only the beginning of a costly relationship; Cuba was a brilliant strategic and political prize.

Before long, the USSR was supplying not only essentials but almost everything Cuba needed, including most of its raw materials, equipment, and even some foodstuffs. A telling indicator of the extent of Soviet aid is the list of Soviet exports to Cuba—in 1987, for example, longer than for any other country except Mongolia (and Soviet exports to the latter were a third of those to Cuba). The Soviet Union became the main supplier of such important products as oil and oil products (100 percent), fertilizer (91 percent), grain (94 percent), iron and nonferrous metals (70 percent), trucks and light vehicles (70 percent), and autobuses (37 percent).[21]

Oil

Cuba was most dependent on the USSR for oil, meeting 90 percent or more of its needs with Soviet imports. The USSR tried every strategy to help Cuba find its own oil, but these efforts filled less than 10 percent of Cuba's domestic needs. Cuba still hopes to strike oil offshore, but exploration and extraction require investment beyond Havana's and Moscow's means. Until new sources of oil are found, the USSR has the power to bring the Cuban economy to a halt. Soviet oil output began to fall in 1988, and economic decline and management problems associated with perestroika threatened shipping and other export distribution systems. The fall in oil and coal production might seem manageable, except that the USSR depends for about half of its foreign exchange on oil exports. (See table 3.2.)

Declines in Soviet oil output and in other exports have created further complications for Cuba; Cuba had been receiving far more oil than necessary for its domestic needs—or rather getting credit from Moscow under the trilateral arrangements with Venezuela (to be discussed later). It needed about 10 million tons a year, while the USSR before its oil crisis

TABLE 3.2
Soviet Energy Production and Energy Exports, 1986–1991

YIELD OF PETROLEUM, GAS, AND COAL

	1986	1987	1988	1989	1990	1991 (est.)
Petroleum, oil, and liquified gas (millions of tons)	614.5	523.8	623.9	606.6	570.4	518.1
Gas (billions of cubic meters)	686.0	727.3	770.1	796.1	814.8	811.0
Coal (millions of tons)	751.0	760.0	772.0	740.0	703.0	642.0

CENTRALIZED SOVIET DELIVERIES FOR EXPORT OF PETROLEUM, PETROLEUM PRODUCTS, AND GAS

	1986	1987	1988	1989	1990	1991 (est.)
Petroleum, oil (millions of tons)	116.7	121.1	122.4	114.9	99.3	46.0
Petroleum products (millions of tons)	56.8	59.2	61.0	57.4	44.5	30.0
Gas (billions of cubic meters)	79.2	84.4	88.0	101.0	108.7	103.0

USSR OIL EXPORTS AS PERCENTAGE OF TOTAL EXPORTS, 1980–1989

	1980	1985	1986	1987	1988	1989
Fuels and energy	46.8	52.7	47.3	46.5	42.1	39.9
Of which: Oil and oil products	36.4	38.9	32.9	33.5	29.4	27.1
Natural gas	7.4	10.6	10.8	9.4	8.8	8.9

Energy Production by the Commonwealth of Independent States, 1991

	Coal		Oil		Natural Gas	
	Total Production (millions of tons)	% Change (compared to 1990)	Total Production (millions of tons)	% Change (compared to 1990)	Total Production (billions of cubic meters)	% Change (compared to 1990)
Azerbaijan	—	—	11.7	-6.0	8.6	13.0
Kazakhstan	130	-0.7	26.6	3.0	7.9	11.0
Russian Federation	353	-11.0	461	-11.0	643	0.4
Turkmenistan	—	—	5.4	-3.0	84.3	-4.0
Uzbekistan	5.9	-8.0	2.8	0.8	41.9	3.0
Ukraine	136	-18.0	4.9	-6.0	24.4	-13.0

Sources: G. Yavlinskogo, "Ekonomika SSR: preodolenie naslediia totalitarnoi sistemy," short report of the leader of the official delegation of the USSR at the annual combined meeting of the executive councils of the International Monetary Fund and the World Bank, October 15 – 17, 1991, p. 18; International Monetary Fund, *A Study of the Soviet Economy* (Washington: IMF, 1991), p. 103; ibid., *Economic Review: Common Issues and Interrepublic Relations in the Former USSR* (Washington: IMF, 1992), p. 44.

supplied about 13 million tons through a European intermediary. Cuba sold the 3 million ton difference to hard-currency purchasers, its second largest source of hard currency. The USSR first cut deliveries to the intermediary to 10 million tons in 1990 and to 7–9 million in 1991. Cubans foresee declines to 6 million tons or less in 1992. (See chapter 5.)

To save transport costs, Soviet oil enterprises, Venezuelan producers, and Cuban consumers made quadrilateral arrangements to supply Cuba with oil. Soviet enterprises delivered Soviet crude oil (much of it type Ural) to FEVA, a German company based in Rotterdam, which made it available to European consumers. FEVA bought Venezuelan crude (for example, type Lago Medio, similar to Ural) and arranged for its delivery to Cuba.[22] This satisfied much of Cuba's need for crude oil. Meanwhile, the USSR, which arranged for Cuba to receive petroleum products directly or through other sources, has spent 105 million pesos on an oil refinery at Cienfuegos.[23]

At the end of 1991, Soviet crude oil was piling up in Soviet ports, as was Cuban sugar, because of the breakdown of distribution systems in the former USSR. In October 1991, FEVA refused to deliver crude to Cuba, since the USSR had suspended deliveries to Rotterdam.

Various oil-producing countries, among them Mexico, Venezuela, and Libya, have been unwilling to sell Cuba crude oil on credit. Several governments, such as that of Venezuela, refuse to aid countries that do not meet certain human rights and democratic criteria.

Sugar

Having produced over 9 million metric tons of sugar in 1990–91, the USSR was the world's third largest sugar producer after the European Community and India. It produced more beet sugar than Cuba produced sugarcane, but Soviet production fell far short of domestic needs. (See table 3.3.) The USSR's sugar yield per hectare was only half that of Denmark, and its recovery rate in refining only two-thirds that of Denmark's. Thus it produced only about one-third as much sugar per hectare as Denmark. Denmark's production is used for comparative purposes because it is near West European averages and its soil and climate are similar to Russia's.

The USSR is the largest consumer of sugar in the world, surpassing Europe, India, the United States, and China, partly because shortages of

TABLE 3.3
Major Sugar Producers and Selected Yields, 1988–1990

SUGAR PRODUCTION IN SELECTED EUROPEAN COUNTRIES
(in millions of metric tons, raw value)

	1989–90	*1990–91*
European Community		
(includes United Germany)	16.00	17.01
India	12.9	13.24
USSR	9.53	9.16
Cuba	8.00	7.62
Brazil	7.79	7.90
United States	6.01	6.27
China	5.62	6.65
Australia	3.80	3.52
Thailand	3.50	3.95
Mexico	3.10	3.60
World Total	108.27	112.98

SELECTED SUGAR YIELDS AND RECOVERY RATES

	Unit	*Denmark*	*Poland*	*USSR*
Area harvested	1,000 ha	67	425	3,334
Yield	Mt/ha.	51.6	35.4	15.7
Recovery rate	Percent	16.1	13.0	10.4
Sugar per ha.	Mt/ha.	8.3	4.6	2.8

Source: Ron Lord, U.S. Department of Agriculture, "Restructuring in Centrally Planned Economies and the Outlook for Sugar," presented to the annual Agricultural Outlook Conference, December 4, 1991, Washington, D.C., pp. 13–14.

meat, cheese, and high-quality seafood have caused consumers to turn to sweets. As a reporter once remarked, "Misha has a sweet tooth." Recognizing the political importance of satisfying consumer needs, authorities have made the provision of sugar, like nutritious dark bread, a high domestic priority. Visitors comment on the excellent ice cream in the USSR. Also, the anti-alcohol campaign causes sugar to be hoarded for private distilling. (See table 3.4.)

Thus Soviet consumption of sugar has exceeded production by about 4 million tons a year, roughly the amount imported from Cuba and about one-third of Soviet sugar consumption. As table 3.5 indicates, the USSR

TABLE 3.4
World Sugar Consumption, 1989–1991
(in millions of metric tons, raw value)

	1989–90	1990–91
USSR	13.70	13.60
European Community (includes United Germany)	12.92	12.82
India	11.26	11.85
United States	7.74	7.96
China	7.45	7.50
Brazil	6.80	6.80
Mexico	4.04	4.24
Japan	2.83	2.80
Indonesia	2.34	2.42
Pakistan	2.27	2.40
Philippines	1.47	1.5
Iraq	0.67	0.32
Total	107.76	109.35

Source: Lord, "Restructuring," p. 14.

imported 3.5 million tons of Cuban sugar in 1989. Note that the Soviet share of Cuba's sugar exports was near an all-time high in 1987, the latest year on the table.

With the breakup of the Soviet Union and the formation of the Commonwealth of Independent States, the question arises whether the former Soviet republics will continue to demand Cuban sugar. Theoretically, these countries could as a group become self-sufficient by various means, including modernizing refining facilities, expanding acreage, or both. Ron Lord, a U.S. Department of Agriculture economist, estimates that by increasing yields and recovery rates halfway to the level of Denmark (see table 5.3), sugar production in the former USSR would rise from 9.3 to 17.3 million tons, that is far in excess of domestic demand.[24] Lord estimates that if the former republics' economies could get back on their feet, such an increase could be achieved without massive capital investment—an estimate based partly on the Polish experience.[25]

In the USSR, instead of renovating inefficient and outdated refining facilities (perhaps half of them built before 1917), officials bought sugar from Cuba instead. Political considerations facilitated such a decision—the need to support the Cuban economy—but possibly they believed foreign purchase was more cost-effective than investing in expanded

TABLE 3.5
Soviet Imports of Sugar from Cuba, 1971–1989

| | All Cuban Exports | Exports to the USSR | | Soviet Share of Exports (%) |
		(in thousands of tons)	(in thousands of rubles)	
1971	5511	1536	185,642	27.87
1972	4139	1101	131,465	26.60
1973	4797	1603	323,058	33.42
1974	5491	1856	610,782	33.80
1975	5744	2964	1,344,312	51.60
1976	5764	3068	1,397,830	53.23
1977	6238	3652	1,675,346	58.54
1978	7197	3797	2,117,209	52.76
1979	7199	3707	2,037,903	51.49
1980	6170	2647	1,857,934	42.90
1981	7055	3090	1,825,665	43.80
1982	7727	4224	2,476,334	54.66
1983	7011	2966	2,408,314	42.30
1984	7007	3508	3,209,285	50.06
1985	7206	3685	3,312,053	51.14
1986	6697	3861	3,091,475	57.65
1987	6479	3750	2,937,183	57.88
1988	—	3004	2,613,296	—
1989	—	3468	2,596,095	—

Source: A. D. Bekarevich and N. M. Kukharev, *Sovetskii Soiuz Kuba: Ekonomicheskoe Sotrud-nichestvo (70-80-e gody)* (Moscow: Nauka, 1990), pp. 9, 205.

production at home. Although the cost of renovation may not seem great in Western terms, alternatives were more promising.

The breakup of the USSR also means that the republics' interests surely will take precedence over those of the former Union. Ukraine produces more than half of the former nation's sugar beets, Russia about a third, and small amounts are grown in Moldova, Byelorus, Kazakhstan, Lithuania, Latvia, and Georgia; Azerbaidjan, Armenia, and Estonia produce none. The bulk of the sugar refining takes place in Ukraine, Russia, and Kirghistan. Now an independent state, Ukraine becomes the largest beet sugar producer in the world, and Russia is in fourth place, after the Ukraine, France, and the United States, in world production.

Ukraine and Moldova produce more sugar than they consume and are not likely buyers of Cuban sugar, except for refining. The republics that most need imported sugar are Russia, Central Asia, Byelorus, the

Caucasus, and the Baltic states. Cuba's most promising customer in terms of need is Russia—which conveniently is the major source of oil. Although Russia is a big producer, its large population consumes far more sugar than it yields. The Slavic states have high consumption per capita (44–49 kg per year), the Caucasus less (34–39 kg per year), and Central Asia, other than Kazakhstan, low (25–36 kg per year).[26] Cuba's best prospects for bartering sugar for oil are Russia and Kazakhstan. (See table 3.6.)

The USSR imported much of its raw sugar from Cuba through the Black Sea port of Odessa. When possible, shipments arrived after the refining of Ukrainian sugar in order to coordinate the processing of domestic and imported sugar. Cuba has already sought hard-currency payments for sugar from Kazakhstan, but has accepted meat instead; Latvia has agreed to pay in hard currency.

Sugar-deficient states may try to expand production to meet local needs, and Ukraine may export more to sugar-deficient republics. Some

TABLE 3.6
Sugar Beet Production and Consumption in the USSR, 1990
(in thousands of tons)

	Beet Production	Domestic Beet Consumption	Net Balance
RSFSR	2,675	7,240	−4,565
Ukraine	5,784	2,850	+2,934
Byelorus	175	500	−325
Kazakhstan	95	680	−585
Georgia	4	200	−196
Lithuania	83	170	−87
Moldava	309	210	+99
Latvia	34	130	−96
NON–SUGAR PRODUCING REPUBLICS			
Uzbekistan	—	550	−550
Azerbaidjan	—	300	−300
Kirgizia	—	170	−170
Tadzhikistan	—	140	−140
Armenia	—	130	−130
Turkmenia	—	110	−110
Estonia	—	70	−70
Total	9,159	13,450	−4,291

Source: The Czarnikow Sugar Review (London) 1812 (September 18, 1991): 131.

states besides Ukraine may achieve self-sufficiency. In the past, sugar producers have not been encouraged to compete in distant markets whose retail prices for sugar have been heavily subsidized—that is, kept low—as a matter of state policy. Now, however, Russia is discontinuing subsidies for sugar, thereby dampening exaggerated demand, and the resulting higher prices will encourage expanded imports from other republics and Central Europe.

Sugar-short states could buy sugar on the world market, but this would require payments in hard currency. U.S. officials estimate that the USSR was paying Cuba about 24 cents a pound for raw sugar in 1991.[27] Raw sugar brought about 9 cents a pound on the world market in 1991, but there were virtually no surplus stocks available.[28] Only about 10 to 15 percent of the world sugar product is traded at the world market price.[29] Thus, even with hard currency, the USSR could not have met its needs for raw sugar on the world market, and any purchases in the amount of 3 or 4 million tons would have sent prices skyrocketing. In 1972–73 and 1979–80 the USSR was forced to buy 1–3 million metric tons on the free market to supplement shortfalls from Cuba, which drove prices up to about 30 cents a pound.[30]

All this suggests that Russia and certain other republics will continue to import sugar from Cuba in the near future. (See chapter 5.) The disorganization caused by the social revolution in the former Soviet lands rules out any large investment in the sugar industry or surge in production in the short run. Similarly, there is little surplus in the world market, and the former USSR is not likely to spend scarce foreign exchange to buy sugar.

In the longer term, the outlook is much less clear. Higher retail prices will check demand. Certain republics may introduce or expand sugar production, and the former socialist countries of Eastern Europe could export in quantity to Russia. In these circumstances, Russia and other republics will be less likely to buy from Cuba for both economic and political reasons, and Cuba will need to develop new markets for its sugar.

Nickel. Nickel's importance in Soviet-Cuban relations exceeded its relatively small value in trade between the two countries. In 1987, for example, Soviet imports of Cuban metal ores and concentrates, mainly nickel and cobalt, represented 5 percent of all imports from Cuba. But nickel is a strategic mineral, often in short supply in the USSR. Soviet

imports of nickel-cobalt from Cuba constituted about 20 percent of Soviet consumption of these metals.[31] Russia's need for Cuban nickel ore is
often cited as a reason for a continued relationship between the two countries. Also it has been used to justify large investments by the USSR and
other socialist countries in Cuban plants.

Soviet specialists came to Cuba in 1961 after the nickel plants at
Nicaro and Moa had been nationalized and the U.S. staff had left. The
USSR provided technical assistance, raw materials, fuel, and spare parts
to help get them back to production. Annual Soviet expenditures averaged about $3 million up to 1972.[32] Most operations were completed in
1980–82 and the plants established "direct ties" with the Soviet mining-
metallurgical complex at Norilsk, a city in the Krasnoiarsk district in
Siberia.[33]

Among the more recent heavy commitments to the industry made by
the USSR and by the Council for Mutual Economic Assistance (CMEA)
was establishing new smelters at Punta Gorda and Las Camariocas, both
with projected capacities of 30,000 tons a year. The former, named for
Che Guevara, had projected an investment of 740 million pesos.[34] The
Cubans were to pay off these Soviet commitments by delivering to the
USSR 50 percent of the sulfite nickel-cobalt concentrate from these mining operations.[35] In 1988 the Punta Gorda plant established "direct ties"
with the Soviet metallurgical complex, Severonickel, a former penal
colony[36] in Murmansk Oblast, which could be interpreted to mean Soviet
smelting of these concentrates at this plant.[37] The other major project at
La Camariocas was granted 600 million rubles' credit under a 1975
CMEA agreement, which was also to be paid off by deliveries of the enterprises' product.[38] The investments of the 1980s were designed to lift
Cuban production of nickel-cobalt to more than 100,000 tons a year.

In the 1980s the USSR received 50–60 percent of Cuba's nickel-
cobalt concentrates, other CMEA countries up to 20 percent, and the balance went to market economies. (See table 3.7.) Information about the
Soviet nickel industry, together with military matters, has been among
the most difficult subjects to research. As a strategic raw material, nickel
was out of bounds for discussion with foreigners. In 1991, I had an introduction to knowledgeable specialists through a colleague who lived in
Norilsk, but none would see me.

Norilsk is a remarkable city a few hundred kilometers south of the
Arctic Circle. Much of its original labor was provided by penal colonies

TABLE 3.7
Cuban Exports of Nickel-Cobalt

	Total Exports	To the USSR	%	To Socialist Nations	%	To Capitalist Nations	%
1981	39,076	19,453	49.78	6,488	16.6	13,135	33.62
1982	38,005	18,093	47.61	6,703	17.64	13,209	34.75
1983	37,807	19,193	50.77	6,135	16.23	12,479	33.00
1984	36,658	18,205	49.66	7,167	19.55	11,286	30.79
1985	33,376	20,709	62.05	6,450	19.32	6,216	18.62
1986	34,913	20,501	58.72	5,722	16.39	8,690	24.89

Source: Bekarevich and Kukharev, *Sovetskii*, p. 203.

in the 1930s,[39] and it was populated by highly paid managers and workers who were granted privileges to hold them there. For many years—perhaps even now—outsiders required permission to visit Norilsk. Soviet pamphlets extolling the city's extensive health, educational, and cultural facilities testify to the considerable importance Soviet leaders attached to its production and refining capacities and what may be their continued interest in access to Cuban ores.

Technical Assistance

The Soviet Union provided considerable technical aid to Cuba, covering enterprises from agriculture to nuclear power. Aid was given not merely out of generosity and ambitions for a client state in the Americas, but also to encourage the survival and growth of a monocultural Third World economy cut off from most of its natural economic partners. The extent of the program over three decades is remarkable. Soviet assistance to Cuba rose from 3.78 percent of its technical support programs in 1970 to 8.56 percent in 1988.[40] The USSR provided 52 percent of Cuba's imports of equipment for comprehensive enterprises in 1970, and 68 percent in 1987.[41] The Czechoslovak government provided 8.22 percent in 1987, but the participation of the rest of Eastern Europe was negligible. (See table 3.8.)

In agriculture, for example, Soviet cooperation touched all kinds of production: mechanizing the sugarcane harvest, producing mineral fertilizers, expanding output, and refining sugar and citrus fruits.[42] Soviet specialists worked in various Cuban provinces—irrigating some lands,

TABLE 3.8
Selected Indicators of Soviet Economic and
Technical Cooperation with Cuba, 1970–1988

	1970	1975	1980	1985	1988
Total exports to the Republic of Cuba (in millions of rubles)	580.0	1141.30	2288.40	3752.90	3726.80
Machines and equipment (in millions of rubles)	205.18	278.10	741.50	1029.52	1190.00
Equipment of comprehensive enterprises (in millions of rubles)	62.41	89.40	352.30	398.49	401.81
Percent share of deliveries of machinery and equipment in comprehensive enterprises	30.42	32.15	47.51	38.71	33.76

Source: Bekarevich and Kukharev, *Sovietskii*, p. 191.

draining others. In 1978 there were 300 Soviet technicians in agriculture, but only 70 in 1989. Soviet technicians also worked in the cattle, poultry, forestry and lumbering, and chemical fertilizer industries. Equipment delivered included tractors, excavators, trucks, bulldozers, graders, pumps, and compressors. The USSR provided a wide variety of implements and training personnel to launch the Cuban fishing industry, which has grown to a substantial fleet with a large catch.

Fuel and electric power constituted the largest part of Soviet aid—for example, 29 percent of the total in 1986.[43] In the 1960s the USSR cooperated in the construction of two thermal electric power stations with a combined output of 300 thousand kilowatts—or nearly 40 percent of the electrical energy produced in 1970.[44] Even larger power stations were built in the 1980s, so that stations built with Soviet cooperation were supplying 42 percent of the nation's capacity.[45] In the meantime, work continued on a nuclear power station, Juragua, at Cienfuegos, with a capacity of 850 megawatts, with possible expansion to twice that figure.[46] The Soviet contribution to that project was more than 1 billion pesos.[47]

Soviet specialists have been working with Cubans repairing oil refineries and oil product plants and building new ones in Havana, Marianao, Cienfuegos, Santiago de Cuba, and Holguín Province. Soviet and Cuban teams, who have been prospecting for oil for many years, conclude that the most promising areas are the northern coastal shelf of Cuba to depths up to ten meters in the Bay of Cardenas and the coastal waters of Havana and Matanzas.[48] Small wells are already open in these two provinces, including pumps near the Varadero beaches. By 1986 oil output had risen to 938,000 tons, or nearly 10 percent of consumption, but declined thereafter (see chapter 6).[49]

Help in mining and metallurgy was another large Soviet commitment, constituting 22 percent of the total by 1986.[50] The Soviets assisted in mining operations for nickel-cobalt (described above), copper, lead, zinc, sulphur, iron ore, and other metals. Steel production rose from virtually nothing to 400 thousand tons in 1985.

The USSR also collaborated in many other industries, including auto maintenance, agricultural machinery, chemicals, textiles, construction, paper, and pharmaceuticals. In addition, there was some involvement in transport and communication, as well as education and health.

Yet, in spite of such massive aid, economic cooperation between the partners should not be viewed in too rosy a light. Viktor Gorbachev, a Soviet journalist, reported at the beginning of 1990:

> First, about the joint construction projects. Last year work proceeded on 150 of them, 20 were completed. Most of them are working productively. But there are serious drawbacks too; for example, the large textile mill in Santiago de Cuba did not cope with its target. Plans for the supply of products were not reached at other Soviet-Cuban ventures, with both countries to blame. There are delays in the supply of Soviet equipment, and the equipment often does not meet international standards. Short supplies by the Soviet Union were worth an impressive figure of about 150 million rubles. The USSR failed to honor its pledges on oil products and on a number of consumer goods, including refrigerators and television sets for a various reasons. One reason is the shortage of these products in the USSR itself and the other reasons—strikes at a number of Soviet plants as well as breakdowns in the work of Soviet transport. I may also note that the Soviet industrial facilities that have access to foreign markets find it more profitable to sell their products not to Cuba but to other socialist countries and, quality permitting, to capitalist countries.[51]

An expansion of technical assistance was authorized in 1986, when ten new projects were added. By early 1991 the USSR was responsible for eighty-two projects, some of which have been terminated, like the nuclear power plant, others modified, and a few completed.[52]

Foreign Trade

Socialist Cuba was a longtime beneficiary of the centralized monopoly of the Soviet Ministry of Foreign Trade, but also became the victim of Gorbachev's reforms, which broke that monopoly. Soviet foreign trade reforms were introduced to respond to Soviet domestic and foreign policies, needs that had little or nothing to do with Cuba but had a profound impact on Cuba.

Before Gorbachev, Soviet-Cuban economic, scientific, and technical cooperation was managed by the Joint Commission, set up in the early 1970s to help make the Cuban economy more effective, to bring order to the bilateral relationship, and to integrate the two economies. The key Cuban on the commission was Carlos Rafael Rodríguez, who had Castro's confidence. The Soviets were also pleased with his appointment because he was a leader of the former Partido Socialista Popular, the Cuban Communist party. Thereafter Soviet aid grew rapidly and Cuba became a member of the CMEA. One outcome of the Joint Commission was the dovetailing of Cuban and Soviet export-import agencies. The Cubans had a major planning and controlling agency to turn to and a major supply agency—the Soviet Ministry of Foreign Trade with its foreign trade monopoly.

All these arrangements were demolished when Soviet leaders under Gorbachev decided to reform the entire foreign trade structure. Leaders judged the Soviet foreign trade monopoly—that is, funneling all foreign trade management through Moscow—a failure. The Ministry of Foreign Trade dampened initiative and was a choke point for foreign trade. Soviet agencies, under Moscow's thumb, could not compete with more independent, flexible, motivated, and vigorously competitive Western companies. Decentralization did not cure inefficiency or the often low quality of Soviet manufactured goods, but it did liberate Soviet traders from the paralyzing embrace of Moscow. Another aspect of the reform was allowing Soviet firms engaged in foreign trade to receive a share of foreign-currency receipts.

Whereas previously the Cubans could deal at a fairly high political level with the Foreign Trade Ministry, they now had to negotiate with hundreds of trade or manufacturing representatives, most of whom had little interest in sugar or nickel. The Cubans were forced to decentralize their own trade to some extent to cope with this new challenge. (See chapter 5.) Perhaps even more threatening was a provision in the Soviet foreign trade reform that allowed Soviet enterprises to retain a percentage of their foreign sales in foreign currency. As a result, few wanted to sell to Cuba; they preferred hard-currency customers.

The Cuban Debt

Beginning in the late 1980s, Soviet leaders began to accept a reality that neither party has been willing to articulate publicly and the Cubans have not admitted even to themselves: the Cuban economy is not viable at established levels, and with its then partners, without extensive foreign aid. Cuba's excessive dependence on sugar prevents it from having a viable, diversified economy. In the main, Soviet aid was provided through subsidized prices, grants, and repayable loans, the latter often to finance a trade deficit. In fact, Cuba has made virtually no interest—much less amortization—payments to the USSR. The Soviets concluded that it was better to write off Cuban trade deficits on current accounts through price subsidies than to send the debt out of sight.

The Soviets were drawn deeper and deeper into this morass, trapped in a way by their own rhetoric. One purpose of their generosity has allegedly been to show the difference between Soviet relations with less developed countries and those of capitalist, or imperialist, countries. Soviet policies were to reflect the generous and humane sentiments of proletarian internationalism, so different from the exploitation and cruelty of market relations. The Cubans were quick to pick up these leads, and turned Soviet ideology against Soviet negotiators who repeated Cuban platitudes about Soviet higher morality in matters commercial.

Determined in the tight circle of the Politburo and lacking genuine popular approval, the volume of Cuban aid and of the Cuban debt were long kept secret. As perestroika and glasnost gathered momentum, more and more voices criticized foreign aid and newly elected deputies sought more information on its magnitude, especially aid to Cuba. An influential speech in the Supreme Soviet and reported in *Kommunist* revealed that the USSR was owed over 85 billion rubles.[53] Cuba was the largest debtor, at more than 15 billion rubles, followed by Mongolia and Vietnam.[54] This revelation hardened public opposition and bolstered the determination of officials to make cuts. If carrying charges on the Cuban debt were counted as aid (and using close to commercial rates), in 1990 the cost to the Soviet Union of carrying Cuban interest was about 1 billion rubles. Soviets leaders have not taken kindly to cavalier Cuban comments that "Nobody pays their debts these days" and do not approve of Castro's repudiation of foreign debts. Press reports from Havana suggest that Russian officials are insisting on some debt payments as part of the negotiations designed to put Soviet-Cuban relations on a new footing.

Why the Partnership Ended

Two Defining Events

Two events that quickly led to the end of the partnership were the Soviet-Cuban economic agreement of December 31, 1990, and, following the failed coup, Gorbachev's announcement of the withdrawal of Soviet troops from Cuba on September 12, 1991.

The radical change in the bilateral economic relationship was the result of developments in the Soviet economy that had been under way for some years. The USSR had long provided 90 percent or more of Cuba's oil, a feasible operation as long as the Soviet oil supply held up. This became impossible when the USSR minister of oil and gas reported in mid-1990 that oil production would begin to fall rapidly in two years.[55] Cuba sometimes paid more than the world market price for oil, but was receiving from the USSR far more than the world price for sugar. Trading oil—a scarce commodity—for Cuban sugar was costing the USSR dearly. The crisis in the Soviet oil industry, a major source of foreign exchange, was one of the catalysts that precipitated the review of Soviet aid to Cuba.

The new principle underlying Soviet aid to Cuba was mutual or reciprocal interest—a polite way of saying that the relationship should no longer mainly benefit Cuba. Exchanges would follow world market prices and be denominated in dollars. The market, not the abstract concept of proletarian internationalism, would govern economic relations. The new arrangment was clearly meant to relieve the pressure of Cuban needs on the Soviet oil supply and reduce resource transfers to Cuba through subsidized prices, grants, and deficit financing. Another benefit was that the new accounting procedures would help Soviet leaders know in market terms how much the Cuban tie was costing them.

The five-year Soviet-Cuban agreement expired at the end of 1990. A cliff-hanger, the new agreement was announced December 31, 1990, and provided only for 1991—not, as the Cubans had hoped, for 1991–95. Its major features were:

1. Soviet oil deliveries were cut from 13 million to 10 million tons, but with an escape clause permitting lower deliveries if Soviet supplies of oil and oil products were insufficient to maintain this level.[56] The ratio of Soviet oil shipped to Cuba to the amount of sugar sent to the USSR has been steadily declining; 3 tons of oil for each ton of sugar in 1989; 2.5 tons in 1990; and less in 1991.[57]

2. Soviet payments for sugar were reduced from about 850 to 500 rubles per ton.[58] Although foreign exchange rates do not necessarily reflect reliable comparative values, a Soviet economist informed me in July 1991 that the 1991 Soviet price for sugar was about the same as what U.S. buyers pay. According to a U.S. official, while reluctant to compare rubles to dollars, the Soviet price is about 24 cents a pound. The new agreement provided for clearing sugar and other commodity exchanges in dollars.

3. The USSR will deliver no more consumer durables like refrigerators and other electrical appliances to Cuba.

4. Cuban purchases of machinery and equipment will be conducted through individual enterprises, not through centralized ministerial structures. Cuba is to pay 10 percent of shipping, which costs in the past were totally borne by the USSR.[59]

Shortly after the one-year agreement was announced, on January 11, 1991, the Supreme Soviet approved development grants to Cuba of 55.7 million rubles, more than was appropriated for any country except Afghanistan.[60] But at the same time, the USSR reduced its technicians and advisors in Cuba from 3,200 to 1,000.[61]

The failed coup of August 19, 1991, resolved most of the remaining issues in the bilateral relationship. The early fallout was a reversal of the fortunes of the old-guard intelligence and military officers, who favored the Castro regime. Among those forced into retirement was KGB General Nikolai Leonov, long an influential voice on Cuban policy.

Although Castro's public reaction to the coup attempt did not come until two days later and he did not take sides, his failure to support Gorbachev and critical Cuban editorial commmment on the situation after the coup leaves open the possibility that he may, in fact, have favored it. Four of the eight coup leaders were his political and ideological allies.[62]

After the abortive coup, the elimination of military and economic aid to Cuba ceased to be a foreign policy embarrassment and came to be viewed as progressive by Soviet reformists. Many of Castro's Soviet defenders were out of the picture, and the authoritarian nature of the Cuban regime became a legitimate reason to cut Soviet aid. Official sympathy for Castro's totalitarian model came to an end.

These developments led to the second defining event, the announcement of a troop withdrawal from Cuba. After a meeting with the U.S. secretary of state, Gorbachev unexpectedly announced on September 12, 1991, that many Soviet troops would be withdrawn from Cuba without previous consultation with Castro and without any concessions from the United States. The Cubans resented not having been consulted and insisted that Soviet troops not be removed until the United States left Guantánamo. The withdrawal was a staggering blow to the Castro regime, not so much because of its immediate practical importance, but because of its symbolic political implications. On top of the economic cutbacks, the announcement spelled the end of Cuba's status as a favored client of the USSR. Gorbachev sought both to reduce Cuba's drain on the Soviet budget and to placate the United States as a highly valued political partner. Also Soviet leaders must have been aware that troop withdrawals cut the USSR's vulnerability and potential involvement in the event of nasty civil strife over regime succession in Cuba.

The Triangle Implodes

The triangular relationship linking the Soviet Union, Cuba, and the United States was an exquisitely balanced combination of stalemates that lasted for about thirty years. The Soviet Union found Cuba an irresistible pied-à-terre in the Americas and was unable to shake off the Cuban burden until economic crisis gave it no other choice. Cuba offered the USSR some of the psychological and political benefits of empire, while Castro's anti-American posture, with Soviet support, was evidence of Soviet anti-imperialism.

Castro may never have wanted reconciliation with the United States—not in 1959, not even thirty years later, or at least not until his partnership with Moscow cracked. Castro's steady stream of vitriolic anti-American rhetoric, his support for revolution in the Americas, and his hosting of Soviet nuclear weapons in 1962 demonstrated his stubborn intent. From Castro's perspective, giving the United States an unforgiving cold shoulder made sense. Castro was fully aware of the danger of sleeping with elephants, whether American or Soviet. U.S. trade and tourism would have sent the Cuban economy in uncontrollable directions. Washington's insistence on human rights and a multiparty system would have loosened Castro's monopoly of power. But the price of independence from the northern neighbor was high. Crippled by the unending U.S. trade embargo, Castro was irremediably dependent on Moscow. The United States' implacable hostility toward Cuba constituted the third obstacle that locked the triangle. Washington remains the last to change, even in the face of a complete Soviet turnabout and evidence that Castro might be more tractable now than ever before.

The deadlock among the three nations was the result of the ossification not only of foreign policy, but of domestic politics as well. Moscow could not have transferred such a huge volume of resources to Cuba if state power had not been concentrated in a few Politburo members and the Soviet public kept ignorant. Castro justified his political control partly by citing U.S. hostility and threat. Moscow was the lesser evil because it was farther away and posed no serious threat to that control.

U.S. policy toward Cuba was also closely linked to domestic politics. Washington has been hostile to Castro in part because Castro has no viable political constituency in the United States and Cuban emigres here have nursed a long simmering hatred of the revolutionary regime. Each succeeding administration has had strong political reasons not to reverse U.S. punitive policies, especially the embargo, and there were no persuasive domestic pressures to lift it.

Why and how then was this triangular equilibrium breached? Washington was not responsible; the essentials of its policies in the early 1960s were still in place in 1992. The Bush administration seemed firmly committed to not loosening the embargo in the belief that the Cuban regime might be about to succumb.

The Soviet Union broke up the triangle for domestic reasons more than foreign policy considerations. In fact, it began to back out of its commitments to Cuba in the late 1980s, all the while professing fidelity to the Cuban regime and sympathy for its many problems. Even a few critics believed for a while that the Soviet Union should continue to help Cuba because it had done so much to shape the Cuban system. And Soviet military and intelligence officials were reluctant to give up the strategic advantages Cuba offered.

The Soviet economic crisis was the definitive cause of Moscow's retreat from Cuba—in fact, the drop in Soviet oil output forced the withdrawal even before the full extent of the crisis was known. But even if
economic difficulties would have forced the retreat even without glasnost
and perestroika, those ideas created pressures in legislatures, the press,
and the public that accelerated the reversal of policy toward Cuba. The
cost of aid to Cuba could no longer be hidden from view. Faced with such
severe sacrifices at home, public officials and private opinion could no
longer justify billions in foreign aid. Finally, the fact that the USSR was
also undergoing a change of regime meant that the Cuban issue became
entangled in the struggle over the union's future.

As the Soviet republics moved away from the neo-Stalinist system toward a market economy, and from the unitary USSR to a Commonwealth
of Independent States, attitudes toward Castro hardened. Sympathy
turned to resentment, concern to indifference, and tolerance to criticism.
Lacking personal or official ties to Castro, new leaders found Cuba a
kind of nuisance and association with Castro ideologically embarrassing.
Then, after the failed coup, the Soviet economy deteriorated rapidly as
economic restructuring went forward. The breakup of the Soviet Union
in 1991 ended aid to Cuba, and enterprises of the former USSR struggled
to fulfill trade agreements in the face of severe production and distribution difficulties.

The Soviet-Cuban Future

What are likely to be the relations of the new CIS and its member states
with Cuba? Gorbachev, the Communist party, and the USSR itself have
been swept away. Many government, military, and party officials who
had personal and official commitments to Cuba have been replaced by
people who don't care. Instead of one government to deal with, there are
now a dozen. One republic, Russia, whose size and economy might be of
significant help to Cuba has already decided against foreign aid.

In the waning days of the USSR, officials left the impression that
they wished to salvage something from the huge Soviet effort and expenditure over the previous thirty years. At a minimum they wanted normal economic and political relations with Cuba. That seemed possible as
long as Castro remained in power; thus some Soviet leaders appeared to
be willing to make minor accommodations to him even if aid itself dis-

appeared. Some states continued to buy Cuban sugar and nickel, and the Russians hoped for at least token payments on Cuba's huge debt.

Russian diplomats, like their Soviet predecessors, have wanted to avoid violent political upheaval in Cuba partly because they do not want their government to be ushered unceremoniously out of Havana by a hostile successor regime. That may be one reason Soviet leaders, and Russian representatives later, were in touch with Cuban emigres in Miami, hedging their bets. What they clearly preferred was a gradual transition on the island that would avoid bloodshed and protect whatever remaining influence the former Soviet Union possessed there.

Trade could be the most enduring common interest between Cuba and the CIS. Cuba offers sugar and nickel, but there are no more political reasons for massive Soviet purchases. The USSR needed at least partial hard-currency payment for the food, fuel, raw materials, and equipment it sent to Cuba, but Cuba paid primarily in sugar. So the USSR let its sugar-producing land and equipment languish and took what Cuba had to offer. The new states' decisions about planting and refining sugar will be based on domestic and economic rather than foreign policy criteria; they could move toward self-sufficiency, buy from neighbors, or turn to the world market. But it will take time to develop these new sources, so Cuba may fill immediate shortfalls in supply.

Russia has the largest demand for sugar, but much of what it consumes will pass through Ukrainian refineries. Russia probably will continue to want Cuban nickel if it can find the means to buy it. Oil is the logical exchange commodity, but it is far more precious than it used to be. Other Cuban exports are primarily luxury goods: citrus, seafood, rum, and tobacco. All were popular in the former USSR, but Russia's buying capacity will be limited for many years.

The CIS states will still have traditional (or rather residual), ties with Cuba of a technological, economic, and cultural nature because of the USSR's dominant presence there for thirty years. Successor states will, for example, want to protect the interests of over 4,600 Soviet women in Cuba, once married to Cubans and now divorced, who are having difficulty returning home.[63] Much of Cuba's industrial plant and military equipment is of Soviet origin and will continue to need Soviet-style maintenance and parts. But when the present transition is over, trade won't amount to much. Whether under Castro or his successor, Cuba is unlikely to pay off its Soviet debt.

Cuba's economic lifelines with the United States were severed in 1960, and the nation relied for more than thirty years on an economy on the other side of the world. These ties were artificial, inefficient, and depended on an unreliable and, in many ways, backward Soviet economy. The triangular relationship between Cuba, the USSR, and the United States was based on political strategies rather than economic advantage. Before the USSR rescued Castro, Cuba's greatest vulnerability was its heavy dependence on sugar exports, with which it bought essential raw materials, machinery, and equipment. Cuba continues to suffer from this dependence even after the Soviet withdrawal. The collapse of the USSR, and with it the triangle, showed once again that Cuba's strongest natural ties—economic and political—are with the Americas, not with distant friendships based on ideology. It will now be principally to the Americas and Western Europe that Cuba must turn to overcome this critical weakness.[64]

NOTES

Sergei Tagor, whose comment on this paper was entitled "From Assistance to Trade," made many helpful suggestions, as did Nikolai Zaitsev (both of the Institute of Latin America, Russian Academy of Sciences).

1. Edward Gonzalez, "Institutionalization, Political Elites, and Foreign Policies," in *Cuba in the World*, ed. Cole Blasier and Carmelo Mesa-Lago (Pittsburgh: University of Pittsburgh Press, 1979), p. 30.

2. Vladimir I. Stenchenko, "The Soviet Role in Latin America," *Washington Quarterly*, Summer 1990, pp. 193–94. See also his "Soviet View of the Caribbean and Central America 1985–1991," presented at the Latin American Studies Association Congress, Washington D.C., June 1990.

3. I refer to state interests as they are perceived by the governments concerned. I make this clarification in response to Tagor's constructive criticism in his comment, "From Assistance to Trade."

4. For example, see Cole Blasier, *The Giant's Rival: The USSR and Latin America*, rev. ed. (Pittsburgh: University of Pittsburgh Press, 1987), pp. 103–32; and Nicola Miller, *Soviet Relations with Latin America 1959–1987* (Cambridge: Cambridge University Press, 1989, pp. 58–126.

5. Tagor, "From Assistance to Trade."

6. For an interesting account of high-level party politics, see Zhores A. Medvedev, *Andropov* (New York: Penguin, 1984). Vitali Vorotnikov, former Soviet ambassador to Cuba, is discussed on p. 203.

7. *Latinskaia Amerika* 1 (1979): 5–7. See also Christopher Andrew and Oleg Gordievski, *KGB, the Inside Story* (New York: Harper Collins, 1990), p. 466 and *passim*.

8. Nikolai Leonov, "Me entiendo facilmente con los Latinamericanos," *América Latina* (Moscow) 8 (1991): 36–55.

9. Information on the Soviet apparat was gleaned from interviews with Soviet and U.S. colleagues since 1958, biographic publications of the Central Intelligence Agency, Robert H. Kitsinos, "International Department of the CPSU," *Problems of Communism* 5 (1984): 47–75, and works cited therein.

10. For Soviet relationships to social revolutions in Latin America, see Cole Blasier, *The Hovering Giant: U.S. Responses to Revolutionary Change in Latin America 1910–1985* (Pittsburgh: University of Pittsburgh Press, 1985); see "U.S.S.R.," p. 339.

11. Office of Research and Policy, Radio Martí Program, *Cuba Annual Report: 1988* (New Brunswick: Transaction Books, 1991), describes the differences and gives quotes from Cuban and Soviet leaders in chapter 1. Note, for example, Gorbachev's reference to the "primacy of universal human values" in his speech to the United Nations, December 8, 1988.

12. *Dagens Nyheter,* Stockholm, October 8, 1988, in FBIS-AFR, December 22, 1988, pp. 9–10; Office of Research and Policy, Radio Martí Program, *Cuba Annual Report: 1988,* p. 69.

13. Owen Ellison Kahn, ed., *Disengagement from Southwest Africa: The Prospects for Peace in Angola and Namibia* (New Brunswick: Transaction Books, 1991).

14. *Krasnaia Zvezda* (Moscow), the organ of the Ministry of Defense, carried two articles, sentimental and patriotic in tone, favoring the Castro regime and the maintenance of the "traditions" of Soviet-Cuban relations on May 8 and 19, 1990.

15. *Sovetskaia Rossiia,* May 27, 1990, p. 6.

16. Irina Zorina, "Osen Patriarkha, ne gotovit li Fidel Kastro pyshnye pokhorony svoemu narodu?" *Megapolis-Express,* August 30, 1990, p. 20.

17. V. Borodayev and G. Leyvikina, though in a restrained fashion, give a coherent account of opposition to the Castro regime and of Cuba's economic difficulties in "Cuba: The Difficult Path to Socialism," *Argumenty i Fakty* (Moscow), March 17–23, 1990, p. 4.

18. See also A. Snam, "Earning Money in the Tropics," *Komsomol'skaya Pravda,* September 19, 1990.

19. International Institute for Strategic Studies (IISS), *The Military Balance 1990–1991* (London: IISS, 1990), pp. 192–93.

20. Office of Research and Policy, Radio Martí Program, *Cuba Annual Report 1988,* p. 246.

21. Ibid.

22. A. D. Bekarevich and N. M. Kukharev, *Sovetskii Soiuz-Kuba: Ekonomicheskoe Sotrudnichestvo (70-80-e gody)* (Moscow: Nauka, 1990), p. 9.

23. Ibid., p. 12.

24. Ron Lord, "Restructuring in Centrally-Planned Economies and the Outlook for Sugar," presented to the Annual Agricultural Outlook Conference, December 4, 1991, Washington, D.C., p. 7.

25. The Russian Sugar Beet Research Institute has prepared a plan which proposes to more than double sugar output in ten years, but implementation seems unlikely at present

because of the huge investment required and attendent technical problems (*Czarnikow Sugar Review* [London], no. 1812, September 18, 1991, p. 131).

26. Ibid., p. 130.

27. Annual Agricultural Outlook Conference, December 4, 1991, Washington, D.C.; the official pointed out that the purchase was not in dollars and that the estimate is dependent on arbitrary exchange rates and other unreliable factors.

28. A. C. Hannah, "World View on Sugar Trade and Prices," presented to the Annual Agricultural Outlook Conference, December 4, 1991, Washington, D.C.

29. Interview with U.S. Department of Agriculture official, October 23, 1991.

30. A. C. Hannah, "World View on Sugar Trade and Prices."

31. *Pravda* (Moscow), April 9, 1990, p. 5.

32. Bekarevich and Kukharev, *Sovetskii Soiuz-Kuba*, p. 76.

33. Ibid., p. 78.

34. Bekarevich and Kukharev, *Sovetskii Soiuz-Kuba*, p. 78.

35. Ibid., p. 79.

36. David J. Dallin and Boris I. Nicolaevsky, *Forced Labor in Soviet Russia* (New York: Octagon, 1974), p. 69.

37. Separate references about Cuban ties to Norilsk and to Severonickel do not explain their relationship. Norilsk has mines, Severonickel refining capacity. The former is located in western Siberia and the latter in Murmansk Oblast on the Arctic Ocean (Bekarevich and Kukharev, *Sovetskii Soiuz-Kuba*, p. 79; V. N. Molchanova, "Ekonomicheskaia tselesoobraznost' proizvodstva poroshoviz oborotinykh zhelezistykh kekov kombinata 'Severonikel,' " *Nauchno-tekhnicheskii progress i razvitie proizvodstva Murmanskoi Oblasti* [Kol'skii filial AN SSSR (Apatiti), 1987], pp. 39-45).

38. Bekarevich and Kukharev, *Sovetskii Soiuz-Kuba*, pp. 12, 79.

39. Dallin and Nicolaevsky, *Forced Labor in Soviet Russia*, p. 61. See also Ievhen Krytsiak, *Korothzi zapys spohadiv, dlia sehi samoho* (Munich: Ukrainisches Institut für Bildungspolitik, 1984) for the Norilsk uprising.

40. Bekarevich and Kukharev, *Sovetskii Soiuz-Kuba*, p. 189.

41. Ibid., p. 190.

42. Ibid., p. 21.

43. Ibid., p. 52.

44. Ibid.

45. Ibid., p. 53.

46. Ibid., p. 56.

47. Ibid., p. 12.

48. Ibid., p. 66.

49. Ibid., p. 68.

50. Ibid., p. 70.

51. FBIS-SOV-90-015, January 23, 1990, p. 36.

52. Bekarevich and Kukharev, *Sovetskii Soiuz-Kuba*. Interview with Soviet Latin Americanist, July 1991. For a summary account in a Western journal, see Jorge F. Pérez-López, "Swimming Against the Tide: Implications for Cuba of Soviet and East European Reforms in Foreign Economic Relations," *Journal of Interamerican Studies and World Affairs* 33 (March 2, 1991): 98f.

53. "Pervyi S'ezd Narodnykh Deputatov SSSR 25 maia-9 iiunia 1989g." Stenograficheskii otchet. Tom III. Izdanie Verkhovnogo Soveta SSSR. Speech by N. P. Shmelev. Boris Sergeyev, *Kommunist* (Moscow) 11 (July 1990): 79–82.

54. *Rabochaia Tribuna* (Moscow), November 3, 1990, p. 3. Cited by FBIS.

55. *Narodny Deputat* (Moscow), August 1990, p. 4.

56. EFE (Madrid), January 19, 1991.

57. Statement of Bernard Aronson, assistant secretary of state for Inter-American Affairs, before the Subcommittee on Western Hemisphere Affairs, House of Representatives, July 11, 1991, p. 10.

58. *Trud* (Moscow), April 18, 1990.

59. EFE (Madrid), January 19, 1991. See Pravda (Moscow), April 8, 1990, for a critical article about high costs of Soviet shipping to Cuba.

60. Vladimir Neklesov of Novosti, "Cuba, una deuda moral de la URSS," *El Espectador* (Bogotá, Colombia), January 19, 1991.

61. *Washington Post*, January 27, 1991; *EFE* (Madrid), March 2, 1991.

62. Letter from Carmelo Mesa-Lago, April 25, 1992, citing the *Independent*, August 26, 1991; Reuters, August 25, 1991; *Wall Street Journal*, August 27, 1991; *Washington Post*, August 27, 1991.

63. Sergei Tagor, "From Assistance to Trade."

64. See Cole Blasier, "Moscow's Retreat from Cuba," *Problems of Communism* 40, no. 6 (November–December 1991): 91–99.; I want to acknowledge the hospitality, interviews, or both, with: Anatolii Bekarevich; V. Borodayev; B. Davidov; Anatolii Glinkin; Alexandr Gorin; Igor Ianchuk; Lev Klochkovskii; Yurii Korolev; Boris Koval; G. Leyvikina; Elida Litavrina; Sergo Mikoyan; Vladimir Neklesov; Victor Paschuk; Victor Sheinis; Alexandr Sizonenko; Vladimir Stanchenko; Sergei Tagor; Victor Volskii; Oleg Yaroshin; Nikolai Zaitsev; Vladimir Zaemskii; Irina Zorina; Gennadii Zuikov.

4

The Political Impact on Cuba of the Reform and Collapse of Communist Regimes

❖ ❖ ❖

Jorge I. Domínguez

THE IDEAS, organizational designs and practices, and experiences of the European and Asian communist regimes have been of the utmost importance to Cuba's domestic politics since 1960. Their influence has varied, however. This chapter seeks to explain why the reforms of communist regimes in Europe and Asia in the mid- and late 1980s had only a modest impact on Cuba, while the subsequent collapse of communist Europe had a markedly greater effect on Cuba's domestic politics.

The explanation of the first phenomenon seems simple. From late 1984 and especially from April 1986, President Fidel Castro's government adopted a Rectification Process (RP) that deemphasized the role of market forces associated with perestroika, thus nipping reform-communist ideas in the bud. Yet reform-communist ideas about political and economic *apertura* influenced Cuba around 1987 and did so to some degree until late 1989. Why did reform-communist ideas have any impact at all, and what was that impact? Cuba's regime has been sufficiently complex so as to allow a certain freedom of expression with regard to thinking about changes in communist Europe, even as Cuba's leaders gradually edged away from those experiments. Similarly, an opening had developed in Cuba's intellectual life that was not caused by the political and intellectual changes associated with Soviet glasnost.

The explanation of the second phenomenon also seems simple. Cuba had depended so much on Soviet economic, military, and political support that the collapse of the Soviet system had an enormous impact on every facet of Cuba's life. But this fails to explain the form of the impact: Cuba did not shut itself off from news about the Soviet Union or Eastern Europe, but chose instead to teach Cubans lessons to vaccinate them from the virus that killed communism in Europe.

This chapter pursues these questions. I will assess whether or not openings in Cuba (especially in the intellectual sphere) were caused by Soviet ideas about glasnost. We consider next the obstacles in Cuba to the reception of ideas about reform communism, but we also show that such external ideas shaped much of Cuba's political debate in the late 1980s. Ideas from abroad legitimated alternative courses of action, clarified strategic choices, provided practical advice, and permitted an indirect discussion of Cuba's own problems. I look also at the social sectors and journals through which those ideas became influential, and on which those ideas had an impact. Finally, I discuss the ideological and political factors in Cuba that resisted new ideas from abroad and the actions taken by Cuban leaders to prevent the repetition in Cuba of the East European experience.

This chapter is not a study of economic and political reforms in Cuba since the mid-1980s—or the lack or insufficiency thereof—nor does it address all international influences on Cuba's domestic affairs. My focus is the impact on Cuba of the ideas and practices of European and Asian reform communism and, subsequently, of the collapse of European communist regimes. Therefore, changes or continuity in the climate of ideas and policies in Cuba are pertinent to my discussion only if they can be traced explicitly to events elsewhere in the communist or former communist world. My references to "political imports" or to "receptivity toward external ideas" must be read within this framework.

Deriving Hypotheses from Cuba's Past

Before the mid-1980s, the ideas, organizations, and experiences of European and Asian communist regimes had an impact on Cuba at three moments. The first was the early 1960s, when Cuba's political regime shifted toward socialism. The second was the late 1960s, when Cuba instituted its most radical political and economic experiment and differentiated its practices from those found in other socialist regimes. The third was the early to mid-1970s, when Cuba adopted, though in modified ways, many of the formal institutions of mature socialist regimes.

Political imports were therefore influential in the first and third periods, but not in the second. How can this variation be explained and what hypotheses might this analysis generate to help us understand the most recent period?

These analytical factors are especially important: the worth of the ideas themselves at given historical junctures; the institutional links between the carriers of ideas and top decision makers; the state-structural features of the crisis of the moment; the nature of Cuba's relations with the Soviet Union; the political coalition that sees new ideas as a way to address a given crisis; and the decisions of top leaders.[1]

The following empirical hypotheses examine these factors within a stylized historical record:

1. Severe state-structural crises (early 1960s, early 1970s) made Cuba more receptive to ideas from abroad, while moderate state-structural crises (mid-1960s) were dealt with by closing off receptivity to external ideas. Emergencies forced the collective mind to open and accelerate the circulation of state leaders, some of whom responded to new ideas, while mere "problems" were addressed with one's own intellectual resources.

2. Political and organizational unity on "core" issues facilitated the reception of ideas from abroad (early 1960s, early 1970s), while breakdowns in coalitions that occurred concurrently with divergences over ideas were associated with less receptivity to ideas from abroad (mid-1960s).[2] Divisions among the elite facilitated the penetration of external ideas into one elite segment but not the conquest of the state by those ideas. In contrast, coalitional unity speeded up the adoption and adaptation of external ideas.

3. The nature of Cuban-Soviet relations explains much about the influence and receptivity of socialist ideas from abroad. Good relations fostered receptivity (early 1960s, early 1970s) partly because the Soviets funded the adoption of their ideas; deteriorating relations reduced receptivity (mid-1960s), in part because the Soviets spent less money in Cuba.

4. The presence or absence of institutional links between idea carriers and top decision makers affects outcomes. Economists were close to decision makers in the early 1960s and early 1970s, but much less so in the mid-1960s.[3]

5. The worth and nature of the ideas (e.g., using some market procedures within central planning) and Fidel Castro's preferences (to rely

on the market as little as possible) seem to be constants. They matter greatly, but they do not explain variations in their ideological influence or reception.

These reflections suggest that Cuba's situation in the mid-1980s resembled—analytically, not in empirical details—that of the mid-1960s. Consequently, one might expect Cuba's leaders to be unreceptive to new ideas in the mid-1980s because (1) there was no severe state-structural crisis; (2) the elite was divided about the course of economic policy; (3) Soviet-Cuban relations were deteriorating; and (4) economists suddenly became less influential in policy making.

The situation of the late 1980s and early 1990s is more difficult to account for. The crisis within the state began to unfold and there was much greater elite unity; these factors would suggest that external ideas should be welcome. Nonetheless, relations with the USSR deteriorated markedly, and economists were much less influential in policy making; these factors should explain closure to external ideas. What light does the historical record shed on these forecasts?

The Irrelevance of Glasnost: Trends in Recent Cuban Poetry and Prose Fiction

Not all changes in Cuba can be explained in terms of imported reform-communist ideas. This allows us to isolate more precisely which processes of change can be connected to external ideas and which seem to have developed endogenously in Cuba. This is the first analytical task.

We adopt the analytical strategy of examining the "most likely" case—that is, one in which the impact of external ideas is most apt to occur. If external influence is modest in this case, it would surely be less in others; one could thus establish the endogenous origin of many recent changes in Cuba. The most likely case must have two features: (1) it must have been a realm of significant change in other communist countries; (2) the Cuban government should have little to lose if change occurred in such an area and thus would not block the influence of external ideas.

The political and intellectual opening called glasnost was particularly important for intellectuals in the Soviet Union, Czechoslovakia, Poland, and Hungary. To assess the influence of glasnost on Cuba, we focus on intellectual life as the most likely case. Cuban leaders might have blocked access to new ideas regarding politics or the economy, so for the most likely case we chose instead on a low-stakes area: recent Cuban poetry and prose fiction.

An important issue in the evolution of Cuban poetry and prose fiction after the revolution is the extent to which content is social or personal. Do poems deal with the epic issues of the revolution and the construction of a new society, or with the life of personal love and sorrow? The spirit of glasnost would presumably permit, perhaps even foster, a transition from social to personal themes in literature. But in Cuba that transition occurred before glasnost and therefore could not have been caused by it; in the 1960s poetry dwelled on social themes and collective action at the expense of intimate personal issues. But already in the 1970s, poetry, especially by young poets, came to focus on personal morality and on love. This was no longer a collective love or a "love for persons unknown," but a love of two people for each other. Poetry referred to specific situations in daily life, explicitly commented on sex, and generally reflected a "rediscovery of the body."[4]

In prose trends were similar. In the 1960s and early 1970s stories had focused on the revolution, on the class struggle, and on the need to become socially conscious; by 1979 the literature of daily life had become much more important. The violence discussed in the narrative fiction of the 1980s was no longer that between political enemies or between men of action, but between individuals—between adolescents and children, for example. The new prose, like the new poetry, focused on love and its disappointments, relations between parents and children, or disagreements among friends that lead eventually to pain.[5]

Some of these changes depended on favorable state policies, for all publications were in the hands of state institutions. The state continued to support a wide variety of literary expression even though some criticized the new forms of writing as too distant from heroic or epic themes.[6]

To say that literary themes were personal does not mean that there were no political implications. Consider the following lines from passages from two poems. They can be read in purely personal terms, as reflections on friends or loved ones, yet can also be read politically. The first, entitled "This Will Be the Only Lie in Which We Will Always Believe," contains the lines: "It is a sad history / To play the game of becoming perfect."[7] Both the title and the quoted lines express disillusionment with the government's policy of constructing the "perfect" socialist citizen. The passage from the second poem, "Days of Anger," reads: "How many suffering corpses / Rotting in the name of survival!"[8] suggests the futility of sacrifices made by citizens in contemporary Cuba.

Glasnost encouraged similar changes in the USSR, but there is no causal relationship between glasnost and thematic changes in Cuban literature. Reform communism in Europe takes no blame and claims no praise for the shifts in Cuba's arts and letters; the main reasons for such intellectual changes in Cuba are to be found in Cuba itself.

An Inauspicious Time: State Structures and Political Coalitions in Cuban-Soviet Relations, 1984–86

The second analytical task is to explain why the ideas of reform communism had such a limited impact on Cuba. Cuba's intellectual and policy milieu in the months preceding and following the rise of Gorbachev was inimical to glasnost and perestroika. At the end of 1984, President Castro sharpened his critique of the economic strategy that Cuba had followed for the preceding decade and began to take steps that would months later result in the removal of Central Planning Board President Humberto Pérez, architect of that economic strategy and the main advocate for using some market mechanisms within the context of central planning (for details, see chapter 5).

In the 1970s and early 1980s, the Central Planning Board had become the key for building coalitions around the notion of market-responsive central planning. The board, which allocated resources, had the discretion to favor certain enterprises over others. The board often yielded to pressures from ministries, and it did so on an ad hoc basis. Such discretion enhanced the board's power because it had to approve every exception to established policy. So too with the budget, which typically reflected an aggregation of responses to organizational demands, as opposed to systematic choices among them. As a result, Fidel Castro charged, "Rather than regulating spending, [the budget] promoted it."[9] There was thus a moderate structural crisis within the state as a result of this pattern of relations among the state's institutions, even though the economy had one of its best years in 1984. Attacking the board was to attack the process of organizational accommodation and coalition building. Because the board was also associated with the use of market-reliant ideas that in the USSR would lead to perestroika, the attack on the board had the anticipatory effect of weakening the institution that might have been most receptive to perestroika.

On April 19, 1986, Castro formally announced the Rectification Process (RP) to guard against those who were becoming too enamored of the market and its mechanisms. Government policy shifted away from reliance on material incentives. Castro attacked both the coalition that had supported some market ideas under central planning and also the ideas themselves.

Further dismissals of high-ranking personnel got under way in the political and internal security realm. In addition to the dismissal of Central Planning Board President Humberto Pérez (noted above), in 1985 Castro dismissed the Cuban Communist party's ideology secretary Antonio Pérez Herrero and Minister of the Interior Ramiro Valdés. All three, who had emerged after the Second Party Congress (1980) as the most important leaders next to Fidel and Armed Forces Minister Raúl Castro and Vice President Carlos Rafael Rodríguez, were dropped from their posts in the party's Political Bureau and Secretariat in 1985. Their removal led to President Castro's remarkable recentralization of power, which continued into the late 1980s.

For separate reasons, Soviet-Cuban relations deteriorated in 1984–85. During Konstantin Chernenko's brief leadership of the Soviet Union, economic strains appeared in Soviet-Cuban relations. These included increases in the price of petroleum to be paid by Cuba, declines in the price of sugar sold to Soviet Union, and disputes over how much support Cuba could expect from the Soviet-led Council for Mutual Economic Assistance (CMEA). There were also political differences, most notably the weak Soviet response to the U.S. invasion of Grenada in late 1983 while Cubans fought U.S. forces on that island. When Chernenko died in early 1985, Fidel Castro did not attend his funeral.[10]

The destruction of the political coalition most receptive to perestroika on the eve of its birth, the reshaping of state structures to emphasize once again President Castro's role, and the deterioration of Soviet-Cuban relations made it much more difficult to welcome external ideas into Cuba, especially ideas from the Soviet Union.

The Influence of Perestroika on Cuba

If important changes in Cuba had endogenous origins and if such formidable barriers were erected to insulate Cuba from foreign ideas, how did reform-communist concepts have any impact at all? The answer is that

Cuba's political regime was complex enough to allow some freedom of expression for a time regarding thinking about the experiments in communist Europe, even as Cuba's leaders were moving in another direction. Moreover, these ideas were so presented as to encourage a favorable reception in Cuba.

Legitimizing Proposals for Major Policy Changes

One reason to import ideas from outside the prevailing national discourse is, of course, to change the content and direction of that discourse when appeals to ideas existing within the country would not lead to change. One way to discredit an idea in Cuba, however, is to say that it has been "copied" from some other country.[11] In the mid-1980s, invoking external ideas in Cuba was even more problematic because the government had adopted the RP to move away from reliance on certain market mechanisms, opposite to what was occurring in nearly all European and Asian communist regimes.

How, then, might Cubans argue that their country should learn from reform-communist ideas? Those who supported a greater use of market mechanisms had to advance their cause in language that was familiar to their intended audience, while retaining their credentials as Cuban communists, not stalking horses for foreigners. In those circumstances, the safest way to borrow from abroad was to invoke the sacred texts of international socialism.

In 1989, Minister of Culture Armando Hart, a Political Bureau member, began to reintroduce ideas from Lenin and Engels into the public discourse as a way of recalling the utility of market mechanisms in socialist countries. It was pedagogically sound, he said, to reread Lenin "from a modern perspective." Hart noted the importance of avoiding schisms and maintaining party unity—an essential Leninist principle. Having established his Leninist credentials, he argued:

> Lenin's focus on the New Economic Policy (NEP) shows the dramatic circumstances that took him to propose, as a pragmatic matter, a change that he recognized was not the one that Marx and Engels had considered in their theories, nor one that he had considered himself, with regard to socialism. We must recall the conjunctural nature of those political and economic decisions, but it is also clear that the most important conjunctural decisions carry also important lessons.[12]

Substitute *Cuba in the late 1980s* for Lenin's *Soviet Union,* and *Fidel Castro* for *Lenin,* and this statement becomes an appeal to adopt NEP-like market mechanisms in Cuba.

In his next article on Engels's thought, Hart attacked dogmatism as an obstacle to making necessary changes:

> Our purpose with these texts . . . is to remind the reader about those classical texts connected with practical and immediate concerns that we have before us. Among them is the need to combat, with reasoning, the calumnies hurled at Marxism-Leninism in presenting it as a "dogma" or as a doctrine that prevents the advancement of knowledge and the analysis of new realities.

Even Marxists, he said, have contributed to this "infamy" because they "have attempted to turn the ideas of the classics into a catechism."[13] To criticize dogmatism within Marxism-Leninism is, of course, to advocate change within the system.

Although it was easier for someone of Hart's stature to use the sacred texts to attempt to redirect government policy toward markets and away from dogmatism, he was not alone. Writing in the more technical journal *Economía y desarrollo,* Félix Gómez Rodríguez followed the identical strategy by quoting Lenin's comments on NEP made in 1921:

> We should not give in to a romantic socialism . . . that feels an unconscionable disdain for commerce. All economic forms are admissible during the transition . . . [and] are necessary . . . to reactivate the economy. . . . [Thus] it is important to continue to study forms of commerce (especially in consumer items) that are used in the capitalist countries which can foster an improvement of commercial activity under socialism once they are drained of their capitalist content.[14]

This strategy illustrates the utility of foreign ideas; reference to the revered texts legitimized the arguments for policy change and enabled their advocates to make a case in terms familiar to the audience in form, though not in specific content.[15] They could not be criticized for referring to current experiences in the Soviet Union and Eastern Europe.

Clarifying Strategic Choices

Some Cuban academics, especially those associated with the Centro de Investigaciones de la Economía Mundial (CIEM), have the task of analyzing international economic relations and the economic ideas and performance of other countries. CIEM reports on the CMEA countries have been particularly professional and informative; their purpose seems to be academic analysis to clarify strategic choices for Cuban decision makers.

The CIEM reviews were never favorable toward Hungary's market-oriented reforms. This was evident both before and after Mikhail Gorbachev's installation as general secretary of the Communist party of the Soviet Union, which suggests a continuity of professional judgment as well as at most lukewarm support among Cuban leaders for market mechanisms, even in the early 1980s. In general, CIEM authors were much more impressed with the centralized efficiency of the German Democratic Republic than with Hungary's market socialism.[16]

In contrast, Norka Clerch's 1985 article on Yugoslavia—which preceded Gorbachev's perestroika—can be read as an effort to clarify the strategic choices for a socialist country that had relied for many years upon market mechanisms under socialism. Cuba's relations with Yugoslavia had not been warm. Nonetheless, Clerch stated, "Yugoslavia's economic growth showed notable results during the postwar period, which allowed it in a few years to grow beyond its underdeveloped agrarian structure to become a country with a middle level of industrial development." Clerch's assessment both of Yugoslavia's accomplishments and of its difficulties with regional economic disparities, inflation, and foreign debt were professional. On a more ideological level, she noted the "overvaluing of private interests, and of those of groups, at the expense of social and national interests" and commented that this configuration of values "causes the imbalances inherent in the operation of the self-management system."[17] In short, there was much to be gained in terms of economic growth and economic structural transformations from using market mechanisms under socialism, but there were also economic and ideological problems. Clerch used Yugoslavia to clarify strategic choices for Cuba's decisions makers.

In late 1988 the CIEM published its first article about the economically successful reforms in the People's Republic of China, followed in 1989 by an article on Vietnam's economic reforms. These editorial decisions are noteworthy because Cuba's political relations with China had been poor from the mid-1960s to the mid-1980s, when they began to improve.[18] The CIEM professionals recognized that China's economic reforms had been more successful than Hungary's or Yugoslavia's.

China's economic reforms after 1978, according to Gladys Hernández Pedraza, "caused rapid economic growth" in national income, averaging 9.5 percent. There was also an "improvement of the people's living standards" and an end to economic stagnation. Because her task was to clarify choices for Cuba's decision makers by writing about a foreign experience, she reported that the costs of China's market-socialist strategy were mainly in the political-ideological realm. There was a "deepening of private relations of production" in the agrarian sector; there was a general growth of income inequality; and, in late 1986 and early 1987, there were "ideological deviations" evident in urban student protests calling attention to "how dangerous" the implementation of reform could be. Although new controls had been announced, she wondered whether they could be effective, "given that the extent of decentralization is already so high."[19]

Maritza Bauta's article on Vietnam's economic reforms criticized that country's past economic policies for "inadequate understanding of the role of monetary-mercantile relations under socialism"—a criticism that could be made about Cuba with equal force. She presented Vietnam's economic reforms thoroughly, noting the tendency toward improved economic performance. Her attention to the constructive role of foreign direct investment preceded the Cuban government's decision to implement more flexibly its 1982 law on foreign investment in order to foster such ventures.[20]

These CIEM researchers went beyond mere reporting to highlight the choices before Cuba's leaders. These were not works of advocacy, but they bolstered the views of those who believed that fostering economic growth on pragmatic grounds was worth some ideological flexibility—as, for example, rereading Lenin's views of the NEP along with Armando Hart.

Providing Practical Technical Suggestions

Ideas from abroad sometimes have narrower but still important objectives: to encourage particular changes in Cuba on the grounds that the new techniques developed elsewhere would serve practical goals. The form of this argument is to demonstrate practical gains at low cost.

Typical of this approach is Jorge Valdés Miranda's exhortation that Cuba should learn trade techniques from the German Democratic Republic (GDR). He showed how the GDR demanded that its market-economy suppliers purchase its exports to improve its trade balance with their countries. He was impressed that the GDR had institutionalized such a policy, whereas the Soviet Union had not. "In Cuba," he noted, "we have not been able to make use of such possibilities to acquire technology," implying that Cuba should learn from the GDR.[21]

Aesopian Language to Discuss Cuban Politics

Cuban intellectuals and journalists knew that there were similarities between events in Cuba and those in Eastern Europe and the Soviet Union; one could write about events in Europe as if one were writing about Cuba. In late 1989, Elsa Claro covered events in Eastern Europe for *Bohemia,* Cuba's leading general-circulation magazine. She wrote about the unraveling of the GDR:

> (1) Workers complained that their ideas received no hearing in the organizations and channels created toward that end; . . . they felt that they were not taken seriously, given the fact that they were taken into account only with regard to whether or not they fulfilled the plan. . . . (2) The labor unions . . . were losing their purpose and, as with other organizations, stuck to following directives without taking into account the interests of the workers. . . . (3) There had developed a tendency not to admit attitudes or criticism about things that worked badly; . . . the mass media reflected successes (of which there was no doubt) but failed to portray the domestic and international reality in their full diversity. . . . (4) The parliament's sessions . . . had no debate and/or interesting participation, with no one objecting, even if the subject were pertinent, until a unanimous decision was reached. . . . (5) [Local government] got used to following orders "from above." . . . (6) The existence of friends and relatives "on the other side" [in the Federal Republic of Germany] or the impact of direct broadcasting by radio and television facilitated [negative] comparisons.[22]

With but slight changes, these statements could have been written about Cuba. Cuban workers have had difficulty getting a hearing and their participation in the workplace is problematic at best. Labor unions have all too easily followed directives from the top.[23] Cuba's National Assembly meets only a few days a year, mainly to listen to lengthy reports followed by little debate and virtually unanimous approval of legislation. Cuba's local governments could potentially foster more popular participation in public affairs than those of many East European countries, but have also suffered from the weight of the national bureaucracy.[24] And the existence of a large Cuban-American community in Miami and Radio Martí and other broadcasts help Cubans to make invidious comparisons.

Cuba's mass media has been triumphalist regarding the accomplishments of government or state enterprises, but reluctant to discuss poor performance because such criticism is typically not allowed. In December 1986 *Granma* published a remarkable account of corruption and abuse of power at a major cement manufacturing plant. Days later, President Castro made it clear that the party had explicitly authorized and requested the article's publication. "No one should imagine," Castro noted, "that some individual could write an article putting the state on trial, nor the party, nor the laws; . . . no one has the right to pass judgment on the party."[25]

Another example of using the East European experience to discuss events in Cuba was Mercedes Santos Moray's review of a Czech film.[26] Although she criticized it—the acting was bad—she welcomed "the clear improvement" of Czech cinema in its "attempt to represent the Czechoslovak reality." She recalled that the Czech film industry "in the 1960s produced with great intensity works that were important and beautiful." This was a time of massive changes in Czechoslovakia, eventually suppressed by Soviet military intervention (though she did not mention it). She noted that the film focused on "bribery, illegal gains, blackmail, professional malpractice" and other matters. Cubans witnessed similar practices on the eve of the scandal that led Division General Arnaldo Ochoa to the firing squad and revealed extensive corruption in top echelons of the government, the party, the internal security forces, and the armed forces.

Despite the endogenous source of many changes in Cuba and though it was an inauspicious time for the reception of reform-communist ideas, in the late 1980s such ideas affected debates in Cuba, forcing people to think about long-range strategies as well as about more immediate choices, enabling some to consider borrowing practical techniques while permitting others to discuss Cuban affairs by indirect means. Thus ideas were influential both for reasons intrinsic to them (content, structure, logic, and familiarity) and their manner of presentation.

The Receptivity to Glasnost and Perestroika in Cuba

Few Cubans have acknowledged publicly their support for the ideas behind glasnost or perestroika, but warnings against the diffusion of such ideas suggest that they had become known and were admired. Unguarded public endorsement for these ideas may have peaked in 1987, although some support lasted through 1989, as we have seen.

The best evidence for public support for external ideas comes from intellectual circles. In late 1987, for example, *Unión*, the journal of the official National Union of Writers and Artists (UNEAC), announced its "new age" with a "new format, new authors, new helmsmen, and new energy." This edition, which "happily coincide[d] with the seventieth anniversary of the October Revolution," contained a special section on Soviet writers "at this moment of the Soviet Union's blossoming . . . [because] debates among the Soviet people . . . underlie the nation's health and endurance."[27]

The key official concerned with the reception of these ideas was Party Ideology Secretary Carlos Aldana, later responsible also for international relations. At the UNEAC's Fourth Congress in January 1988, Aldana referred—without mentioning any country—to those who "were understandably enthusiastic about the disappearance, in other latitudes of the globe, of official state doctrines about esthetics." Speaking in the first-person plural, he said, "We of course respect, hail, consider with hope, and must study [those processes]." But Aldana's enthusiasm for reform communism was limited. In the same speech, he cautioned his audience not to "pretend to identify our . . . current changes with those processes abroad" because Cuba's government had never made the mistakes committed in those unnamed countries and thus did not need such changes.[28]

Aldana's choice of words may have sought to express his preferences, and those of many others, for wider openings while allaying Fidel Castro's suspicions. In draft form, Aldana's original phrase for this speech had been to extend *respect, understanding, confidence, analysis,* and *sympathy* to changes occurring in the Soviet Union. When in late 1987 Aldana discussed this language with Castro, the president approved the words *respect, understanding,* and *analysis* but rejected *sympathy* and questioned *confidence.* Aldana dropped these two concepts from his UNEAC remarks and substituted the more ambiguous verb *to hail* (*saludamos*). More important, he turned his remarks away from truly hailing the processes of change and, instead, warned against copying them.[29]

Retrospectively, Castro too dates his change of heart about the processes of change in the USSR and Eastern Europe from late 1987. In November he led a Cuban delegation to the Soviet Union and participated in CMEA meetings, where he cautioned against excessive reliance on market mechanisms and began to worry about the trend of events.[30] Just after this time, he and Aldana had the conversation, reported above, that would change Cuban policy.

The Role of Social Sectors

Aldana has noted that there was substantial support for reform-communist ideas within Cuba's Communist party, perhaps including himself. He gave a persuasive explanation for the diffusion of those ideas: "We idealized the Soviet Union . . . and led people to think that everything that came from there, whatever it might be, was good and better even than our own practices." For Aldana, recent changes abroad had brought "a most difficult ideological moment [to Cuba] . . . one of the most difficult that we have experienced," though "not at the level of the people, but at the level of many intellectual circles in our country."[31]

Aldana's explanations seem accurate. Intellectuals were most receptive to ideas from abroad, even if important changes in the content and style of Cuban literature of the 1970s and 1980s were not caused by Soviet glasnost. Leaders of the Communist Youth Union expressed unusual concern about younger intellectuals and especially about social scientists.[32] But, separately, those who had always thought well of the USSR were also more responsive to any ideas from the USSR. To my surprise, in interviews in 1991 and in 1992 I was told that many former members of the prerevolutionary Communist party tended to sympathize with changes in the Soviet Union, while those who had been close to Che Guevara in the 1960s were more skeptical. Thus responses to ideas and events of the late 1980s ware partly shaped by experiences and alignments from the 1950s and 1960s.

In the late 1980s, the most stirring argument on behalf of an intellectual opening in Cuba was made by the senior "old communist" Carlos Rafael Rodríguez, though not once did he refer to "copying" from the Soviet Union. He condemned the view that there was only "enough room for apologists and acolytes" among Cuba's intellectuals. He recalled Fidel Castro's saying to Cuban intellectuals in 1961 that "outside the revolution, nothing" was permissible in their work. Rodríguez argued against interpreting that phrase too narrowly so as "to impose inopportune decisions or minority views in the name of the revolution and the party." The motto he proposed was: "Those who are not against us are with us." He defended a cosmopolitan vision: "If knowing how to handle a rifle in our nation is nowadays necessary for every citizen, let us not overlook the fact that appreciating Degas or Picasso, Beethoven or Prokofiev is also important."

Rodríguez commented on the UNEAC Congress resolution that asked Cuban intellectuals to be "as far removed from dogmatism as from liberalism, as far removed from intolerance as from complacency." He reminded the UNEAC Congress, "We must not forget, however, that although liberalism is dangerous and complacency is unacceptable, more dangerous still are intolerance and dogmatism in the field of culture and science."[33] This argument was surely consistent with glasnost, but the vice president made a point of ignoring the connection. As with the changes in Cuban intellectual life that had occurred independently of events in the USSR, so too (he seemed to say) there were enough "Cuban reasons" to define a more open policy toward intellectual life.

The Role of Journals

Reform-communist ideas were disseminated through Soviet journals, interviews with foreigners in Cuban journals, and specialized academic publications in Cuba that kept the windows open to news about communist Europe and Asia.

Some Soviet publications that allowed Cubans to express ideas about changes in Cuba became conduits for new ideas, even if their expression did not imply that Cuba ought to emulate Soviet trends. Consider the views of Roberto Fernández Retamar, director of the Casa de las Américas publishing house. In 1990 he expressed views in the Soviet journal *América Latina* that he had not published in Cuba. He discussed the works of Guillermo Cabrera Infante and Heberto Padilla, exiled Cuban authors whom he called "openly hostile toward the revolution." Nonetheless, "they are Cuban authors of important works and sooner or later they will be published in Cuba, and they will enter the flow of Cuban literature of which they are part." Moreover, he noted that a dictionary of Cuban literature, published in Cuba, had failed to mention Cabrera Infante: "My personal opinion is that this is dumb."[34]

Some Soviet publications attacked the Cuban government and its policies. Written mainly by Soviet authors, these assaults raised the suspicions of Cuban leaders toward the reform processes in the USSR. The first mild but pointed rebuke of Cuba appeared in the Soviet publication

New Times in August 1987, eliciting a strong response from Vice President Rodríguez.[35]

Another way of importing foreign ideas was to interview foreigners who would connect the events of communist Europe to those in Cuba. In May 1989, the director of *Casa de las Américas,* Cuba's most internationally influential journal, interviewed the left-wing Brazilian intellectual Darcy Ribeiro, who had just received a medal from Cuba's Council of State. Ribeiro asserted, "[I] found a sclerotic Marxism in the Soviet Union, dated, and given to the repetition of slogans. And I find the same in Cuba." Ribeiro called for the inclusion in Cuban publications of "different voices" so that "voices that seek to contest [prevailing views] would also have space." Ribeiro criticized the "ritualistic" teaching of Marxism in Cuba, the prevalence of censorship even of some of his works, and concluded that "it is necessary not to be afraid to think."[36] Minister Hart replied to Ribeiro, "European formulas are not the ones that can shed light on our paths." The journal's designer liberally sprinkled the issue in which Hart's reply appeared with pictures of buffoons, some of whom wore the faces of journalists known to advocate official positions.[37]

Several key journals published articles about changes in other communist countries. *Cuba socialista,* the official party journal, responds to party directives and follows a political logic. From 1981 through 1985, it published 100 major articles with by-lines, of which eleven were by Soviet authors and another seven by Cubans on topics bearing on the USSR or Eastern Europe. (I exclude unsigned pieces, book reviews, reprints of Fidel Castro's speeches, and so forth.) In 1986 and 1987, fifty-two such articles were published, but only five were by Soviet authors and none by Cuban authors on topics bearing on communist Europe. In 1988 and 1989, the journal published seventy-seven such articles, of which two were by Soviets, and again none by Cubans on communist Europe. Through 1987, therefore, the official journal's receptivity to Soviet authors was a nearly constant 10 percent, although it declined slightly in Gorbachev's early years and Cubans no longer published comments on communist Europe. After early 1988, articles by Soviet authors became rare (2.6 percent).

The CIEM's editorial decisions for its journal, *Temas de la economía mundial,* responded to a more academic logic—for example: those economies had not become less important for Cuba in the late 1980s even if

Cuban leaders had come to disagree with political trends in those countries. *Temas* rarely printed articles by foreigners; when it did, they were from the United States or Western Europe. *Temas* typically published one article per issue on the economies of communist countries. In 1984, it published twelve articles, three of which dealt with the economies of communist countries; the respective proportions were nineteen to five in 1985, seventeen to six in 1987, and twelve to one in 1988. This pattern suggests that intellectual curiosity rose in the early Gorbachev years and, as with *Cuba socialista,* nearly vanished in 1988. While *Temas*'s continued coverage of communist Europe was consistent with its professional mission, the pattern of publication suggests that *Temas* was more interested than *Cuba socialista* in the early Gorbachev experiments but, by early 1988, *Temas* had pulled back as much as *Cuba socialista* had— both reflecting the shift in attitude of Cuba's top leaders.

This differential pattern of journal publication is not accidental. It bears directly on a hypothesis mentioned earlier: that institutional links between idea carriers and top decision makers affect the likelihood of the receptivity of the ideas. Some Cuban economists play multiple roles: as academics they express a full range of views, but as advisors to policy makers, they support prevailing policies. Therefore, the fact that an academic economist is close to policy makers need not imply influence, though at times that may be; at critical junctures the effect is reversed— namely, the policy maker affects the economist's published ideas.

Consider for example two nearly identical articles, using literally many of the same paragraphs and sentences, published in 1990 by José Luis Rodríguez.[38] The version in the party journal, *Cuba socialista,* has some harsh criticism about economic policies and performance during 1981–85 (when some market mechanisms existed under central planning) and significant praise for economic policies and performance during 1986–89 (when the role of market forces was reduced); this mirrored the party's official position. In contrast, the version in *Economía y desarrollo,* the principal academic journal in economics, omits sections 3 and 4 of the *Cuba socialista* version and, consequently, is much less critical of the 1981–85 period and much less laudatory of the 1986–89 period; this is consistent with the view of many academic economists in and outside Cuba, as well as with Rodríguez's other work on Cuba, that some market mechanisms are appropriate under central planning. The following paragraph on the 1981–85 period, for example, was present in *Cuba socialista* (p. 93) and absent in *Economía y desarrollo:*

> The distorting use of material incentives in economic management advanced individual interests in opposition to the interests of the whole society. An individualist ideology came to be felt through the corrupting actions of speculators and intermediaries as well as that of self-employed workers who profited at the people's expense . . . managers who followed a mercantile strategy in their enterprises . . . and bureaucrats who persisted in following a technocratic approach to the solution of economic problems.

On the other hand, the article in *Economía y desarrollo* makes it clear—unlike the *Cuba socialista* version—that the performance of all economic sectors except agriculture was very positive during 1981–85, while during 1986–89 economic growth stopped and productivity fell.

In sum, Cuban intellectuals, including academic economists, were the most receptive to some features of Gorbachev's early reforms. Intellectuals used academic publications in Cuba (and occasionally in the USSR) to advance their views, at times interviewing friendly foreigners who made their own points. Those who had long been sympathetic to ideas from the Soviet Union, no matter what their content, were also more receptive to reform communism. In late 1987 and early 1988, however, the Cuban leadership's attitude toward the Gorbachev policies changed, and these forms of expression became less common.

More subtly, the links between economists and policy makers were not severed, but the flow of influence was reversed: while economists remained free to publish as they wished in academic journals, before a wider public they became advocates of official policies rather than proponents of alternatives. Thus the policy milieu changed even if on the surface the organizational channels remained the same.

The Ideological Domestic Resistance to External Ideas

In 1987–88, a battle of ideas developed between those who favored using some market forces within the context of central planning and close collaboration with the Soviet Union, and those who were allergic to the market and suspicious of the USSR's long-term ideological reliability. One form this debate took was an argument about Ernesto (Che)

Guevara's ideological legacy. Although Guevara spent only about a decade of his life in Cuba—and thus his ideas are also a foreign import—he became an adopted patron saint of the Cuban government after his death in Bolivia in 1967. His works have become sacred texts used to protect the integrity of the communist project in Cuba. After the official launching of the Guevara-flavored RP in 1986, no one sympathetic to opening up Cuban politics or economics could publicly oppose Guevara's ideas. The preferred strategy was to "domesticate" this revolutionary tiger, preferably with help from abroad.

In a stunning revision of history, Vladimir Mironov argued that Guevara was a precursor of Gorbachev. He noted (accurately) that the "theoretical and practical work of Che Guevara during the initial stage of building socialism in Cuba was considered by some a leftist deviation (for instance, the emphasis he placed on the human factor)." Nonetheless, Mironov tells us, it "appears to have in fact been a scientific and moral precursor of a new stage in the socialist movement." Guevara's "notion of building a new kind of man is very close to the profoundly humane goals of the process of restructuring [perestroika] under way in the Soviet Union [in 1987]."[39]

In Cuba, those who favored some market reforms had to argue that Che's ideas were not inconsistent with the recommendations of academic economists and government technocrats. "A great many of Che's principles are found incorporated" in Cuba's official economic management system, wrote Carmen León and Adelaida Arias in 1988. They appear in "the need to combine the centralized planning of the economic activities of state enterprises and the recognition and use of monetary and mercantile relations," and in a system that features "a high centralization at the top" with "operational economic autonomy" for the enterprise.[40] The main tendency of Guevara's views was, of course, the opposite. Without oversimplifying: Guevara did not advocate reliance on monetary and mercantile relations, nor did he favor antonomous state enterprises to any great extent.[41]

In the late 1980s, exponents of Guevara's ideas used his hallowed texts to warn against the Soviet Union's potential perfidy. Part of that perfidy was intellectual: the "theoretical vulgarization or impoverishment" of Guevara's thought in the USSR, reducing it to simplistic political and military tactics.[42] This warning about the USSR's unreliability became urgent as the prospects of Cuban-Soviet trade at market prices (no longer at preferential prices) drew nearer: "With great honesty, courage, and realism Guevara discussed the asymmetrical exchanges found between the more developed socialist countries and the underdeveloped countries when trade occurs at market prices," noted Osvaldo Martínez, CIEM's director, who quoted Guevara's dictum that "the socialist countries are, to some degree, the accomplices of imperialist exploitation."[43]

The shift in the quality of economic relations between Cuba and other communist countries impaired Cuba's ideological receptivity to ideas from abroad. The critique of the Soviet Union's international behavior and of the treatment of Guevara by Soviet intellectuals did not, however, necessarily mean that those who made these arguments were opposed to greater political and economic openings. My argument is narrower: In making these critiques of the Soviets, Cuban authors weakened the legitimacy of importing ideas from the USSR and thus made it more difficult to foster openings in Cuba, even if that was not their intention.

The Ideological Assault on Reform Communism

Attacking reform communism was Fidel Castro's responsibility. "Che [Guevara] would have been appalled if he had been told that money was becoming man's main concern, man's fundamental motivation," Castro argued, as he radically rejected the influx of reform ideas.[44]

Three years before the dismemberment of the Soviet Union, Castro noted that "there are also some brains around," perhaps referring to Cuban intellectuals, "people who have no confidence in themselves, no confidence in the nation, no confidence in their people, no confidence in their revolution—who right away say we have to copy what others are doing." The official newspaper reported that applause followed this remark, though it is unclear whether copying was being applauded. Castro left no doubt: "That is an incorrect stand . . . no two countries are the same."[45]

Months later Castro argued that Cuba's "errors" often "stemmed from imitating the experience of other socialist countries." "Learning from the Soviet Union," seen as positive in the early 1960s and again in the early 1970s, by the late 1980s was perceived as mistaken. More copying would be even worse: "We do not want anyone saying ten or twenty years from now that some of the things they are doing today were no good." Therefore "we must base ourselves on our experience, our own ideas, our own interpretations of Marxism-Leninism." In addition, "the people of Cuba could say with satisfaction that they have not committed many of the errors committed by others."[46] Castro expounded on these ideas during Gorbachev's visit to Cuba in the spring of 1989. "We never experienced some of those things that happened in the Soviet Union during the Stalin era; . . . we did not have the problem of forced collectivization. . . . It would be absurd for us to start worrying about the problem of nationalities in Cuba."[47] In short, Cuba had little need to change, and ideas about change had better be home-grown.

By December 1989, the Berlin Wall having fallen, there was no longer room for ambiguity. On Armed Forces Day (December 2), the lead speaker was Rear Admiral Pedro Pérez Betancourt, chief of the navy. His theme was the demand for proven "loyalty" and the repudiation of "some chicken-hearted and mediocre people. . . . They are those who . . . only know how to copy others." Whenever Cubans made "room for imitation and mechanically cop[ied] foreign solutions, that was precisely when [they] erred most."[48] Fidel Castro's response was plain: "It is disgusting to see how many people, even in the USSR itself, are engaged in denying and destroying the history-making feats and extraordinary merits of that heroic people."[49]

In 1990 and 1991 Cuba's economy plummeted as a result of the disappearance of communist regimes throughout Eastern Europe and especially as a result of the Soviet Union's economic collapse. The crisis in Cuba's economy (see chapter 5) was much more profound than anything experienced in the 1960s.

By spring 1991, Castro's views on reform had hardened: "We are in no way responsible or to blame for past and present errors of any kind made by others . . . they allowed themselves to be penetrated by reactionary ideas, by the ideology of capitalism and imperialism."[50] In December 1991 the Soviet Union collapsed.

Will Cuba Be the Next Domino to Fall?

Cuban leaders have designed various strategies to assure the survival of communism in their country. First, they have adopted severe measures to adjust to the cutback in economic assistance from and trade with the former communist countries and have reemphasized the state's central role in economic management. The main policy shift toward a more open market was the liberalization of rules to promote foreign direct investment. Cubans, however, were still not allowed to form truly private firms to take advantage of a market opening that remained restricted to foreigners. Proposals to allow Cuban farmers to participate again in limited private markets were rejected at the October 1991 Fourth Party Congress (discussed in chapter 5).

In international relations, as early as August 1989 the Cuban government was banning Soviet publications that criticized Cuba.[51] Over the next year, various East European governments cut back their diplomatic and economic presence in Cuba and shut down the cultural institutions that had once worked with their Cuban counterparts. The Cuban government eagerly cooperated with this dismantling of the organizational channels that could have spread the reform-communist virus.[52] The government repatriated most Cuban students and workers—a few sought asylum—stationed in the former communist countries. In domestic politics, a mass media campaign responding to changes in Europe was one of several strategies adopted.

Cuba's Mass Media Explains "What Went Wrong" in Communist Europe

A failure of leadership, not a failure of the system, is the central explanation for what went wrong in communist Europe. Making concessions was especially wrong, for the enemies of socialism are never satisfied. And when the political regime changes, the standard of living of ordinary citizens drops. To make these three points, the Cuban government flooded the mass media with tales of woe from Eastern Europe and the Soviet Union.

By December 1989, Cuba's leaders had at last arrived at a clear and decisive rejection of reform communism. Thus journalists who only weeks earlier had written about the problems of bureaucratic socialism evident in both Europe and Cuba adopted the new line. At first, however, some hoped that reform communism was still possible and need not lead to the destruction of socialism. Let us focus on *Bohemia*'s Elsa Claro.

Claro wrote about the fall of Czechoslovak communism in terms of "problems related to the violation of principles, not [problems of] the system . . . that is [the problem was with] aspects of the model, not with socialism." Czechoslovak socialism, she said, fostered an industrial economy with extensive social welfare policies and support for families.[53] Writing in February 1990 about the changes in Bulgaria, she reported that foreign direct investment "would permit productive increases in all spheres" of the economy. "Despite all the mistakes and the corruption in politics and economics," she argued, "the prevailing conditions in this country would have permitted other alternatives" to the dismantling of socialism.[54] Reform was still possible and not inherently antisocialist—and socialism itself was still good.

A year later Claro's writings had changed: "In our judgment, under the cover of democratization, there have arisen and endured attitudes contrary to socialism. . . . Persons and groups who appeared as defenders of improving socialism have become open opponents of that system. . . . I believe it useful . . . to expose those who desire such a stunning change toward capitalism."[55] Reform communism was, she now believed, a fraud.

Thus those who abandon a communist regime are bound to suffer. By spring 1991, Claro reported that "90 percent of Czechoslovaks were dissatisfied with their standard of living. . . . Remember that the regime that had governed the country, despite its many deficiencies, granted its citizens a set of supports and guarantees unknown by people in other regions; . . . no one knows what one has until one loses it." She discussed inflation, currency devaluation, and unemployment. She cited a letter from a Czech friend: "I was one of those who a year ago went to the streets but also one who quickly reconsidered after the 'drunkenness' and thus I came to figure among the unemployed."[56]

In the fall of 1991, Claro wrote, "Today's Poland takes little pride in having been the first East European nation to shift course in a direction that has come to seem questionable for many. Ordinary folk no longer feel they are masters of their destinies." Inflation, unemployment, and the loss of government services "that had been enjoyed for four decades . . . [have] provoked a decline in living standards and forced thousands of people to emigrate in search of another life."[57] Claro's transition from potential sympathizer with reform communism to sharp critic was slow but, in the end, clear.

Others opposed reform communism sooner. Consider the daily newspaper *Trabajadores,* under the supervision of Cuba's labor confederation. By early October 1989, it reported that Poland was on the "eve of a social explosion because of the massive unemployment and the reduction of living standards that stem from the adjustment process." Despite its many changes, Poland had yet to get relief from its creditors.[58] The paper reported events in Hungary as "a step backward"[59] and commented on the flight of large numbers of East Germans toward West Germany as follows:

> Behind them, they left the German Democratic Republic, where no one went shoeless, was illiterate, hungry, or unemployed, for no one would find there the conditions that one finds [in West Germany] with greater frequency than is often supposed: marginality, crime, and social decay.[60]

The transition to a non-Marxist-Leninist regime implies suffering for many people, Cuban elites argued. This point would be made as well about Nicaragua after the defeat of the Sandinistas in the February 1990 elections: "Those who voted for the river full of dollars announced by the [anti-Sandinista opposition coalition] UNO are still awaiting the overflow of this 'horn of plenty,' while the crisis grips the nation more than ever before," wrote Néstor Núñez in 1991, citing inflation, currency devaluation, and unemployment in Nicaragua.[61]

Two more specific points were made. Fidel Castro argued: "You all know what has been happening elsewhere: they were asked to accept pluralism, so they accepted pluralism. The communist parties held multiparty elections . . . and even won several of them by a large margin. . . . But the reactionaries and imperialists were not satisfied with that; the Communists had to be swept away anyway." Thus he concluded, "Once a single concession is made, all sorts of concessions are demanded until they ask for your head."[62] Do not make any concessions, therefore.

Writing about the collapse of the Mengistu regime in Ethiopia, Juan Marrero noted in 1991:

> In revolution or in politics, making concessions about principle leads sooner or later to the equivalent of suicide. This has happened not just in Eastern Europe where the presumed brilliance of the market economy confused the eyes and minds of politicians, governments, and parties but even in Third World countries which, facing more severe difficulties, turned back on the ideas and behavior that had been the pillars of their national independence. . . . The lesson of Ethiopia demonstrates that, if revolutionary processes act with weakness, they cannot survive.[63]

Third World socialist countries, too, must resist promarket changes, for there too the events of Eastern Europe could recur.

Making concessions was not only strategically unsound but also empirically unnecessary. Cuba is different; the difference is Fidel. The military magazine *Verde olivo* talked to young Cubans watching anticommunist Czech street protests on television. One young Cuban is quoted as saying: "That does not happen here, because here anyone who wants can talk with Fidel and say anything." But, another noted, "not all the leaders reach the people as Fidel does." A third, identified as a practicing Roman Catholic, observed that other such leaders do exist, naming Armed Forces Minister Raúl Castro and Communist Youth Union leader Robertico [*sic*] Robaina, but he cautioned: "in those European countries many communists turned their back on the people."[64] The danger, therefore, is that some Cuban leaders might, unlike Fidel, turn their backs on the people. Failures of leadership must be avoided because socialism is judged to be sound.

Cuban Leaders Narrow the Political Space

In the discussions leading up to the October 1991 Fourth Party Congress, significant political changes were considered. The Congress dropped the article in the statutes committing the party to atheism, thus opening membership to some religious believers. The Congress recommended the direct election of deputies to the National Assembly. More far-reaching changes, however, were not approved. The Congress ratified the Communist party as the only lawful party. In late 1991 and in 1992, the shift toward direct elections of deputies moved slowly; more fundamental changes in the electoral law to permit greater electoral competition seemed unlikely for the time being.

The Political Bureau chosen at the Fourth Congress was constituted mainly of politicians. Only the elderly Vice President Rodríguez and new member Carlos Lage had technical knowledge about the workings of Cuba's economy. The distance between red and expert widened. Armando Hart was dropped from the Political Bureau; during the preceding two years, many officials in the Ministry of Culture had been replaced and the Ministry's powers curtailed. The likelihood of either glasnost or perestroika "from above" narrowed markedly.

The Interior Ministry authorized the activities of "rapid action brigades"—in effect, licensed mob attacks on the regime's opponents—which became especially conspicuous after mid-1991. The brigades attacked individuals on the streets as well as in their homes; they broke up meetings of dissidents. Though not unprecedented, this use of targeted informal violence to stifle dissent was in many ways new. In late 1991, the government intensified repression of the small human rights and opposition groups, arresting and sentencing to jail many of the leaders and a fair number of activists. Harassment and surveillance of dissidents increased markedly. At least one Roman Catholic church was desecrated, and Roman Catholic bishops were warned to stay away from potentially counterrevolutionary behavior.[65]

Cuba's political milieu has changed. In an address to the National Assembly in December 1991, Carlos Aldana, the only leader ever to have implied he thought well of reform communism, intoned a mea culpa. He thanked Castro for rescuing him from the error of expressing sympathy for the processes of change occurring in the Soviet Union. He noted, however, "More than a few of our comrades became supporters of perestroika and of Gorbachev. They echoed in our midst the changes and proposals then being implemented in the Soviet Union and suggested that we should adopt them." Aldana said he could understand why so many comrades had become "confused," but he "could not break bread with those who still lack the intellectual honesty and moral courage to recognize that they were wrong."[66] He called on them to recant. (For various reasons, Aldana was dismissed from his post in September 1992.)

By early 1992, it had almost become subversive to advocate changes in Cuba akin to those undertaken in communist Europe. The Sixth Congress of the Communist Youth Union denounced the "traitors" and the "pseudo-enlightened" who espoused views similar to those that caused the collapse of the USSR; it attacked those whom it called *perestroikos* who criticized everything but refused to recognize their own errors.[67] In interviews, I discovered that discussing one's earlier views about events in the former USSR had become a virtual taboo.

In the economy and in domestic politics, leaders acted to forestall a repetition in Cuba of the collapse of communism elsewhere. The prospects that Cuba can endure its new economic and political hardships are not good, but it is difficult to envision anything other than the survival of the status quo.

Conclusions

Since 1959, Cuba has been the willing recipient of many ideas from the Soviet Union and other communist countries. New concepts were influential in the early 1960s, when the means of production were socialized, and in the early 1970s, when Cuba's economic institutions and policies were reorganized. Cuba was more receptive at those junctures because of a severe crisis within the state about the management of the economy, because of Cuba's excellent relations with the Soviet Union, because of the unity of the leadership coalition on core issues, and because national and international economists carrying the new ideas had access to top Cuban policy makers.

At times of crisis, a united Cuban leadership (renewed with new idea carriers) has used advice consistent with its good relations with the Soviet Union. In the mid-1960s, by contrast, when there was only a modest state-structural crisis in managing the economy, the elite coalition had split, and relations with the USSR had deteriorated, Cuban leaders disdained ideas and advisors that they had embraced at other times; problems were to be solved using Cuba's own political resources. The worth and nature of new ideas, such as using some market elements within central planning, and Castro's preference for relying on the market as little as possible, were constants. Despite obvious empirical differences, at the analytic level conditions of the mid-1980s matched exactly those of the mid-1960s.

In the late 1980s and early 1990s, Cuba's leaders resisted external ideas as never before. There was a crisis in the state's structure because the rapidly failing economy could no longer finance the state and in 1989 the government presented evidence of widespread corruption in its midst. There was considerable unity among the top elite. At one time, such circumstances had facilitated the reception of fresh ideas from abroad. In recent years, however, the collapse of the Soviet economy and of the USSR itself prevented such a response. The content of the ideas was no longer a constant; at issue was preserving central planning, state ownership of the means of production, and the political regime.

Since 1959, therefore, the nature of Soviet-Cuban relations has been the most important and consistent explanation for Cuba's receptivity to new ideas. It is the only factor that accounts for trends in all five episodes when ideas from abroad were either welcomed or spurned. At issue is not Cuba's "sovietization"; we seek instead to account for both the rise and fall of Soviet ideological influence.

One might object that because I have focused on a period (1984–92) when Cuba's political leaders were especially unreceptive to new ideas, perhaps external ideas have had no impact whatsoever in Cuba. But the pattern is more complex. Glasnost had little impact on Cuban literary life in part because autonomous changes in Cuba's domestic intellectual world and government policy anticipated the Soviet opening. This case study indicates that there is some truth to the claim of Cuban leaders that, having avoided many of the errors committed by Soviet leaders, they had little to learn from the USSR. And Cuba's intellectual life has been freer than that in the Soviet Union. But notions of political and economic opening imported from abroad did inform aspects of Cuba's political debate up to 1989.

For some, ideas borrowed from communist Europe legitimized calls for policy change and enabled advocates to make their case in terms that were familiar in form, though not in content, to their audience. Second, references to changes in communist Europe and East Asia clarified the strategic choices faced by those regimes—and, by extension, by Cuban leaders if they followed in their footsteps. Third, some academics argued that Cuba could learn specific practical techniques from countries undergoing change. Finally, some found it easier to discuss Cuba's problems by writing about the problems of socialism in communist Europe—using Aesopian language. In these ways, ideas were influential because of their content, their structure, their logic, their familiarity, and also their presentation.

Despite the inauspicious timing for receptivity to new ideas, for a while there was in Cuba considerable interest in external ideas. Intellectuals, including academic economists, welcomed or at least were intrigued by them, as were many whose careers predisposed them to accept innovations from the Soviet Union. At the top of the regime, those most closely associated with ideas of opening were Carlos Aldana, Armando Hart, and Carlos Rafael Rodríguez.

At the institutional level, intellectual and academic publications were the most effective carriers of innovative ideas, as were journalists who regularly covered events in Eastern Europe. Soviet publications at times facilitated the expression of ideas aimed at a Cuban public. Interviews with foreigners in Cuba's journals occasionally advanced an agenda for change. But idea carriers had limited influence; while economists remained free to publish as they wished in academic journals, before a wider public they endorsed official policies rather than proposing alternatives.

By the end of 1987, the tide had turned within Cuba's top leadership, though not yet in the regime's middle ranks. Beginning in 1988, explicit support for ideas from communist Europe dimmed; coverage of events in those countries shifted in tone. Within Cuba, elite alarm at the trends in the USSR toward greater reliance on market principles in international trade led some Cuban scholars to launch an ideological counterattack based on Ernesto Guevara's criticisms of such policies; this critique delegitimized reliance on ideas from the Soviet Union. Finally in the summer of 1988, Fidel Castro opened a public attack on ideas coming from communist Europe about politics and markets—a critique sharpened over the next eighteen months.

The collapse of communism in Europe ended public arguments in Cuba that sought to legitimize reform communism. For some, such arguments approximated advocating the overthrow of Cuba's political regime. A sustained assault was launched on notions of "copying" from abroad, blaming Cuba's past mistakes on such copying. Instead, Cuban leaders argued, Cuba would follow its own path to socialism; they defended socialism even though they admitted that specific European communist leaders had performed badly.

Cuba's leaders asserted that they would not fail. The mass media responded to this policy direction by reporting on all the economic ills evident in formerly communist Europe, to dissuade would-be Cuban sympathizers with reform communism. Cuba should make no concessions to those who wanted to modify the regime, conscious of the superiority of its leaders over those of communist Europe. Cuban leaders narrowed the regime's political space—never wide—and jailed dissidents. Cuban leaders knew how to face the future. Change may come to Cuba yet, but now more than ever it must be for native reasons, the leaders argued, as Cuba seeks to adjust to a new world that is hostile to its brand of socialism.

NOTES

I am very grateful to Pedro Monreal, of Cuba's Centro de Estudios sobre América, for his excellent critique of an earlier draft of this chapter, entitled "Coping with the Collapse of Communist Governments in Europe: An Alternative Explanation of Cuba's Recent Developments" (Center for Latin American Studies, University of Pittsburgh). I am also grateful to Carmelo Mesa-Lago, Susan Eckstein, and other conference participants for their comments. The errors that remain in this work are my sole responsibility.

1. This analysis owes much to Peter A. Hall's introduction to *The Political Power of Economic Ideas: Keynesianism across Nations,* ed. Hall (Princeton: Princeton University Press, 1989).

2. Cuban leaders were divided about various issues in the early 1960s. They were united, however, on key points of concern to this work, such as the expropriation of all foreign firms and of most private firms outside of agriculture and certain services, the utility of comprehensive state planning and management of the economy, and learning from the Soviet Union's conduct of its economy.

3. José Luis Rodríguez, *Estrategia del desarrollo económico en Cuba* (Havana: Editorial de Ciencias Sociales, 1990), pp. 82–84, 117–19, 134–35.

4. Víctor Rodríguez Núñez, "En torno a la (otra) nueva poesía cubana," *Unión,* no. 4 (1985): 29–30, 32; Virgilio López Lemus, "Poetas en la Isla (treinta años de poesía cubana: 1959–1989)," *Unión,* no. 7 (1989): 65, 69–70.

5. Francisco López Sacha, "Tercio táctico," *Unión,* no. 4 (1985): 63–64, 67, 73–74.

6. Imeldo Alvarez, "El carácter polisémico de la narrativa de la revolución cubana," *Unión,* no. 11 (1989): 32.

7. Damaris Calderón, "Esta será la única mentira en la que siempre creeremos," *Unión,* no. 4 (1985): 61.

8. María Elena Cruz Varela, "Dies Irae," *Unión,* no. 9 (1990): 73. Although Cruz Varela would soon thereafter become an opposition activist and is in prison at this writing, she was not so when she wrote this poem, when it was published in an official journal and when she received Cuba's "Julián del Casal" national poetry prize.

9. Fidel Castro, "Main Report: III Congress of the Communist Party of Cuba" (Havana: 1986), pp. 31, 35.

10. Jorge I. Domínguez, *To Make a World Safe for Revolution: Cuba's Foreign Policy* (Cambridge: Harvard University Press, 1989), pp. 106–08.

11. I have observed this in countless conversations in Cuba during my trips in 1979, 1980, 1985, 1988, two trips in 1991, and 1992.

12. Armando Hart Dávalos, "Leamos de nuevo a Lenin," *Cuba socialista,* no. 43 (January–March 1990): 2–3.

13. Armando Hart, "Volvamos a leer a Engels," *Cuba socialista,* no. 44 (April–June 1990): 1.

14. Félix Gómez Rodríguez, "Reflexiones sobre la circulación mercantil en el socialismo," *Economía y desarrollo* (November–December 1989): 44–45.

15. For a similar argument about the impact of ideas that seem familiar and useful, D. Michael Shafer, *Deadly Paradigms: The Failure of U.S. Counterinsurgency Policy* (Princeton: Princeton University Press, 1988), pp. 43–78.

16. José Luis Rodríguez, "La evolución de la economía de los países socialistas durante 1983," *Temas de la economía mundial: revista del CIEM,* no. 10 (1984): 27–94; Edith Felipe, "Los cambios más recientes en los sistemas de dirección económica en Europa socialista," *Temas de la economía mundial: revista del CIEM,* no. 12 (1984): 77–116; Norka Clerch, "Problemas actuales que plantea la elevación del nivel de vida en los países socialistas europeos miembros del CAME," *Temas de la economía mundial: revista del CIEM,* no. 22 (1988): 95–142.

17. Norka Clerch, "Yugoslavia. Algunas consideraciones sobre la situación actual y perspectivas de su economía," *Temas de la economía mundial: revista del CIEM*, no. 13 (1985): 121–23.

18. *Granma*, April 8, 1987, p. 6; ibid., December 16, 1989, p. 1; *Granma Weekly Review*, November 26, 1989, p. 9.

19. Gladys Hernández Pedraza, "La evolución de la economía de la República Popular China en los últimos años," *Temas de la economía mundial: revista del CIEM*, no. 25 (1989): 119, 124, 135. See also Gladys Hernández Pedraza, "El sector agrícola en China," *Economía y desarrollo*, no. 116 (May–June 1990): 96–109.

20. Maritza Bauta, "La situación actual de la economía vietnamita," *Temas de la economía mundial: revista del CIEM*, no. 26 (1989): 75, 86.

21. Jorge Valdés Miranda, "Acerca de la compraventa de plantas completas u objetivos industriales," *Economía y desarrollo*, no. 71 (November–December 1982): 168–69.

22. Marifeli Pérez-Stable, "Class, Organization, and Conciencia: The Cuban Working Class after 1970," in *Cuba: Twenty-five Years of Revolution, 1959–1984*, ed. Sandor Halebsky and John Kirk (New York: Praeger, 1985), pp. 291–306.

23. Elsa Claro, "RDA: Bordeando la encrucijada," *Bohemia* 81, no. 46 (17 November 1989), 68–70.

24. See the discussion by Cuban authors Haroldo Dilla Alfonso, Gerardo González, Ana T. Vincentelli in "Cuba's Local Government: An Experience Beyond the Paradigms," *Cuban Studies* 22 (1992).

25. Fidel Castro, "En la reunión informativa del Comité Provincial del Partido de ciudad de La Habana," *Cuba socialista*, no. 26 (March–April 1987): 13.

26. *Trabajadores*, January 23, 1989, p. 11.

27. *Unión*, no. 4 (1987): 1, 20.

28. *Unión*, no. 2 (1988): 43.

29. *Granma*, January 1, 1992, p. 5.

30. *Bohemia*, October 25, 1991, pp. 32–33.

31. *Granma*, January 1, 1992, p. 5.

32. *Juventud Rebelde*, March 22, 1992, p. 7.

33. *Granma Weekly Review*, February 14, 1988, p. 7.

34. Roberto Fernández Retamar, "En el mundo están ocurriendo cosas importantes," *América Latina*, no. 6 (1990): 81.

35. Vladislav Chirkov, "An Uphill Task," *New Times*, no. 33 (August 17, 1987): 16–17; Carlos Rafael Rodríguez, "A Difficult but Steady Ascent," *New Times*, no. 41 (October 19, 1987): 16–17.

36. Esther Pérez and Arturo Arango, "No tener miedo a pensar: entrevista con Darcy Ribeiro," *Casa de las Américas* 30 no. 176 (September-October 1989): 105–06, 110.

37. Armando Hart Dávalos, "Carta a Darcy Ribeiro," *Casa de las Américas* 30, no. 180 (May–June 1990): 117. A journalist who was offended at being portrayed as a buffoon was Luis Sexto, "En Cuba: el turno del ofendido," *Bohemia* 83 no. 12 (March 22, 1991): 25.

38. José Luis Rodríguez, "Aspectos económicos del proceso de rectificación," *Cuba socialista*, no. 44 (April–June 1990): 86–101; and "La economía cubana en 1986–1989," *Economía y desarrollo*, no. 116 (May–June 1990): 26–43.

39. Vladimir Mironov, "A Revolutionary by Calling," *New Times*, no. 43 (November 2, 1987): 26–27.

40. Carmen León and Adelaida Arias, "El Che acerca de la efectividad de la producción social," *Economía y desarrollo*, no. 105 (1988): 121, 124.

41. For translations of Guevara's texts in debate with his critics, see Bertram Silverman, ed., *Man and Socialism in Cuba: The Great Debate* (New York: Atheneum, 1971).

42. Luis Suárez Salazar, "Che: un creador heroico," *Cuba socialista*, no. 31 (January–February 1988): 76.

43. Osvaldo Martínez, "Notas sobre el pensamiento de Ernesto Che Guevara en las relaciones económicas internacionales," *Cuba socialista*, no. 35 (September–October 1988): 81. See also María del Carmen Ariet García, "Che's Role in the Foreign Policy of the Cuban Revolution," *Tricontinental*, no. 113 (May 1987): 59. For a prescient early warning and technical discussion (though without reference to Guevara), see José Luis Rodríguez, "Los precios preferenciales en los marcos del CAME: análisis preliminar," *Temas de la economía mundial: Revista del CIEM*, no. 9 (1984), esp. p. 23.

44. *Granma Weekly Review*, October 18, 1987, p. 5.

45. Ibid., August 7, 1988, p. 4.

46. Ibid., December 18, 1988, p. 5.

47. Ibid., April 16, 1989, p. 2.

48. Ibid., December 10, 1989, p. 3.

49. Ibid., December 17, 1989, p. 2.

50. *Granma Weekly Review*, May 5, 1991, p. 12.

51. Ibid., December 17, 1989, p. 2.

52. Interviews in 1990 and 1991 with East European diplomats.

53. Elsa Claro, "Checoslovaquia: en el vórtice de la tormenta," *Bohemia* 81 no. 48 (December 1, 1989): 76–78.

54. Elsa Claro, "Bulgaria: las variantes de Sofía," *Bohemia* 82 no. 8 (February 23, 1990): 60–62.

55. Elsa Claro, "URSS: Cuitas y riesgos, entronque de esperanzas," *Bohemia* 83 no. 1 (January 4, 1991): 44.

56. Elsa Claro, "Trágico testimonio: crónica para un final de siglo," *Bohemia* 83 no. 19 (May 10, 1991): 40–41.

57. Elsa Claro, "En el mundo: ni fáciles ni promisorios," *Bohemia* 83 no. 43 (October 25, 1991): 43.

58. *Trabajadores*, October 7, 1989, p. 11.

59. Ibid., October 11, 1989, p. 11.

60. Ibid., October 12, 1989, p. 11.

61. Néstor Núñez, "Nicaragua: pasaje para un sueño," *Bohemia* 83 no. 19 (May 10, 1991): 42.

62. *Granma Weekly Review,* May 5, 1991, p. 15.

63. *Granma,* July 9, 1991, p. 9.

64. Pedro Prada, "¿Conflictivos?" *Verde olivo,* no. 7 (1990): 26.

65. *Americas Watch* 4 no. 1 (February 24, 1992); and interviews in Havana during three visits in 1991 and 1992.

66. *Granma,* January 1, 1992, p. 5.

67. *Juventud Rebelde,* March 22, 1992, p. 8.

5

The Economic Effects on Cuba of
the Downfall of Socialism in
the USSR and Eastern Europe

Carmelo Mesa-Lago

This study of the domestic and external changes in the Cuban economy since 1986 briefly reviews the main economic features of the antimarket Rectification Process, analyzes the dramatic deterioration in Soviet-Cuban economic relations and the disappearance of economic relations with Eastern Europe, and evaluates the socioeconomic impact of these changes.

The Rectification Process

From 1976 to 1985, Cuban leaders gradually introduced a modest market reform (the System of Direction and Planning of the Economy, or SDPE) that resembled the Soviet reform of the mid-1960s. The SDPE authorized some decentralized decision making such as: giving more power to managers of enterprises; using some market mechanisms (such as profit as a major indicator of managerial performance, free peasant markets, private self-employment—particularly in services); supporting self-financing of enterprises based on bank credit; and expanding economic incentives (for example, wage differences, production bonuses, prizes). Although the SDPE was flawed and never fully implemented, the Cuban economy grew vigorously in this period. However, the expanding trade deficit had to be covered with huge Soviet credits, while income inequality, bureaucratism, and corruption increased. These problems, combined with the USSR's changed leadership and growing economic crisis, as well as

Fidel Castro's politico-ideological objections to the SDPE, set the scene for a dramatic change in economic policy.

In 1986 Castro launched the Rectification Process (RP) that set Cuba against the worldwide trend of market-oriented reform in socialist economies. RP policies have further restrained private ownership and the market: abolishing free peasant markets; integrating more small private farms (8 percent of total farmland) into state-controlled cooperatives; eliminating small private manufacturers, truckers, and street vendors; reducing self-employment (at least until 1991), and restricting private construction, selling, rental, and bequest of housing. The vacuum left by these measures was to be filled by the state by the expansion of procurement (*acopio*), marketing agencies, the parallel market, and production of state enterprises, as well as by the resurrection of construction minibrigades and new "contingents" (state-managed, military-style groups of construction workers centrally assigned to priority targets).

A second cluster of RP measures was enacted to increase control of labor and wages and to fight corruption: reducing surplus labor; tightening labor output quotas or "norms" (usually increasing them); revising (usually reducing) wages, production bonuses, prize funds, and overtime payments; reemphasizing unpaid voluntary labor and nonmaterial or "moral" incentives (but with selective use of material incentives in tourism and for construction contingents); and creating new categories of crime to fight corruption.

A third set of policies pursued macroeconomic stabilization (that is, reducing trade and budgetary deficits) by promoting exports (establishing investment priorities), cutting imports, and reducing domestic consumption (lowering state subsidies to prices, ration quotas, and free meals, as well as increasing some prices). The least precise and least known RP policies pertain to key macroeconomic aspects such as planning, management and financing of enterprises, and price reforms.[1]

The RP has not yet produced an integrated model of economic organization to replace the SDPE. Theoretically, the RP is expected to find a middle point between the "idealistic errors" of the Guevarist-Castroite model (1966–70) and the "economicist mistakes" of the SDPE (1976–85). Several laws have been enacted and policies launched, but no comprehensive model of the RP has been published. As a result, there has been much contradiction and confusion on the role of economic tools, such as the nature of the central plan, the role of profit as a major indicator of managerial performance, price reform, how to measure efficiency, and so forth.

As in 1966 when Castro took over many functions of the Central Planning Board, in the 1986–92 period he launched and personally supervised numerous economic projects, but failed to produce an integrative model fundamental for a socialist economy, especially one that eschews markets. In 1990 Cuban social scientists began to call for definitions and a blueprint. Finally admitting the problem, the Communist party's Central Committee postponed discussion until the Fourth Party Congress, which simply reiterated the need to search for "new forms of organization and economic management, as well as the structure and functioning of enterprises."[2]

Economic Features of the Rectification Process

Little is known about the economic characteristics of the RP.[3] In 1986 a new National Commission of the System of Direction of the Economy (SDE—which dropped "planning" from the former title) proposed several modifications of the old system that were approved by the party in 1988. In 1990 the SDE's president was dismissed, and his successor immediately began restructuring the system. The Fourth Congress did not even mention the SDE, let alone evaluate its performance.

Planning. An experiment in "continuous planning" began in 1988 to promote more flexibility and active participation among managers and workers; although this technique was criticized as "abstract," it was expected to be used in elaborating the 1991 plan. However, the National Assembly extended the 1990 laws of the plan and budget to 1991, and a formal plan was apparently not elaborated. The Fourth Congress ratified planning as a key economic instrument but did not define its character and failed to mention continuous planning, probably because it was unsuccessful.

Decision Making. Castro has asserted that centralized decision making must totally control investment, the use of hard currency, and other crucial economic resources. The Fourth Congress ratified these elements (adding central control of enterprises) and granted exceptional powers to the party's Central Committee, presided over by Castro, to make economic decisions, enact laws (in lieu of the National Assembly), and take any needed actions during the current crisis.[4] Merging enterprises into bigger trusts or *unions* has paralleled macroeconomic recentralization since 1986, with the possible exception of tourism.

Directive Indicators, Prices, and Financing. Castro warned that profit cannot be the most important goal of an enterprise but should be subordinated to the national interest, a point ratified by the Fourth Congress (which replaced the term *profit* with *private interest*). The problem is that the national interest has not been defined in practical terms. Reforms to correct highly distorted prices were postponed by the Fourth Congress until the current economic crisis ends; in the meantime, central allocation of materials has been extended to cover virtually the entire economy. After two years of secret discussions, in 1988 the party approved continued self-financing of enterprises (a key element of the former SDPE that appeared to be in limbo after the RP); however, publication of that resolution in the official gazette was delayed by one year. The Fourth Congress ratified the principle of self-financing, particularly in enterprises that operate in hard currency (a tiny minority), but allowed the continuation of centralized budgetary financing.

Integral System of Enterprise Improvement. This system has been used mostly in military (MINFAR) enterprises, reportedly with good results. It reinforces the managers' power and the connection between worker performance and remuneration; workers who repeatedly fail to fulfill output goals are demoted or dismissed. Yet difficulties in applying the system to civilian enterprises, concerns about unemployment, and delays in revising output norms seem to have obstructed the universalization of this system. The Fourth Congress praised the MINFAR experiments but did not evaluate the integral system's results.

Uncertainty in Planning; Increased Centralization. The previous sections strongly suggest that the SDE either is in serious trouble or has been discarded without another planning mechanism to replace it. The vagueness of the domestic economic model is compounded by uncertainty about international trade. In the Special Period in Time of Peace (a euphemism for the state of emergency that began in 1990), a highly centralized crisis strategy to maximize resources and establish priorities has been forged, but it can hardly be called a plan. Furthermore, market tools have been further reduced, except for foreign investment enclaves.

Unsuitable State Substitutes for the Market. Most of the state mechanisms that were expected to fill the gaps created by the RP's elimination or reduction of market tools have apparently not achieved that goal:

(1) the system of *acopio* continues to be inefficient and state enterprises and farms, as well as cooperatives, have not been able to increase production (see chapter 6); (2) the parallel market has virtually disappeared and all consumer goods are rationed; and (3) Castro has criticized construction minibrigades as inefficient, and it is doubtful that new construction contingents are self-financed, while their expansion has been restrained by the crisis. (In late 1991 Castro warned that they might be disbanded.)[5]

Asked by a journalist if the state had been able to fill the output vacuum created by eliminating the free peasant markets, a government official answered yes in terms of quantity, but not in assortment and in effective supply, because organizational deficiencies have resulted in spoilage and losses; he noted that a majority of the population wanted the markets to be reintroduced.[6] But in a long speech delivered at the Fourth Congress, Castro forcibly opposed that action, arguing that agricultural production could be increased only by the state and the cooperatives. Congress voted against the markets but agreed to authorize individuals to cultivate produce in urban gardens, under proper permits and regulation.[7] It approved self-employment in private activities but with significant restrictions: it should be subsidiary to the role of the state, be performed after regular public-sector working hours, be confined to minor service activities, and be strictly regulated to ensure that it does not conflict with socialism and the limitations imposed under the Special Period. In addition, self-employed persons cannot hire anyone outside the immediate family. Reportedly, these restrictions (and the fresh memory of harsh public criticism in 1982 and curtailment of self-employment in 1986) have impeded a resurrection of this type of work.[8]

In summary, the RP and the SDE launched economic policies that resemble those applied in the idealistic antimarket period of 1966–70. There is neither a real central plan nor clearly integrated mechanisms to measure managerial performance; rather, decision making has been recentralized under Castro and his inner group, who essentially govern the economy on subjective criteria. Some institutions that were discredited in the 1970s have been reintroduced (such as construction minibrigades) with equally inefficient outcomes. The partial militarization of production (MINFAR enterprises, labor minibrigades and contingents), the massive transfer of labor to agriculture under the Food Program, and the excessively optimistic economic strategies and goals (see chapter 6) echo some of the doomed practices of 1966–70. The Fourth Congress ratified the RP and its programs but failed to design a new economic model; Congress rejected the reintroduction of free peasant markets but allowed self-employment (although crippled by restrictions). Paradoxically, in his opening speech, Castro referred to some of the RP programs as belonging to the past, promising measures that had been paralyzed or hurt by the collapse of socialism elsewhere and by the economic crisis at home.[9]

The Dramatic Deterioration of the Soviet-Cuban Economic Relationship

The Cuban economy depended heavily on foreign trade (see table 5.1). From 1962 to 1974, Cuba's average trade turnover as a percentage of the Global Social Product (GSP) was 24 percent, and it rose to 50 percent in 1985–89. Furthermore, trade with the USSR grew from an average of 45 percent in 1961–65 (60 percent with the Council for Mutual Economic Assistance, or CMEA) to 71 percent in 1985–88 (85 percent with CMEA).

Because of this concentration on one trade partner, in 1988 83 percent of Cuban trade was in transferable rubles, 8.7 percent in barter and dollar agreement, but only 8.3 percent in convertible currency.[10] In 1988, Cuban exports to the USSR were 85.2 percent sugar, 5.4 percent nickel, 2 percent citrus, 0.3 percent alcohol and tobacco, and 7.1 percent other goods. In turn, imports from the USSR were 48 percent oil and oil products, 17.3 percent machinery and equipment, 9.8 percent manufactured goods and spare parts, 8.1 percent foodstuffs and raw materials, and 16.8 percent other products. Finally, since the revolution, Cuba's foreign trade has systematically resulted in a deficit: between 1959 and 1989 there was a small surplus only during two years and the cumulative deficit in the entire period was 21 billion pesos ($23 billion at the official exchange rate); in the 1980s, 70 percent of it was with the USSR.[11] As a Cuban scholar recently said:

> Cuba's economic performance is tied, in large measure, to the behavior of its external sector. . . . External trade [dependency on GSP] is astronomical and makes our economy extremely sensitive to external sources of instability. . . . Insufficient [domestic] production fosters the adverse impact of external factors. . . . The economy still needs considerable imports to supplement both domestic output and the needs of society.[12]

TABLE 5.1
Cuba's Trade Turnover by Trade Partner, 1965–1989
(in percent)

	1965	1970	1975	1980	1985	1988	1989
SOCIALIST COUNTRIES	77.2	71.9	59.9	75.8	86.3	87.1	83.2
CMEA	61.7	63.8	56.4	71.6	83.1	83.6	78.9
USSR	48.2	51.7	48.0	60.0	70.5	69.1	64.7
All other CMEA countries	13.5	12.1	8.4	11.6	12.6	14.5	14.2
East Germany (GDR)	3.4	4.2	2.4	3.3	3.7	5.0	4.8
Czechoslovakia	5.2	3.3	1.3	2.0	2.2	3.1	2.6
Bulgaria	2.4	2.2	2.6	3.0	2.7	2.5	2.6
Rumania	0.3	1.5	0.3	0.9	1.2	2.1	2.1
Poland	0.8	0.4	0.5	1.2	1.1	0.8	0.8
Hungary	0.6	0.4	0.5	0.9	1.3	0.8	1.0
China	14.3	6.6	2.7	2.6	2.7	3.1	3.5
Other	1.2	1.5	0.8	1.6	0.5	0.4	0.8
MARKET ECONOMIES	22.8	28.1	40.1	24.2	13.7	12.9	16.8
Western Europe	14.4	17.6	21.0	10.9	7.1	7.0	8.4
Spain	5.2	3.4	6.2	2.2	2.0	1.7	2.0
United Kingdom	4.1	3.2	2.3	1.1	0.9	0.8	1.4
France	1.9	3.2	2.0	1.7	1.1	0.7	0.6
Italy	0.7	2.9	1.9	0.7	0.5	1.0	0.7
West Germany (FRG)	0.4	1.6	2.4	1.2	0.7	1.0	1.1
American continent[a]	1.7	1.8	5.6	6.2	3.2	3.5	5.6
Canada	1.3	1.5	2.7	2.6	0.6	0.5	0.7
Latin America	0.3	0.2	2.6	2.9	2.3	3.0	5.0
Mexico	0.2	0.2	0.4	2.4	0.5	0.9	0.7
Argentina	0.1	—	1.7	—	1.4	1.0	1.3
Asia	2.1	7.5	10.8	4.3	2.4	1.8	1.6
Japan	1.6	6.0	9.6	3.4	2.1	1.5	1.1
Africa	2.9	1.2	1.9	2.7	0.7	0.6	0.9
Other countries	1.7	0.0	0.8	0.1	0.3	0.0	0.3
Total	100.0	100.0	100.0	100.0	100.0	100.0	100.0

Sources: Based on Comité Estatal de Estadísticas (CEE), *Anuario Estadístico de Cuba (AEC) 1989.*
a. Includes North and Latin America.

Declining Trade Turnover and Increasing Deficit

Until 1990 Cuba was the USSR's sixth largest trade partner (see chapter 3). Total trade turnover increased 77 percent in 1976–80 and 92 percent in 1981–85 (with a peak of $10.7 billion in 1985) but declined by

11.5 percent in 1986–89 ($8.8 billion in 1989). The decline in turnover hid an important fact: the value of Soviet imports remained basically the same in 1985–89, but Cuban exports to the USSR fell by almost 28 percent; as a result, the trade deficit increased by 144 percent from $937 million to $2,291 million.[13] Official statistics are not available for 1990 (but see "Effects of the Crisis on the Economy," below).

The 1989 Soviet-Cuban trade pact set total trade between the two countries at 9,000 million rubles or 9,990 million pesos (at the official exchange rate of 1.11 pesos per ruble) but actually only 8,753 million pesos were exchanged, 12 percent less than planned. The Soviet-Cuban trade pact for 1990 raised the target to 9,200 million rubles (10 billion pesos). According to then Soviet Vice Chairman Leonid I. Abalkin, Cuba agreed to increase exports by 7.5 percent over 1989, while Soviet exports were to rise by 5.9 percent to reduce the trade deficit.[14] There are no official data on actual total trade for 1990, but, according to Castro, Soviet imports represented by the end of September only 3,838 million rubles (75 percent of the agreed amount) or 4,249 million pesos—23 percent below the 1989 level.[15] Official data have not been released on exports and the trade balance for 1990.

A trade and economic pact was signed for 1991, but no data were released on turnover, amounts of key commodities to be exchanged, prices, or economic aid. Cuba's minister of foreign trade said later that the exchange of sugar for oil products would be roughly the same as in 1990, but total trade turnover would decline because (1) sugar exports would be about the same as in 1990, but at a lower price than in 1986–90; (2) nickel exports would decline (although there were planned increases in biotechnology-medical products and citrus exports); (3) there would be a 64 percent cut in imported equipment (equal to a 16 percent reduction in total imports); and (4) no more imports of nonessential manufactured goods (such as television sets, refrigerators).[16] According to Castro, the planned value of Soviet imports for 1991 was initially set at $3,940 million, but later reduced to $3,363 million, and only $1,305 million had been delivered by September 30. The final value of Soviet imports, at the end of 1991, was given as $1,673 million, 71 percent below the 1990 level.[17] The value of exports is impossible to assess: whereas the value of sugar exports was halved and nickel exports declined, there might have been more exports of biotechnology and medical products. The net value of most exports has declined, but probably less than imports, thus possibly resulting in a trade surplus.

During 1976–90, the Soviet Union and Cuba signed three five-year trade agreements that provided significant security to Cuba. The 1991 pact, for only one year, expired on December 27, 1991. Despite intense negotiations, no five-year agreement was signed for 1991–95. With the disintegration of the former USSR and the creation of the Commonwealth of Independent States (CIS), Cuba now has to negotiate individually with fifteen republics or states. In early 1992, Cuba had signed partial trade pacts with Belorus, Kyrgyzstan, Lithuania, and Tajikistan (for five years); Ukraine (three years); Estonia, Kazakhstan, and the city of St. Petersburg (for 1992 only); and Russia (for the first quarter of 1992).[18] A Cuban official has reported that imports from CIS will fall in 1992 to less than half the 1991 level—that is, to about $800 million, or 15 percent of the peak achieved in 1985.[19] It is impossible to estimate the value of Cuban exports and the corresponding trade balance for 1991.

Castro has said about the situation: "For decades our plans . . . were based on the existence of the socialist camp . . . with which we worked out agreements, . . . reliable markets for our products and [guaranteed] supply sources for important equipment and merchandise; . . . the socialist camp no longer exists. We have total uncertainty for 1991 through 1995."[20] And Vice President Carlos Rafael Rodríguez adds: "The only certainty is that . . . the situation will worsen."[21]

Deterioration in Terms of Trade Against Cuba

Previous analysis of Soviet-Cuban terms of trade, based on a sample of 90 percent of Cuban exports and 39 percent of its imports, showed a constant improvement for Cuba in 1968–74 but a deterioration in 1975–84 (1968 = 100, 1974 = 187, 1984 = 86). The loss in 1981–84 was 36 percent; but if Cuba had conducted its trade with the USSR at world market prices, the deterioration would have been much worse—a decline of 81 percent.[22] Based on 80 percent of all Cuban exports and 60 percent of all imports, two Cuban economists have estimated the deterioration as 21 percent in 1981–85; a third economist calculates a loss of 6 billion pesos for the period, of which about 4 billion might have been with the USSR.[23] An accurate evaluation of the terms of trade in 1986–90 is not possible because data for 1989–90 are lacking; however, table 5.2 summarizes the information available for 1986–88 and includes estimates for 1989–90.

TABLE 5.2
Comparison of Prices in the Soviet-Cuban Market and the World Market, 1980–1990

	Raw Sugar (cents per pound)					Nickel Sulfide (cents per pound)					Crude Oil (pesos/dollar per barrel)				
	Soviet		World	Ratios[a]		Soviet		World	Ratios[a]		Soviet		World	Ratios[a]	
Year	Pesos	Dollars	Dollars	Pesos	Dollars	Pesos	Dollars	Dollars	Pesos	Dollars	Pesos	Dollars	Dollars	Pesos	Dollars
1980	33.7	47.5	28.2	1.20	1.68	2.26	3.19	2.96	0.76	1.08	10.87	20.67	28.67	0.38	0.72
1981	27.5	35.2	16.6	1.65	2.12	4.90	6.27	2.70	1.81	2.32	13.87	17.75	32.50	0.43	0.55
1982	29.8	35.7	8.4	3.54	4.25	4.90	5.88	2.19	2.24	2.68	17.21	20.65	33.47	0.51	0.62
1983	39.6	45.9	8.5	4.65	5.40	4.90	5.68	2.12	2.31	2.68	20.42	23.69	29.31	0.70	0.81
1984	39.3	44.4	5.2	7.55	8.53	4.92	5.56	2.16	2.28	2.57	23.80	26.90	28.47	0.83	0.94
1985	44.7	48.7	4.1	10.90	11.87	4.92	5.36	2.22	2.21	2.41	26.19	28.55	26.98	0.97	1.05
1986	39.3	47.5	6.1	6.44	7.67	4.93	5.96	1.76	2.80	3.38	26.38	31.92	13.82	1.91	2.31
1987	38.6	38.6	6.8	5.67	5.67	4.94	4.94	2.21	2.24	2.24	26.56	26.57	17.79	1.49	1.49
1988	41.8	41.8	10.2	4.09	4.09	4.94[b]	4.94[b]	6.25	0.79	0.79	26.55	26.55	14.15	1.88	1.88
1989	41.8	41.8	12.8	3.26	3.26	4.94[b]	4.94[b]	6.04	0.82	0.82	26.55[b]	26.55[b]	17.19	1.54	1.54
1990	41.8	41.8	12.5	3.34	3.34	4.94[b]	4.94[b]	4.02	1.23	1.23	26.55[b]	26.55[b]	22.05	1.20	1.20

Sources: USSR prices in pesos are author's estimates based on CEE, AEC 1986 to 1988 and CEE, Compendio Estadístico de Energía 1989; world prices from IMF, International Financial Statistics 1980 to 1991; ratios calculated by the author (conversion of Cuban pesos to U.S. dollars based on country. AEC 1989 discontinued the series on exports and imports by product and country.

a. Ratio of Soviet-paid prices (in pesos and converted to U.S. dollars) over world market prices (in U.S. dollars).

b. Estimate assuming price remained constant.

Both Soviet and Cuban sources assert that prices of commodities traded by both countries in 1986–90 were frozen and based on 1985 prices.[24] Table 5.2 confirms that assertion for nickel and oil prices but not for sugar prices: in 1986 the price of sugar paid by the USSR (in pesos) was 12 percent below the 1985 price (although equal to 1984), and it remained practically unchanged in 1987. Although the price increased by 8 percent in 1988, it was still 6 percent below the 1985 base price. However, Vice President Rodríguez told me in July 1990 that the cost per ton of sugar for the Soviets was 850 rubles (42.7 Cuban centavos per pound) in 1985–90.[25]

To facilitate the analysis, table 5.2 assumes that Soviet prices of the three commodities, as well as exports, remained unchanged in 1988–90. The table compares Soviet prices, in pesos and converted to U.S. dollars, with the world market price in U.S. dollars, and gives the corresponding price ratios. The reason for including a series of Soviet prices in pesos (assuming an equal exchange with the dollar) is to avoid the wide fluctuations and distortions caused by the unilaterally set Cuban peso-dollar exchange rate (for example, 1980 = 1.41; 1981 = 1.28; 1985 = 1.09; 1986 = 1.21; 1987–90 = 1.00). In any event, the difference between Soviet prices in pesos and the conversion to dollars was very small in 1986–90 because the peso exchange rate was set at par in the last four years. Finally, it should be noted that most sugar transactions in the world are not set at world market prices but conducted under bilateral agreements with preferential prices; comparing the latter to Soviet prices (more generous than most preferential prices set among market economies) results in smaller ratios than comparing to world prices.

According to table 5.2, while the Soviet price of crude oil (in pesos) remained unchanged in 1986–90, the world price declined sharply in 1986 and then oscillated—but always at a level substantially below the 1985 price level. Therefore, the price ratio that was about par in 1985, deteriorated to 2:1 in 1986, and then improved to 1.2:1 in 1990. In that period, Cuba paid much more than world market prices for Soviet oil. Conversely, the Soviet price for sugar apparently declined about 6 percent in the period, while the world price increased threefold; hence the price ratio that was 11:1 or 12:1 in 1985 declined to 3:1 in 1990.

In other words, in relation to world prices, the USSR cut its subsidy to Cuban sugar by more than a third; however, if Cuba had sold that sugar

TABLE 5.3
Gross Estimates of Cuba's Gains and Losses in Trade
with the USSR, 1986–1990
(in millions of dollars)

Year[a]	Sugar Exports			Nickel Exports			Oil Imports			Total
	Soviet Prices	World Prices[b]	Gain/ Loss	Soviet Prices	World Prices	Gain/ Loss	Soviet Prices	World Prices	Gain/ Loss	
1986	4,081	523	3,558	236	70	166	1,763	763	−1,000	2,724
1987	3,240	570	2,670	200	90	110	1,561	1,045	−516	2,264
1988	3,138	765	2,373	200[c]	254	−54	1,496	796	−700	1,619
1989	3,138[c]	960	2,178	200[c]	245	−45	1,476	977	−499	1,634
1990	3,138[c]	938	2,200	200[c]	163	37	1,476	1,126	−350	1,887
Total	16,735	3,756	12,979	1,036	822	214	7,772	4,707	−3,065	10,128

Sources: Author's calculations based on table 5.2 and CEE, AEC 1988.
a.In 1987–90 the Cuban peso-dollar exchange rate was at par; the rate in 1986 was $1.21 per peso, thus increasing the dollar totals for the period by 1 million.
b.In the case of sugar, comparing the Soviet price with preferential prices set in bilateral agreements would result in lower subsidies than comparison with world prices.
c.Unchanged value of exports and Soviet prices are assumed.

on the world market instead of to the USSR, it would have received only 22 percent of what the Soviets paid. Finally, the Soviet price for nickel remained unchanged in the period, while the world price fluctuated. Over the period, the average price of Soviet-subsidized nickel was above the world price, so that Cuba gained about 26 percent in nickel export value, but, compared to 1981–85, the Soviet subsidy was cut by 68 percent.

In summary, Cuba's terms of trade (limited to three homogeneous commodities for which we have information) continued to deteriorate in 1986–90. And yet, as in the previous quinquennium, Cuba gained significantly by trading with the USSR vis-à-vis the world market, mostly because of the high Soviet subsidy paid for Cuban sugar. The estimated overall net gain for the entire period was $10.1 billion ($1 billion lower if estimated in pesos) disaggregated as follows: $13 billion in sugar, -$3.1 billion in crude oil, and $214 million in nickel (see table 5.3). However, Cuba's net gain on these three commodities in 1981–85 was $15.7 billion; hence the gain in 1986–90 declined 36 percent.[26]

A few Cuban and Soviet authorities have discussed terms of trade, but for isolated commodities and without showing their calculations or integrating their estimates for several commodities, resulting in contradictions. For instance, V. Venediktov, a Russian, estimated that Cuba lost 1.3 billion rubles annually (or 6.5 billion rubles during the period, equal to 7.2 billion pesos) in buying all oil and oil products from the USSR. Assuming that the overprice paid by Cuba on oil products was the same as for crude oil, and taking into account that the latter represents about 60 percent of all oil products imported by Cuba, Venediktov's estimate was 2 billion pesos higher than mine (5 billion pesos for all oil products). Venediktov also claimed that according to "experts," prices of Soviet machinery and equipment were twice as high as world prices for the same products (a difficult evaluation to make because of the lack of information on their quality) and that in 1988 Cuba overpaid 600 million rubles (666 million pesos) for that reason. He concluded that these losses "ate up" part of the Soviet aid in the form of subsidies for sugar.[27] Even if we accept Venediktov's figures (on oil and other import losses), Cuba would have had a net gain of 5 billion pesos in its trade with the USSR during the period.

Vice President Rodríguez told me in 1990 that Cuba lost 4.7 billion pesos (in comparison with world prices) in oil and oil products in 1986–90, near my estimate of 5 billion pesos, but 2.5 billion pesos less than Venediktov's. We concur that Cuba had a "slight gain" in terms of nickel. Rodríguez did not compare Soviet and world prices of sugar (which obviously would have reflected a significant gain) but shifted the discussion to the deterioration in trade with the USSR. He complained that if the Soviets had raised the price of sugar (frozen in 1985) to the world market price, Cuba would have earned 50 percent more for its sugar exports. And yet, if Cuba had not enjoyed a subsidy, it would have earned only 22 percent of what it actually received. A Cuban economist therefore puts Cuba's sugar gain in 1986–87 at 4 billion pesos, 2 billion lower than my estimate.[28]

In a speech delivered in late September 1990 after Iraq's invasion of Kuwait (followed by a world embargo) sent oil prices skyrocketing from $14 to $40 a barrel, Castro said that two tons of sugar were needed to buy one ton of oil. Therefore, to maintain the island's consumption level of 13 million tons of oil and oil products, Cuba would have to export 26 million tons of sugar.[29] This statement was shrewdly confusing. Castro referred to the world market, but 100 percent of Cuba's oil imports came from the USSR in 1988, and the island sold half of its sugar to that country. In 1990, under the Soviet-Cuban trade terms, one ton of sugar bought 4.6

tons of oil; it was precisely the price security offered by the five-year trade agreement that protected Cuba from the wide fluctuations of the world market.

No concrete data have been released officially on volume and prices of sugar exports and oil-product imports under the 1991 trade pact. However, Cuba's minister of foreign trade stated that the volume of both commodities in 1991 would be roughly the same as in 1990, which means about 4 million tons of sugar and 10 million tons of oil and oil products. He added, "For the moment only in the case of sugar a preferential rate has been maintained, which is less than in the last five years [$0.42] but more than that of the world market [$0.09 in early 1991]." The rest of the exchanged goods must still be determined according to the world market, even for fuel, he said, but he could not use current world prices—about $20 a barrel in the first two months of 1991—as a point of reference for the entire year.[30]

A Cuban scholar reports that the Soviets paid $0.25 per pound for sugar in 1991, or 60 percent of the price they paid in 1990, but twice the world price at the end of that year. A Western source adds that in 1991 the Russians charged $20 per barrel of oil (much less than both the Soviet price of 1990 and the world price in December).[31] In 1992 the Russians eliminated the subsidy paid for Cuban sugar and set the price at the world market level ($0.09 to $0.10); hence in 1992 Cuba was expected to receive 40 percent of what the Soviets paid in 1991 and 24 percent of what they paid in 1990. The price of oil also was to be set at the fluctuating world market level.

A Soviet economist refuted the claim that in 1986–90 the Soviet Union benefited from its economic relationship with Cuba. He argued: (1) oil is a much more competitive commodity in the world market than sugar (Cuba's citrus exports are even less competitive than sugar because of inferior quality); (2) under the 1986–90 Soviet-Cuban trade terms, one ton of sugar bought about five tons of oil, while on the world market the ratio was one for three (but in 1992 the Cuban-Russian ratio became either 1:1 or 1:1.8); (3) Soviet preferential prices for sugar in 1990 were triple world prices (but in 1992 the price was the same); (4) sugar exports to the USSR were lower than planned in some years, forcing Cuba to borrow 3.5 million tons from a French firm (actually 6.5 million tons to meet all sugar commitments with a value of $1.8 billion), a debt guaranteed by the USSR in convertible currency (but canceled in September

1990); and (5) the USSR's concession on oil "reexports" resulted in an equal loss of hard-currency revenue for the Soviets (an agreement canceled in 1990).[32] As noted, none of these benefits for Cuba existed in 1991.

A final point is that Cuba's large and increasing trade deficits with the USSR in 1986–90 were not only a result of the explained deterioration in the terms of trade but also of the decline or stagnation in the quantity of Cuban exports. In 1988, sugar exports to the USSR (85 percent of total exports to that country) were 6 percent below the 1985 level. Nickel exports (5 percent of total exports) increased 4 percent, but were at the same level as 1980; furthermore, the closing of one of the major Cuban nickel plants in 1990 (66 percent of whose exports were committed to the USSR) cut exports substantially. Citrus exports jumped 23 percent in the same period, but constituted only 2 percent of total exports to the USSR. Finally, tobacco exports were stagnant and alcoholic beverages declined sharply.[33] (On the sluggishness in Cuban exports, see chapter 6).

Termination of Soviet Aid

Soviet economic aid to Cuba assumed three forms between 1960 and 1991: credits to cover trade deficits, development loans, and price subsidies (see table 5.4). The first two were to be repaid (thus are debt), while the third was nonrepayable grants. In 1992 all aid ended.

Trade deficit credits are the most accurate figures on the table because the USSR automatically extended them every year. Figures on development loans are based on announcements in the Cuban press but, in the 1980s, only an aggregate figure for each quinquennium was provided and no disaggregated information on annual loans was released. Price subsidies (for sugar, oil, and nickel) are the most difficult to estimate for these reasons: (1) When Soviet prices are compared with world market prices or preferential prices set in bilateral trade agreements, the first comparison normally results in larger subsidies than the second (which involves a wider range of prices). This problem is most important in estimating sugar subsidies, but less so for nickel subsidies and even less for petroleum. (2) The bulk of Soviet imports are nonhomogeneous products, and the lack of data on their quality and sophistication impedes serious evaluation. Most experts agree that such imports are overpriced, but there is no agreement on their magnitude (transferable rubles paid by the USSR for Cuban goods have to be spent in buying Soviet goods).

TABLE 5.4
Soviet Economic Aid to Cuba, 1960–1990

| Period | Trade Deficit | Repayable Loans (Debt) | | Nonrepayable Price Subsidies[a] | Total Aid |
		Development	Subtotal		
1960–70	2,083	344	2,427	1,131	3,558
1971–75	1,649	749	2,398	1,143	3,541
1976–80	1,115	1,872	2,987	11,228	14,215
1981–85	4,046	2,266	6,312	15,760	22,072
1986–90	8,205[b]	3,400	11,605	10,128	21,733
Total	17,098[c]	8,631[c]	25,729	39,390	65,119

| | Distribution (%) | | Growth (%) | |
	Loans (Debt)	Subsidies (Grants)	Loans (Debt)	Subsidies (Grants)
1960–70	68.2	31.8	—	—
1971–75	67.8	32.2	97[d]	101[d]
1976–80	21.0	79.0	24	882
1981–85	28.6	71.4	111	40
1986–90	53.4	46.6	83	−36
Total	39.5	60.5	—	—

Sources: Author's calculations based on Carmelo Mesa-Lago and Fernando Gil, "Soviet Economic Relations," p. 219, revised and updated with table 5.3, and *AEC 1988.* Also J. L. Rodríguez, "Las relaciones económicas entre Cuba y la antigua URSS" (Havana: CIEM, 1992), p. 12. *Note:* The table excludes military aid, reported as $13.4 billion in 1960–85.

a. Subsidies to sugar and nickel exports and petroleum imports are all estimated in comparison with world market prices. Includes an insignificant negative subsidy to grains in 1960–85. Excludes additional revenue in hard currency obtained by Cuba in the 1980s by "reexporting" subsidized Soviet oil.

b. Includes an estimate of $1 billion for 1990. According to a former Cuban trade official, the initial credit for the period was set at 2.5 billion rubles ($4 billion) as in 1981-85 but it was insufficient and later was increased by an equal amount.

c. According to a Cuban economist, cumulative aid for trade credit was 13.8 billion pesos while it was 6.6 billion pesos for development loans. (The difference is due to conversion of the pesos into dollars.) He also reports that the distribution of the *debt* by source in 1990 was: 62% trade deficits since 1972, 35% development loans since 1972, and 3% debt accumulated until 1972. Such distribution is close to the *debt* distribution in the table: 66% trade deficits and 34% development loans.

d. Over the estimated average for 1966–70.

(3) Estimates of Soviet subsidies must be calculated in U.S. dollars to allow comparisons with world market and bilateral agreement prices set in that currency, but the arbitrary peso-dollar exchange rate set by Cuba creates erratic fluctuations and distortions. (4) Cuban "re-exports" of Soviet oil add further complications.[34]

Trade deficit credits steadily increased from 1960 to 1990 except for the 1976–80 period because in 1975–78 there was a surplus in favor of

Cuba. In those four years, the price of Cuban exports was adjusted to the price of a basket of Soviet imports, which greatly benefited the island as Soviet aid shifted from repayable trade deficit loans to nonrepayable price subsidies. The Soviets reportedly terminated this arrangement because it became very expensive.[35] The trade deficit reappeared in 1979 and grew rapidly in the 1980s: out of the cumulative deficit in 1960–88, two-thirds was concentrated in the 1980s and almost half in the last four years of that period.

Development loans also increased steadily, particularly after 1975, with two-thirds granted in the 1980s. Subsidies increased in 1971–75 and jumped almost nine times in 1976–80, but growth slowed to 40 percent in 1981–85 and declined by 40 percent in 1986–90. Cumulative economic aid in 1960–90 reached $65 billion, 60 percent in grants and 40 percent in loans. The total figure should be smaller due to an overestimation of the subsidy (already explained) and a possible double counting of development loans within trade deficit credits.[36] On the other hand, that figure excludes $13.4 billion in free military aid in 1960–86, a figure supplied by the head of Cuba's armed forces. A Soviet critic, however, suggests that military aid has been much higher: "Considering that Cuba has one of the world's largest armies [in per capita terms] . . . it can be presumed that Soviet [military] aid is well matched with civilian aid or is even more lavish." Also, a Soviet economist has questioned whether all Soviet military aid has been free: "Unpaid-for military shipments make up part of the debt of Cuba."[37]

Despite these problems, table 5.4 detects significant changes in trends in the size, growth rate, and composition of Soviet aid: in 1960–75 aid increased slowly and more than two-thirds was in loans; in 1976–80 aid jumped 300 percent and almost four-fifths was in nonrepayable subsidies; in 1981–85 total aid kept rising but at a much slower rate (51 percent), and the share of subsidies declined while that of loans increased; and in 1986–90 the amount of aid declined slightly and the bulk of it became repayable loans.

According to a former Cuban foreign trade officer, during tense discussions in Moscow in early 1990 the Soviets informed Cuba of their intention to substantially reduce aid both in subsidized prices and trade deficit financing starting in 1991 and to terminate oil supplies exceeding Cuban needs in 1990.[38] Under the 1991 trade pact, the Soviets approved an undisclosed amount of credit to support ongoing projects in Cuba, but not to start new ones. Concerning trade deficit financing, in 1991 Cuba's minister of foreign trade vaguely mentioned "the Soviet willingness to grant a credit for the trade deficit that will develop this year."[39]

At the beginning of the 1990s, President George Bush began to pressure the USSR to stop economic aid to Cuba as a condition for receiving U.S. aid.[40] The USSR's economic deterioration and growing criticism in the Soviet media of aid to Cuba and its allegedly inefficient use strengthened the U.S. position. In his campaign for the Russian presidency, Boris Yeltsin echoed that criticism and in mid-1991 told a group of U.S. lawmakers that he favored eliminating all economic aid to Cuba.[41] Nevertheless, Castro and other Cuban leaders publicly rejected the possibility that the Soviet leaders would yield to U.S. pressure and denied that Yeltsin was an adversary; instead, he was "a friend of Cuba."[42] At the Bush-Gorbachev summit held in Moscow in August 1991, a few weeks before the failed Soviet coup, the U.S. president stated that Soviet aid to Cuba was one of the few remaining obstacles in U.S.-Soviet relations.[43]

Although Cuba adopted a cautiously neutral position during the attempted coup in the USSR, its failure sealed the fate of Soviet economic aid to the island: top orthodox officials who strongly supported aid (in the KGB, the army, the party, and the central economic bureaucracy) vanished; moderates like Gorbachev who favored a gradual instead of abrupt reduction in aid saw their power weakened; and reformers who favored eliminating aid, such as Yeltsin, soon were in full control. Furthermore, some of the institutions in which aid supporters worked were swept away (like the Communist party and the KGB).[44]

In a television interview broadcast in the United States after the coup, Gorbachev was asked if aid to Cuba would be terminated; he answered that mutually beneficial economic relations would continue. But Yeltsin responded to a question on withdrawing Soviet troops from Cuba by stating that the process that had started in East Europe would continue in Cuba. Finally, after a September meeting with Secretary of State James Baker in Moscow, Gorbachev declared that in the immediate future economic relations with Cuba would be limited to mutually beneficial trade and that "other elements from that relationship [aid] that were born in a different time and era would be removed." In addition, he said that discussions would begin with Cuban leaders about removing 11,000 Soviet troops. Baker praised that declaration,[45] but Cuba criticized it, saying that it was a "unilateral decision" taken without previous consultation: "It is obvious that [Gorbachev] negotiated and made concessions to the United States concerning Cuba, yielding to their pressure." The Cubans would accept the withdrawal of Soviet troops only if U.S. military troops were withdrawn from Guantánamo.[46]

All economic aid from the former USSR was indeed terminated in 1992 and trade dramatically reduced. By April of that year, Soviet troops were still stationed in Cuba, but there had been a gradual withdrawal of other personnel: out of 3,500 technicians, 2,400 had left Cuba before the coup and the Soviets had requested that the remaining 1,100 be paid in hard currency. Cuban workers stationed in the USSR (such as 1,000 lumbermen in Siberia) were called home, most Cuban students had been repatriated at the beginning of 1992, and the number of diplomats and journalists was drastically cut. After the coup, out of 174 Soviet projects in Cuba, 80 were completed, 70 remained unfinished, and 20 were shelved. Castro bitterly complained of the waste of hundreds of million of pesos invested in unfinished Soviet-supported projects.[47]

Cuba's Debt to the Former USSR

Until 1990, there were no official data on Cuba's external debt to the USSR; conversely, since 1982, there have been statistics on the hard-currency debt, which reached $7.3 billion in 1990. Table 5.4 indicates that total Soviet repayable loans to Cuba under the revolution were $25.7 billion; I estimate that amortization of principal and payment of interest have been very small.[48] Early in 1990, Nikolay I. Ryzhkov declared that on November 1, 1989, the Cuban debt was 15.49 billion rubles and that the USSR had deferred 2.4 billion rubles in 1986–89 for amortization and interest. The Cuban debt to the USSR was the highest among all debtor nations (both socialist and developing); it made up 37 percent of the total debt of developing countries and 18 percent of the total debt of sixty-one nations.[49] (Release of these data surprised the Cubans because there had been a gentlemen's agreement not to publish them—an agreement honored by the Cubans when they refused to supply this information to the Paris Club.)[50]

At the Soviet official exchange rate (the rate used to calculate the foreign debt to the USSR), in November 1989 the Cuban debt was equivalent to $24.5 billion, or $27.6 billion at the November 1990 rate (see table 5.5). It could be argued that using the official exchange rate inflates the debt because other rates are considerably lower (e.g., $8.6 bil-

TABLE 5.5
Estimates of Cuba's Total External Debt, 1989–1990

| | | *Dollars (millions)* | | |
| | *Rubles (millions)* | *Official November Rate* | | *Commercial Rate* |
		1989 = 1.58	*1990 = 1.78*	*1990 = 0.56*
To the Soviet Union (November 1989)	15,490	24,474	27,572	8,674
(as percent of total)	—	(71.4%)	(73.4%)	(50.0%)
To Eastern Europe[a] (June 1990)	—	2,498	2,717	1,407
Czechoslovakia	600	948	1,068	336
Bulgaria	300	474	534	168
Hungary	170	268	303	95
East Germany (GDR)	2,000[b]	808	808	808
In Hard Currency (September 1990)	—	7,300	7,300	7,300
Total	—	34,272	37,589	17,381

Sources: Soviet debt from Nikolay I. Ryzkhov, *Izvestia*, 2 March 1990, p. 3; East European debt from *El Nuevo Herald*, 14 June 1990, p. 3B, "CMEA Trade: Down but Not Out," *Cuba Business* (August 1990), pp. 2, 15; Peter Jacina, Ministry of Foreign Trade, Prague, 7 August 1991; exchange rates from the *New York Times*, November 1989 and 1990; J. L. Rodríguez, "Las relaciones económicas entre Cuba," p. 6.

a. According to José Luis Rodríguez, Eastern Europe loaned Cuba 2.3 billion pesos in 1959–89 to finance the trade deficit, plus 500 million more in development loans for a total of 2.8 billion pesos. However, he has given the debt as only 1.5 billion pesos.

b. 2,000 million GDR marks exchanged in FRG marks (DM) at exchange rate of 1.649 = 1,212 million DM = U.S. $808 at 1.5 exchange rate. Or 2,000 GDR marks = U.S. $600 at 3.33 rate.

lion at the 1990 commercial rate). However, it is difficult to believe that Cuba's debt, contracted over a thirty-year period, would be converted by using current lower exchange rates. When asked which exchange rate should be used to estimate the debt, Vice President Rodríguez (surprisingly) told me in July 1990 that Cuba might lose if a lower rate was applied because servicing the debt was a long-run problem, whereas the Soviets could apply the lower rate to sugar export prices and cut their value in the short run. In September 1992 Russian minister of foreign trade Pyotr Aven stated that the Cuban debt was $28 billion and that the Cubans refused to discuss repayment.[51] Table 5.5 shows that Cuba's total debt at the end of 1989, at official exchange rates, was $34.2 billion— $24.4 billion to the USSR, $2.5 billion to Eastern Europe, and $7.3 billion in hard currency (other estimates of the total are $37 and $17 billion). Cuba's debt per capita in 1989 (excluding that to Eastern Europe) was the highest in Latin America.[52]

This comparison has to be qualified by the generous terms of the Soviet debt (80 percent of the total). Trade loans have an amortization period of twelve years and a 2–4 percent interest rate, and payment is not due until one or two years after delivery; for development loans, the amortization period is twenty-five years and the rate of interest 2 percent, and many of these loans are to be repaid with Cuban products. Rescheduling of such loans has been extremely flexible; for instance, the payment of debt and interest accumulated in 1963–75 was postponed until 1986 (free of interest) to be paid in twenty-five years; when it became due in 1986, it was postponed for another five years, and then again in 1991.

In 1989 enterprises established with Soviet aid generated 15 percent of Cuba's gross industrial output: 100 percent in sheet steel, sugarcane combines, television and radio sets; 70 percent in electricity; 60 percent in textiles; and 50 percent in the machine tool industry.[53] However, there are complaints that many Soviet development projects are defective or burdensome for Cuba: (1) the Che Guevara nickel plant, which cost 1 billion pesos, is only half as efficient as plants dating from the 1950s; furthermore, it had to be shut down in 1990 due to high operating costs and the fuel shortage; (2) the Soviet-built oil refinery of Cienfuegos, with a 3-million ton capacity, faces serious difficulties in beginning operation; and (3) the nuclear power plant has endured long delays and increased its initial building costs by $800 million due to additional safety measures introduced after the Chernobyl accident. Castro has questioned whether the last two projects will ever be completed.[54]

Despite these problems, in the 1980s—particularly the first half—the USSR protected Cuba from the worst regional economic crisis since the Great Depression. Two major causes of the crisis were the heavy debt burden and declining prices of raw materials. By subsidizing Cuban exports and postponing debt repayments free of interest, the USSR greatly contributed to the high economic growth rates the island enjoyed in 1981–85 and postponed the time of reckoning. But perestroika and the collapse of the USSR changed that rosy situation.

In 1985, largely with Moscow in mind, Castro asked the developed world to cancel all foreign debt and, during a meeting in Havana, urged Latin Americans to repudiate the debt. In a speech to the UN in December 1988, Gorbachev was more cautious, proposing to write off part of the debt (particularly for small countries) and establishing a lengthy moratorium for the rest. This raised hopes in Havana that the Soviet leader would cancel Cuba's debt during his 1989 visit. In a joint news conference, Castro said: "We are in favor of abolishing the debt we owe the USSR. We have been waiting to abolish it for thirty years."[55] But the debt has not been canceled; in fact, Ryzhkov's report showed that the USSR had written off only part of Vietnam's debt, which accounted for 0.5 percent of the total debt owed by all nations to the USSR.

According to a former Cuban trade officer, in April 1990 Leonid I. Abalkin told the Cubans that the debt would be payable in dollars beginning in 1995 at an exchange rate to be determined by both sides in 1990 or 1991; this point was ratified by Minister Katushev during his visit to Havana in June.[56] A spokesman for the Soviet embassy in Havana said in October 1991 that "the question of the debt must be settled" to continue future trade, a position also maintained by some East European countries. The head of the Cuban Department of the Russian Chancery stated publicly in 1992 that payment of the debt (which rose to 17 billion rubles at the end of 1991) is a major obstacle in relations with Cuba; another problem is how to distribute that debt among CIS republics.[57]

Cuban economist José Luis Rodríguez argues that 62 percent of Cuba's debt is owing to trade deficits resulting in part from deterioration in the terms of trade with the USSR in the 1980s. But he denies that Cuba asked the Soviets to cancel the debt and believes an agreement will be reached eventually.[58] However, a top Cuban leader told me candidly (but off the record) in mid-1990, "I don't know if the Soviets will cancel the debt or not, but we are not going to pay it." Despite this bravado, the Cubans are in a vulnerable position, as they need to salvage as much as possible of their economic relationship with the former USSR.

Dissolution of the CMEA

The Council for Mutual Economic Assistance (CMEA), based on barter trade under Soviet hegemony, isolated Eastern Europe and Cuba from the discipline of international competition. Exchanged goods were priced in "transferable rubles" that could be spent only within the community. East European countries paid for Soviet oil with manufactured products difficult to sell on the world market, while Cuba paid basically with sugar. Until the energy crisis of 1973–79, the system probably helped the USSR, but since then booming world oil prices and Soviet-subsidized prices turned the tables to favor other CMEA members.

To cut losses, the USSR gradually closed the price gap. Ryzhkov said that the transferable ruble became an accounting unit "unrelated either to the national currencies of the CMEA members or to freely convertible currency, and therefore could not serve as a fully valid means of payment." In the forty-fifth meeting of CMEA held in Sofia in January 1990, Ryzhkov proposed that at the start of 1991 multilateral and bilateral trade be conducted in freely convertible currency and world-market prices. The need to integrate into the world economy—he said—forced the shift.[59]

The proposal favored the USSR, as it would be able to sell oil at market prices in hard currency while the other members would find it difficult to sell their low-quality manufactured goods in the world market. The countries most seriously harmed would be those dependent on Soviet energy and developing members enjoying Soviet price subsidies for their exports: Cuba fell into both categories. Although practically all East European countries accepted the Soviet proposal, several of them (as well as Cuba) tried to delay its implementation: while the USSR wanted a quick transition, other members asked for a five-year grace period in which the trade deficit would be written off as Soviet aid. Several CMEA members began discussion of a market-oriented group of the most developed countries, excluding the least developed ones such as Cuba. A commission was appointed to study these issues.[60]

The Soviet proposals were criticized in Havana and attempts were made to circumvent them. Because 84 percent of Cuban exports went to CMEA, less than 9 percent of its trade was in convertible currency (part of Cuban trade with market economies was in barter), and the island extracted in 1986–90 a $10 billion net gain from the USSR, mainly subsidies for sugar exports. Vice President Rodríguez declared that restructuring the CMEA should not mean renouncing basic socialist principles and should not harm developing members: "We have been unable to come up with adequate prices for a socialist [economy], but let's not idealize the prices on the world capitalist market that we may be obliged to use."

Rodríguez then reasserted that eliminating unequal terms of trade was a key principle of the CMEA, including fixing prices of raw materials (such as sugar) much higher than world market prices:

> All solutions of the issue of CMEA prices must uphold the principle of the grad-
> ual equality of levels between Cuba, Mongolia, and Vietnam and the most de-
> veloped European countries. . . . [Because] ours is still an economy in which
> central planning plays a key role, pacts with other countries must include guar-
> antees for our imports which in most cases cannot depend on [direct] relations
> between enterprises.

Finally, he argued that according to a paragraph in the CMEA protocol
signed in Sofia, the shift should be done in stages and payments in convertible currency be governed by bilateral agreements, taking the special
conditions of developing members into account.[61]

President Castro was more blunt in his criticism:

> The CMEA still exists formally [but is significantly changed]. . . . We are
> struggling to keep [it] alive [but] it will be a mixed association [instead of] a
> union of socialist countries with socialist goals. . . . Will they try to buy our
> sugar at the price prevailing in the world garbage heap, the so-called world mar-
> ket price? . . . Are we going to sell our sugar at [that] price? . . . We are not a
> country of beggars . . . our sugar has commanded a [Soviet] price higher than
> the world price, it has been a just price because it put an end to . . . unequal
> terms of trade [tantamount to "robbery, plundering"].[62]

At the beginning of 1991, the commission studying reform of the
CMEA announced its dissolution (because it could not operate under current conditions) and the intention to create a new Organization for International Economic Cooperation, a market-oriented group whose
members would be free to trade with any nation.[63] But such an organization failed to materialize.

Concerning special treatment for the developing members during the
transition, Ryzhkov said, "[It] will be particularly difficult for Cuba,
Vietnam, and Mongolia; [to mitigate the damage] the humane principle
of helping weaker partners will remain in force. But [any] proposal to
continue to pay for Soviet petroleum in nonconvertible currency can
hardly be expected to be met with understanding." On the issue of a state
guarantee for Soviet imports, Abalkin commented: "Our partners over-
seas must know [that] no one is going to be bound to supply them with
a given product."[64] Cuban negotiators struggled to get a grace period,
while the Soviets opposed it; they insisted that prices of commodities
should be based on world market prices, while Cubans argued that in the
case of sugar the world price did not take into account the large percentage of sugar sales that took place under bilateral agreements at prefer
ential prices.[65]

The trade pact of 1991 included "transitional protocols" for the new forms of payment that, although maintaining the new principles, introduced several exceptions on behalf of Cuba. (1) During a grace period of three months (which ended March 31), traditional practices would continue, such as calculations in rubles and arbitrarily set prices. (2) Payments in hard currency (U.S. dollars) began on April 1, but so that each trade operation would not require a direct exchange payment, a mechanism was set up to settle accounts (over an unspecified period) without necessarily involving cash transfers. (3) All traded commodities were fixed at world prices beginning in April, except for sugar, which retained a preferential price for 1991 only. (4) The world price was not fixed at the beginning of the year, but fluctuations were accounted for and there was an adjustment or balance at the end of the year. (5) The Soviet state guaranteed a central supply of certain commodities, while directly contracting with decentralized enterprises for others (see next section).[66] These special concessions ceased in 1992, and trade is (in principle) now conducted in hard currency at world market prices, although some exchange is in barter.

Problems with Contracting and Shipping

Soviet enterprises are expected to be increasingly decentralized, autonomous, and competitive, as well as to fix prices closer to real costs and to maximize profits, which means cutting price subsidies. In contrast, Cuban enterprises are still highly centralized, there is no competition among them (except perhaps in tourism), they are heavily subsidized, and although there is an attempt to cut costs, profit is not a major indicator of performance. These differences have created serious problems in relations between Soviet and Cuban enterprises. Whereas Cuban trade was once carried out with only sixty-two Soviet centralized institutions, at the beginning of 1991 there were 25,000 entities to deal with.[67]

In mid-1989 Vice Chairman Abalkin said, "Foreign economic links will not be intergovernmental agreements in which the volumes of deliveries for [oil] . . . or other goods are determined in advance for five years to come but, to an increasing extent, direct links between enterprises and firms based upon business cooperation . . . and the strictest responsibility on each side. There will be no guarantee that we will conclude these contracts no matter what [the other side does] and deliver products if our conditions are not met."[68]

Almost at the same time, the Soviet trade representative in Cuba, P. I. Kormilitsin, reported serious difficulties in establishing direct linkages. For instance, Cuba's major export (sugar) was needed by the USSR as a whole, instead of by individual enterprises; sugar was bought and sold in the USSR through a centralized trade network. Soviet supply enterprises received transferable rubles for their deliveries to Cuba, but they could buy little with that special currency.[69] Soviet trade organizations insisted on compliance with the provision of contracts: "If a barter transaction called for delivering Soviet onions in exchange for Cuban potatoes and the latter were unsuitable for table use due to nitrates, the onions would not be delivered."[70]

According to an advisor to Cuba's State Committee on Economic Collaboration (SCEC), three types of Cuban enterprises have been licensed to export and/or import and can directly negotiate with Soviet enterprises: (1) Ministry of Foreign Trade enterprises that export sugar, nickel, citrus, and tobacco; (2) SCEC enterprises licensed to export and import goods related to development projects, hiring of technicians, and contracting services for foreigners; and (3) independent enterprises that export fish, pharmaceuticals, and medical products.[71] Another Cuban economist reported that seventeen direct links had been established by mid-1990 between Soviet and Cuban enterprises and that there were, in addition, four joint enterprises and thirty seven agreements on cooperative production. These are minuscule figures compared with the above-cited 25,000 Soviet institutions involved in foreign trade; by mid-1990 the Cubans were working on 173 linkages but only one-third had materialized in agreements.[72]

The 1991 trade pact unveiled the complexity of the tasks Cuba faces. In that year the Soviet government retained control of certain products for foreign trade, but most were handled by decentralized enterprises. The most important Cuban export, sugar, continued to be bought (in 1991) by one Soviet central institution which, in turn, had to contract with numerous Soviet enterprises for key supplies to be sent in exchange to Cuba. It appears that nickel and other Cuban exports as well as medical services had to be contracted with individual enterprises. In addition, Cuba dealt separately with republics interested in buying Cuban products. The Soviet state was expected to secure most essential supplies (through the internal contracting process), such as fuels, some foodstuffs, equipment for top priority projects, fertilizers, and industrial chemicals.

For other imports, Cuba had to deal directly with suppliers and producers; in some cases contracts had to be signed with several Soviet enterprises for a single product. Even for "guaranteed" imports, there was no assurance that they would be delivered (or delivered on time) for three reasons: domestic economic problems in the USSR, the complexity of Soviet internal contracting for Cuban supplies in competition with other demands, and the fact that centralized contracts for vital products such as sugar and oil were not signed in December 1990 but were discussed later in 1991. (As the next section shows, most products were not delivered.)

The timing and complexity of the contracting process also affected trade: in previous years, when the annual trade pact was signed, about 80 percent of the contracts were ready, while under the new system all the contracting processes (both with central institutions and decentralized enterprises) began after the pact was signed. New contracts were more complex and took more time than old ones because prices must be set at world prices in hard currency, and for many Soviet commodities such evaluation was very difficult (in comparative technological level). A frustrated Castro complained: "We have to run all over the USSR talking to who knows how many firms to buy a spare part."[73]

After the dissolution of the USSR, things became worse: in 1992 exchanges among republics through GOSNAB (the central ministry) were terminated, and all trade agreements now have to be negotiated with each republic separately and with many independent enterprises within each. New problems arose. As already noted, early in 1992 Cuba had signed trade pacts with eight of fifteen CIS republics, but the agreement with Russia (the most important republic in size and population as well as in oil exports) was confined to the first quarter of that year, with the option for renewal for the remainder. In mid-1992, the Russians said that such agreement would not be renewed for the second half of the year, and conversations for future exchanges had been canceled.[74]

Cuban-Soviet trade is also limited by the inadequacy of Cuban docks and reduced Soviet shipping capacity. Until 1990 some 300 Soviet ships annually carried 24 million tons of cargo (almost one a day) in bilateral trade with Cuba. There was abundant evidence of the inefficient loading and unloading process in Cuban ports: ships stayed unnecessarily long, stevedores did not work at night or on weekends, hauling equipment frequently broke down (only 54 percent were operative in 1989), and labor effort was low.

In 1989 these problems cost almost 1 million pesos at the Havana docks alone. Soviet pressure produced some improvement: Minister Katushev reported that, in the first half of 1990, the stay of Soviet ships in Havana's ports had been reduced by 20 percent, the tonnage handled daily increased by 28 percent, and a surplus of half a million pesos was achieved. Reasons for these changes were: adding a night shift that handled 10 percent of the total operation (it should be 33 percent) and weekend working hours; payment by task (loading and unloading) rather than by the hour; and more rigorous inspection and repair of the equipment (even though only 45 percent of it was operative).[75] On the other hand, fewer Soviet merchant ships were available to handle Cuban trade because many were decrepit and had been written off. This forced the hiring of foreign vessels to deliver cargo (usually paid in hard currency); in 1989, 30 percent of total trade volume was carried by hired ships, with substantial losses to the USSR.[76]

In the 1991 pact, Cuba agreed to transport a significant part of the tonnage: half of the fertilizers brought from the USSR were to be carried on Cuban ships, which were washed and reloaded with sugar; Cuban vessels were expected to handle dry cargo of cereals. In addition, the reduction of certain Soviet imports (machinery, manufactured goods) reduced trade cargo. Still, a mechanism had to be set up in the USSR regarding charter payments.[77] Castro acknowledged that despite the growth of Cuba's merchant fleet, "it does not have sufficient capacity to take care . . . of even a significant part of [Soviet] imports."[78] In 1992 CIS vessels stopped carrying Cuban freight unless paid in hard currency. (Freight costs were $150 million in 1991 and expected to be higher in 1992.) Furthermore, Cuba now has to negotiate transport with each independent republic and their autonomous enterprises.[79]

Delays and Cuts in Soviet Deliveries and Purchase of Cuban Products

From the end of 1989 through 1990, President Castro and the Cuban press reported cuts and delays in Soviet supplies of the following products: foodstuffs (wheat, grains, fodder); crude oil and oil products; items essential to agriculture and industry (some cut by 50 percent) such as fertilizers, lumber, metals, and tires; manufactured goods (TV sets); and spare parts. No problems were reported with imports of machinery, but it was noted that they might not be needed due to the lack of fuel.[80]

In 1988, all of Cuba's flour imports came from the USSR, as well as 89 percent of wheat and 50 percent of corn.[81] Imported fodder was essential to the production of eggs and poultry meat.[82] In December 1989 and January 1990, scheduled deliveries of flour, grain, and poultry fodder did not arrive, forcing Cuba to cut by 20 percent the bread ration in Havana (to 3 ounces daily) and to raise by 30 percent the price of bread outside the capital, where it was not rationed. The price of eggs also was increased nationally. According to Western sources, Cuba used desperately needed foreign reserves to buy some grain and flour on the world market.

Pravda attributed the delays to lack of ships and administrative errors, while foreign observers blamed domestic shortages in the USSR.[83] A Soviet embassy official indirectly blamed the Cubans' lack of foresight for the shortage; wheat had routinely been delivered one month or more before its due date, and the Cubans had been repeatedly advised to stockpile that month's supply to cover any possible contingency. Furthermore, the Soviet news media argued, the shortage was greatly exaggerated because the Soviet grain arrived in Havana only a few days after rationing was intensified, but the new measures were not lifted.[84] The chief of Cuba's Institute for Domestic Demand acknowledged Cuba's error and said that the restriction in consumption was meant to develop the needed stockpile.

In September 1990 *Granma,* the principal Cuban newspaper, reported that the USSR was up-to-date on grain deliveries, but complained that no agreement had been reached for such deliveries in the last trimester of the year (an indication that the 1990 trade pact did not set the amount of certain imports for the entire year).[85] In fact, a new postponement occurred, this one due—according to Cuban sources—to problems faced by the USSR in negotiating with countries that actually supplied the grains (Argentina, Canada).[86]

Coinciding with the first "cereal confrontation," in December 1989–January 1990, Cuba failed to deliver to the USSR 36 percent of planned exports of citrus fruits. Because Cuba has very few refrigerated ships, the USSR used to provide the necessary 180 vessels at the peak of the citrus harvest. But Poland and the GDR were requesting hard-currency payment for rental of their vessels. A surplus of nonexported citrus had to be rapidly distributed for domestic consumption.[87] Soviet sources also reported that in the first half of 1990 Cuban exports of sugar and nickel were 332,000 and 1,500 tons short, respectively. The Cubans acknowledged the latter, but argued that it was due to problems in the Soviet-built Che Guevara nickel plant. In early 1991 there were delays in exports of sugar due to a lack of Soviet ships.[88]

In 1984–88 Cuba imported 99 percent of all its crude oil from the USSR (including reexports), which accounted for about 7 percent of total Soviet fuel exports. According to Cuban statistics, Soviet deliveries of oil and oil products declined 3.6 percent in 1987–89, from 13.5 to 13 million tons; the later was still more than enough to meet Cuba's domestic needs, but Cuba lost almost 500,000 tons that it used to "reexport." This problem was compounded by a 28 percent decline in domestic crude oil production in 1986–90 (a loss of 267,000 tons) due to technical problems.[89] (See chapter 6.)

In 1989, the USSR reduced by 7 million tons its crude oil exports to the world (including socialist countries), alleging domestic disruptions in production and priority needs. In June 1990, Castro said that the USSR was delivering less oil, putting the sugar harvest in jeopardy and halting other economic activities.[90] In August *Granma* announced that until the end of that month there was a shortfall in Soviet deliveries of "2 million tons of oil and oil products" which made it necessary to cut fuel consumption. (However, Castro later confused the issue by referring to a shortage of 1.7 million tons of crude oil alone.)[91]

Articles in the two major Soviet newspapers denied Castro's charge of a 1.7 million ton shortfall of crude oil in 1990 and claimed that the overall shortfall of oil *and oil products* was not 2 million tons but 580,000 tons. The Soviet publications offered two reasons for Cuba's attitude: due to the Soviet termination, in 1990, of "reexports" of oil, Cuba's reduction in oil consumption was to enable it to export the oil saved and thus obtain desperately needed hard currency; and the cut in consumption was to create stockpiles or to prepare the population for worse shortages in the future, or both. The Soviet figures, in turn, were refuted by the Cuban press.[92]

The Soviet ambassador in Havana diplomatically acknowledged the 1990 shortfall in supplies (refusing to give figures), but justified it by saying that the USSR had reduced oil exports (39 million tons in 1988–90) not only to Cuba but to all East European partners because a sharp drop in Soviet oil output (down by 23 percent in 1989–91) had created severe shortages that had harmed agricultural production and cut consumption.[93]

At the end of 1990, Castro claimed a shortfall in oil and oil products of 3 million tons (from 13 million in 1989 to 10 million in 1990). The supply of Soviet oil and oil products declined to 8.6 million tons in 1991 and was expected to be cut further to 4–6 million tons in 1992, for a decline of 55–70 percent over the 1987–92 period.[94]

At the Fourth Party Congress, Castro reported that by the end of September 1991, the nonfulfillment in total Soviet deliveries averaged 42 percent, but was higher for many key products: 100 percent in rice, cotton, detergents, pulpwood, and chemicals (sulfur, caustic soda, sodium carbonate); and 43–75 percent in cooking oil, condensed and powdered milk, canned meat, fertilizers, paper, steel, soap, tires, and spare parts (the 66 percent shortfall in the last was especially serious—affecting the maintenance of Cuba's physical plants and equipment imported from the USSR). Nondelivery was about 30 percent in grains, wheat, and butter.[95]

What are the possibilities for Cuba to continue to sell its products (particularly sugar) to CIS countries? On the positive side, Cuba should continue to enjoy a comparative advantage with former USSR states, whose domestic sugar consumption is 12 to 13 million tons; since the CIS only produces about 8 to 9 million tons, there should be a need for Cuba's 4 million tons, which once accounted for 30 percent of the USSR's domestic needs. According to a Western expert, sugar yields per hectare are about twice as high in Cuba as in the former USSR and Cuba has 50 percent more daily processing capacity, giving it a significant comparative advantage. (But Cuban yields are lower than those of other leading exporters.)[96]

To expand domestic sugar production in some republics (particularly Ukraine, which exports 3.8 million tons of refined sugar), the CIS would have to start production on new, less fertile land or shift crops. However, that is problematic; other crops (such as wheat) are more needed and more profitable than sugar. CIS republics could buy sugar in the world market, but would be paying the same price and in hard currency, while transactions with Cuba could be barter, with accounts settled at the end of the year. Finally, some refineries in the former USSR republics had been adapted to process raw sugar from Cuba and hence have surplus capacity.[97]

In spite of the potential advantages just noted, for the first quarter of 1992 Cuba was committed to sell only 700,000 tons of sugar to CIS republics: 500,000 to Russia (with an option to buy an additional 500,000 quarterly) and 200,000 to Kazakhstan (with a similar option). Of the other republics that have signed trade pacts with Cuba, Ukraine is a major sugar exporter (Kyrgystan and Lithuania are minor exporters), while Byelarus, Tajikistan, and Estonia are minor sugar importers. A Russian scholar argues that sugar consumption in Russia has declined sharply because of price increases. Cuban and Western experts estimate that total sugar sold to CIS nations by Cuba in 1992 might reach 2 million tons, or half what Cuba exported in 1990.

The Russian republic is the major oil exporter within CIS, while Kazakhstan exports a relatively small amount. (Uzbekistan exports gas but not oil, and Azerbaijan is an oil producer but not an exporter.) Under the quarterly trade pact, Russia seemed committed in the first quarter of 1992 to export 900,000 tons of oil in exchange for 500,000 tons of sugar (at a beneficial ratio for Cuba of 1.8:1); that exchange could be renewed in the remaining three quarters, for a total of 3.6 million tons of oil (but the exchange was not renewed in the second half of the year). We lack information on Kazakhstan's committed oil exports, but they could possibly be 400,000–500,000 tons. Therefore, maximum total exports of oil and oil products to Cuba from the CIS would be about 4 million tons.[98]

Cuba used to supply 20 percent of the Soviet need for nickel and, without it, steel mills in the Urals would not be able to function. However, the shutdown of the Che Guevara nickel plant must have reduced Cuban export of that mineral since mid-1990. No data are available on actual exports in 1991 and potential commitments for 1992. The USSR meets 40–50 percent of its needs with Cuban citrus, even though of less than standard quality, because they would have to pay hard currency for a better product.[99] However, due to the severe food scarcities in CIS, citrus probably will not be a high priority there.

Finally, in 1990, Cuba exported 550 million rubles (610 million pesos) of biotechnical and medical products to the USSR, and 800 million rubles (880 million pesos) were scheduled for 1991; no data are available for 1992.[100] Impressive as these amounts are, these exports (if they indeed materialize) represent one-fourth of the value of Cuban exports in 1989 and would not compensate for the huge losses in sugar and nickel, and possibly citrus.

Cuba's Adjustment Policies

In May 1990 the Cubans launched a modest conservation program in forty-five major industrial plants to save 150,000 tons of crude oil through more efficient use of equipment. Workers at one of the largest steel mills burned wood for fuel. But the easiest conservation measures had been taken in previous years and Cuba lacked sufficient foreign exchange to buy oil in the world market.[101] The first round of tough policies to cut oil consumption were taken at the end of August 1990, immediately following the news of the Soviet shortfall in oil delivery.

Euphemistically labeled a "Special Period in Time of Peace," the plan included (1) shutting down the Che Guevara nickel plant, two-thirds of whose output went to the USSR in payment of its Soviet investment (perhaps a message that to get a return on investment, the Soviets must keep up oil supplies); (2) delaying the opening of the oil refinery in Cienfuegos, also built with Soviet aid; (3) cuts in gasoline and fuel deliveries of 50 percent to the state and 30 percent to the private sector; (4) cutting electricity consumption by 10 percent in industries, farms, and homes; (5) exhorting farmers to use draft animals (bulls, oxen, mules) instead of fuel-operated machinery for plowing and transportation.[102]

The crisis had serious repercussions. As a result of the first two measures, 400 Soviet technicians returned home. Electricity conservation is enforced by threats of power shutoffs at peak hours one day a week and for thirty days for families who do not cooperate; further drastic cuts were implemented in October 1990. Shortage of airplane fuel at Havana's international airport led to such long flight delays that Aeroflot moved its headquarters for Central and South America to the Miami airport. More than 200 cars, sometimes waiting for days, lined up at gas stations.[103]

A second round of stringent measures was introduced in September 1990. These included: (1) shutdown of a bus factory and attempts to turn it into a bicycle factory; (2) reducing textile production to a minimum; (3) cuts in cement and construction materials production by two-thirds— from 4 to 1.5 million tons (but Castro later said that the Mariel cement factory was being expanded to produce 400,000 more tons and a new cement factory was under construction); (4) canceling social programs "for a number of years," including new schools, day-care centers, hospitals, and urban housing (priority is given to agriculture, key industries, and

housing for rural labor camps); (5) reducing the number of buses in circulation (urban bus trips were first cut by 25 percent and then by another
50 percent); (6) reducing the work week from five and one-half to five
days (if necessary it will be cut to four) with no loss in pay; (7) a 50
percent cut in the Communist party bureaucracy and reassigning government administrative workers to "productive" tasks in agriculture and industry; (8) reduced publication of books, newspapers, and magazines
(*Juventud Rebelde* and *Trabajadores* went from daily to weekly issues
and in October many newspapers and magazines were shut down); (9)
rationing liquid gas for cooking; and (10) rationing once again 28 food
products and 180 consumer goods (such as clothing, footwear, household
appliances). In October, 321 factories of the Ministry of Light Industry
cut operations to twenty-four hours per week, and twenty-six factories
were shut down.[104]

A third round of measures came in late 1991 and early 1992, after the
announcement of the shortfall in Soviet deliveries, notably of fuel, and
the gloomy prospects for 1992. Because electricity consumption (both
state and private sectors) reportedly takes 3 million tons of fuel (50–75
percent of the expected 1992 supply), most measures have focused on
conserving electricity: (1) state-sector consumption was cut by 19 percent in 1990–91, with provinces exceeding a day's quota asked to stop or
reduce service on following day; (2) private consumption was reduced by
less than 4 percent in 1990–91 (instead of the decreed 10 percent), therefore the 40 percent of consumers who did not reduce consumption according to the plan had their service cut for three days and backsliders for
ten days; (3) air conditioners are to be shut down, carnivals canceled,
television transmissions further reduced (from 129 to 81 to 48 hours
weekly), some theaters and restaurants closed, sports activities scheduled for daylight hours, street lighting reduced, and newspapers shut
down or their pages further decreased (the army newspaper was suspended as well as many provincial newspapers). The Committees for the
Defense of the Revolution have been instructed to check the implementation of these measures block by block. A top official reported in early
1992 that there will be more factory shutdowns.

Another adjustment target has been to limit gasoline for transportation: (1) daily bus trips in Havana have been cut further (trips in mid-
1991 were only 25 percent of those made in 1990), and at the beginning
of 1991, there were only 80 buses operating, while 900 were paralyzed

due to lack of tires and spare parts, motor damage, or the gasoline short-age; (2) there have been further cuts of 30 percent in gasoline for state vehicles, state taxis are restricted to the most essential services (emergencies, funerals), and gasoline for private taxis has been eliminated (half of the *total* number of taxis are paralyzed); and (3) gas for cars belonging to professionals (such as physicians) has been cut by 70 percent, and a further decrease of 30 percent for private cars.[105]

Because the above measures mean reduced employment needs, the government is reducing personnel, particularly in the central administration. Unneeded workers (*sobrantes*) have two options: retraining or transfer (temporary or permanent) to other "useful" jobs, particularly in agriculture. Retrained workers receive 70 percent of the corresponding salary with a minimum of 100 pesos monthly. Workers that cannot be transferred to another job receive 100 percent of their salary in the first month and 60 percent in subsequent months until a job is found. (Payments are stopped if a worker refuses a legitimate job offer.)

The government is also encouraging job swaps to get workers jobs closer to home, thereby reducing transportation costs and time wasted in commuting. Young graduates who cannot find jobs are placed in a "skilled labor reserve": middle-level technicians are paid 75 pesos monthly and take retraining courses; university graduates can either continue their studies or be retrained and be paid 130 pesos monthly, or wait for a job offer and be paid 100 pesos monthly.[106]

Finally, "social consumption of food" (in state enterprises, agencies, schools) is to be reduced and rationing made tougher. In addition, prices of agricultural products were increased in February 1992 for the following official reasons: (1) such prices have been kept artificially low for many years in spite of rising costs of inputs and imports (fertilizers, seeds, pesticides, herbicides); (2) state subsidies to cover the price gap, although reduced in 1980–81, steadily increased thereafter—the subsidy for nonsugar agricultural products was 447 million pesos in 1991 excluding distribution costs, and according to a survey conducted by the Ministry of Agriculture, 84 percent of agricultural products are subsidized (for example, 10 million pesos for potatoes alone); and (3) some subsidized products are used to feed animals in the private sector. Prices will be raised gradually, the first round of increases embraced twenty-five products, including potatoes, yucca, plantains, bananas, green vegetables, tomatoes, carrots, and beets.[107]

A fourth round of adjustment measures was expected in 1992 if Soviet deliveries were lower than expected. Castro has warned: ''We
should be prepared for greater difficulties . . . even for the 'Zero Fuel
Option' in the most extreme case.'' In late 1991 and early 1992, he added
that Cuba had not entered ''the most critical phase of the Special Period . . . the worst is not here yet.''[108]

The Disappearance of Economic
Relations with Eastern Europe

Cuba's trade with Eastern Europe (excluding the USSR) averaged 12 percent in 1965–89. In the last year, the four largest partners were the GDR
(4.8 percent), Czechoslovakia (2.6 percent), Bulgaria (2.6 percent), and
Romania (2.1 percent); Poland and Hungary averaged about 1 percent
each (see table 5.1). Total turnover with all Eastern Europe increased
tenfold in the period; however, peaks were reached with Hungary and Poland in 1985 (with Bulgaria in 1983 and Romania in 1987), while trade
with the GDR and Czechoslovakia rose steadily. In 1985–88, 14.7 percent of Cuba's sugar exports went to Eastern Europe, nearly two-thirds
of it to Bulgaria and the GDR (Hungary and Poland are net exporters and
Czechoslovakia is self-sufficient)

Sugar prices paid by Eastern Europe in 1988 were 2.4 times higher
than the world market price but half the Soviet price; prices paid by Vietnam and China were one-fourth and one-third, respectively, those paid
by Eastern Europe. Cuba exported 24 percent of its nickel to Eastern Europe, mostly to Czechoslovakia and less to the GDR. Prices paid by these
countries in 1988 (for sinter and oxide) were about double the world market price; the USSR bought all of Cuba's nickel sulfide, so none went to
Eastern Europe. Finally, 48 percent of Cuba's exports of citrus were
bought by these countries, mostly by the GDR and Czechoslovakia. The
price of citrus paid by Eastern Europe was about the same as the Soviet
price and slightly higher than the world price (see table 5.6).

Cuba imported from Eastern Europe a wide variety of goods: foodstuffs, agricultural and irrigation equipment, fertilizers, and pesticides;
plants and equipment for sugar processing, for electricity, cement, fertilizer, pharmaceutical and metal-processing industries; construction
equipment (cranes, bulldozers, excavators); oil extraction and production

machinery; telecommunication and transportation equipment (buses, trucks); merchant and fishing vessels; engines, steel, computers, textiles, tires, medicines, and other manufactured goods; and spare parts.[109] The lack of detail and disaggregation of Cuban statistics on East European imports makes it impossible to construct a table similar to that for Cuban exports.

In the 1970s, Cuba's trade with Eastern Europe resulted in a deficit that rapidly increased, reaching almost half of Cuba's total deficit in 1983; thereafter the imbalance gradually declined to 8.4 percent of the total in 1989.[110] According to a Cuban economist, Cuba received 1.8 billion pesos in credits from Eastern Europe to cover the trade deficit alone. Table 5.5 presents several estimates of the Cuban debt with Eastern Europe: at the Soviet official exchange rate it was $2.5 billion in 1989–90 ($1.4 billion at the Soviet commercial rate in 1990). These estimates do not include loans granted by Poland and possibly Romania, as well as by the CMEA's International Collaboration Bank and International Investment Bank (17.4 million pesos from the latter in 1980).[111] In 1991 an official of the National Bank of Cuba declared to the press that East European countries were seeking to convert Cuba's debt to them from rubles to hard currency.[112]

The move toward market economies in Eastern Europe preceded the shift in the Soviet conception of the international division of labor: from two sectors—socialist and capitalist—to only one—the capitalist. Some of those countries wanted to strengthen their links with the world market to reduce their dependence on the USSR.[113] Hungary and Poland, the most advanced in that movement, were the first to reduce trade with Cuba in the mid-1980s. With the demise of socialism in Eastern Europe, that trend intensified and became more universal.

In 1988–89, Cuba exported about 1 million tons of sugar to four East European countries (either zero or very small amounts to Poland and Hungary), but sugar exports declined in 1990 to 50 percent and in 1991 to 5 percent (68,000 tons) (see table 5.6). Hence Cuba has to export about 1 million tons of sugar elsewhere. Furthermore, Cuba lost East European subsidies to sugar for as much as $300 million. When world sugar prices were high, it was advantageous for Eastern Europe to meet sugar needs as much as possible with Cuban imports in exchange for their products (which are not very competitive in the world market), but as the world price of sugar declined in 1991–92, such an advantage disappeared.

TABLE 5.6

Cuba's Foreign Trade and Exports, 1985–1992

	Sugar (1985–88)				Sugar (1989–92) Exports (1,000 tons)			
	Exports (1,000 tons)	% Distribution	Cuban Share in Total Imports	Cuban Centavos per pound (1985)	1989	1990	1991	1992[a]
CMEA	4,720	69.0	n.a.	n.a.	4,618	4,167	3,893	2,040
USSR/CIS	3,701	54.1	76	41.8	3,469	3,576	3,835	2,000
Bulgaria	323	4.7	71	19.8	309	146	43	40
Czechoslovakia	157	2.3	100	23.0	159	89	0	0
GDR	293	4.3	95	24.9	357	97	0	0
Hungary	22	0.3	—	29.8	0	0	0	0
Poland	73	1.1	72	n.a.	58	0	0	0
Romania	137	2.0	100	n.a.	266	260	15	0
Mongolia	2	—	—	n.a.	n.a.	n.a.	n.a.	n.a.
Vietnam	12	0.2	n.a.	6.0	n.a.	n.a.	n.a.	n.a.
Other socialist countries	803[d]	11.8[d]	n.a.	n.a.	988	955	831	960
Albania	25	0.4	n.a.	n.a.	24	24	10	10
China	746	10.9	32	7.66	889	892	796	900
North Korea	28	0.4	n.a.	n.a.	n.a.	n.a.	n.a.	n.a.
Yugoslavia	—	—	—	—	18	0	0	0
Market economies	1,314	19.2	n.a.	10.2	1,517	2,050	2,043	2,350
Total	6,837	100.0	n.a.	n.a.	7,123	7,172	6,767	5,350

| | Nickel[b] | Citrus[c] | Trade in 1989 (millions of dollars) | | | |
	% Distribution (1987)	% Distribution (1988)	Exports	Imports	Turnover	Balance
CMEA	76.3	n.a.	4,068	6,590	10,658	-2,522
USSR/CIS	52.6	41.9	3,231	5,522	8,753	-2,291
Bulgaria	—	n.a.	177	178	355	-1
Czechoslovakia	11.7	12.2	136	216	352	-80
GDR	5.5	24.9	286	359	645	-73
Hungary	2.2	3.3	55	80	135	-25
Poland	1.6	7.4	54	58	112	-4
Romania	2.7	n.a.	122	156	278	-34
Mongolia	0.0	n.a.	1	1	2	0
Vietnam	0.0	n.a.	6	20	26	-14
Other socialist countries	0.7	n.a.	236	342	578	-106
Albania	0.0	n.a.	3	3	6	0
China	0.0	n.a.	216	255	471	-39
North Korea	0.7	n.a.	13	20	33	-7
Yugoslavia	0.0	n.a.	4	64	68	-60
Market economies	23.0	n.a.	1,087	1,192	2,279	-105
Total	100.0	100.0	5,391	8,124	13,515	-2,733

Sources: AEC 1988, 1989; G. B. Hagelberg, "The Sugar Side of Perestroika," International Sugar and Sweetner Report 122, no. 6 (February 1990): 91–95; Jorge Pérez-López, "Sugar and the Sugar Economy: Implications After Thirty Years," Journal of International Food and Agrobusiness Marketing 3, no. 3 (1991): 36; ISO, Statistical Bulletin 50 (December 1991): 9–10; Peter Buzzanell, "Cuba's Sugar Industry Facing a New World Order," Sugar and Sweetner (March 1992): 24–41; Nicolás Rivero, "The Future for Cuban Sugar," International Sugar and Sweetner Report, 124, no. 10 (20 March 1992): 157–65.

a. Estimate. For the first quarter of 1992, agreed exports to CIS were only 500,000 tons; the figure of 2 million tons assumes that Russia will buy a similar amount of sugar in the remaining three quarters.
b. All nickel products; exports to "others" have been assigned to market economies; 1988–89 not available.
c. In addition to the countries listed, there was 10.3 percent exported to "others"; 1989 not available.
d. Includes a small sum of "others."

Since the end of 1989, East European exports to Cuba have also dwindled; there have been significant delays in deliveries, prices have sharply risen, and payments in hard currency were demanded.[114] In 1990, Castro bitterly complained: "We are slowly getting into a situation just like in the early years of the revolution when the United States imposed their blockade on us: there were not any spare parts for our machinery, for our equipment, for our factories, for anything. We confront the same situation now, except it is [with] the Eastern European countries that have joined the United States."[115]

German Democratic Republic

Cuban trade with the former GDR reached $645 million in 1989. Imports consisted of equipment for the sugar industry (two-thirds of all sugar mills have East German machinery) and for the nickel-processing, cement, textile, oil-refining, chemical, pharmaceutical, bakery, and fertilizer industries; computers (practically all those installed in banks, hospitals, and libraries), and military trucks and weapons. (Lack of spare parts from GDR may paralyze important Cuban industries and services.)

In January 1990, the East German authorities halted all military supplies and recalled advisors from Cuba; in July they requested payment in hard currency for all their exports to Cuba as well as for fuel and maintenance of Cuban airplanes landing in Berlin. The number of East German tourists in Cuba declined dramatically. Cuba's major export to GDR was sugar: compared with 357,000 tons in 1989, 290,000 tons were scheduled for 1990, but only 97,000 were delivered. After the German unification on July 1, 1990, and with the sugar surplus generated by the FRG, the incorporated East German population does not need Cuban sugar any more; in October they ceased buying it (see table 5.6). Exports of citrus (second only to those of the USSR) and nickel sinter either stopped or are insignificant.

Cuba owed $600 to $800 million to the GDR for twelve-year loans granted at 2 percent interest that was seldom paid. Castro did not criticize the GDR (as he had Czechoslovakia, Hungary, and Poland), hoping to get economic aid from a unified Germany. In July 1990, Vice President Rodríguez was hoping for an agreement to export 200,000 tons of sugar to Germany (half of the 1989 exports). However, in November 1990 German leaders declared that they were terminating all former GDR aid to Cuba but will continue projects in other developing countries (the Cuban debt to the GDR could be renegotiated and requested to be paid in Deutschmarks). The exclusion of Cuba was explained by the "notorious misguidance" of its economy and violation of human rights. As Cuba does not have any major export to sell to the FRG, trade has been drastically reduced to the most essential spare parts, to be paid in DM. Cuba might have lost $300 million for that reason. Furthermore, 9,000–10,000 Cuban workers who earned $3 million annually in the GDR returned home in 1991 (50,000–70,000 had previously returned), and some 300 students probably lost their fellowships (100,000 Cubans had received technical training in the GDR).[116]

Czechoslovakia

Cuba's trade turnover with Czechoslovakia was more than $400 million in 1988 and $352 million in 1989. Principal imports were machinery, equipment (one-third of Cuban sugar mills have Czech centrifuges), parts for thermoelectric plants, nickel processing, vehicles, tires, medicines, textiles, footwear, barley (for beer), and so on. The major Cuban export was sugar (although Czechoslovakia is self-sufficient and refines Cuban sugar for export). Other exports were nickel (important for the steel industry), citrus, and copper concentrate.

In 1989 Cuba exported 159,000 tons of sugar; at the end of 1990, due to deteriorating political relations between the two countries, Havana suspended sugar exports (only 89,000 of the 203,000 tons committed had been delivered) as well as nickel exports (see table 5.6). However, the Czechs kept exporting to Cuba in 1990 to complete the delivery of thermoelectric plants and other planned products they could not sell elsewhere. (But with fewer Cuban ships to transport this merchandise, it accumulated in Polish ports).

As Cuba exported little and Czech imports continued, the trade deficit expanded and so did the debt. Cuba's debt to Czechoslovakia was about 1 billion dollars in 1991 and was slowly being paid by Cuban exports. The Czechs want payment in convertible currency, but it is difficult because the two parties have to agree on an exchange rate; according to a top official of the Czech Ministry of Foreign Trade, resumption of trade must be linked to an agreement on debt payment. In a trade pact signed in June 1990, the two countries failed to agree either on debt repayment or prices (Czechoslovakia requested immediate payment in convertible currency and Cuba asked for a postponement until 1991; no agreement had been reached in the summer of that year).

In July 1991, a grave crisis occurred when several Cubans who took asylum in the Czech embassy in Havana (others took asylum in the embassies of Spain, Italy, Switzerland, and Belgium) were denied exit visas by the Cuban government; they eventually gave themselves up. As a result, thirty Czech diplomats left Cuba and trade relations were suspended. This action cost Cuba about $200 million in exports. By mid-1990, all Cuban students in Czechoslovakia had been called home and 5,300 Cuban workers were to be repatriated by the end of the year. In December, Czechoslovakia stopped being Cuba's representative and providing Cuba with facilities in the United States.[117]

Bulgaria

Turnover trade with Bulgaria was $355 million in 1989. Cuba's imports included foodstuffs (canned meat, dairy products, poultry, wheat, corn, lard), fertilizers, steel, textiles, forklifts, and agricultural equipment. Cuba's only major export was sugar (average of 300,000 tons in 1985–89). Cuba owes about $500 million to Bulgaria. A trade agreement was signed in mid-1990 for 1990–91, sugar exports declined to 146,000 tons in 1990 and 43,000 tons in 1991 (see table 5.6).

Reportedly, Cuba has a significant comparative advantage in sugar production over Bulgaria, whose sugar-beet production costs are the highest in Eastern Europe. Cubans hoped in 1990 that Bulgaria would pay $0.20 per pound of sugar (more than twice the world price) in exchange for Bulgarian foodstuffs. However, many Bulgarian exports to Cuba have been delayed or not delivered at all—such as 12,000 tons of chicken. In addition, Castro has criticized the quality of Bulgarian equipment: "Forklifts are worthless; . . . we are the only ones who buy them; . . . thousands stand idle in our warehouses [due to malfunction or lack of spare parts and batteries]."[118]

Romania

In 1989, Cuban trade with Romania was $278 million. Cuba's major export was sugar: about 260,000 tons in 1989–90, but only 15,000 in 1991 (see table 5.6). Major imports were oil-extraction equipment, cranes, excavators, ships, railway equipment, tractors, spare parts, and chemicals. Cuba completed a trade agreement with Romania in 1989, just before the downfall of Ceaucescu; in mid-1990 the new Romanian minister of foreign trade visited Cuba, but no trade agreement was signed; however, a pact to buy sugar was signed in 1991.[119]

Hungary

Trade with Hungary halved during the period 1985–88 and stood at $135 million in 1989, consisting mostly of imports of buses (about four-fifths of all buses were imported from Hungary in 1985–88), gasoline pumps, telecommunications, port modernization and thermoelectric equipment. In exchange, Cuba sent sugar (the smallest amount among Eastern Europe, which was reexported by Hungary since it is self-sufficient) and relatively small amounts of citrus and nickel. In 1989 all sugar exports stopped (see table 5.6).

Cuba owes about $300 million to Hungary. In the fall of 1989, Ikarus bus manufacturing increased by 20 percent the price of spare parts (40 percent over the average price in 1986–89) to be delivered in the first half of 1990, and another increase of 30 percent occurred in the second half of the year. Cuba accepted those terms, but complained that trade relations with Hungary were "a far cry from what we view as a fair practice among socialist countries." In 1990, Castro said that practically no spare parts would be coming for Ikarus buses, but that was not a great loss because such buses got only 6 kilometers to the gallon, used 30 percent more fuel than other buses (using more gas than the entire sugar harvest), and poisoned the people with exhaust fumes.

Conversely, Castro acknowledged that Hungarian thermoelectric plants were of good quality, but spare parts were not available. No trade agreements were signed with Hungary for 1990 or 1991, and commerce has practically stopped. All Cuban students in Hungary have been called home, and the Magyar embassy staff in Havana was cut from thirty to three by the end of 1990.[120]

Poland

In 1989 Cuba's trade turnover with Poland was the smallest among East European partners ($112 million). Cuba imported Polish equipment for shipyards, the sugar industry and paper production, spare parts for transportation, steel, jeeps, and light bulbs, in exchange for sugar (58,000 tons in 1989, the smallest amount after Hungary because Poland is also a net exporter), citrus, and nickel. In 1990 all sugar exports stopped. Cuba did not sign trade agreements with Poland in 1990–91, but there were negotiations on nickel exports.[121]

Effects on the Cuban Economy

Between 1986 and 1992 the Cuban economy deteriorated and entered the worst crisis under the revolution. There is no doubt that, since 1990, such deterioration has been principally the result of the collapse of socialism in USSR and Eastern Europe. However, the negative economic performance began in 1986 when the RP was launched—long before the collapse of socialism. The debate continues as to whether the economic deterioration in 1986–90 was caused by the RP or by external factors or a combination of both. Furthermore, the antimarket features of the RP have possibly played a negative role in the 1991–92 crisis.

Official Cuban publications and economists have blamed exogenous, conjectural variables as exclusive causes of the 1986–90 deterioration, such as adverse climate (drought), deteriorating world prices (sugar), and lack of fresh hard-currency credit, while arguing that the RP has had a positive, compensatory effect. Most U.S. scholars, including myself, without disregarding external variables, have noted serious inconsistencies in the official argument and have pinpointed the importance of negative effects of the RP, such as the decline in private output and services, the state's inability to substitute the eliminated market mechanisms, and lack of a coherent new model.

A few Cuban economists have acknowledged that the crisis cannot be explained by external factors alone; they admit that the state—overburdened with too many functions—has been unable to fill the vacuum left by quashing the free peasant markets and self-employment. On the other hand, Carlos Aldana, the third most powerful political figure until he was dismissed in the fall of 1992, declared in mid-1991 that the crisis (and particularly rationing) is "not a consequence of inefficiency or incompetence on our part but has been imposed on us by external factors beyond our control."[122] As it is impossible to separate the causes of the crisis, I will evaluate its socioeconomic effects.

Effects of the Crisis on the Economy

Table 5.7 summarizes the state of the Cuban economy in the year prior to the introduction of the RP and compares the booming performance of 1981–85 with the economic deterioration of 1986–90. (1) The Global Social Product (GSP: based on the Soviet Material Product System instead of the Western System of National Accounts) grew at 41.6 percent in 1981–85 but declined by 6.3 percent in 1986–90 (in per capita terms, there was an increase of 36 percent and a decline of 10 percent, respectively).[123] (2) Labor productivity grew at 41.4 percent in 1981–85 but declined 10.3 percent in 1986–89. (3) The average annual nominal wage in 1989 was at the same level as in 1985 (no data are available in constant prices). (4) There was a cumulative surplus of 287 million pesos in 1981–85 but a cumulative deficit of 5.5 billion pesos in 1986–90 (the deficit increased 645 percent in 1985–90). (5) Housing construction increased 17.8 percent in 1981–85 but declined 6 percent in 1985–87 (aggregate comparable data were not published after 1987). (6) Total merchandise trade increased 63 percent in 1981–85 and declined 6.6 percent in 1981–89. (7) The growth rate in the trade deficit slowed down significantly (from 209.5 percent in 1981–85 to 33.6 percent in 1986–89), but the deficit level remained above 2 billion pesos (data for 1990 are not available). (8) The trade deficit with the USSR increased from 44.2 percent in 1981–85 to 144.5 percent in 1986–89. (9) The trade deficit in hard currency worsened by 148 percent in 1981–85 but only by 18.3 percent in 1986–89; this was achieved not by increasing exports (which were stagnant) but by reducing hard-currency imports and shifting the trade deficit to the USSR. (10) International reserves declined 13.2 percent in 1981–85 but decreased by 74.8 percent in 1986–89. (11) The hard-currency debt increased 14 percent in 1981–85 but 101.6 percent in 1986–90.

Foreign trade figures for 1990 are rough estimates by a Cuban economist and have not been used in the comparison; these figures indicate a decline in the total trade turnover, but a reduction in the global deficit mostly due to a sharp decrease in imports; the turnover with the USSR increased, and the deficit was cut dramatically due to increased exports and reduced imports. None of the annual planning targets set in 1986–90 was met (on GSP growth, productivity, average wages, imports and exports, housing construction); real performance was half of the target.[124]

TABLE 5.7

Deterioration of the Cuban Economy, 1986–1990

(in millions of pesos)

Indicators	1980	1985	1986	1987	1988	1989	1990	% Comparison	
								1985/80	1989–90/85
GSP[a]	19,111	27,070	27,390	26,350	26,921	27,208	25,360[h]	41.6	–6.3
GSP per capita[ac]	1,971	2,681	2,685	2,558	2,585	2,586	2,406[h]	36.0	–10.2
Labor productivity[bd]	6,626	9,373	9,235	8,826	8,677	8,404	n.a.	41.4	–10.3
Average annual wage[bc]	1,774	2,252	2,255	2,208	2,242	2,260	n.a.	26.9	0.4
Budget balance[b]	n.a.	(253)	(188)	(609)	(1,146)	(1,624)	(1,985)	n.a.	684.6
Housing units[e]	60,576	71,367	70,914	67,099	n.a.	n.a.	n.a.	17.8	–6.0
Total merchandise trade[b]	8,594	14,027	12,894	13,013	13,098	13,516	13,000	63.2	–6.6
Exports	3,967	5,992	5,322	5,401	5,518	5,392	5,932	51.0	–7.9
Imports	4,627	8,035	7,596	7,612	7,579	8,124	7,068	73.6	–5.6
Balance	(660)	(2,044)	(2,274)	(2,211)	(2,061)	(2,732)	(2,015)	209.5	33.6
Trade with USSR[b]	5,158	9,901	9,248	9,363	9,047	8,753	8,978	92.0	–11.6
Exports	2,654	4,482	3,935	3,867	3,683	3,231	4,064	68.9	–27.9
Imports	2,904	5,419	5,337	5,496	5,364	5,522	4,914	86.6	1.9
Balance	(650)	(937)	(1,402)	(1,629)	(1,681)	(2,291)	(850)	44.2	144.5
Trade in convertible currency[b]	2,295	2,473	2,082	1,915	2,020	2,287	n.a.	7.8	–7.5
Exports	1,284	1,171	896	975	1,049	1,066	n.a.	–8.8	–8.9
Imports	1,011	1,302	1,186	940	971	1,221	n.a.	28.7	–6.2
Balance	273	(131)	(290)	35	78	(155)	n.a.	–148.0	18.3
International reserves[bf]	403[g]	350	242	196	234	88	i	–13.2	–74.8
Hard-currency debt[f]	3,170	3,621	4,985	6,094	6,450	6,165	7,300	14.2	101.6

Sources: CEE, *AEC 1987, 1988, 1989; BEC, 4,* 1987 and 1, 1988, *La economía Cubana en 1989,* March 1990; BNC, *Cuba Informe Económico Trimestral,* December 1982, 1987, 1988, *Informe Económico,* June 1989, *Selected Statistical Information of the Cuban Economy,* May 1990; *Gaceta Oficial,* December 30, 1987; *GWR,* January 24, 1988 and January 1, 1989; *Granma,* December 24 and 26, 1988; *Cuba Business,* April 1989; Reuters, Havana, May 3, 1991; José Luis Rodríguez, "Las relaciones económicas entre Cuba y los países socialistas: Situación actual y perspectivas," Conference on Cuba, Halifax, November 1989, pp. 32–33, and "La economía de Cuba ante la cambiante coyuntura internacional," *Boletín de Información sobre Economía Cubana* 1, no. 2 (February 1992): 9.

a. Constant 1981 prices.

b. Current prices.

c. Pesos.

d. Productive sphere only (exclude commerce).

e. Built by the state, coops, and population; 1981 instead of 1980 (no comparable data available).

f. December 31, except international reserves in June 1989 and debt in September 1990; reserves in 1981 instead of 1980 due to lack of data.

g. 1981.

h. Based on information provided by a Soviet scholar, Miami, November 1991.

i. Daniel Legra, an official of Cuba's National Bank, reported a decline vis-à-vis 1990.

CARMELO MESA-LAGO

TABLE 5.8
Losses to Cuba from Cuts in Soviet Aid and Impact on GSP, 1989–1992
(in millions of dollars)

	1989	1990	1991	1992
Price subsidy to sugar	2,178	2,200	1,100	0
Price subsidy to nickel	−45	37	0	0
Credits to cover trade deficit	2,291	850[b]	0	0
Development loans	680	680	0	0
Petroleum reexports[a]	162	0	0	0
Total Soviet aid	5,266	3,767	1,100	0
Loss in Soviet Aid		1,499	2,667	1,100
Loss in Eastern European aid		500	500	—
GSP (without Soviet aid)[c]	27,208	25,709	23,042	21,942
GSP (without all aid)[c]	27,208	24,209	22,042	20,942
GSP rate (Soviet loss only)[c]		−5.5	−10.4	−4.8
GSP rate (all losses)[c]		−7.3	−12.5	−5.0

Sources: Author's estimates based on CEE, *AEC 1989*; Fidel Castro, "Discurso en la inauguración del IV Congreso del Partido Comunista de Cuba," *Granma*, 14 October 1991, pp. 7–12; Santiago Pérez, "The USSR and Cuba: An Uncertain Future" (Havana: CEA, October 1991), p. 6; *Trabajadores*, 27 January 1992; G. Zuikov et al., "Informe sobre la Economía de Cuba," Miami 1992.

a. Soviet payments in hard currency for the value of committed exports of fuel not consumed by Cuba.

b. Based on rough estimates from table 5.7.

c. Estimate; excludes domestic impact.

Specific objectives of the RP such as reduction of the budget and trade deficits have not been realized, either.

Cuba has not released any data on macroeconomic indicators after 1989; hence it is impossible to estimate the impact of the collapse of socialism on the Cuban economy accurately. Table 5.8 attempts to roughly measure the impact on Cuba's GSP of lost Soviet and East European economic aid, but the table takes into account neither the reduction of Cuba's imports from and exports to those countries, nor their impact on domestic production. The table suggests that, combining all aid lost, GSP declined 23 percent in 1989–92; obviously, the decline would be greater if the other factors were taken into account.

Another estimate of GSP focuses on the decrease in total imports, estimated to be 60 percent in 1989–91 and another 50 percent in 1992. Based on the share of import/GSP (38 percent in 1989), the study calculates that GSP declined by 22 percent in 1989–91 and should fall in 1992 by more than 9 percent. These figures, like those in table 5.8, exclude the domestic repercussions of the decline in imports, the loss in export value, etcetera.[125]

A team of Soviet scholars has reproduced Cuban figures (not available elsewhere) on "mercantile production" in 1990; this magnitude is smaller than GSP, but gives a better picture of overall economic performance than the previous estimates. According to these data, the overall decline in 1990 was 6.9 percent, and other sectors had worse decreases: 26.2 percent in paper and cellulose, 23.9 percent in textiles, 21 percent in steel, 19.5 percent in petroleum, 18 percent in construction materials, 15 percent in fishing, 9 percent in chemicals, and 7.8 percent in food. A member of the team estimated the overall GSP decline in 1990 as 5 percent, with a further contraction of 20 percent in 1991.[126]

A sympathetic U.S. scholar has released the gloomiest estimates of economic decline (although giving no basis for them): 35–40 percent in Cuba's national income in 1989–91 and another 7–12 percent in 1992; he foresees a "slow turnabout after 1992."[127] Cuban scholars have not published any estimates on the GSP decline. Some argued first that the economy would bottom out in 1991 and then in 1992. In the latter year, J. L. Rodríguez referred to the crisis as a "depression" and said that the economy would bottom out in 1992 or 1993.[128]

Social Effects of the Crisis

According to table 5.9, in 1979, before the liberalization measures introduced in the early 1980s (for example, free peasant markets), certain goods were freely sold and others could be bought in the state parallel market at higher prices than the rationed price. By the end of 1991, not only were some 200 consumer goods added to the list of rationed items (hence none was freely sold in the market), but the rationed quotas of two-thirds of the goods had been cut (barely guaranteeing a subsistence level), and the parallel market had disappeared. Medicine is in very short supply, as well. The quality of goods also has deteriorated; for instance, coffee is mixed with green peas and beer is very inferior. Quotas are not guaranteed; hence long queues form in the early morning (reducing the population's leisure time), and many products disappear from the state shops for months.[129]

Few will contest that Cuba has one of the most egalitarian systems in the world, but the crisis is conspiring against it. Rationing has always

TABLE 5.9
Monthly Quotes of Selected Rationed Consumer Goods
in Havana, 1979–1991
(in pounds)

	1979[a]	1991[b]
Beef[c]	2.5	0.75
Fish	free[d]	0.67d
Rice	5	5
Beans	1.25	0.62[f]
Cooking oil and lard	1.5	1.5
Eggs (units)	free	20
Butter	free	[g]
Coffee	0.375	0.25
Milk (canned)[e]	3	3
Suger	4	4
Bread	free	5[h]
Cigarettes (package)	4	4
Gasoline (gallon)	10	7
Detergent (medium package)	0.5	0.3
Soap (cake)	1.5	1[i]
Toilet paper (roll)	1	1[j]
Toothpaste (small tube)	0.33	1[j]
Cigars (units)	4	4
Beer (bottle)	free	24[j]

Sources: Carmelo Mesa-Lago, *The Economy of Socialist Cuba* (Albuquerque: University of New Mexico Press, 1981), p. 158; interviews with Cuban visitors to Europe and Miami in mid-1991; Ana Santiago, "Libreta en Cuba abastece poco," *El Nuevo Herald,* 19 January 1992.

a. Also free in 1979 were macaroni, spaghetti, and yogurt; cakes and vegetables (according to season); and bread (after 4 p.m.).

b. October–December.

c. Chicken is alternated with beef, about 2 pounds per month.

d. Small fish. Seafood has not been available for more than two decades.

e. Children under seven had a daily ration of two-thirds of a liter of fresh milk and adults over sixty-five received six cans of condensed or evaporated milk monthly in 1979; in 1991 they received double rations of canned milk.

f. Black, red, and white beans; the first is seldom available; the quota was reduced to 0.125 in January 1992.

g. Not available in the market at all.

h. One small roll daily.

i. Bath soap; laundry soap had not been supplied for two months.

j. Per family; toothpaste for up to four people.

been justified as protection to low-income groups. But the severe scarcity of consumer goods has produced a phenomenal expansion of the black market with skyrocketing prices; for instance, the official price of a pound of chicken is 70 centavos, but a two-pound chicken is sold on the black market for 20–30 pesos.

Other goods, such as cigars and rum, are sold at 7–10 times the official price. The average monthly salary is 190 pesos (the minimum salary is 100 pesos), while the minimum pension is 90 pesos. Therefore, the lowest income groups cannot supplement their meager rations by buying on the black market. Furthermore, since February 1992 official food prices began to rise—150 percent for potatoes, 125 percent for tomatoes, 75 percent for plantains. Finally, the elite has always had access to goods and services not available to the masses such as special stores, separate hospitals, medicines, cars, gasoline, social clubs, recreational villas, and trips abroad. The gap between the elite and the masses is therefore expanding.[130]

Inflation in Cuba is probably the lowest in Latin America, but price increases in 1992 should generate some degree of inflation. There is a more perverse trend, however: as consumer goods become increasingly scarce, surplus money in circulation has grown, as there is nothing to buy with it outside the rationing system except black-market goods. In 1970 the monetary surplus per capita peaked at 388 pesos, declined to 216 pesos in 1980, and then began to climb again. In 1988 it reached 347 pesos and kept rising, thereafter probably surpassing the 1970 level.

The Fourth Party Congress declared that it was urgent to reduce the monetary surplus because of its negative effects on labor productivity and absenteeism, which in 1970 reached 20 percent of the labor force, and that situation may recur soon. Since it is not possible to expand the supply of consumer goods to reduce the monetary surplus, the government is trying desperately to encourage people to save by increasing interest rates from 2 percent to 4 percent and 5 percent, according to different plans. But this measure cannot make a dent in the surplus: in 1991 net savings totaled 600 million pesos, but that sum was probably no more than 15 percent of the monetary surplus. Hence the government is attempting to control labor discipline, wasted work hours, and labor absenteeism by treating violators more rigorously and stiffening penal sanctions. Even some of the celebrated labor contingents are now subject to criticism because of inefficiency and have been threatened with dissolution.[131]

Open unemployment in Cuba rose from 3.4 percent to 6 percent in 1981–88 and should be higher now due to the shutdown of enterprises and reductions in other activities. As discussed above, there is a comprehensive system of protection for the unemployed and the *sobrantes* consisting of compensation, retraining, and transfers (particularly to agriculture). However, as surplus labor expands, the burden on the economy both in subsidies and declining labor productivity will grow. Most young graduates entering the labor force are headed for the "reserve," and their frustration and disappointment rises as they are unable to get adequate jobs.

The claim that the RP would reduce crime and corruption has not materialized; the growing scarcity of consumer goods has become a fertile ground for robbery, black-marketing goods and foreign currency, and even prostitution. Despite harsher penal sanctions in 1988, there are many reports of food thefts from state farms and cooperatives, warehouses, and cafeterias, attacks on trucks, and even of a huge container stolen from the docks. Castro has denounced these crimes and requested the army, police, security forces, and groups of armed workers and peasants to protect the food. The Fourth Congress demanded a tougher policy to fight crime and, by the end of 1991, the National Assembly enacted new laws for integrating all "forces of order" into a United System of Vigilance and Protection, modifying criminal procedures to expedite trials, and selecting judges who will take a tougher stand with criminals.[132]

Conclusions

There has been a dramatic deterioration in Soviet-Cuban economic relations between 1986 and 1992, particularly in the last three years. No five-year trade agreement was signed for 1991–95 and Cuba confronts medium-term uncertainty in placing its exports, securing key imports, and determining prices of both. The trade pact of 1991, although making some concessions to Cuba, left for contract negotiation the determination of specific quantities and prices of most commodities, hence adding uncertainty as well.

The dissolution of the USSR has forced Cuba to negotiate individually with independent states; at the time this chapter was finished, trade agreements for 1992 had been signed with only half of them and the pact with Russia was for the first quarter of the year, and it was not renewed in the second half of the year.

After the CMEA was disbanded at the beginning of 1991, there was a radical shift from mutually agreed subsidized prices and payment in transferable rubles to world prices and hard-currency payments. As 84 percent of Cuban trade was with the CMEA and 92 percent in nonconvertible currency or barter, such a shift has had an enormous impact. The 1991 trade pact upheld preferential prices for sugar, but left all other commodities to be set at world prices and in hard currency (U.S. dollars) after April 1; beginning in 1992 sugar prices are set at world market levels. The trade turnover between the two countries declined by 11.5 percent in 1985–89; this was due to a 28 percent decrease in the value of Cuban exports while the value of Soviet imports was stagnant. But the value of the latter fell by 70 percent in 1989–91 and possibly by another 50 percent in 1992.

Cuba's trade deficit increased by 144 percent in 1985–89 (no data are available for 1990–92). The USSR ended two special concessions to Cuba in 1990: reexporting for hard currency crude oil supplies exceeding the island's needs, and guaranteeing Cuba's debt to a French firm that provided credit for buying sugar on the world market to meet export commitments. The terms of trade continued to deteriorate against Cuba in 1986–88, at least concerning three major trade products. Yet Cuba still enjoyed an estimated net gain of $10 billion in 1986–90, but that was 36 percent lower than in 1981–85. Although not enough data are available, the situation must have worsened in 1991–92, particularly because the Soviet price paid for sugar was cut to one-fifth of the 1990 level. (However, the ratio of the sugar-oil exchange with Russia for the first quarter of 1993 apparently was 1:1.8, still suggesting some preferential treatment for Cuba.)

Total Soviet aid granted to Cuba declined only slightly in 1986–90 (compared to the previous quinquennium), but its composition shifted from 29 percent in repayable loans and 71 percent in nonrepayable subsidies to 54 percent and 46 percent, respectively. All Soviet economic aid to Cuba ended in 1993. Cuba's debt with the USSR at the end of 1989 surpassed $24 billion at the official exchange rate and kept growing in 1990–91; the USSR apparently has requested repayment at a mutually agreed exchange rate or with exports. Cuba's enterprises must deal with increasingly decentralized, competitive, and profit-maximizing Soviet counterparts. Under the 1991 trade pact, Cuba's sugar exports were handled by a central Soviet institution that, in turn, contracted with numerous enterprises; the rest of foreign trade was conducted with thousands of decentralized enterprises. Under the old system, 80 percent of the contracts were ready when the annual trade pact was signed, but in 1991 all contracting started after signature. Since 1992 the central buying and selling mechanisms have virtually disappeared. Moreover, the complex new contracts (to be set at world prices and in hard currency) take much more time to negotiate and have been one cause of delayed Soviet deliveries.

Additional limitations to Cuba's trade with the USSR has been a dramatic decrease in the number of Soviet merchant ships (since 1992 virtually none) and the insufficient capacity of Cuban docks. In 1989–91 Cuba reported delays and cuts in numerous Soviet supplies; in the last year close to half of planned imports were not delivered. Most important were cuts in crude oil and oil products of 36 percent in 1987–91, with a projected further decline of 53–70 percent in 1992.

Fragmentary information shows that Cuba would export about 2 million tons of sugar to the CIS in 1992, half of what it used to export, and would import up to 4 million tons of oil and oil products. Cuba will probably sell less nickel and citrus than before, and the expansion of biotechnology products cannot compensate for the huge losses from other exports. Cuba's trade relationship with the CIS will continue, but at drastically reduced levels, without the previous advantages, and facing increasing difficulties and challenges.

Cuban trade with the former GDR and Czechoslovakia (the two major trade partners in Eastern Europe), as well as with Hungary and Poland, has either stopped or is reduced to a trickle. Trade with Bulgaria and Romania continues, but at a very low level. Estimates indicate that by 1992 Cuba might have lost $1.8 billion, or 95 percent of trade turnover with Eastern Europe. The latter include about $800 million in export value of sugar (a loss of exports of 1 million tons) at twice the world price. Loss of key East European imports has seriously disrupted the Cuban economy. Trade deficit financing with Eastern Europe has stopped altogether. Cuba owes at least $2.5 billion to Eastern Europe, and an agreement on repaying that debt is a precondition for resuming trade with some of these countries.

In 1986–89, before the collapse of socialism, economic deterioration was occurring in Cuba. The RP and some external factors were responsible: virtually all macroeconomic indicators showed a decline, compared with the previous quinquennium, including 10 percent in GSP per capita. The cut in economic aid and the elimination or reduction of trade with USSR and Eastern Europe created a crisis in 1990–92 that is the worst since the revolution. Three series of adjustment measures have drastically reduced consumption of fuel, electricity, foodstuffs, services, and entertainment; transportation facilities and mechanization in agriculture have been cut; many factories have been shut down and construction of new plants paralyzed; employment has shrunk and labor hours reduced.

The decline of GSP in 1990–92 has been grossly estimated as 23 percent based on the loss of more than $6 billion annually in economic aid, and 30 percent based on a 70 percent to 85 percent loss of imports alone; these calculations exclude the domestic repercussion of external factors. Even rougher estimates of the decline in GSP (as a whole) are 25 percent in 1990–91 and 40–47 percent in 1989–92. Rationing has been extended to virtually all consumer goods, and current quotas are the most stringent since the revolution, barely at a subsistence level. The poor suffer most because they cannot supplement the meager rations by buying goods at the high prices charged by the expanding black market; increasing official prices aggravates the situation.

The monetary surplus per capita has probably surpassed the 1970 record, harming labor productivity and stimulating absenteeism, despite tightened discipline. Unemployment has increased, but the government has provided a safety net; however, the welfare burden is becoming heavier as the labor surplus rapidly expands. Food scarcity has provoked an increase in crime, combated ineffectually with tougher penal sanctions and vigilance by unified "forces of order." The worst is still to come in 1992, a year of severe testing of the viability of the Cuban model of socialism.

NOTES

Abbreviations used in notes:

AEC: *Anuario Estadístico de Cuba*
BEC: *Boletín Estadístico de Cuba*
BNC: Banco Nacional de Cuba
CEE: Comité Estatal de Estadísticas
CeC: *Cuba en Cifras*
GWR: *Granma Weekly Review*

I greatly appreciate the bibliographical help provided by my research assistants, Ivan Brenes and Rafael Tamayo, the materials supplied by José Alonso, the typing by Mimi Ranallo, and the preliminary editing by Shirley Kregar. I am also grateful for the financial support of the Latin American Studies Association for a trip to Cuba in 1990 and of the Mellon Foundation for research in Western and Eastern Europe in 1990–91.

1. For divergent views on the RP, see C. Mesa-Lago, "Cuba's Economic Counter-Reform (*Rectificación*): Causes, Policies and Effects," *Journal of Communist Studies,* 5, no. 4 (December 1989): 98–139; "On Rectifying Errors of a Courteous Dissenter," *Cuban Studies* 20 (1990): 87–108 and "Rectification Round Two: An Answer to Eckstein's Rebuttal," *Cuban Studies* 21 (1991): 193–98; Carlos M. García Valdés, "El proceso de rectificación: Motivación y fuente para el desarrollo de la economía política del socialismo en Cuba," *Cuba Socialista* 38 (March–April 1989): 13–36; José Luis Rodríguez, "Aspectos económicos del proceso de rectificación," *Cuba Socialista* 44 (April–June 1990): 86–101; Susan Eckstein, "The Rectification of Errors or the Errors of the Rectification Process in Cuba," *Cuban Studies* 20 (1990): 67–85; "More on the Cuban Rectification Process: Whose Errors?" *Cuban Studies* 21 (1991): 187–92; and Jorge Pérez-López, "The Cuban Economy: Rectification in a Changing World," *Cambridge Journal of Economics* 16, no. 1 (March 1992): 113–26.

2. "Resolución sobre el desarrollo económico," *Granma,* October 23, 1991, p. 6. Subsequent references in the text to Fourth Congress resolutions are based on this source. José Luis Rodríguez disagrees that the RP lacks a comprehensive model and implies increased centralization ("Commentary," pp. 6–7).

3. For a detailed analysis of the RP economic features, see, in addition to the sources cited in note 1, Carmelo Mesa-Lago, "Cuba: An Unique Case of Anti-Market Reform," World Bank Conference on "Economic Reform: Recent Experiences in Market and Socialist Economies," Madrid, July 6–8, 1992. See also Comisión Nacional del SDE, *Normas sobre la unión y la empresa estatal* (Havana: April 1988), and *A problemas viejos soluciones nuevas: El perfeccionamiento de las empresas del MINFAR* (Havana: Editora Política, 1990).

4. "Resolución que faculta al Comité Central," *Granma,* October 23, 1991, p. 6.

5. Fidel Castro, "Discurso de Clausura del V Congreso del Sindicato de Trabajadores Agropecuarios," *Granma,* November 26, 1991, p. 5.

6. "P'atrás ni para coger impulso (Entrevista con Darío Machado)," *Areíto* 3, no. 9 (June 1991): 27–28.

7. Fidel Castro, "Intervención sobre el mercado libre campesino en el IV Congreso," *Granma,* October 29, 1991, pp. 3–6; and "Cuba: Congreso elige," *El Nuevo Herald,* October 15, 1991, p. 4A.

8. "Resolución sobre el desarrollo," p. 6; Gillian Gunn, paper presented at UCLA Seminar on Cuba, Los Angeles, February 28, 1992.

9. Fidel Castro, "Discurso en la Inauguración del IV Congreso del Partido Comunista de Cuba," *Granma,* October 14, 1991, pp. 7–12. He repeated these ideas in "Discurso de Clausura del V Congreso."

10. Interview with Tania García, head of international relations, National Bank of Cuba, Havana, July 12, 1990.

11. Carmelo Mesa-Lago, Fernando Gil, and Ivan Brenes, "Relaciones Económicas de Cuba con la URSS y el CAME: Pasado, Presente y Futuro," paper presented at the second meeting of the LASA Study Group on Cuba's International Economy, Havana, CIEM, July 9–10, 1990.

12. Ramón Martínez Carrera, "Cuba: Crecimiento económico e inestabilidad externa," *Economía y Desarrollo* 1 (January–February 1990): 18–57.

13. Author's estimates based on Comité Estatal de Estadísticas (CEE), *Anuario Estadístico de Cuba (AEC) 1988;* and CEE, *Cuba en Cifras (CeC 1989).*

14. *Granma Weekly Review (GWR)*, April 29, 1990, pp. 1, 3; "Cuba, Soviet Union Sign $14.7 Billion Trade Pact," *Wall Street Journal*, April 19, 1990, p. 10A; Leonid I. Abalkin, *Sovetskaya Rossiya*, May 5, 1990, p. 5; CEE, *AEC 1989.*

15. Castro, "Discurso en la Inauguración del IV Congreso." A higher figure for imports (5.8 billion pesos) has been given in "Algunas cifras sobre las dificultades," *Trabajadores*, January 27, 1992, p. 2. See also table 5.7.

16. "Interview with Minister Ricardo Cabrisas Regarding Cuban-Soviet Trade," *GWR*, February 3, 1991, p. 3.

17. Castro, "Discurso en la Inauguración del IV Congreso" (Castro mixed figures in pesos, rubles, and dollars in a confusing way); "Algunas cifras sobre las dificultades."

18. *Cuba Info* 4, no. 1 (January 27, 1991): 6; "Siege Economy," *Oxford Analytica*, February 5, 1992; J. L. Rodríguez, "Commentary," pp. 3–4.

19. "Meléndez on Decrease in Crude Oil Imports," FBIS-LAT, February 24, 1992.

20. Fidel Castro, "Speech at the Closing Session of the 16th Congress of the CTC," *GWR*, February 11, 1990, pp. 2–3.

21. As quoted in "Cuba's Predicament: A Fate Worse than Imperialism?" *NPQ* (Winter 1991): p. 10.

22. Carmelo Mesa-Lago and Fernando Gil, "Soviet Economic Relations with Cuba," in *The USSR and Latin America: A Developing Relationship*, ed. Eusebio Mujal-León (Boston: Unwin Hyman, 1989): pp. 213–15.

23. Mario Fernández and Nieves Pico, "Consideraciones sobre la evolución de la industria y el sector externo de la economía cubana durante el período revolucionario" (Havana: INIE, 1988), pp. 11–12 (quoted by José Luis Rodríguez in "La evolución económica de Cuba, 1985–1989," [Havana: CIEM, 1990], pp. 4, 20); Martínez Carrera, "Cuba: Crecimiento," pp. 36–38.

24. Abalkin, *Sovetskaya*, p. 5; Carlos Rafael Rodríguez, interview, Havana, July 12, 1990.

25. C. R. Rodríguez, interview. Russian press reports in 1990–91 corroborated that the price of sugar was fixed at 850 rubles per ton in 1986–90. If these reports are accurate, then data on sugar from the *AEC* are incorrect.

26. Mesa-Lago and Gil, "Soviet Relations," revised and updated with *AEC 1988.*

27. V. Venediktov, "Azúcar, naranjas y una cucharada de hiel," *Bohemia* 27 (July 6, 1990): 62. At the end of 1990 Castro said that the quality of equipment imported from socialist countries was poor because of technological backwardness and low quality of metals. Yet Cuba bought them because it lacked hard currency to buy better quality products from market economies. "Fidel at Closing Session of Fifth National Forum on Spare Parts," *GWR*, December 30, 1990, p. 2.

28. C. R. Rodríguez, interview; Isis Mañalich Galvez, "Lo que afecta a las exportaciones cubanas," *Tribuna del Economista* 1, no. 12 (May 1990): 10.

29. Fidel Castro, "Speech at the 30th Anniversary of the CDRs," *GWR*, October 7, 1990, p. 1.

30. "Interview with Minister Ricardo Cabrisas," p. 3.

31. Santiago Pérez Benítez, "The USSR and Cuba: An Uncertain Future," Havana, CEA, October 1991, pp. 6, 11; Mauricio Vincent, "USSR mantiene trato favorable," *El Nuevo Herald,* 20 January 20 1991, p. 1.

32. Victor Pyatigorsky, "An Oil Drum Plus a Strong Box Stuffed with Dollars," *Moscow News* 19 (May 20–27 1990): 12. See also *Moscow Selskaya Zhizn,* May 19, 1990, quoted by Radio Martí, *Cuban Situation Report,* July 1990, p. 4; ibid., September 24, 1990, p. 4.

33. *AEC 1988.* The *AEC 1989* does not provide desegregated Cuban export products by trade partners.

34. For different estimates and a discussion of these issues, see Central Intelligence Agency, *Handbook of Economic Statistics 1986* (Washington D.C.: Directorate of Intelligence, 1986): p. 115; Jorge Domínguez, *To Make a World Safe for Revolution* (Cambridge: Harvard University Press, 1989): pp. 290–93; Mesa-Lago and Gil, "Soviet Relations," pp. 217–19; Andrew Zimbalist and Claes Brundenius, *The Cuban Economy: Measurement and Analysis of Socialist Performance* (Baltimore: Johns Hopkins, 1989): pp. 150–52; Archibald R. M. Ritter, "The Cuban Economy in the 1990s: External Challenges and Policy Imperatives," *Journal of Inter-American Studies and World Affairs* 32, no. 3 (Fall 1990): pp. 124–33; and Jorge Pérez-López, *The Economics of Cuban Sugar* (Pittsburgh: University of Pittsburgh Press, 1991).

35. As reported by J. L. Rodríguez, interview, Havana, July 10, 1990.

36. Ritter, "Cuban Economy" (p. 126) has eliminated development loans because he believes that imported Soviet plants financed with such loans are also counted as imports and thus are part of the trade deficit. Questioned about this issue in Havana, Cuban economist J. L. Rodríguez stated that there is no double counting because development loans are under separate agreements (collaboration) and are excluded from the trade deficit. Ritter retorted that *AEC 1988* (pp. 488–91) lists industrial plants (*plantas completas*) as imports (personal letter to the author) but these could be different than those acquired through development loans.

37. The Cuban figure (10 billion rubles) was released by Raul Castro in April 1987 as cited by Alfonso Chardy, "Armed Waste Admitted by Cuban Raul Castro," *Miami Herald,* September 12, 1987, p. 1A. The Soviet sources are Pyatigorsky, "Oil Drums"; and Ye. Arefyena, *Izvestia,* March 2, 1990, p. 3.

38. Howard W. French, "Cuban Defector [González Vergara] Tells of Soviet Cuts," *New York Times,* September 13, 1990, p. 3A.

39. "Interview with Minister Ricardo Cabrisas," p. 3.

40. Santiago Pérez Benítez, "Cuba en la política norteamericana hacia la URSS," Columbia University, Papers on Latin America, no. 24, 1991.

41. RFE/RL, *Daily Report,* no. 116, June 20, 1991, p. 6.

42. "Gorbachev and Aldana Meet," *Granma International,* July 14, 1991, p. 3; Carlos Aldana, "Anyone Who Wants Can Leave the Country," *Granma International,* July 22, 1991, p. 2; Fidel Castro, "Discurso en el XXXVIII Aniversario del Asalto al Cuartel Moncada," *Granma,* July 29, 1991, p. 3.

43. *El Pais* (Madrid), August 5, 1991, p. 3.

44. Pérez Benítez, "The USSR and Cuba."

45. Thomas L. Friedman, "Gorbachev Says He is Ready to Pull Troops Out of Cuba and End Castro's Subsidies," *New York Times*, September 12, 1991, pp. A1, A6.

46. "Editorial," *Granma*, September 14, 1991, p. 1.

47. "Castro's Warnings Take on Urgency for Isolated Cuba," *Washington Post*, August 27, 1991, p. A14; *El Pais*, January 20, 1991; *ABC*, January 22, 1992, p. 28.

48. For 1988 I estimated the outstanding debt at more than $19 billion with an amortization of only $500 million (Mesa-Lago et al, "Relaciones," pp. 42–45). J. L. Rodríguez estimated the debt in 1987 at 13.6 billion pesos (9.8 for trade deficit and 3.8 for development loans) but in the same document he gave it as 10.1 billion pesos (6.6 and 3.5 billion, respectively) without explaining whether the difference of 3.5 billion pesos was for amortization ("Las relaciones ecónomicas entre Cuba y los países socialistas: Situación actual y perspectivas," Conference on Cuba, Halifax, November 1989, pp. 1, 3, 4, 14 n. 13). My estimate of the debt was conservative in comparison to the official figure published in the USSR.

49. Nicolay Ryzhkov, *Izvestia*, 2 March 1990, p. 3. The debt table was provided by the Leningrad journalist union newspaper *Chas Pik*, no. 1, February 1990. Reportedly, the debt rose to 16.4 billion rubles by the end of 1990 and 17 billion in 1991 (J. L. Rodríguez, "Commentary," p. 2).

50. Tania García, interview.

51. C. R. Rodríguez, interview. According to Ramón González Vergara, the former vice secretary of the Cuban delegation to CMEA, Rodríguez told him that—based on Cuban calculations—Ryzhkov's figure on the debt was underestimated by 2 billion rubles ("Will Castro Survive if Cuba Is Forced to Pay Its Bills?" *Wall Street Journal*, September 28, 1990, p. 15A). Minister Aven debt figure from "Russia Cites Debt Crisis with the Third World," *Journal of Commerce* September 14, 1992, p. 3A.

52. Mesa-Lago et al., "Relaciones," pp. 45–47.

53. J. L. Rodríguez, "Las relaciones," and "El contexto internacional en las relaciones Estados Unidos-Cuba: Los cambios en Europa del Este," Washington D.C., Seminario CEA-Woodrow Wilson Center, May 3–4, 1990.

54. French, "Cuban Defector"; p. 3A; González Vergara, in "Will Castro Survive?" p. 15A; Castro, "Speech at the 30th Anniversary of the CDRs," pp. 2–5.

55. Havana TV, April 6, 1989.

56. Reported by González Vergara, in "Will Castro Survive?" p. 15A.

57. Reported by Werner Stanzl, "Facing the Economic Void," *Der Standard* (Vienna) October 8, 1991, p. 6; and Euguéni Umerenkov, "Cuba desde la nueva perspectiva de Moscú," *Tiempo* (Mexico), February 21, 1992, pp. 2–3.

58. J. L. Rodríguez, interview, and "Commentary," p. 13.

59. "CMEA—On the Threshold of Major Changes—At the 45th Session of the CMEA," *Pravda*, January 10, 1990, pp. 1, 6; and "Press Conference Given by Nicolay Ryzhkov," Tass, January 12, 1990.

60. Clyde Haberman, "Moscow Proposes that Trade Bloc Begin Using Real Market Prices," *New York Times*, January 10, 1990, pp. 1, 7; Peter Passell, "Unsnarling a Tangled Trade Alliance," ibid., p. 7; Haberman, "Soviet Trade Group Says It Needs Big Changes," ibid., January 11, 1990, p. 6; *GWR*, January 21, 1990, p. 9.

61. C. R. Rodríguez, "Speech at the 45th meeting of the CMEA," *GWR*, January 21, 1990, p. 10; see also "Restructuring CMEA," ibid., p. 9.

62. Castro, "Speech at the Closing Session of the 16th Congress," pp. 2–3.

63. *El Pais*, January 6, 1991, p. 4; *Wall Street Journal*, January 7, 1991, p. 10A.

64. Ryzhkov cited by A. Kapralov, "Radical Renewal," *Izvestia*, January 12, 1990, p. 4; "Press conference by L. Abalkin," Moscow, April 9, 1990.

65. José de Córdova, "Castro Remains Firmly in Control of Cuba," *Wall Street Journal*, April 19, 1990, p. 11A; "Interview with Minister Ricardo Cabrisas," p. 3.

66. "Interview with Minister Ricardo Cabrisas," p. 3.

67. Ibid.

68. "Press Conference by L. A. Abalkin"; Abalkin, *Sovetskaya*, p. 5.

69. Kormilitsin, *Izvestia*, March 29, 1989, p. 5, quoted by Nicola Miller, "Soviet-Cuban Relations in the Era of Perestroika," paper presented at the LASA XV International Congress, Miami, December 1989.

70. "Cuban Economic, Trade Balance Problems," *Literaturnaya Gazeta* 16, April 18, 1990, p. 14.

71. Miguel Figueras, interview, Havana, July 11, 1990.

72. J. L. Rodríguez, "Las relaciones económicas," p. 10.

73. "Interview with Minister Ricardo Cabrisas," p. 3; Fidel Castro, "Speech on the 30th Anniversary of the Victory at the Bay of Pigs," *Granma International*, May 5, 1991, p. 12.

74. Ken Gluck, "Cuba recibe última gota de crudo ruso . . . ," *El Nuevo Herald*, July 20, 1992, p. 1A.

75. "Disminuído en un 20 percent el tiempo de estancia de buques soviéticos," *Granma*, July 7, 1990, p. 2.

76. N. P. Tsakh, deputy minister of the Soviet Marine, *Pravda*, April 8, 1990.

77. "Interview with Minister Ricardo Cabrisas," p. 3; Vincent, "USSR mantiene trato favorable," p. 1.

78. Castro, "Speech on the 30th Anniversary of the Victory at the Bay of Pigs," p. 12.

79. Arleen Rodríguez Derivet, "Lo que no es eficiente no es socialista" [interview with Carlos Lage, secretary of Executive Committee of Council of Ministries], *Juventud Rebelde*, January 26, 1992, p. 6; and Fidel Castro, "Discurso en la clausura del VI Foro Nacional de Piezas de Repuesto," *Granma*, December 18, 1991, pp. 3–6.

80. Fidel Castro, "Speech at the Main Rally for the 37th Anniversary of the Assault on Moncada," *GWR*, August 5, 1990, pp. 3–5; "Speech at 30th Anniversary of the CDRs," pp. 2–5.

81. CEE, *AEC 1988*. Part of these imports actually came from Argentina and Canada (which are paid by the USSR) but appear in Cuban statistics as coming from the USSR (Figueras, interview).

82. Carlos Martínez Fagundo, "Presencia e influencia de los factores de desequilibrio," *Economía y Desarrollo* 19, no. 5 (September–October 1989): 182.

83. Paul Lewis, "As Shipments of Soviet Grain Lag," *New York Times*, February 7, 1990, p. 10A.

84. A. Novikov, "Turn Out the Lights," *Konsomolskaya Pravda,* September 1, 1990, p. 3.

85. The reference to the chief of the Institute for omestic Demand, Eugenio Balari, comes from Don A. Schanche, "Castro's Power, Cuba's Future," *Los Angeles Times,* May 6, 1990, p. 12A. See also *GWR,* September 23, 1990, p. 3.

86. "Interview with Minister Ricardo Cabrisas," p. 3.

87. Lewis, "Shipments Lag," p. 10A; *Newsweek,* April 30, 1990, p. 35; Figueras, interview.

88. A. Kamorin, "What are the Causes?" *Izvestia,* August 31, 1990, p. 5; *GWR,* September 23, 1990, p. 3; Fidel Castro, "Discurso en las conclusiones de la Asamblea Provincial del Partido," *Granma,* February 5, 1991, p. 3.

89. CEE, *AEC 1988 , 1989,* and *Anuario de Comercio Exterior 1989.*

90. Fidel Castro, "Speech at the Ceremony to Present the Blas Roca Construction Contingent," *GWR,* June 17, 1990, p. 3.

91. *Granma,* August 29, 1990, p. 1; Fidel Castro, quoted in "University of San Marcos granted Fidel honorary degree," *GWR,* September 23, 1990, p. 2.

92. Kamorin, "Causes?" p. 5; Novikov, "Turn Out the Lights," p. 3. Both articles were reproduced in *GWR,* September 23, 1990, p. 3, together with the Cuban rebuttal by Felix Pita Astudillo, "Clear Accounts on Oil Delivery," p. 3.

93. "Soviet Ambassador Explains Delays in Deliveries to Cuba," *GWR,* September 16, 1990, p. 9. The collapse in Soviet exports was reported by Deborah Hardgreaves, "The Coup Collapses, Soviet Energy a Priority," *Financial Times,* August 22, 1991, p. 5; the decline in Soviet oil production by Pérez Benítez, "The USSR and Cuba," p. 7.

94. "Fidel at Closing Session of 5th Congress of the FMC," *GWR,* March 18, 1990, p. 2; Rodríguez Derivet, "Lo que no es," p. 6; "Meléndez on Decrease"; Castro, "Discurso en la clausura del VI Foro," pp. 3–6.

95. Castro, "Discurso en la Inauguración del IV Congreso," pp. 7 12.

96. G. B. Hagelberg, "The Sugar Side of Perestroika," *International Sugar and Sweetener Report* 122, no. 6 (February 8, 1990): 94. There is no agreement on the comparative advantage for the Soviets of buying Cuban sugar. According to C. R. Rodríguez (interview), in 1986 the USSR paid 850 rubles per ton for Cuban sugar but the average cost of production of sugar beet in the USSR was 700 rubles per ton (thus a disadvantage for the latter to buy from Cuba). Conversely, J. L. Rodríguez ("Las relaciones económicas," pp. 6, 16) said that in 1980 the USSR paid $540 per ton of Cuban sugar versus a domestic cost of production of $988 (hence an advantage for the USSR to buy from Cuba). However, with the elimination of the price subsidies (down to the world market level) the USSR should have an advantage in buying from Cuba.

97. Nicolai Zaitsev, deputy director of Latin American Institute of Moscow, AAASS meetings, Miami, November 22, 1991.

98. Peter J. Buzzanell, "Cuba's Sugar Industry Facing a New World Order," *Sugar and Sweetener* (March 1992): 35–37; G. B. Hagelberg, "Bleak Crop and Export Prospects," *Cuba Business,* February 1992, p. 2; Nicolas Rivero, "The Future for Cuban Sugar," F. O. Licht's *International Sugar and Sweetener Report* 124, no. 10 (March 20, 1992): 162–64; J. L. Rodríguez, "Commentary," pp. 3–4, and "La economía de Cuba

ante la cambiante coyuntura internacional," *Boletín de Información sobre Economía Cubana* 1, no. 2 (February 1992): 6–7; and conversations with Soviet scholars Nicolai Zaitsev and Sergei Tagor at the University of Pittsburgh Conference on Cuba, 27–28 April 1992.

99. The percentage of Soviet dependency on Cuban exports was given by Abalkin, *Sovetskaya*.

100. Castro, "Speech on the 37th Anniversary," pp. 3–5; and "Interview with Minister Ricardo Cabrisas," p. 3.

101. Córdova, "Castro Remains," p. 11A.

102. *Granma*, August 29, 1990, p. 1.

103. Kamorin, "Causes?" p. 5; Novikov, "Turn Out the Lights," p. 3.

104. Castro, "Speech at the 30th Anniversary of the CDRs," pp. 2–5; information from Cuban news media; "Fidel Closing Speech at 8th," p. 3; Pérez-López, "The Cuban Economy: Rectification," p. 122.

105. "Información a la población sobre las medidas adicionales con motivo de la escasez de combustibles y otras importaciones," *Granma*, December 20, 1991, p. 1; Rodríguez Derivet, "Lo que no es," p. 7; *Cuba Info Newsletter* 4, no. 1 (January 27, 1992): 5–6; *Granma*, 8 January 8, 1992, p. 1; ibid., January 21, 1992, p. 2.

106. "Precisiones acerca de las implicaciones laborales y sociales de las últimas medidas acordadas," *Granma*, February 1, 1992, p. 2.

107. "Adecuación de precios agrícolas a los costos de producción," *Granma*, February 14, 1992, p. 4.

108. Castro, "Discurso en la Clausura del Congreso de la FEU," *Granma*, December 31, 1990, pp. 2–3, "Discurso en la Inauguración del IV Congreso," pp. 7–12; and "Discurso en la Clausura del VI Foro," pp. 3–6.

109. J. L. Rodríguez, "Las relaciones económicas," p. 2; and *AEC 1988*.

110. Author's calculations based on *AEC 1975* to *AEC 1989*. See table 5.6 also.

111. Jorge Ferrer Martín, "El Banco Internacional de Colaboración y el Banco Internacional de Inversiones en las relaciones de colaboración económicas de los miembros del CAME," *Cuestiones de la Economía Planificada* 6, no. 16 (January–April 1983): 110–44.

112. Daniel Legra, reported by Reuters, Havana, May 31, 1991.

113. Pedro Monreal, Havana, July 10, 1990.

114. Eugenio Balari, quoted by Anne Marie O'Connor, "East Bloc Upheavals Upset Castro," *Pittsburgh Post Gazette*, January 2, 1990, p. 2.

115. Castro, "Speech at the Closing Session of 5th," p. 11.

116. *AEC 1988, AEC 1989;* Juan O. Tamayo, "Cuba to Pay Stiff Price for German Reunification," *Journal of Commerce*, July 6, 1990, p. 10A; C. R. Rodríguez, interview; Hagelberg, "Sugar Side," p. 2; "No German Aid for Cuba," *Wall Street Journal*, November 19, 1990, p. 10A; IRELA, "Cuba: The Challenge of Change," Madrid, Dossier 27, October 1990, p. 11; interview with Peter Jacina, director general for developing countries, Ministry of Foreign Trade, Prague, August 7, 1991.

117. *AEC 1988;* "Workers Now in Czechoslovakia to be Repatriated," AFP, Prague, March 27, 1990; "Cuba reconvertirá comercio exterior," *El Nuevo Herald*, June 14, 1990, pp. 3B, 4B; C. R. Rodríguez, interview; "CMEA Trade: Down but not Out,"

Cuba Business, August 1990, pp. 2, 15; "Crisis at the Embassies," ibid., pp. 1–2; "Fidel at 4th Congress" p. 8.

118. Castro, "Speech at Closing of 5th," p. 11; C. R. Rodríguez and J. L. Rodríguez, interviews; Hagelberg, p. 2; "CMEA Trade," p. 15; *AEC 1988.*

119. *AEC 1988;* C. R. Rodríguez, interview; Pérez-López, "Sugar," p. 36; J. L. Rodríguez, "La economía cubana y los desafíos de un mundo cambiante" (Havana: CIEM, 1991), p. 9.

120. Ibid., and "Unilateral Change in Hungarian Enterprises Terms with Cuba," *GWR,* October 1, 1989, p. 9; *GWR,* March 18, 1990, p. 11; "Fidel at Closing Session of 5th," p. 2.

121. Ibid.

122. The first view is from two Cuban economists who participated in a LASA-sponsored seminar held in Havana, CIEM, July 10, 1990; the second view is from Carlos Aldana, "Anyone Who Wants Can Leave the Country," *Granma International,* July 21, 1991, p. 2.

123. Castro has boasted that, in spite of the crisis, Cuba's official cumulative growth rate of GSP in 1981–90 was still the highest in Latin America; for that purpose he used ECLAC's series which exactly reproduces Cuban official data without any comment on their lack of comparability nor an evaluation of their reliability. A critical revision of the official series of GSP in 1975–87 results in rates 22 percent to 64 percent lower; see Carmelo Mesa-Lago and Jorge Pérez-López, "Cuba's Economic Growth in Current and Constant Prices, 1975–88," *Statistical Abstract for Latin America* 29, pt. 1 (1992): 598–615.

124. Annual targets in the economic plans for 1986–90 were published in *Granma,* January 12, 1986, p. 8; ibid., December 29, 1986; *Gaceta Oficial,* December 30, 1987, p. 96; *Granma,* December 24, 1988, p. 3; ibid., December 26, 1988, p. 4; and *Gaceta Oficial,* December 30, 1989, pp. 1, 110.

125. "Siege Economy."

126. S. Zuikov, O. Panivshkina, A. Mijailov, and M. Tregubenko (all from the Soviet Academy of Sciences), "Informe sobre la Economía Cubana," Miami, 1992; and O. Panivshkina, cited by Rivero, "The Future for Cuban Sugar," p. 164. J. L. Rodríguez reports a decline of GSP in 1992 of 2.6–4.4 percent ("La economía cubana y los desafíos," p. 19).

127. Andrew Zimbalist cited in "Cuba and the Future," Donald E. Schultz, ed., U.S. Army War College, January 16, 1992, p. 3, quoted in Richard Boudreaux, "Can Castro Weather the Storm?" *Los Angeles Times,* April 6, 1992, p. A8.

128. Conversation with Jorge Domínguez, Washington, D.C., September 27, 1991; J. L. Rodríguez, statement at the University of Pittsburgh Conference on Cuba, April 27, 1992.

129. F. Orgambides, "La tristeza hace presa entre los cubanos," *El Pais,* August 5, 1991, p. 9; Ana E. Santiago, "Libreta en Cuba abastece poco," *El Nuevo Herald,* January 19, 1992.

130. "Lucha contra el auge del mercado negro," *El Nuevo Herald,* November 22, 1991, p. 3A; Anne Marie O'Connor, "Fidel's Last Resort," *Esquire,* March 1992, pp. 104, 156.

131. Excess money in circulation from *AEC 1986* to *1988*. See also "Resolución sobre el desarrollo económico"; "Nuevas medidas del Banco de Ahorro Popular," *Granma*, February 11, 1992, p. 2.

132. "Fidel en la reunión del Comité Ejecutivo," p. 3; Castro, "Intervención sobre el mercado libre," pp. 36; "Elaboran proyectos legistativos en la Asamblea Nacional," *Granma*, December 27, 1991, pp. 1–3.

6

Cuba's Economic Policies and Strategies for Confronting the Crisis

◆ ◆ ◆

CARMELO MESA-LAGO

CHAPTER 5 SHOWS that Cuba's economic relationship with Eastern Europe has ended, while that with the former USSR has been drastically reduced; the bulk of the 84 percent of the island's trade with the defunct Council for Mutual Economic Assistance (CMEA) must be shifted urgently to market economies. Sugar continues to generate more than three-fourths of Cuba's exports, and the island must sell its 3 million ton surplus elsewhere; in view of the depressed world price of sugar and its gloomy prospects in the world market, Cuba must rapidly promote new nontraditional exports. In the last three years, Cuba lost socialist economic aid of more than $6 billion annually; therefore, it must find other external sources of capital and technology in the capitalist world. In addition, the island needs to obtain fuel supplies to cover 50–80 percent of its needs. Last but not least, the Cuban people face the worst food scarcity in the thirty-four years of the revolution.

To save socialism, Cuba must solve these phenomenal problems, in a relatively short period, in the midst of increasing international isolation, and with a type of economic system that either has collapsed or is being dramatically reformed all over the world. In this chapter I evaluate the viability of Cuba's policies under the Special Period in Time of Peace to cope with those problems: (1) reintegrating Cuba into the capitalist market through trade-partner diversification; (2) searching for new exports and other sources of revenue and foreign capital; (3) pursuing alternative sources of energy; and (4) expanding agricultural output to achieve food self-sufficiency (the Food Program). Finally, I discuss whether a market-oriented reform is the only option to the crisis and the political feasibility of that alternative under the current regime.

Potential New Trade Partners and Investors

Cuban economists and officials optimistically argue that changes in Eastern Europe and the USSR have some benefits for Cuba, as they should force the island to reach out to new trade partners, increase economic self-sufficiency, and diversify exports. A top trade official asserts that just as the U.S. embargo in the 1960s pushed Cuba to industrialize, the collapse of the socialist camp would help to introduce the above changes; he added that in the 1980s Cuba was forced, for lack of alternatives, to increase its economic dependence on the USSR in spite of a strong desire to diversify trade partners.[1] This section analyzes Cuba's realistic alternatives for shifting its trade to new partners, both socialist and market economies.

Socialist Partners: China

Apart from China, in 1989 Cuba's trade turnover with other socialist countries (Albania, North Korea, Mongolia, Vietnam, South Yemen, Yugoslavia) was $135 million, or 1 percent of the total, and showed a declining trend; at its peak in 1980, commerce with these countries reached 1.6 percent of total trade. Cuba signed a trade agreement with Albania in 1990, but turnover with that country in 1989 was $6 million; political relations with North Korea have improved, but trade in 1989 was less than $33 million; and in spite of Cuba's close political links with Vietnam, trade in 1989 was $27 million, a 50 percent decline from 1983. Political relations with Yugoslavia have never been good, and trade in 1989 was $67 million; further economic reforms and the civil war in Yugoslavia must have led to a decrease in trade. These countries cannot provide substitutes for most East European imports; they either are not in great need or lack resources to buy Cuban sugar or citrus. In spite of Iraq's enormous oil resources and need for sugar, Cuba's trade with that nation was just $12 million in 1989.[2]

Therefore, China is the best hope Cuba has within what is left of the socialist camp. Trade turnover with China in 1988 was $402 million, a twofold increase over 1987, and rose to $472 million in 1989 (3.5 percent of Cuba's total trade) and $500 million in 1990, according to that year's trade pact. In 1991 Cuba and China signed a five-year trade agreement for $500 million annually, and in 1992, an agreement for economic and commercial collaboration.[3] With a 24 percent jump in trade in 1990 over 1988, China's share of Cuba's total trade in 1990 probably did not exceed 4 percent, considerably below the 1965–70 trade shares (see chapter 5, table 5.1). Because of the disappearance of trade with the GDR, today China is Cuba's second largest trade partner (after the former USSR).

According to the cited agreements, Cuba mainly exports sugar (95–99 percent of total exports) and nickel, citrus, and medical products. Chinese imports include food and fodder, textiles and clothing, raw materials, chemicals, machinery, and road vehicles (bicycles). In addition, China is building assembly plants in Cuba to produce bicycles and electric fans in line with the imperative to reduce fuel consumption. By 1991, 1.2 million Chinese bikes had been purchased, and the plant is to produce 500,000 in 1992. Some problems have been reported, such as improper assembly, lack of lights, frequent broken brakes, lack of spare parts, and need to import air pumps (gas stations lack air hoses). Chinese bikes mainly come from the huge and notoriously inefficient Flying Pigeon Factory, which in 1991 had an unsold inventory of 1 million. These are the bikes exported to Cuba and sold for 130 pesos, about 68 percent of the average monthly salary.[4]

Sugar exports to China averaged 890,000 tons in 1989–90, a 19 percent increase over the 1985–88 average of 746,000, and, according to the five-year agreement, exports will rise to 900,000 tons in 1992. The overall increase (150,000 tons) is only 15 percent of the 1 million ton reduction in Cuba's exports to Eastern Europe and 5 percent of the overall reduction of exports to CMEA. Furthermore, if the price paid in 1988 was maintained in 1980–90, sugar sold to China conveyed only one-third of the earnings resulting from sales to Eastern Europe and one-fifth of that paid to the USSR. In the 1990s China will be paying the world market price for Cuban sugar (see table 5.6).

Since 1987, Sino-Cuban relations have improved. In a 1990 interview for U.S. television, Castro—capriciously interpreting history—stated that market reforms in China had caused widespread discontent, thus prompting the student uprising which, in turn, forced Chinese leaders to reestablish order. Cuba did not condemn the events of Tiananmen Square; on the contrary, a few days later, Castro visited the Chinese embassy in Havana and then received the Chinese foreign minister. Justifying the massacre, he said that "repression of students is common all over the world," and the Chinese "did not have experience on how to deal with the uprising."[5] Castro was soon after invited to visit China. Despite the fact that the Chinese have implemented a profound economic reform, political affinity and a desperate trade need have induced Cuba's rapprochement with China. At the end of 1991 Castro praised "the extraordinary miracle" accomplished by the Chinese of feeding more than 1 billion people, but he conveniently omitted that such a feat has been accomplished mainly through market reform in agriculture.[6]

The possibility of Cuba's expanding trade with China beyond current levels is practically nil for the following reasons: (1) China has a program to achieve self-sufficiency in sugar (with sugarcane in the south and beets in the north); (2) although China is the second most important importer of Cuban sugar, this is for political reasons, since the Chinese do not have a great craving for sugar; (3) most of China's trade is with Asia (70 percent exports and 60 percent imports), and China could buy sugar from Thailand and Australia at much cheaper freight rates than from Cuba; (4) China cannot send Cuba the capital goods and most manufactures that were previously supplied by Eastern Europe and the USSR—furthermore, China has only enough oil for itself and cannot export any, nor can it provide aid or price subsidies to the island; and (5) Cuba has no strategic or ideological significance for China. In addition, there is a long history of quarrels between the two countries; the current rapprochement could change.[7]

In summary, the share of Chinese trade will continue to be small and stagnant, trade will consist mostly of an exchange of sugar for rice and bicycles, and the additional sugar that Cuba exports to China is only a fraction of the surplus left by the closing or reduction of Cuba's markets in Eastern Europe and the former USSR.

Market Partners

There is a consensus among top Cuban government officials and academic economists that, in order to survive, Cuba must reintegrate itself in the capitalist market.[8] It must diversify exports, increase domestic efficiency, find a solution to the hard-currency debt, set a more realistic exchange rate, and attract foreign capital.

To increase efficiency and export competitiveness, rather than improve the current system—a Cuban scholar says—the island needs a "radical restructuring of the socialist model . . . a new system." At least until the Fourth Party Congress, Cuban economists debated how the market could raise efficiency.[9] My view is that the debate did not focus on whether or not the market should play a role, but to what degree and how to control its negative effects.

Expanding trade with market economies is severely limited by Cuba's significant hard-currency debt (which is not being serviced), the six-year deadlock in negotiations with lender nations, and the island's scarce international reserves and lack of external credit. In 1984–90, Cuba's hard-currency debt with developed countries increased 2.5 times, reaching $7.3 billion. Cuba stopped payments of principal and interest in 1986, and new loans were virtually halted.

Yet adding unpaid interest to the principal and the gradual devaluation of the dollar have steadily increased the debt. Accounting on the debt is conducted in dollars, but real operations are done in other currencies; therefore, as the value of the dollar has declined, other currencies have appreciated and the value of the debt has risen. Major creditors are Spain, France, Canada, Italy, West Germany, and Japan. Cuba wants to unblock stalled debts with such creditors, but argues that it cannot pay without fresh loans. The Paris Club, in turn, refuses to extend new credits until Cuba starts repaying. As a result, at least until the end of 1992, there had been no agreement among the parties.

Lacking fresh credit, Cuba's trade volume in hard currency declined by close to $200 million in 1985–89. Hard-currency reserves at the end of 1989 were down to $88 million, which covered less than one month's imports (see table 5.7). According to a Western expert, one solution for Cuba might be a multiyear rescheduling with a relatively onerous repayment schedule, perhaps following a grace period. However, if that agreement is reached, Cuba would have to generate a significant trade surplus to pay interest and principal, thus moving back to square one: how to increase exports. The Fourth Party Congress passed a resolution saying that Cuba is willing to negotiate its foreign debt and consider new payment methods. Debt equity swaps and debt payment with exports were being negotiated with several developed and market economies at the end of 1991 and in 1992.[10]

In 1982 Cuba enacted a law that allowed foreign investment in joint ventures up to a maximum of 49 percent of the shares (higher in certain cases). There were few takers (basically only Spanish investors) until the end of the 1980s when conditions became more flexible. In 1991 the

Fourth Party Congress approved a resolution legitimizing what was being done informally and allowing various types of foreign investment such as joint ventures, cooperative production, marketing agreements, and shared accounts.

Foreign partners now enjoy the right to own a majority of shares in enterprises the government has given priority to (such as tourism—which accounts for more than half of all foreign investment), total or partial exemption on profit tax (as much as ten years in tourism) and customs duties, freedom to hire foreign executives, free repatriation of profits and salaries of foreigners, state intervention to dismiss unruly or unproductive workers, a ban on strikes, low wages, special government services (legal, architectural), and accounting and management control by each party.

A top Cuban official reported in early 1992 that 50 joint ventures had been approved (30 of them already in operation) and another 100 were under negotiation, but little is known about who these investors are, what business they are involved in, the amount of investment, and so forth. Official secrecy is explained by concern that U.S. pressure might force investors away or cancel their contracts. It is reported, however, that many of these joint ventures do not entail financial capital, but access to markets or expertise, and that Castro is directly involved in authorizing each one.[11] In a lengthy study on how to do business with Cuba, Business International considers the nation a "problem locale" because of risks: in 1991 the island was ranked 116th among 129 countries in terms of investment safety.[12]

The value of Cuba's peso is not set in the international market but unilaterally fixed by the government, supposedly in relation to a group of foreign currencies. The peso-dollar exchange rate for foreign trade transactions oscillated widely in 1972–86, reaching a maximum of $1.41 per peso in 1980. Since 1987 the rate has been fixed equal to the dollar (it fluctuates with other foreign currencies) allegedly because the peso was overvalued and to facilitate calculations and operations.[13] The exchange rate for tourists in 1990 was $1.39 per peso, but Cuban-Americans received $0.50; in the black market the normal rate was $0.13.

Some Cuban economists have acknowledged that the exchange rate is a key instrument for measuring productive domestic efficiency and effectiveness of export-import transactions: when properly set—they say—the rate can contribute to increased competitiveness of exports, labor productivity, savings in inputs, and advances in technology. To achieve those ends, the exchange rate has to be based on a system of domestic prices as close as possible to real domestic production costs and world prices. They add that incorrectly setting domestic prices of export and import commodities (as is the case in Cuba although not explicit) leads to economic errors. Furthermore, differences between domestic prices of import-export commodities and world prices converted into national currency applying the foreign trade rate are absorbed or subsidized by the state.[14]

As Cuba becomes integrated in the world market, there is increasing pressure for peso convertibility, setting more realistic prices of imports and exports, and reforming the exchange rate. But since 1985, there has been a debate in the National Bank of Cuba and the National Association of Cuban Economists on crucial questions: (1) whether the exchange rate should be merely a mechanism for measurement or control, or also for stimulation; (2) what base should be used; (3) whether the rate should be applied to the whole economy or to only a sector—and if so, which one; and (4) whether it should be set for the capitalist world alone or include the remaining socialist countries as well.[15] To the best of my knowledge, by April 1992 decisions had not been made on any of these fundamental issues, nor had the needed price reform been implemented. Until these steps are taken, Cuba's integration in the world market will be problematic at best.

In 1989 the share of market economies in Cuba's total trade was 17 percent, two-fifths of what it was in 1975 when record sugar prices in the world market allowed Cuba to dramatically increase trade with developed market economies. Major industrialized trade partners in 1989 were: Spain (2 percent), the United Kingdom (1.4 percent), Japan and the FRG (1 percent each), and France, Italy, and Canada (about 0.6 percent each). In 1975–89, the combined trade share of all these partners declined from 33 percent to 10 percent. Latin America's share in Cuba's trade was 5 percent in 1989; Argentina and Mexico accounted for three-fifths of that. The remaining share of market economy trade partners share was only 1 percent in 1989 (see table 5.1).

Developed Market Economies: Western Europe, Japan, Canada, USA. The European Community (EC) trade share with Cuba declined from 21 percent to 8 percent in 1975–89. The EC has shifted from a net sugar importer to a net exporter (the EC is the biggest sugar producer in the world: 15 million tons in 1988), and it has not granted fresh credits to Cuba since 1986 for reasons explained above. Cuba exports nickel, tobacco, and fish/seafood, and imports capital and manufactured goods.

Spain's trade with Cuba peaked in 1975, when it reached $458 million; it declined to $271 million in 1989 after Spain stopped buying Cuban sugar toward the end of the 1970s. Cuba exports cigars, tobacco leaf, nickel, sinter, and fish/seafood to Spain in exchange for industrial, agricultural, and construction equipment and manufactured goods. In addition, Spain has invested in a chain of hotels and granted Cuba $2.5 million in educational aid. Spanish corporations were the first to become economic partners with Cuba. Most of this investment of more than $100 million has been concentrated in tourism (discussed below).

In the fall of 1991, two large Spanish trade delegations from Galicia and Asturias (the two regions that sent most emigrants to Cuba in the nineteenth and early twentieth centuries) went to Cuba. The second delegation signed nine trade and investment agreements (for a total of $12 million) dealing with laser technology, computers, dairy products, steel, tourism, and bank training. However, the delegation said that it was searching for "ways to finance those trade agreements."[16]

Spain's socialist government had a close and long relationship with Cuba, but was apprehensive because of the island's orthodox leadership and its reluctance to democratize. Anxious to change that policy and make it closer to that of the EC, in 1990 the Spaniards opened contacts with Cuban exiles in the United States, and this news probably reached Havana. Spain found a justification to reduce its involvement in Cuba in Castro's rude handling of the July 1990 diplomatic crisis created when eighteen Cubans took asylum in the Spanish embassy in Havana. They were denied visas and Castro accused Madrid (together with the United States and other Western governments) of provoking the crisis. In turn, the Spanish government claimed that the crisis was manipulated by Cuban agents posing as asylum seekers. Spain recalled its ambassador for consultation, suspended the aid program, and recommended that the EC follow its example (the European Commission interrupted all its cooperative programs—$3.6 million—and the FRG eventually cut all its aid as well). Castro retorted by accusing Spain of behaving like a European imperialist power and mobilized supporting public opinion in Latin America.

Although both sides eventually agreed to stop the war of words, Madrid announced at the end of 1990 that aid to Cuba had been terminated.[17] In April 1991 the Spanish vice minister of foreign relations officially received a delegation of Cuban exiles who favor a peaceful democratic transition in the island.[18] Castro and Spain's Prime Minister Felipe González met several times in July 1991 during the first meeting of Iberian and Hispanic American presidents in Guadalajara, where reportedly González unsuccessfully tried to convince Castro to introduce democratic and market-oriented reforms. During the second summit, held in Madrid in July 1992, Castro was given a cold shoulder by González and the Latin American presidents who also made Cuba a target of their criticism. Castro cut short his visit (the day after he left, a group of Cuban exiles was officially received by González), and subsequently the Cuban media denounced the summit as a trap to humiliate Castro.[19]

Another incident occurred when a Spanish joint venture (a discothèque) was seized and shut down by the Cuban government; later, a Cuban official explained that the operation of such business was ''improper'' (possibly involving prostitution) and that the Spanish businessman had been reimbursed for his investment.[20] In spite of the political conflicts, Spanish investment in tourism in Cuba continues, although so far there has not been any significant expansion of trade by the two countries.

Cuban trade with Japan peaked in 1975 ($705 million) with the sugar price boom and declined thereafter to $155 million in 1989. Cuba exports sugar and fish/seafood to Japan in exchange for industrial and construction equipment, manufactured goods, and raw materials for medicines. In 1985, Cuba exported 511,000 tons of sugar to Japan, but that sum declined to 162,000 tons in 1990. However, exports increased to 411,000 tons in 1991 due to a decline in Australian sugar exports to Japan because of a drought. That increase was temporary, as Japan prefers to buy sugar from Australia, Thailand, and Fiji because of proximity and considerably higher trade exchanges with them. In 1986–89, Japanese imports were halted (steel, textiles, trucks, buses); such cuts probably continued in 1990–92, given Cuba's worsening economic crisis. Cuba's lack of credit and export variety have been the major reasons for the decline in trade with Japan.[21]

Trade with Canada increased from $33 million in 1960 to $319 million in 1980 under Trudeau (making Canada the principal market-economy trade partner); thereafter trade declined to $92 million in 1989. Such trade created a steady deficit for Cuba and good business for

Canada, which exported grain and flour, as well as minor industrial, chemical, and wood products, in exchange for sugar, seafood, and cigars. However, sugar exports increased from 180,000 to 332,000 tons in 1989–91. In addition, a Canadian corporation (Sherritt Gordon) has reportedly been considering the investment of $1.2 billion in Cuba for a new smelting technology to improve efficiency in the nickel industry, although an agreement had not been signed as of April 1992. In spite of these positive developments, trade with Canada is not expected to recover its 1980 level due to Cuba's lack of credit and the free trade agreement between the United States and Canada.[22]

Cuban trade with the United Kingdom, the FRG, France, and Italy peaked in the first half of the 1970s and declined sharply thereafter (although there was a slight increase in 1989) when the EC, once a net sugar importer, became a net exporter; moreover, since the mid-1980s, Cuba has lost its credit. Cuban citrus exports are basically excluded also because of competition with Mediterranean products. As noted in chapter 5, the FRG terminated all former GDR aid to Cuba in 1990, and West Germany's sugar surplus eliminated the need for imports from East Germany.

There were no realistic possibilities of lifting the U.S. embargo and reestablishing trade with Cuba under the Bush administration. With the collapse of socialism in Europe, the U.S. government has tightened its embargo and exerted pressure on allies to isolate the island. Liberal Democrats are afraid to oppose those moves, fearing accusations of helping Castro survive and avoid liberalization. In 1992 the U.S. Department of the Treasury enacted new regulations to cut Cuban revenue from the United States. Remittances from Cuban emigres have been reduced from $500 to $300 per quarter; aid to relatives in Cuba who want to travel to the United States is limited to $500, which can be sent only once; and packages of food and other essential goods have been limited to $200 a month. These remittances, however, are very small (about $300 million annually) and serve a humanitarian purpose.[23]

The most important U.S. trade and investment with Cuba is handled through subsidiaries abroad (legally authorized in 1975 to conduct such business). These subsidiaries are mostly located in Switzerland; the rest are in Argentina, the United Kingdom, Canada, France, and Mexico. The total annual value of trade with Cuba by these subsidiaries rose from $331 to $705 million in 1989–90; the cumulative value in 1980–90 was

$3.3 billion.[24] Some U.S. subsidiaries involved in these activities are Dow Chemical, Du Pont, Ford, General Electric, IBM, Union Carbide, Otis, AT&T, and Business International. The latter considers, however, that U.S. pressure and sanctions are not the major factors limiting international business involvement in Cuba but the island's political and economic system itself.[25] One of these subsidiary operations has been approved by the U.S. government: AT&T's installation of an underwater cable between Palm Beach and Cojímar in Cuba (completed in 1989 but not operational by October 1992) that would increase lines by 50 percent and pay Cuba a partial share of call revenues ($1 to $2 million yearly) plus $60 to $100 million deposited in an escrow account in the United States for shares unpaid since 1966. However, Castro rejected the request for payment of the full shares.[26]

Several attempts have been made by Congress to prohibit trade with Cuba by U.S. subsidiaries. In the spring of 1990, a bill empowering the president to withhold federal assistance to countries that buy sugar from Cuba was passed by both houses of Congress, but Bush did not act on it and it was pocket-vetoed. The bill by Senator Connie Mack (R-Fla.) was reintroduced in the fall; it was approved by the Senate and the House in 1991 and was going to committee in the spring of 1992. Another bill was presented in February 1992 by Congressman Robert Torricelli (D-N.J.); it has the support of Bill Clinton. This bill adds a ban (for six months) from U.S. ports of ships that dock in Cuban harbors and was passed by Congress in September.[27] The United Kingdom, Ireland, Canada, and France, among other countries, opposed the bill, but it had the strong support of Cuban exiles, crucial for Bush's attempt to win Florida in the presidential elections. Bush then signed the bill in October.[28]

Toward the end of 1991, Cuba proposed a draft resolution to the United Nations to terminate the U.S. embargo. The draft argued that Cuba had lost $15 billion because the United States had (1) exerted pressure on foreign enterprises to avoid deals or cancel export contracts signed with Cuba; (2) successfully closed most traditional Cuban markets for nickel exports (including embargoing shipments of steel suspected of containing Cuban nickel); (3) impeded imports of sweets that allegedly contained Cuban sugar; and (4) prohibited the use of dollars in financial transactions indirectly related to Cuba.[29] The draft resolution was never submitted to the UN General Assembly, probably because Cuba did not have enough votes to get it passed.

U.S. stubbornness has its counterpart in Castro, who has not yielded an inch either: "Never will our country accept conditions to change our domestic policies in order to reestablish relations with the U.S."[30] The two countries should try to reach an understanding and negotiate their differences. Many in the United States argue that the policy of economic aid and exchanges with East European countries contributed to their dramatic transformation. In view of that, the policy of economic isolation of Cuba appears counterproductive. I have argued for years that the embargo caused many difficulties to Cuba in the 1960s and first part of the 1970s (the Cubans estimate the total cost of the embargo to be from $13.6 to $30 billion), but later it ceased to be a major problem as the island expanded economic relations with Western Europe, Japan, and Canada.

The principal obstacle to Cuban trade has been the lack of saleable exports and excessive concentration on sugar exports, now aggravated by the disappearance of socialist trade partners and subsidies. Furthermore, the U.S. embargo has solidified the position of the ideologues in Cuba and served as a scapegoat to justify domestic errors. On the Cuban side, the political changes introduced by the Fourth Party Congress are positive but insufficient to promote significant political openness, while the repression of peaceful dissidents and the organization of gangs to attack opponents are negative opposite trends.

Developing Market Economies: Latin America. Cuban trade with Latin America was basically stagnant from 1980 to 1988. In 1988, out of a Latin American share of 3 percent of Cuba's turnover trade, two-thirds was with Argentina and Mexico, and most of the remainder was with Brazil and Venezuela. In 1980–88, Cuban imports from Latin America increased 253 percent, while exports declined by 72 percent; hence the trade balance shifted from a $166 million surplus to a $272 million deficit. The total cumulative deficit in this period was $1.5 billion, mostly with Argentina and Mexico, and trade was done on credit, which explains Cuba's debt with those two countries.

In 1989 Cuba's total trade with Latin America and the Caribbean suddenly increased by 71 percent and the trade share rose from 3 percent to 5 percent. The latter still remained very low and Cuba's trade deficit expanded to $285 million. There were no significant increases with the major trade partners, the increase being concentrated elsewhere (probably Brazil). Cuba's major exports do not sell in the region, and the lack of credit impedes the import of needed commodities from the most industrialized Latin American countries; barter and compensated trade have been only partial ways out of that dilemma.[31]

Despite allegedly good Cuban-Mexican relations, commerce between the two countries decreased by three-fourths in 1980–89, from $413 to $98 million. Mexico imports some sugar from Cuba, but its domestic output is rapidly increasing; by 1992, its import needs had been reduced to one-third (400,000 tons). In addition, increasing integration of the Mexican and U.S. economies will have a negative impact on trade with Cuba. Trade with Argentina fell in 1985–89 (from $211 to $181 million) due to Argentina's demand that Cuba pay $900 million in debt before new credits were offered. Prior to 1989, Cuba's trade with Brazil was negligible (0.5 percent of total turnover in 1988) but during his trip to that country Castro closed a deal to sell $100 million of biotechnical products (meningitis B vaccine) in exchange for engines, refrigerators, and oil products; even if trade turnover reached $200 or $300 million in 1990 it would be about 1.4 percent of total turnover. With Noriega's downfall, the Panamanian front companies that circumvented the U.S. embargo (and earned $70 million for selling visas to Cubans) were shut down. Trade with Nicaragua ($32 million in 1989) vanished with the Sandinistas' electoral defeat. Trade with Colombia ended in 1990 because Cuba had not paid a $38 million debt and suspended payments for $3.4 million in imports from that country. However, at the end of 1991, Cuba agreed to restructure the debt with Colombia and pay it in 1992–96 with half of its exports. With the restoration of democracy in Chile, there might be some resumption of trade with Cuba but, even at its peak under Allende's administration, trade between the two countries was only about $6 million.

Trade with non-Latin Caribbean countries grouped in CARICOM has been practically nil, at least until 1992, because of Cuba's refusal to recognize the government of Grenada (an action pragmatically taken in 1992). Finally, Cuba has tried unsuccessfully to obtain petroleum at preferential prices from Mexico, Venezuela, and Ecuador, although some triangular oil trade was conducted through the USSR.[32]

A few recent joint ventures have been or were being negotiated with Cuba by major Latin American countries at the end of 1991, but it is doubtful that any is operational yet, and at least one has floundered:

Mexico was discussing a $300 million trade agreement to sell industrial machinery and equipment as well as raw materials to build a hotel in Cuba. The credit would be provided by the Mexican Ministry of Foreign Trade, raising Cuba's total debt to Mexico to $600 million, which would be paid by exports, possibly sugar. Venezuela signed an agreement for a joint venture in fertilizer production and cooperation in pharmaceuticals. Brazil's airline VASP signed an agreement to renew the antiquated equipment of Cuban Airlines in exchange for shares, but it was canceled—allegedly under U.S. pressure.[33]

Castro made an unscheduled appearance in 1991 at the meeting of presidents of Mexico, Colombia, and Venezuela held in Cozumel. These three countries have joined in a pact to help Central American and Caribbean countries, but one of the presidents said that the pact was already closed and Cuba could not be admitted; another dignitary said that no oil concessions were granted to Cuba and acknowledged that some changes in the latter's political systems had been introduced but not as much as desired. Cuba's National Assembly reacted to that disappointing outcome by criticizing the Cozumel meeting (as well as the previous one held in Guadalajara) because it requested political democratization and market-oriented reforms in Cuba instead of demanding that the United States cease hostilities against the island; by that conduct—the declaration said—those Latin Americans act as agents of U.S. policy.[34]

A Cuban scholar, Pedro Monreal, recently denied that Latin America and the Caribbean is a region for the "natural" integration of Cuba.[35] First, there is the growing integration of Latin America into an economic trade zone subordinate to the United States; the latter would exercise power to block Cuba's insertion and, even if it were feasible, Cuba would be reluctant because it would lead to its indirect entry into the U.S. economy and increased economic and political vulnerability. Second, Cuba would have to deal with multinational corporations (MNCs) and impose restrictions on them but, due to intense competition in the region, MNCs would reject those restrictions and go elsewhere. Third, Cuba cannot export large quantities of sugar to the region (most countries are self-sufficient in sugar and many are exporters); hence it would have to develop new products and focus on market corners (a reduced number of products where Cuba has an advantage) but there would be high costs for the initial penetration of each new product. Fourth, to make entry in market corners feasible, Cuban exports would have to be more competitive, which, in turn, would require a significant improvement in domestic efficiency (Monreal does not tackle the question of how this could be done without a market-oriented reform but his analysis leads to that point).

In summary, there are no real possibilities for Cuba's expansion of trade and economic links with Latin America and the relationship will continue to be marginal. Furthermore, it would be difficult in the 1990s for Cuba to continue to import goods from the region, as in the 1980s, because it lacks credit and its imports are too few and too little diversified.

Potential New Exports and Other Sources of Revenue

Cuba's inability to diversify its exports has been studied by several Western experts but only recently by Cuban economists, one of whom argues, "Contrary to Latin America where the 1980s recession encouraged vigorous policies of export promotion and diversification, the Cuban economy has not been able to modify [export concentration]" because of the traditional "great asymmetry of its foreign trade dominated by the high concentration on sugar exports." The most significant factor in Cuba's export growth in the 1980s was the expansion of fuels (a gain of 6 percent) an important component of which was the reexport of Soviet crude oil; "the remaining groups [of exports] have not shown any significant structural changes."[36] Another Cuban economist ratifies and elaborates on the argument: Cuba has not been able to develop "new export products," which have very low weight in total exports—only 600 million pesos or less than 11 percent of exports in 1988 concentrated in a few products, e.g., 70 percent are crude oil (reexports), gasoline and so forth.[37]

Table 6.1 shows that when oil reexports are properly excluded, the percentage of sugar exports (column 7) is significantly higher—especially in 1983–85—than in the first column. Some scholars have argued, with data from column 1, that the share of sugar exports has declined.[38] For instance, in 1984, at the peak of oil reexports, the share of sugar export was 75 percent (column 1) a significant decline from 90 percent in 1975 but, when the adjustment was done, the real sugar share increased to 83 percent (column 7). If one compares column 7 in 1959 and 1989 the sugar share is about the same. And the percentage of non-traditional exports (column 6) is the same in 1959 and 1989.

TABLE 6.1
Cuban Exports by Product, 1959–1989
(in percent)

	Sugar (1)	Minerals[a] (2)	Tobacco (3)	Total (4)	Oil Reexports (5)	Nonoil Other[b] (6)	Sugar Exports over Nonoil Exports[c] (7)
					Other		
1959	75	3	9	13	0	13	75
1965	85.8	7.4	4.7	2.1	0.0	2.1	85.8
1970	76.9	16.7	3.2	3.2	0.0	3.2	76.9
1975	89.9	4.7	1.8	3.6	0.1	3.5	90.0
1980	83.7	4.9	0.9	10.5	4.2	6.3	87.6
1981	79.1	7.9	1.3	11.7	4.2	7.5	82.7
1982	77.2	6.1	2.1	14.6	5.5	9.1	81.7
1983	74.0	5.4	1.9	18.7	9.3	9.4	81.5
1984	75.2	5.5	1.0	18.3	10.0	8.3	83.4
1985	74.5	5.1	1.5	18.9	9.5	9.4	82.3
1986	77.0	5.9	1.5	15.6	4.6	11.0	80.7
1987	74.3	6.1	1.7	17.9	6.5	11.4	79.5
1988	74.6	8.2	1.8	15.4	3.4	12.0	77.2
1989	73.2	9.2	1.6	16.0	3.9	12.1	76.2

Sources: Author's calculations based on: 1959 from JUCEPLAN, Comercio Exterior de Cuba: Exportaciones 1962 (Havana, 1963); the rest from JUCEPLAN, Boletín Estadístico de Cuba (BEC) 1966 to 1971; CEE, AEC 1972 to 1989, and Banco Nacional de Cuba, Selected Statistical Information 1989.
a. Mostly nickel.
b. Mainly citrus, fish/seafood, and naphta.
c. $1 \div (1 + 2 + 3 + 6)$.

Economists from the island have given three explanations for the slow increase and lack of diversification of exports. First is the absence of an "export culture": traditional Cuban exports are homogeneous or have similar quality all over the world, but this is not the case with manufactured goods and other exports that occasionally have been rejected by clients due to low quality and delays in delivery. Second is the instability of such exports, as very few are in steady supply: they appear and disappear in the world market and, hence, buyers turn to more stable suppliers. This problem is caused by a lack of market studies to determine which products would be profitable to export (distorted domestic prices are a serious obstacle) and to export what is in demand instead of occasional production surpluses. Third, until the 1990s, 80 percent of Cuban export sales were guaranteed by CMEA thus there was no incentive to diversify and improve quality. To overcome these problems, it is necessary—the Cubans say—to transform domestic management, making it responsive to external demand thus promoting investment in the most profitable exports.[39] An analysis of the potential of traditional and non-traditional Cuban exports follows.

Traditional Exports

Cuba's traditional exports are sugar, nickel, and tobacco; under the revolution, fish/seafood and citrus have become important exports as well. The Fourth Party Congress, in addition, has stressed the export of biotechnology and medical supplies as well as pharmaceutical products, but warned that sugar will continue to be the major export for some time.

Sugar. Recent targets for Cuban raw sugar production were 9.6 million tons in 1990, 11 million in 1995, and 13–14 million in 2,000. Apart from the negative impact on world prices and potential lack of buyers, are these goals feasible? In 1981–85 the USSR, GDR, and Bulgaria invested $3 billion in Cuba to reconstruct and modernize twenty-one sugar mills, expand the grinding capacity of another thirty-eight mills, and build four new mills, as well as upgrade the transportation system and reduce excessive trash in cane delivered to the mills. These improvements helped to increase output by 12 percent in 1981–85 and were expected to raise it by an additional 15 percent in 1986–90. Actually, output declined by 2.5 percent in 1986–90; annual averages were 6,929,000 tons in 1976–80, 7,777,000 in 1981–85, and 7,582,000 in 1986–90.

Unable to meet its export commitments with the USSR in 1986–90, Cuba had to spend $398 million buying sugar in the world market, which took 20 percent of its hard-currency export earnings. Shipments to Japan and other market economies were postponed. The 1989–90 harvests slightly surpassed 8 million tons, but they were 15 percent below the target and the 1991 crop declined to 7.6 million tons. Two Western experts project that if the trend fitted to 1950–88 output continues, Cuba would still be producing 8 million tons through the 1990s, but recent events strongly indicate a lower output (see below).[40] Cuban officials blame the drought, but there are more permanent problems: a limited harvest season, deficient irrigation, land scarcity, poor technology, problems with harvesters, low industrial yields, and transportation constraints.[41]

Cuba's wet season extends from May through October and the dry season (optimal for the harvest) from November to April. In the last thirty years, this rainfall pattern has curtailed the harvest: rains impede cutting and rush the spring seeding as well as weeding and repairs. Less than normal rainfall when the crop is growing affects yield; if rains come early in the dry season, field and mill work is slowed.

In spite of a significant increase, irrigation covers only one-fifth of the total area cultivated in sugarcane. Little additional arable land is available without cutting into food crops and export crops such as citrus and tobacco. Cuba's sugarcane yield of 52–55 tons per hectare are comparable to those of Caribbean countries, but lower than the average of 69 tons in similar latitudes and considerably lower than Australia's 77 tons and South Africa's 65 tons. To increase yield, cultivation and fertilization must be improved and cane varieties developed with higher sucrose content and resistance to disease; but these improvements will require years of research and experimentation.

About 67 percent of the crop is harvested by combines, which leave considerable amounts of cane in the fields due to technical flaws in conveyor belts and blowers. The choice of chopper harvesters instead of whole-stalk "soldier" harvesters (used under similar conditions worldwide) is another serious obstacle. Chronic shortages of spare parts, inadequate repairs, and poor maintenance have reduced the efficiency of the combines and extended the period of the harvest. Combines do not clean the cane leaves (an improved machine, KTP-3, cuts the cane tips); cleaning centers were built for that purpose, but they process less than half of the cane, do not function well, and still leave considerable waste, which increases fuel consumption in transportation and grinding. Burning would help clean the cane but is applied to less than one-fourth of the crop because bagasse is used for fuel and the burned cane must be transported and quickly ground to avoid losing sugar.

Two-thirds of the sugar mills are small and over 85 percent were built before 1913; new and upgraded mills only partially compensate. There are constant grinding stoppages, and industrial yields have gradually declined: 12.5 percent in 1959–65, 11.4 percent in 1966–80, 11 percent in 1981–85, and 10.8 percent in 1986–89. Finally, poor transportation causes delays and losses in recoverable sucrose, and excessive trash increases fuel consumption; the oil shortage exacerbates these problems.

Another important issue is that almost half of all sugar sold in the world is refined, while Cuba's output of refined sugar, after a peak of 1 million tons, steadily declined to 665,000 tons in 1989. The probability of increasing that output in the near future is very small.[42]

The Cuban government acknowledged that the 1991–92 sugar harvest was in trouble and would be smaller than the previous one (7.6 million tons). The most quoted Western estimate was 6.5 million tons, but the U.S. Department of Agriculture gave 6 million and a well-known sugar expert calculated 5.8 at best. Reasons for the projected decline were (1) the harvest started two months late, in January, and was not in full swing by mid-February; (2) almost no fertilizer was applied in 1991 and there were problems with weeds and lack of herbicides; (3) the severe fuel shortage, in spite of the priority to sugar given by the government, is a serious obstacle for 150 mills, 75,000 tractors, and thousands of harvesters; (4) massive labor mobilizations (to substitute for someart of the mechanized equipment) apparently have not taken place yet, probably due to transportation and feeding difficulties; (5) transport of the cut cane to the mills, once by truck, is now partly done by 100,000–200,000 supposedly domesticated oxen; (6) mills, harvesters, and cleaning centers lack spare parts; and (7) some of the area planted in sugarcane has been shifted to other crops under the Food Program. In spite of these formidable obstacles, the Cuban government announced in September 1992 that total sugar production was 7 million tons, a figure questioned by most experts.[43]

With a 1992 crop of 6 million tons, Cuba would be able to meet its current export commitments (about 5 million tons) plus domestic consumption needs (900,000 tons), leaving virtually no surplus to sell at higher prices; a 7 million ton crop would result in a 1 million ton surplus. There might be unsatisfied world demand for about 2 million tons from CIS and a couple of East European countries that could increase the world price, but Cuba would not be able to take full advantage of that. Furthermore, a price increase could be short-lived: world sugar production would rapidly expand in 1993, placing Cuba at a disadvantage because of its output limitations (explained above) plus the higher competitiveness of more efficient producers and their proximity to major consumers in Asia. In fact, world sugar prices for future contracts showed a declining trend in early fall 1992.

Nickel. Nickel output was expected to reach 106,500 tons by 1986 (making Cuba the second largest nickel exporter in the world), but table 6.2 shows that output averaged 41,000 tons in 1986–90, an increase of only 4,000 tons over the 1981–85 average and 60 percent short of the target. There are several causes for this failure. First is the low quality

TABLE 6.2
Planned and Actual Nickel Output, 1981–1990
(in thousands of tons)

| | Planned Installed Capacity | | | | | Actual Output | | | |
| | Remodeling | | Construction of New Plants | | | | | | |
	Nicaro[a] (René Ramos Latour)	Moa[a] (Pedro Soto Alba)	Punta Gorda[b] (Che Guevara)	Camarioca-Moa[c] (CMEA 1)	Total	Nicaro and Moa	Punta Gorda	CMEA 1	Total
1981	20.0	19	0	0	39.0	39	0	0	39
1982	22.5	19	0	0	41.5	36	0	0	36
1983	22.5	24	0	0	46.5	39	0	0	39
1984	22.5	24	23	0	69.5	33	0	0	33
1985	22.5	24	23	0	69.5	34	0	0	34
1986	22.5	24	30	30[d]	106.5	35	0	0	35
1987	22.5	24	30	30	106.5	35	1	0	36
1988	22.5	24	30	30	106.5	36	8	0	44
1989	22.5	24	30	30	106.5	36	10	0	46
1990	22.5	24	30	30	106.5	36	6	0	42[d]

Sources: Carmelo Mesa-Lago, *The Economy of Socialist Cuba: A Two-Decade Appraisal* (Albuquerque: University of New Mexico Press, 1981), p. 72, and "The Economy: Caution, Frugality and Resilient Ideology," in *Cuba: Internal and International Affairs*, ed. Jorge Domínguez (Beverly Hills: Sage, 1982), pp. 145–46; Carlos Rafael Rodríguez, "Press Conference on the 39th Session of the CMEA," *GWR*, October 28, 1984, p. 3; "Objetivos integracionistas en la industria niquelífera," *Colaboración* 10, no. 28 (June–September 1986): 26–30; CEE, *AEC 1981 to 1989*; Robert Graham, "Nickel Still No Gold Mine," *Financial Times*, February 17, 1989, p. 36; Fidel Castro, "Intervención en la reciente asamblea del poder popular," *Granma*, December 26, 1988, p. 3; *Tribuna del Economista*, September 1989, pp. 6–7; *GWR*, January 21, 1990, p. 12; "La industria cubana del níquel," *El Níquel*, June 22, 1990, pp. 1, 4; J. L. Rodríguez, "Commentary," p. 4.

a. Overhaul and expansion of existing plants (Nicaro, 1943; Moa, 1958); agreed with USSR in 1973 at a cost of 160 million rubles. Ore extraction is done through leaching with water plus acid: ammonium carbonate in Nicaro and sulfuric acid in Moa. By 1983, combined production of the two plants was planned to be 46,500 tons but it was 39,000 and then declined to 35,000–36,000 due to technical problems.

b. Construction of a new plant began in 1976 with 600 million rubles from the USSR, Czechoslovakia, Bulgaria, and Poland. It uses the same technology as Nicaro. Stage one (11,000 tons) was to become operational in 1984, and stage two (12,000 tons) in 1985; plans were postponed with a new target of 15,000 for 1989, but at most 10,000 were produced. Two-thirds of output was to go to the USSR. This plant was shut down in August 1990 due to the oil shortage and technical problems.

c. Construction of a new plant began in 1984 with 400 million rubles from USSR, Czechoslovakia, GDR, Bulgaria, Romania, and Hungary. It uses the same technology as Nicaro. About half of the output was to go to the USSR and one-fourth to other CMEA partners. It was scheduled to begin operation in 1990 and then postponed to 1993 or 1995.

d. Estimate; output in 1991 was 40,000 tons.

and high cost of extracting Cuban ore: nickel is mixed with other elements (such as iron) and is qualitatively the worst among twenty-seven existing ore varieties.

Furthermore, the nickel ore found on the island is laterite, which is processed by leaching. In other exporting countries, sulfites are processed by burning, and the sulfur contributes to the burning, thus reducing costs; this second process is increasingly more competitive and cannot be used in Cuba. In addition, the leaching done with water and ammonium carbonate (used in Nicaro and predominant in Cuba) is apparently less competitive than other technologies that must be bought in hard currency that Cuba lacks.

Second is the difficulty of modernizing old plants and building new ones under a Soviet and CMEA investment program of $2 billion. The two prerevolutionary plants of Nicaro and Moa were to be practically reconstructed with Soviet-Czech equipment, but, due to technical difficulties, that work has not been completed and output is 36 percent below the target. The new Che Guevara plant of Punta Gorda suffered many delays in construction due in part to defective Soviet casting that required hundreds of Soviet technicians to repair. At most, this plant produced one-third of its capacity and was shut down in 1990 because of technical difficulties and the oil shortage. The Camariocas plant has suffered delays too; in October 1990, a meeting was held by CMEA major investors to revise construction plans, but the plant was not operative in 1992.[44]

According to table 6.1, nickel's share of total exports rose from 6 percent to 9 percent in 1987–89, a result of a 28 percent increase in output combined with a 180 percent jump in the world price. But Cuba could not take full advantage of the latter due to its export commitments to CMEA (76 percent of total exports; the total value of nickel exports in 1987 was $317 million). Output and prices declined in 1990, so the nickel share must have also decreased. As noted, a Canadian corporation is considering investing a significant sum to modernize nickel production in Cuba, but that deal apparently has not been completed and in any case would take considerable time to produce results.

Tobacco.   Tobacco's share in total exports shrank from 9 to 1.6 percent in 1959–89; in the last year the value of exports was $85 million. One reason was the decline in tobacco leaf production (from 52,000 to 8,000 tons in 1976–80) due to blue mold. After a vigorous recuperation in 1981, output has stagnated (averaging 41,500 tons) mostly due to reduced private farming. Output of cigars fell sharply from 657 to 166 million units between 1965 and 1980, then increased, but in 1988 it was 309 million, less than half the 1965 level. In 1990, the international to-bacco firm Davidoff et Cie. ended its dealings with Cuba, alleging a de-terioration in the quality of Cuba's products, and started manufacturing cigars with tobacco grown in other Caribbean countries. This was a se-rious blow to Cuba and should reduce the tobacco export share even more.[45]

Citrus Fruit. Production of one of the most dynamic Cuban exports increased more than tenfold in 1970–89 from 93,000 to 981,000 tons, while the export share jumped from 0.3 percent to 3.1 percent in the same period. In 1987, Cuba was the fifth largest exporter of citrus in the world and sold abroad 59 percent of its production; the value of citrus exports in 1989 was $139 million. However, citrus output declined by 15 percent in 1989 for unknown reasons and its trade share declined to 2.6 percent. Furthermore, because of the low quality of Cuban citrus (combined with strong competition in the world market), practically all exports used to go to CMEA countries.[46] The shutdown of trade with Eastern Europe requires Cuba to sell the surplus citrus in the world market, which will be most difficult unless quality improves. Another alternative is that the new states of the former USSR could increase imports of Cuban citrus fruit, but there are other import priorities in those countries.

Fish and Seafood. Another dynamic Cuban export that faces limi-tations is fish and seafood. Output increased seven times from 30,400 tons in 1961 to 211,100 tons in 1978, but declined because of the uni-versalization of the 200-mile maritime zone. After a strong recuperation, output peaked at 244,600 in 1966 and decreased thereafter: output in 1989 (192,000 tons) was back at the 1976 level. The value of these ex-ports in 1989 was $127 million. The export share increased from 0.4 per-cent to 2.6 percent in 1965–88 but declined to 2.3 percent in 1989. Close to two-thirds of the Cuban catch is harvested outside the island's waters and is increasingly restricted by the maritime zone limit and bilateral agreements (which require sharing the catch). The rich U.S. waters are closed to Cuban vessels. The Cuban fleet is near full capacity and rapidly aging, and the fuel shortage is another obstruction for expanded output.[47]

Nontraditional Exports and Tourism

Oil Reexports. Cuban reexports of Soviet oil were the major source of hard currency (much more than sugar exports) and jumped from 1.6

percent to 10 percent of total exports in 1979–84, but steadily declined to 3.9 percent in 1989 (as the world price of oil decreased) and disappeared altogether in 1990 when the USSR sharply cut oil supplies to Cuba. Therefore, a most significant source of hard currency was halted: more than $600 million, similar to the value of biotechnical and medical products exported in 1990.

Biotechnical and Medicinal Products. In 1980 Castro decided to develop a laboratory to produce interferon, sent a group of Cubans to be trained in Finland (the largest producer of that drug), and in 1982 the lab started operations. A Center of Genetic Engineering and Biotechnology (CIGB) was built in 1986 on the outskirts of Havana at a cost of $65 to $80 million (other figures are as high as $200 million). The complex is made up of nine buildings; I visited the main one in 1990 and was much impressed. The equipment mostly came from Japan, Sweden, the United Kingdom, France, and some from the USSR and United States. The staff has 400 highly skilled technicians, many of whom were trained abroad; they earn $400 to $550 per month (three times the average salary) and, in addition, enjoy free housing, three meals a day, as well as transportation, sports, and recreational facilities. The center reportedly produces 136 items, including interferon, AIDS diagnostic kits, meningitis and hepatitis B vaccines, epidermic growth factor, and enzymes.[48]

Castro has reported that $80 million worth of meningitis B vaccine was sold to Brazil, and other deals were announced with Venezuela, Italy, and Spain. Initially, the Russians were skeptical about these products. At the January 1990 CMEA meetings, Vice President Rodríguez complained that no contracts on biotechnology were signed with Cuba, something he could explain only as a result of Russia's ignorance about Cuban advances. But a few months later, in the 1990 trade pact, the Russians agreed to buy 250 million rubles in biotechnology products, plus another 300 million in pharmaceutical goods and high-tech medical items, as well as rehabilitation services for 10,000 Soviet children who were victims of the Chernobyl accident and for thousands of soldiers wounded in Afghanistan. The total sum, 550 million rubles, was increased to 800 million ($888 million) under the 1991 trade pact.[49] That figure is higher than all revenue for exports of nickel, citrus, fish, tobacco, and tourism.

Although these high-tech goods have been produced for years, Cuba's statistical yearbook of 1989 did not specify any of them as exports;

they might have been lumped together under "pharmaceutical and medicinal products," which accounted for only $55 million. If that was the case, the value of these products increased sixteen times in about two years, an increase as miraculous as those drugs. One Cuban economist, however, reports $200 to $300 million of "medical" exports in 1991 including biotechnology products, while another gives $500 in biotechnology exports alone.[50]

An important concern is the quality and efficacy of these drugs. A U.S. scholar who has intensively studied this field and praises Cuba's accomplishments, cites various Cuban and foreign experts who criticize the rapid commercialization of these products before they are widely tested. Examples are: (1) interferon was only tested in animals and needed more study before advertising and selling it; (2) according to the Pan American Health Organization (PAHO), the meningitis B vaccine has been sold since 1987 without having completing two of the required clinical trials, and the results of the trials done so far have not been published in any journal or submitted to a peer review system (for these reasons Mexico did not buy the vaccine, while Brazil that bought it more for political than medical reasons, used and evaluated it simultaneously, and found one batch of the vaccine either ineffective or contaminated); (3) PAHO also found that the studies conducted on the hepatitis B vaccine were incomplete and that additional tests were needed to assure its safety and efficacy; and (4) sales of a skin-growth treatment (for burns, et cetera) to a European pharmaceutical company were held up for lack of research data on long-term toxic effects.[51]

A second issue is profitability. A Canadian economist argues that basic research in his own country and the United Kingdom is usually not connected with commercialization and profit, as the major interest is on research rather than practical application; a common result is the disregard of costs. Confronted with this question, a CIGB technician candidly stated he did not know about financing—a revealing answer in itself—but ventured that most of the CIGB's resources came from the state budget rather than profits. Castro has recently said, nevertheless, that biotechnology, genetics, and the pharmaceutical industry are self-financing in convertible currency. Still, with distorted prices and hidden costs, that assertion may be meaningless.[52]

One question is whether sales cover only operating expenses or capital expenditures as well. According to a U.S. scholar, the Cubans are good copiers but have not developed the new technology in order to be at the forefront of research and generate real profit-making products. Furthermore, because the Cubans do not pay for foreign patents, their products can also be copied but cannot be sold to countries that honor such patents. The CIS seems to be an important buyer of these Cuban products, but as it becomes integrated into the capitalist market and recognizes patents, it would be under pressure not to buy from Cuba. Also, many developing countries cannot afford these drugs and have more urgent priorities.[53]

Finally, the international market of biotechnology is a difficult-to-penetrate oligopoly tightly controlled by U.S., Japanese, Italian, and European corporations. Cuba has been unable to enter the market as it has failed to establish an association with an international firm; it also must develop tests and publish the results. A Bayer executive, consultant to the Cubans, told them that it was unrealistic to compete with international giants in this field and that marketing each new drug would cost at least $150 million, but the Cubans ignored the advice. The CIGB director has identified its major shortcoming as "the [slow] pace at which we get our products to the market." In 1986 Cuba signed an agreement with an Austrian firm to sell interferon in developing countries, but the deal apparently was canceled in 1988 either due to quality problems or U.S. pressure. Cuba was competing with other countries for an UNIDO-financed international center for genetic engineering and biotechnology, but it was awarded to India and Trieste, Italy.[54]

It is doubtful that Cuba can successfully and profitably sell large quantities of medical equipment and products in the world market until their presentation is improved, consumer confidence increases, and adequate follow-up equipment service is guaranteed. Another problem is the need to import significant quantities of needed costly inputs; for instance, three key Cuban pharmaceutical products require 98 percent of inputs that must be purchased in hard currency. Finally, income by "medical tourism" is small: in 1990, 2,000 patients paid $4 to $5 million for all types of surgery. Despite these difficulties, Cuba keeps trying: at the Fourth Party Congress a new wonder drug was unveiled that supposedly reduces cholesterol levels and, as a side effect, increases sexual potency.[55] Some jokers say that, if successful, this drug could be the savior of the revolution.

Tourism. This sector ranks fourth in generating hard currency, but data are scarce, confusing, and contradictory due to the lack of consolidated figures and coordination among various tourist agencies (three statistical series have been published since 1977; the longest is reproduced in table 6.3). Before the revolution, tourism was called "the second sugar harvest," but the number of tourists declined from 272,000 to 2,000 between 1957 and 1971; thereafter the number increased slowly (except for a sudden jump to 191,400 in 1979 due to the exceptional influx of 100,000 Cuban-Americans that year who paid twice the standard rate) and reached 270,100 in 1989. Thereafter, only individual estimates that do not separate visitors and tourists are available: 341,000–360,000 in 1990 and 350,000– 390,000 in 1991.

TABLE 6.3
International Tourism in Cuba, 1957–1995

	Foreign Visitors			Tourist Revenue (in millions of pesos)[d]		% of GSP	
	All[a] Tourist[b] (in thousands)		Tourist-pole Rooms[c]	Gross	Net	Gross	Net
1957	272			62.1			
1960	86						
1971	2						
1975	40	34					
1979	191	83		87.6		0.11	
1980	130	101		39.6		0.10	
1981	106	94	14,303	43.6		0.08	
1985	172	168	16,003	100.4	60.2	0.37	0.22
1988	247	242	16,946	152.9	91.7	0.58	0.34
1989	276	270	17,600	168.0	100.8	0.62	0.37
1990	n.a.	341	n.a.	250.4	150.0	0.98	0.59
1991	n.a.	360[e]	20,000[e]	400.0[e]	240.0	n.a.	n.a.
1995 (goals)	n.a.	1,500–2,000	50,000	1,000–1,200	n.a.	n.a.	n.a.

Sources: CEE, Estadísticas de migraciones externas y turismo (La Habana: Editorial Orbe, 1982); CEE, AEC 1982 to 1989; Ramón Martín Fernández, "El turismo y su destino," Economía y Desarrollo 18, no. 5 (September–October 1988): 30–37; GWR, July 22, 1990, p. 9; Miguel A. Rodríguez-Espí, "The Cuban Tourist Industry," unpublished, University of Pittsburgh, December 1991; Instituto de Investigaciones Económicas, Situación actual de la economía cubana . . . (Havana: JUCEPLAN, March 1992): 40; José Luis Rodríguez, "La economía de Cuba ante la cambiante coyuntura internacional," Boletín de Información sobre la Economía Cubana 1, no. 2 (February 1992): 5, 9, and conversations in Pittsburgh, April 26–28, 1992; Business International, Developing Business Strategies for Cuba (New York, 1992): 61–62.
a.Another series ("all visitors") available for 1982–86 gives slightly higher figures. All visitors are those in transit or spending one or two days only, while tourists are those staying more time.
b.Another series ("tourists" INTUR) available for 1974-86 gives lower figures. Scattered figures are higher than the series in the table, e.g., 309,200 in 1988.
c."Locations which have most demand from foreign tourism"; another series that gives figures twice as high might include all rooms.
d.The 1979-81 series might be net income. Other series give higher and lower figures than those in the table.
e.Estimate.

The number of rooms given in table 6.3 apparently excludes hotels managed by two state agencies and joint ventures. Data on tourist revenue are even worse, as there are several series: for example, $17.5 and $43.6 million were reported for 1981. Furthermore, since 1985 figures are for "gross revenue" but the "recovery" (net revenue) averages 60 percent of the gross, a $400 million gross in 1991 was reduced to a $240 million net. Finally, the 1990–91 figures include "all direct and indirect income" (for example, tourist expenditures in special shops); hence they are not comparable to previous data. The last column (tourist revenue as a percentage of GSP), based on gross revenue, shows an increase of 0.37–0.98 percent in 1985–90, but based on net revenue, it is only 0.22–0.59 percent.

Targets for 1992 ranged from 400,000 to 600,000 tourists and $420 to $560 million in gross revenue; grandiose goals for 1995 are 1.5–2 million tourists, 50,000 rooms, and $1–1.2 billion in gross revenue.[56] Such inadequate statistics make it impossible to evaluate these targets, but projected four- to fivefold increases over five years (1991–95) appear too optimistic.

The most natural market for tourists, the United States, remains closed because of tight U.S. Treasury regulations; most visitors come from Canada, Germany, Spain, and Italy. Cuba's main hope for expanding the tourist infrastructure and improving service is foreign investment. In 1976 INTUR was created to develop a plan to increase international tourism. As we have noted, the 1982 foreign investment law gave special concessions to joint ventures in tourism. In 1988, a holding company, Cubanacán, was organized to operate as a vertically integrated unit controlling its own finances and allowed to import supplies, keep foreign exchange earnings, establish joint ventures, and hire foreign managers at special salaries.

Two other tourist agencies, CUBATUR and Gaviota, have their own facilities, and the latter has Spanish stockholders. The first joint venture with foreign capital was with Spain (Group Sol Meliá); it completed the Sol Palmeras Hotel at Varadero Beach in 1990 and Meliá Varadero in early 1992; three other hotels are reportedly planned by that corporation, with a total investment of $150 million for 1989–2000. A second Spanish corporation, jointly with Cubanacán, invested $47 million to build the Hotel Cohiba in Havana, but after serious delays, this project was suspended in February 1992 by the Cuban government due to a disagreement with the Spaniards. A third Spanish group built the Marina Hemingway in 1988. A Jamaican corporation, jointly with Cubanacán, refurbished a hotel in Varadero; and three old hotels in Havana are being restored: the Nacional, Copacabana, and Sevilla. Cubanacán projects seven or eight more hotels throughout the island for 1995, and others are planned by Gaviota and CUBATUR. About 80 percent of future hotel rooms are expected to be joint ventures, 14 percent to have foreign financing, with only 6 percent to be built entirely with domestic funds. Castro has promised that investors will recover their investment in three years.[57]

According to Castro, Cuba needs foreign expertise in running tourist facilities and international marketing: "We don't know how to run a hotel, how to handle tourists." He compared the efficiency of two hotels inaugurated at the same time, one managed by Cubans and the other by Spaniards, and noted that the Cuban, with less than half the rooms of the Spanish hotel, had more employees. He concluded that the best indicator of success was the number of tourists who return.[58]

But the record so far is disappointing: only 7–8 percent of tourists return, compared with 20 percent for the Caribbean overall, because of bad food, awful service, frequent breakdowns of air conditioning and elevators, little entertainment outside the hotels, transportation difficulties, and so forth. In 1990, the *Economist* reported that one-third of Cuban hotel rooms were unoccupied. (If there were 270,000 tourists in 17,600 rooms in 1989, that gives an average of twenty-four room days per tourist in a single, or forty-eight room days in a double; these extremely high figures indicate that many rooms were empty; domestic tourists may occupy them in the summer, but that does not generate hard currency.)[59]

Without disregarding the positive economic impact of tourism, it has created "small islands" not accessible to Cubans, a sort of "tourist apartheid." The contrast between the meagerness of everyday life for the common citizen and those oases of opulence has provoked irritation and frustration in a society accustomed to a high degree of equality. Furthermore, it makes evident a dual standard: capitalism is all right for foreigners but not for Cubans.[60] As the foreign enclaves expand, these conflicts will grow.

The combined additional annual revenue from tourism and expanding new exports (biotechnology and medical products) in 1991–92 in the best of cases was $1.5 billion—obviously insufficient to compensate for the loss of more than $6 billion annually in trade and aid from the former USSR and Eastern Europe.[61]

Potential New Sources of Energy

I noted in chapter 5 that Soviet supplies of oil and oil products to Cuba have steadily declined: 13.5 million tons in 1987, 13 million in 1989, 10 million in 1990, and 8.6 million in 1991. Official estimates for 1992 range from 4 to 6 million tons, but at best, Cuba had commitments for a maximum of 4 million tons (in exchange for sugar). Excluding the 1.5–2 million tons that Cuba reexported in 1984–89, there is a need for about 8 million tons.

Domestic crude oil production steadily increased from 31,000 to 938,000 tons between 1963 and 1986 (when it met 10 percent of needs) but steadily declined thereafter: 894,000 tons in 1987, 717,500 in 1988–89, 671,000 in 1990, and 650,000 in 1991 (meeting 5 percent to 6 percent of Cuba's needs). Probable causes for the decline are the deterioration of the protective layer in the Jaruco wells and increasing technical difficulties in drilling and extraction. The extracted Cuban crude has high sulphur and asphaltic contents that limit its use and increase refining costs. The crude extracted in Ciego de Avila is light and of good quality, but represents only 10 percent of total crude extraction. Prospective geological reserves are 308 million tons, but only 36 million are considered extractable; the most important deposits (80 percent of the total) are in Jaruco and Varadero.[62]

Apparently half of the oil potential is under water in the Varadero Beach area. In December 1990 Cuba signed a six-year contract with Total Compagnie Française des Pétroles for offshore exploration to begin in the spring of 1991. The joint venture gives 49 percent of shares to Total, which assumes the cost of exploration; if oil is found, the investment would be paid out of it. To prove its effectiveness, the exploration should take from three to four years, with a couple of years more needed to begin extracting crude oil. Therefore, this potential source of oil, if it materializes, would take five to six years to pay off; hence the Cuban government plans to get out of the Special Period without counting on that oil production.

In April 1992 it was reported that Total's preliminary analyses were disappointing: the oil is very thick, a bitumen sludge difficult to refine, which would bring only $6 a barrel (less than one-third of the current world price). The head of Cuba's Chamber of Commerce acknowledged that the crude quality is not "as good as Texas crude but we are soldiering along." Total is not expected to risk drilling on its own, and the oil's poor quality will make it difficult to find partners. The United States has also informed Total that its area of exploration had been awarded to a U.S. corporation before the revolution and that claims might be brought up in the future.

A small Swedish firm, Taurus Petroleum, has a contract to do exploration in Camagüey's southern shores and Canada's northwest in the northern shore of Matanzas; other corporations negotiating concessions are British Petroleum, Royal Dutch Shell, Brazil Petrobras, and Canada's Sherritt Gordon.[63] But the poor findings in Varadero are a blow to the great expectations of finding a rich deposit and, even if some explorations are successful, it will take years to produce oil.

Other fuel alternatives are nuclear energy and gasohol. In 1976, Cuba signed an agreement with the CMEA to build a nuclear plant with four reactors capable of producing 1,600 MG, or 20 percent of the island's energy needs; the site (Juraguá in Cienfuegos) was chosen in 1979 and the final design approved in 1982. The first reactor was to have begun operation in the late 1980s, then was delayed; increased safety measures and technical problems caused postponement to the mid-1990s. The termination of Soviet aid left the project in limbo, but there were unconfirmed reports that the Cubans were paying hard currency to Russian and East European technicians to complete the plant. The chief of the construction team of 1,400 workers said in March 1992 that they were about to start the installation of the heavy equipment for the first reactor, which should be completed by the end of the year. In September 1992, however, Castro announced that construction of the plant had been halted.[64]

Unlike Brazil, Cuba has never seriously considered producing alcohol from sugar as a source of energy. Castro argued in 1990, during a visit to Brazil, that it was more economical for Cuba to produce sugar than alcohol because it had secure markets (in USSR and Eastern Europe) at a subsidized price and molasses could be made into protein-rich syrup to feed cattle. Now the security of socialist markets is gone, but the obstacles for increasing sugar output make it difficult to use alcohol as an alternative.[65]

Finally, Cuba is trying to get oil from other countries. At the end of 1991, a Cuban government official visiting Iran proposed a sugar for oil (485,000 tons) trade barter; despite a sympathetic response from the foreign minister, no agreement has been reported. Earlier that year, Colombia's foreign minister publicly stated that his country could use Cuba's underutilized oil-refining capacity (Cuba's refinery in Cienfuegos is working only at one-tenth of its capacity) to process Colombian crude and pay with oil. Reportedly, Mexico is also short on refining capacity and could strike a similar deal. But after the Cozumel meeting of the presidents of Colombia, Mexico, and Venezuela, the possibility of those countries exporting significant amounts of oil to Cuba at subsidized prices appeared closed. The presidents said that there would not be a special relationship on oil with Cuba. After the attempted coup in Venezuela, Castro strongly criticized Venezuelan democracy. And Mexico's Pemex (Petróleos Mexicanos) discouraged a private campaign to ship oil to Cuba.[66]

Potential of the Food Program

Agriculture has been the Achilles' heel of command economies, and in Cuba that flaw is even more important because of that sector's significance. Some of the problems in Cuban agriculture are: (1) excessive collectivization—more than 80 percent of the land is in state farms, another 13 percent is in slowly growing but inefficient cooperatives, and less than 7 percent is in the tiny private sector that is most productive; (2) prices for farm products are very low and widely distorted; hence, they fail to stimulate production; (3) yields are reported as the lowest among socialist countries, while labor productivity in agriculture declined 12 percent in 1985–88; and (4) in spite of enormous investment in agriculture, per capita production has either stagnated or declined with very few exceptions (citrus, eggs) throughout the revolution.

Causes, Policies, and Goals of the Food Program

The Food Program (FP) has not solved the problems of Cuban agriculture. The FP, conceived at the end of 1986, was begun in late 1989; the Havana self-sufficiency program (part of the FP) started in the summer of 1990. It was created because of the decline in food imports from Eastern Europe and the USSR and the need—because of cuts in fuel imports—to reduce the cost of transporting foodstuffs from the provinces to Havana: half of the tubers and vegetables consumed by the city (20,000 tons) come from the provinces. In addition, after the free peasant markets were closed under the Rectification Process (RP), there was a noticeable reduction in the supply of tubers and vegetables in the capital. Finally, recurrent severe droughts have necessitated an expansion of irrigation.[67]

According to Castro, Havana's self-sufficiency program was launched after most of the 1990 potato and tomato crop (planted on state land) was lost due to lack of manpower. In May, the students who had been tilling those crops moved to the capital to take their exams, leaving nobody in the fields for the summer harvest. Despite a last-minute mobilization of workers from Havana, little was saved. The result was a grave scarcity of those products. Castro's solution was to assure that Havana achieved self-sufficiency in food.[68]

Some of the Food Program projects are: (1) a national plan to increase production of export crops (sugar and citrus) and foods for domestic consumption (rice, tubers, green vegetables, plantains and bananas, beef, milk, pork, poultry, eggs, fish); (2) a project—just mentioned—to make the city and province of Havana self-sufficient in tubers and vegetables; and (3) a similar project for the city and province of Santiago. Havana and Santiago are even expected to generate a surplus for other provinces. These projects involve a phenomenal effort to expand the area under irrigation through dams, minidams, canals, and various other irrigation techniques. The FP targets are listed below. The target year is not always clear, but short-term goals are usually 1991 and medium-term goals are 1992 to 1995.[69]

Sugarcane. An engineering system combining irrigation and drainage is to be applied to 800,000 hectares of sugarcane land (eventually to 930,000 hectares—about half of the 1989 sugarcane land) to double the current yield. By the end of 1990, 200 brigades were working on 80,000 hectares and 30 more brigades were scheduled for 1991. (At that rate, it would take about ten years to reach the goal.) About 65 brigades are to install irrigation in areas with excess milling capacity, to produce 1.5 million more tons of sugar in 1991 (equivalent to the output capacity of fifteen sugar mills). According to Castro, building these mills would require 45,000 workers, 300,000 hectares of land and 1.5 billion pesos, compared to only 200 million pesos for the irrigation project. The increment in sugar output is partly to be exported and partly to be used for feeding cattle, pigs, and poultry. If accomplished, this plan would overcome some of the limitations described in chapter 5 and increase sugar production by 20 percent over the average output of the 1980s.

Citrus Fruit. Starting in 1992, irrigation is to be expanded to 1,350 hectares of citrus plantations, with the goal of increasing irrigation by 13,400 hectares annually (half of that figure was given in 1992). Eventually, this would double the citrus output.

Rice. A irrigation and drainage system is planned to cover 160,000–175,000 hectares for rice (more than the total rice land in 1989) to increase output by 600,000 tons in 1995, hence converting Cuba from an importer to an exporter of that grain. Castro's arithmetic on the required manpower is confusing and contradictory. In October 1990 he reported 10 brigades working on this project which increased to 15 in December and were to expand to 25 in 1991, 40 in 1992, and 65 in 1995. But in January 1991, he mentioned only 12 brigades. Each brigade should be able to cover 1,000 hectares; thus, to reach the target, 160 to 175 brigades (instead of 65) would be needed.

Tubers and Green Vegetables. The area of irrigated land for cultivating these products should double (meaning an additional 65,000 hectares), thus making Havana and Santiago self-sufficient. Output is to expand by 40 percent to 153 percent in various municipalities of Havana Province; onion production is to increase 100 times in some locations.

Plantains and Bananas. In Havana alone, 8,800 hectares of plantain land are to be planted and irrigated; at the end of 1990, the first 670 hectares were ready. In Santiago 14,800 hectares are to be planted (the area to be added is approximately the size of all the plantain area sown by 1989). According to Castro, exporting the food produced on 1,350 irrigated hectares would pay for all materials needed to grow 33,500 hectares of plantains (but he did not provide specific figures to support this assertion). He added that only 200 hectares of irrigated banana fields would produce in 1991 more than all the total production of Güines, a municipality in Havana Province famous for its fertile land.

Cattle and Dairy Products. Genetically improved herds and dairy production are to receive a big push. Eugenio Balari reported at the beginning of 1991 that 114 cattle development centers (using embryo transplants, artificial insemination, and genetic techniques), 32 breeding centers, and 325 dairies had been built.[70] By 1995, 1,000 new dairies should be in operation at a rate of construction thirty times the rate of 1981–85.

Pigs.   In the second half of 1991, 50 integral hog breeding centers (27 new and 23 expanded) are planned to double pork output. Pigs are fed a liquid fodder made up of sugarcane by-products, leftover food, and other local products. Output in these centers should increase from 4,000 tons in 1991 to 20,000 tons in 1993 (the latter equals 20 percent of the annual average pork output from 1986–89). The planned *acopio* of pork is expected to increase forty times when the program is fully in operation.

Poultry and Eggs.   The goal is to build 1,950 poultry sheds in three years to increase poultry meat output by 40,000–50,000 tons and reach an annual production of 3–3.5 billion eggs—about one egg per day per capita for "one of the highest rates in the world."

Fish and Seafood.   In 1990 fish breeding in freshwater dams produced 49 million fingerlings, and the target for 1992 is 188 million (a nearly fourfold increase in two years). Output of fish, shrimp, and oysters is planned to quadruple too, from 20,000 to 75,000 tons annually.

Castro has proclaimed that the FP is not only an economic and social battle but also a political and ideological one: "We want, we have to prove that socialism can solve problems . . . that socialist agriculture is superior to private."[71] The following sections analyze the key components of the Food Program and the obstacles to fulfiling its goals.

Key Components of the Food Program

Land.   Land is scarce in Cuba. An official report to the National Assembly in 1990 indicated that instead of merely expanding acreage under cultivation—which has reached a limit—Cuba must shift to intensive farming techniques through better technology and particularly through irrigation. Since those improvements will take time, however, the urgent need for food has meant cultivating tubers and vegetables on 67,000 hectares once used to raise sugarcane; a shift of an additional 42,000 hectares is planned.[72] Reducing sugarcane land may create a decline in output, despite compensatory measures (see below).

Transfer of Labor to Agriculture.   As in the mid-1960s when the focus of development strategy shifted from industrialization to sugar production, Cuba now must transfer a growing surplus of urban workers to the countryside to meet the demand for more workers under the FP. The labor surplus has been augmented recently by shutdown of factories, reductions in transportation, cuts in bureaucracy, restrictions on private activities, and the return of troops from Africa. The scarcity of farm workers is the result of migration to the cities and the rural population's shift to nonagricultural jobs.

According to a top Cuban official, lack of manpower is the major weakness of the FP. Castro too has often referred to the labor shortage. He noted that although Havana has 22,800 hectares of state farms planted with tubers and vegetables, it has only 1,900 full-time workers to till them. A rural town in Havana Province (population 32,000) had only 128 agricultural workers, too few to harvest an important crop. Tubers and vegetables are labor-intensive crops; reportedly, the few mechanical cultivators are inefficient and usually do more harm than good.[73]

The leadership has announced that labor mobilization will be necessary for four or five years, particularly in Havana Province. Voluntary (unpaid) labor, which almost disappeared in the 1970s and first half of the 1980s, has been resurrected and has reached "unprecedented heights in the history of the revolution": in November 1990, 2 million workers were mobilized to celebrate Red Sunday. However, fuel scarcity has forced a more cautious approach to labor mobilization. For the Havana self-sufficiency program, 20,000 workers are needed: 10,000 have signed for two years in contingents (with 500 workers in each), and 10,000 are being recruited for fifteen days; this would involve 200,000 workers if mobilized fifteen days once a year, or 100,000 twice a year. (It is claimed that members of labor contingents will have from six to seven times the productivity of regular workers.)

Other types of labor transfers to agriculture are: (1) voluntary extension of military service to farm work; (2) mobilization of entire schools for fifteen days or longer during vacation time ("student working brigades"), cultivation of school vegetable gardens, and linking the Youth Labor Army (established in the 1970s) to the FP; (3) organizing a contingent of women who will sign two-year contracts; and (4) a Turquino Plan to move people back to the mountains to produce their own food. If necessary, Castro has warned, "We will shut down a town for the needed time and send all its inhabitants to work in the harvest."[74]

Payment, Housing, and Other Perquisites for Workers. To keep experienced agricultural workers in the fields, average monthly salaries have been raised from 128 to 225 pesos (higher than the corresponding salary of urban blue-collar workers); salaries are paid during the first few months of work and then linked to output by weight. The monthly salary of contingent workers is much higher: 400 pesos, based on workers' productivity and yields. However, private farmers pay workers 20–30 pesos daily and as much as 50 pesos at the peak of the harvest, equivalent to 480 to 1,200 pesos monthly—as much as five times the average agricultural salary and three times the contingent worker's salary. Therefore, there is concern that private farmers—in spite of hiring restrictions—may steal from the FP's badly needed manpower at the peak of the harvest.

The 20,000 mobilized workers for the Havana self-sufficiency program are being lodged in sixty-two camps, about 320 workers in each. In October 1990 it was reported that half of those camps were already built, but the same proportion was given in January 1991, the other half being under construction. In February Castro first said that forty camps were being built by the city and twenty-two by the province, but later in the month he asserted that all camps were finished. In 1992 he stated that sixty camps had been built "in a few weeks." In addition, from 8,000 to 10,000 new homes are planned for agricultural enterprises; they will be furnished, have separate bedrooms, fans, and kerosene stoves.[75]

The "definitive solution" to the rural labor deficit is to create thirty-two towns or communities (some sources mention as many as forty-five) with permanent personnel fully devoted to agricultural work. Each community would be spread over 1,000 hectares, and houses would be of "optimum quality" not like "boxes" but similar in style to those of the Pan American Games village. Some of the promised amenities are: bedrooms with mattresses and electric fans, one large dining room and communal kitchen with air extractor and two freezers, refrigerators, window screens as protection against mosquitoes, two recreational centers (with swimming pool, color TV, VCR, gym, and table games), a library, wake-up music, "food as good as in Havana Libre" hotel (part of it imported), a school, a day-care center, and a physician, nurse, and ambulance.

In January 1991 models and blueprints for the new towns were being finished and construction was to begin shortly; in February, construction contingents broke ground for three communities, and it was said that the project would take five years. But disagreements arose over locating the communities: Castro criticized the Physical Planning Institute for placing them close to highways and towns without agricultural populations. He demanded that the new settlements be built in the midst of the fields where there would be fewer temptations to leave.[76]

Potential Problems: Labor. This significant mobilization of labor poses many problems. In the span of a year and a half, the magnitude and nature of the proposed mobilization changed several times as fuel constraints grew: at first it was "the more the better"; next, half-day mobilizations were considered a waste (because of time and fuel required for transport); then one-day mobilizations were chastised ("it is better to have 100 men for ten days than 10,000 for one day"); later, it was fifteen-day mobilizations (even better if the same group was mobilized twice a year); then a mix of fifteen-day stints and two-year contracts were considered the best short-term solution; finally, a permanent farm labor force with adequate salaries and living conditions was to be the long-term solution, but this would take five years to set up, according to optimistic estimates.

In the meantime, the short-run solution faces serious difficulties.[77] Construction contingents are expected to build the camps and communities as well as dams, irrigation projects, concentrated markets (explained below), and so forth. Greatly reduced output of domestic cement and cuts in construction material imports raise doubts as to whether these projects can be built. Mobilized workers make up two-thirds or more of the needed labor force in some districts. Therefore, there will be relatively few professional, experienced agricultural workers in the FP; the bulk of the labor force will come from the capital, most of whom will probably lack the needed skills.

Using students and women not employed outside the home would involve similar problems, as well as creating new ones; for instance, female mobilization requires the organization of day-care centers, and students have proved to be unreliable (for example, in 1990 a group of high-school students, frustrated with poor living conditions, left the fields and returned to Havana).[78] Mobilized workers were reported in 1991 to have stopped labor for a week due to lack of fuel. Officials believe that at the peak of the harvest (several crops must be harvested in March, April, and May) there could be a deficit of FP workers (particularly if private farmers succeed in stealing state workers for their own crops) but ignore the magnitude of the deficit—"We will find out at that time."

Services for mobilized workers may be poor. Castro criticized "negative tendencies" in one camp where half of the staff cleaned or worked in the kitchen while the other half filled leadership positions. The mobilization for farm labor could take workers away from important jobs. True, many are unemployed factory hands, returning soldiers, or new entrants to the labor force. But removing workers from productive or service jobs may harm the economy. That situation could worsen if a huge deficit at harvest time requires a rapid massive mobilization to avoid crop losses. Such a scenario would be similar to the 1970 gigantic mobilization for the 10 million ton sugar harvest that ended with a Pyrrhic victory: a record-breaking sugar crop, but a decline in the rest of the economy and a stagnant national product. Castro's intense involvement in the FP and his view of it as an ideological-political-economic battle to prove that socialist agriculture is better than the capitalist dangerously resembles the 1970 campaign and could produce similar results.

Technology.   Throughout the revolution Castro, a lawyer by profession, has conceived of grandiose and complex projects (rapid industrialization, cattle breeding, gigantic sugar crops) without previous scientific study and then has asked technicians for ex post facto plans to make them feasible—usually blaming failure on the experts. This seems to be the case with the FP also, as Castro has set up experiments and criticized scientific institutions. For instance, he proposed to the National Assembly a study to measure the impact of aerial microjet irrigation on sugarcane yield. An engineer suggested that an underground system of irrigation, then under experimentation, could save water and be cheaper. Without further discussion, the assembly agreed to test Castro's idea in Havana; he later proposed a similar experiment in Santiago during that province's party meeting.

Castro also has initiated a search for a new variety of potatoes resistant to heat and rot and using sugarcane by-products as liquid fodder for cattle and pigs. He has criticized the University of Havana's School of Agronomy for its "prehistoric techniques" and amateurism and blamed Cuba's technological backwardness on the failure to link the numerous scientific agricultural institutions established under the revolution with production.[79]

Dams and Irrigation.   At the beginning of 1991, Cuba reportedly had 186 dams and 762 minidams with a maximum capacity of 12.8 billion cubic meters of water, 75 percent of which went to food production.

It is claimed that, in 1986–90, 53 dams and 156 minidams were built, 27 percent and 20 percent, respectively, of total capacity. But these figures appear inflated when compared to those published by Cuba's statistical yearbook, which reports 103 dams (with more than 5 million cubic meters) built before 1985 and 6 dams built in 1986–87. Therefore, to have 186 dams functioning in 1990, 77 should have been built in only three years—an impossible feat. Even if only 53 were built in 1986–90, that would be about 12 per year or almost three times the average built between 1959 and 1985.

Plans for 1991–95 call for the construction of 104 new dams and 31 master canals (for a total of 516 kilometers) as well as related installations such as tunnels and pumping stations to increase water capacity by 4 billion cubic meters. Twice as many dams are scheduled to be built in the current quinquennium (using the very high figures quoted above) as in the previous one—a record number, more than half of all dams built in Cuba up to 1990—and water capacity is planned to increase 32 percent in five years. Furthermore, according to Castro the easiest dams to put to use are those already built: they involved a million cubic meters of earth to impound 150–200 million cubic meters of water. Dams under construction or planned for the current quinquennium are much more complex and expensive. For example, the Yateras Dam requires 4 million cubic meters of earth to impound only 100 million cubic meters of water, while the Agabama Dam will need a 70 kilometer canal.

The more than 200 brigades that began work in 1991 should complete 80,000 hectares of drainage annually, while 55 additional brigades should yearly install irrigation machines for 60,000 hectares. About 12,000 irrigation machines of three types are to be installed in 1991–95: microjet (ground and aerial), drip, and Fregat. The microjet type is very expensive: each costs 170,000 pesos plus $20,000–25,000 for imported parts (if half of all the machines to be installed are of this type, their cost would be 1.2 billion pesos, or 4 percent of Cuba's GSP in 1990). Factories to produce the Fregat machine are planned, but very few were reported in operation in early 1991.[80]

Equipment. The sharp decline in imports of agricultural equipment from Eastern Europe and lack of access to the capitalist market, combined with increased demand for such equipment, are serious obstacles to the Food Program's success. The brigades need massive amounts of machinery—for instance, forty rice brigades will need 300 bulldozers, 320 trucks, 120 cranes, and 880 other machines. Part of that equipment (such as steel tubes for microjets) is expected to come from the former USSR, but there is no assurance that it will be delivered; furthermore, Castro has criticized Soviet-made irrigation equipment for consuming too much fuel, and many machines are paralyzed for lack of spare parts. The Ministry of Iron, Steel, and Machine Industry (MIHSA) has been asked to produce 180 items (to replace imports) directly linked to the FP, such as sugarcane and rice harvesters, harrows for rice planting, plows, irrigation equipment, excavators, bulldozers, forklifts, electric engines, and concrete mixers, as well as spare parts.

Despite his criticism of agricultural technicians, Castro has declared that the ingenuity of domestic engineers and technicians can tackle the immense task of import substitution. He has mentioned inventions of "great importance" such as the "multiplow" whose creator was invited by the Cuban president to a meeting of the Council of Ministers. There are two types of multiplows: one that breaks the surface and a land preparation tiller, more complicated to produce, that penetrates deep into the soil uprooting weeds. A few months after these machines were invented (leaving little time for large-scale scientific testing), Castro ordered their mass production. At the end of 1990, the minister of MIHSA said that 276 multiplows would be manufactured (starting in the spring of 1991), but Castro quickly explained that those were land tillers because 1,000 surface multiplows already had been produced. In 1988 part of the rice crop was lost due to problems with rice combines; to correct that situation, seventy-five combines were imported, but they had to be modified from pneumatic to track wheels; one prototype made in Cuba was in experimentation at the end of 1990. Information is not available on their design and performance.[81]

Fertilizers, Pesticides, Herbicides, Seeds, and Fodder. In 1988, 96 percent of all imported fertilizer came from the USSR and Eastern Europe, but now their provision is subject to drastic cuts and uncertain delivery (in 1991, 59 percent of Soviet planned delivery of fertilizers did not come through). Most herbicides and pesticides came from industrialized market countries (except the GDR); those imports declined 36 percent in 1985–88 due to Cuba's lack of credit and probably have been cut further. A white-fly pest damaged the potato and tomato crops in 1990, and later in the year excessive weeds (due to the lack of herbicides and manpower) did not leave enough potatoes even for seed. Castro first said that the 1991 potato harvest would be reduced (due to the shortages), but later asserted that the pest was "almost fully controlled" by Cuban scientists: "The only blight is absentee workers," he said, "There won't be any weeds left in the fields; . . . we will weed by hand if we have to." In the spring of 1991, Castro reported that 35 percent of Havana's plantations were full of weeds, and that yields had been below expectations due to the lack of pesticides, herbicides, and fertilizers.

Some tuber seeds are imported at great cost, while others are being developed in Cuba. Potato seeds are imported at the cost of $10 million annually. For 1992, 2–5 million plantain seeds will be needed, as well as seeds for *malanga* and *ñame;* there are ongoing biotechnical experiments to develop the last two domestically. Biofactories producing millions of plantain seeds were reported toward the end of 1991 by Castro. Cuts in seed imports or failure or delays in domestic seed production would seriously jeopardize the FP.[82]

A major threat to the FP's livestock program is the decline in imported fodder from the USSR and the West: in 1988 close to 400,000 tons of fodder were imported. Difficulties were created by delays in such imports in 1989–90, and the situation is much worse now. Cubans are using fodder substitutes for livestock such as molasses, pastures, saccharine, and manioc by-products. There is no uniform standard for cattle feeding, and experts warn that new products must be properly mixed with the traditional ones to avoid weight loss and increased mortality. In 1969 Castro quarreled with a team of British advisors because they criticized his idea of substituting sugar molasses and pastures for grain as cattle fodder, but in 1978 a Cuban technical report confirmed that the use of substitutes had been harmful: the number of cattle per capita in Cuba steadily declined from 0.87 to 0.46 between 1967 and 1989. Pigs are being fed a substitute liquid fodder made up of *torula* (a high protein sugar by-product), saccharine honey, and leftovers. Several reports indicate that production of new liquid fodder plants is grossly insufficient and pigs have lost weight. Chickens cannot be fed with such substitutes, and the decline in imported fodder has harmed the production of poultry, meat, and eggs.[83]

In 1991, due to the sharp decline in imports of fodder and fertilizer and the failure to keep up with goals for sowing domestic fodder (two-thirds behind target), a radical shift in cattle feeding was introduced. The Voisin rational pasture method, invented by an obscure French scientist who worked and died in Cuba, was tried in 1964 but abandoned because it required electric fences, irrigation, and skilled personnel. The substitute cattle fodder combines pastures, saccharine, and legumes, like the formula unsuccessfully tried in the later 1960s (which mixed pasture and molasses).

To increase the production of pasture, seeds that do not need to break the ground (and hence do not require machinery and fuel to sow) are being used: the seeds are manually scattered, the cattle push them into the ground, and the land is fertilized by the animals' manure. All cattle ranches were ordered to implement the new method by the end of 1991. Said Castro: "Never in the world has a plan been designed and implemented as fast as this one"; he claimed that, in a few months, they had built factories to produce electric fences, thousands of miles of irrigation hoses, 10,000 multiplows, and mills to produce saccharine. But the electric fences require imports that cost $10 million and increase the use of electricity. He added: "We need to make miracles, to produce more milk and beef with little or no fodder and fertilizer."[84]

Distribution: Flaws in Acopio. An important component of the FP is rapid distribution of food to avoid spoilage. This issue prompted long discussions at the National Assembly at the end of 1990. One deputy stated: "While we are making big efforts and investments in the FP, *acopio* [procurement] is not working well. Delays in gathering produce irritate farmers, and consumers often receive rotten merchandise due to the lack of organization and [quality] control of *acopio.*" Another deputy said that prices are sometimes too high or too low; for instance, prices of poor-quality oranges are too high, nobody buys them, and they are wasted. Pineapples reach the consumer in bad shape because they are loaded improperly into huge trucks—the fruit on the bottom is smashed by the weight. Castro has blamed this problem on the SDPE, and yet the RP has been in operation for more than five years and was expected to solve it. Plans to correct flaws are vague. *Acopio* will continue, but its role in distribution is "under review" and prices of products that do not sell should be reduced, but then the state will not be able to recuperate part of the subsidy, at least to cover costs. When Castro asked for suggestions on how to improve *acopio,* leaders could only come up with the idea of computers.

Distribution: Concentrated Markets. To solve distribution problems, so-called concentrated markets, or refrigerated warehouses, are to be built. They will receive agricultural products from the countryside, keep some of them, and distribute the rest to 500 or 600 small groceries. Products include: bananas, tubers (except yucca, which needs quick distribution), and vegetables (except the most perishable, such as lettuce); citrus will be delivered directly to the grocery stores. Each market is to operate a fleet of delivery trucks—a questionable proposition, given the fuel shortage. Four concentrated markets were to be built in Havana Province, the first to open at the beginning of 1991.

In April 1991 Castro reported that two warehouses were finished (one had been under construction for years), a third was being built, and a fourth would be ready in 1992. He also said that 161 small groceries (25–33 percent of the planned total) had been finished. But he acknowledged that each warehouse cost about $2 million and that many components have to be imported: compressors from Bulgaria and China, steel, pipes, forklifts, and 1,700 cubic meters of wood (which used to come from the USSR). A former Cuban official told me in June 1991 that the first large freezer had to be shut down soon after it was inaugurated because it malfunctioned, and all the produce had to be sold immediately.

There are other distribution problems: milk containers are sometimes unclean and in short supply, and deliveries of milk are delayed; the small groceries are understaffed and inefficient, so that some produce rots. These problems have been "discussed on several occasions by the Executive Committee of the Council of Ministers," to no avail.[85]

Fuel Scarcity and Animal Traction. The decline in Soviet oil deliveries has crippled transportation in Cuba. The FP, however, should increase the demand for fuel for harvesters, irrigation machines, electrified fences, transportation of mobilized workers, operation of equipment to build dams, canals, labor camps, and trucks to distribute foodstuffs. Priority in fuel allocation has been given to agriculture, but even so, will there be enough fuel to satisfy all the FP demands? Despite the planned technological explosion in agriculture, there is an effort to substitute animals for machines. At the end of 1990, it was announced that 100,000 oxen would be trained in six months to do agricultural work; new cuts in the fuel supply raised the target to 400,000 animals, adding bulls, mules, and horses. Are there enough experienced farmers left in Cuba (after three decades of mechanization) to tame and drive these animals? Data have not been published on their performance, either. Cuts in beef supply to the population were to be compensated with imported poultry from Bulgaria, but delays of even normal deliveries of poultry from that country made this substitution unfeasible.[86]

Climatic Factors.   The president of the ANAP has acknowledged that drought or excessive rain would jeopardize the Food Program. In several speeches, Castro has referred to heat waves and particularly hurricanes as imponderable factors: a hurricane would destroy banana trees and damage irrigation hoses and wires. In the same month he expressed opposite views on the effect of hurricanes on the harvests: "The crops would not be lost," yet "We could lose one year of production."[87]

Overall Coordination.   Several deputies to the National Assembly have indicated the need for an all-around approach to the FP because of the huge investment required, the many projects it embraces, and its connections with all sectors of the economy. The lack of a comprehensive integrated economic model as well as a plan could result in serious bottlenecks and projects left incomplete, as in 1966–70. We have mentioned already the damage that can be inflicted on the rest of the economy if its resources are depleted to fulfill the FP targets.

Castro is adamant on giving priority to the Food Program: "These plans cannot be stopped under any condition and I think we are very clear on this point." More realistic, cautious positions probably will not prevail against him. For instance, Eugenio Balari (chief of the Institute of Domestic Demand) has said: "We have 20,000 priority projects to be finished. Last year [1990] we had 3.8 million tons of cement, this year [1991] not 2 million. If we were hoping for 20,000 projects, maybe 10,000 is more realistic."[88] Castro maintains that using sugarcane land for other crops under the FP will not affect sugar output because sugarcane plantations will increase their yields due to expanded irrigation and drainage.[89] But I have noted that experiments related to that plan just began in 1991, and that there will be a sharp decline in sugar output in the 1992 harvest. Recall that in 1962–63, reduction of sugarcane land to diversify agricultural production caused the worst decline in sugar output under the revolution and led to the first change in development strategy.

Viability of the Food Program

Official Views.   Early in 1991, President Castro gave the following optimistic picture of the progress and ultimate success of the FP:

> In the next months . . . concentrated markets will begin to function, first crops will be harvested, we will have an army of 20,000 [mobilized workers] in our

camps and the Student Working Brigades, . . . hydraulic work [will be under way] that will have dams in all rivers, all the island crossed with canals to channel water to crops, all the water reservoirs exploited. . . . Although many think it is naive to strive for fulfillment of these plans amidst a difficult economic situation . . . the food program goals are based on its own resources and make allowances for major reductions in oil imports. . . . We are going to demonstrate what real socialist agriculture is.[90]

A more realistic view on the feasibility of the FP has been offered by Adolfo Díaz, vice president of the National Assembly, in a synthesis of his 138-page official report to that body:

In our report we have not given details on [the output and] yields of various crops and cattle, still low in many lines, but what we hope to accomplish. . . . The international situation and the pressure of our enemies to create a crisis in our economic relations [with the USSR] impede an accurate forecast of the situation we will face in the immediate future. . . . The Food Program has maximum priority but, due to current limitations, it will have to be realized with less resources. . . . Low yields in some agricultural lines are the result of objective problems but also to a large extent to organizational flaws, lack of discipline. . . . We have little time to apply this program . . . and this task has become a principal battle trench. All time lost will have not only an economic cost but political as well.[91]

A Cuban journalist asked the president of ANAP: "Are you not afraid that your efforts might fall short of expectations?" His cautious answer was: "No, [but] solving the food problem is not easy, we must not be idealists and think we can solve things overnight."[92]

As just noted by Díaz, data are very scarce data on the accomplishments of the FP more than two years after its inception; furthermore, quantitative targets and their terms are seldom given. In late 1990 and into 1991, important meetings were devoted to the FP and abundant figures published, but they were fragmentary, confusing, and sometimes contradictory. We lack comprehensive and accurate data on output and irrigated land (current and planned, overall and by crops), yields, investments, domestic production of machines, and so forth. A serious evaluation is, therefore, not possible at this time.

Table 6.4 summarizes the scarce available data on output and irrigated land. Despite its limitations, the table is the first attempt, inside or outside Cuba, to assess the feasibility of the FP. Output targets for 1995 (or earlier years) are compared in the first part of the table with actual production in 1989, the latest data available at the time of writing. In addition, the increase in planned output (1995 over 1989) is contrasted

TABLE 6.4
Feasibility of Output and Irrigation Targets of the Cuban Food Program, 1989–1995

| | Output (000 Metric Tons) | | | | Irrigation (000 Ha) | | | |
| | | | % Difference[a] | | | | | |
Production Lines	Target 1995	Real 1989	Target 1995/89	Real 1989/84	Target 1995[b]	Accomplished 1990–91[b]	% of Fulfillment	Current Area 1989
Sugar[c]	11,200	8,121	37.9	–1.0	800–930	80	9.2	389
Citrus[d]	1,656	825	100.7	10.8	n.a.	n.a.	n.a.	106
Rice[e]	610	536	13.8	–3.3	160–175	12–15	8.0	164
Tubers[f]	1,032	681	51.5	0.0	65	n.a.	n.a.	50
Vegetables[g]	910	610	49.1	2.7				
Plantains[h]	n.a.	291	n.a.	–15.4	8.8	.67	7.6	38
Meat[i]	477	517	–7.7	0.2				
Milk (ML)[j]	1,987	898	121.2	–2.0				
Eggs (MU)	3,250	2,523	28.8	–1.3				
Fish[k]	222	192	15.6	–12.7				

ML = million liters.

MU = million units.

Sources: Output targets from Adolfo Díaz, "Presentación del Informe sobre el Programa Alimentario," *Granma*, December 27, 1990, p. 2; real output and current area under irrigation from CEE, *AEC 1988* and *1989*: irrigation targets and real outcome from calculations for this chapter and *AEC 1989*.

a. Percentage increase of target (1995) over real output (1989) and actual increase in 1984–89.

b. End of 1990 or beginning of 1991 (real); no specific year for target is usually given.

c. Output target is an increase of 30 percent to 50 percent of 1990 output; the middle point (40 percent) was chosen; the date for the target was not released.

d. Target (no year given) is to duplicate output; but also an output target of 900,000 tons of fruit (including all citrus not exported) was set which is actually lower than the 1,079,000 fruit output in 1988. Still another target is 2 million tons in citrus alone. Irrigation target is annual starting in 1992.

e. Output target is rice for population consumption only; real output is total output, probably including seed, 1989–86.

f. Potatoes, sweet potatoes, *malanga*, and others.

g. Tomatoes, onions, peppers, and others, 1989–85.

h. Irrigation targets for Havana Province only.

i. Output of beef, pork, and poultry in 1989 was 8 percent higher than the target; if poultry is excluded, output was 399,100, or 16 percent below the target.

j. Cow's milk; 1989 is state sector only; 1989–84 includes private sector too.

k. Fish and seafood; combined output in 1986 was 244,000 tons, 10 percent above the target, 1989–85.

with actual increases or decreases of output in the previous five years (1984–89).

The FP targets optimistically set increases in output ranging from 14 percent to 121 percent according to the various production lines, but real previous output declined from 1 percent to 15 percent. (Exceptions are citrus and vegetables, whose output increased in 1984–89—10.8 percent and 13.7 percent, respectively.) For the only two products that had actual increases, the target rate of growth for 1995 is enormous compared to the actual rate achieved in 1984–89: 18 times for vegetables and 9 times for citrus. In view of Cuba's external constraints, general agricultural problems, and specific obstacles faced by the FP, these targets are obviously not feasible.

The second part of table 6.4 compares targets (for 1995 or earlier) on irrigated land, with actual accomplishments in the first year or so of the FP and then estimates the percentage of the target fulfilled; it also provides the area actually under irrigation in 1989. If the target period is five or six years (1990–95), the annual percentage of fulfillment should be from 16 percent to 20 percent; if the target period is shorter, the annual percentage of fulfillment should be higher (for example, 33 percent if the target year is 1992). In the three products for which we have data (sugar, rice, and plantains), the target fulfillment ranges from 7.6 percent to 9.2 percent—less than half of what it should have been for the longest target period.

Approximate totals of planned and accomplished irrigated land (about 1,000,000 and 100,000 hectares, respectively) indicates that, at the 1990–91 rate of progress, it would take ten years to reach the goal. The last column of table 6.4 shows the irrigated area of various crops in 1989; the projected expansion of irrigation (1995 targets) involves increases ranging from 100 percent to 222 percent in three products. The total irrigated area covered in thirty-one years (1959–89) was 896,500 hectares, less than the 1 million hectares planned to be added in five years. Targets for six provinces (not shown on the table) set increases of irrigated land ranging from 50 percent to 300 percent in one year, which are too optimistic, to say the least.

In meetings to analyze the FP—all presided over by Castro, who constantly intervened in the discussion—delegates repeatedly acknowledged the failure to fulfill the 1990 targets (both in output and irrigation), explained the failures, and faithfully promised to accomplish the 1991 goals. For instance, in Pinar del Rio the unrealized irrigation target for 1990 was 1,000 hectares, but a target of 3,000 was set for the following year. In Camagüey there was a bad crop of rice in 1990, but the target of 130,000 tons for 1991 was considered feasible. In Matanzas, the head of an agro-industrial sugar complex reported that its output targets had not been met since 1988 due to managerial inefficiency and inadequate manpower, but gave assurances that things would change for the 1991 harvest.[93]

According to Cuban economist J. L. Rodríguez, the initial FP targets set in 1990 for 1995 have been "modified or postponed" because of the substantial cut in imports from the former USSR. He adds that, due to the lag between sowing and harvesting some crops, results might take several years to materialize. Finally, he argues that performance has been better so far in citrus, tubers, and vegetables than in cattle, pigs, and poultry, but he provides figures for few products, scattered over the 1990–92 period and often not comparable with previous data on national production. In April 1992 Castro announced the halting of several key FP projects: the construction of new dams and irrigation systems (including the special ones in sugar and rice), the organization of new labor brigades, and the construction of forty-four permanent camps in Havana.[94] In April 1992 Castro announced the halting of several key FP projects: the construction of new dams and irrigation systems (including the special ones in sugar and rice), the organization of new labor brigades, and the construction of forty-four permanent camps in Havana.[95]

The Other Alternative: Market-Oriented Reform

Faced with a desperate need to reintegrate Cuba into the world capitalist market, raise domestic efficiency, and increase the supply of consumer goods, in 1990 a few Cuban economists began to look at economic reform as the lesser of two evils. There was an ongoing nonpublicized discussion of possibly combining a socialist framework with market mechanisms—which, the Cubans hastened to assure me, are not exclusive of capitalism.

Although I spoke with only a small group of academic economists and other social scientists in Havana, I realized that the debate did not center so much on whether to use market tools, but on how far they should be employed and how to avoid their negative consequences. Two economists argued that it is useless to ignore or repress such mechanisms—they emerge anyway, as the black market demonstrates. Moreover, satisfying the population's urgent needs should transcend the desire to curtail profiteering by a small group that could help to meet those necessities. Finally, some asked, if the state cannot satisfy urgent needs, why not allow a regulated market or private activity to do it?[96]

A U.S. diplomat stationed in Havana noted in the fall of 1990 that midlevel technicians were calling for privatization of personal services the state is unable to provide and reintroducing the free peasant markets, production bonuses, and other mechanisms abolished or greatly reduced under the RP. He cautioned, however, that these technicians did not want a global market reform, merely small gradual changes to avoid further economic decline and promote some improvement. The well-known economist Eugenio Balari told a U.S. journalist: "Why should the state concern itself with running things like ice cream stands and barber shops?" He added that state taxi drivers offer bad service, do not care for the cabs, and pocket part of their earnings, yet if the state sold the cabs to the divers, they would give excellent service and take good care of their cars.[97]

Open-minded Cuban economists and technicians nevertheless harbor many reservations about market mechanisms, often because they have observed the unintended adverse consequences of market reforms in Eastern Europe and the USSR. For instance, they see the private sector as playing a positive role: eliminating the state monopoly and introducing healthy competition to improve state efficiency. But there could be a destructive snowball effect as the private sector demands increasing inputs, accumulates wealth, and presents a frontal challenge to the state.

Problems caused by the disappearance or sharp reduction of the social safety net is a major preoccupation: (1) high unemployment (apparently the Cubans have not discussed remedies such as unemployment compensation and retraining); (2) severe economic inequality (one argument was that equality is the cement that keeps the Cuban people together, but when I rebutted that there were inequalities under socialism— in housing, access to special stores, automobiles—there was no reply); (3) price increases that would sharply reduce consumption for low-income groups (an interesting suggestion was to subsidize people rather than goods); and (4) reduction of social benefits such as free education, health care, and social security. Private ownership of the means of production seemed to be a taboo, as it was never directly discussed.[98]

In light of these stimulating discussions, my meeting with Vice President Rodríguez was anticlimactic. Although he led the proreform forces in the 1963–66 debate against the Guevarists and later took flexible positions when interviewed by foreigners, in this meeting he was quite orthodox: he played down the importance of the 1986 abolition of free peasant markets (arguing that they had a very small role as suppliers of consumer goods), asserted that Cubans do not think for one minute about private property, and stood solidly behind all the RP measures. The most liberal thing Rodríguez said was that the parameters of private activity had to be defined.[99] At age seventy-seven and loaded with honors, he understandably did not want to confront the Maximum Leader who, in Machiavellian fashion, chose him to respond to the first article criticizing Cuba published in the Soviet press.

Rodríguez's safe orthodoxy reflects Castro's stubborn dogmatism. The Cuban president has rejected all market-oriented reforms, even those implemented in countries that are still socialist, such as China:

Reforms? Capitalist reforms? Never! Everybody must know that the revolution won't back up even one millimeter [on this]. . . . We cannot solve the problems of society by copying capitalism. . . . We are not going to "privatize" absolutely anything; on the contrary we must progressively socialize more. . . . The problems of distribution, commerce and marketing, restaurants, small services cannot be solved with "privatization." . . . It is impossible to divide the state land into parcels. . . . In other socialist countries this land was distributed so that private property would solve the [agricultural] problem, as in China [rather than decollectivization, China has used contracts of state farms and factories with families or groups of workers], but they have plenty of people to work the land. . . . [Ownership of the means of production] cannot be by a group of workers as some have tried to smuggle into socialist ideas [this was just after this mechanism was approved in the USSR]. . . . Group property is not and will never be socialist, it will simply be group capitalism. . . . We are waging a battle against them [private farmers, who declined from 101,900 to 70,000 in 1988–90]. . . . The free peasant market could not solve the food supply problem. If we believe we are going to solve that problem with . . . prehistoric production methods we would be nuts. . . . The state is the only one that can do it. . . . If the party squeezes to a maximum the *merolicos* [private street vendors and tiny producers] then I will be happy [to] give all my support to it [because] they are enemies of socialism.[100]

Since 1990 Castro's speeches increasingly include attacks on individuals and groups of people inside Cuba who are "skeptical," "disaffected," "demoralized," "critical," "defeatist," "halting." Economic reformers have become the president's target; he calls them "imperialist puppets," "political snipers," "fifth columnists," and "traitors" and threatens them with harsh retaliation. As I discussed in chapter 5, in the Fourth Party Congress Castro sternly opposed reintroducing the free peasant markets and, in general, the Congress quashed market-oriented reform in Cuba—even the Chinese variant that manages to combine political repression with economic progress.

The following quotations from Castro's speeches in 1990–91 unequivocally show his aversion to market reform, his willingness to smash those who oppose him and to take the whole nation with him in his opposition:

> Some currents entered here . . . people who wanted to introduce things from abroad and began to campaign against socialism, Marxism-Leninism with the pretext of improving it. . . . There might be some disaffected people around ["some second-rate critics"] spreading their ideas in a sneaky way . . . who abhor [our] heroic spirit . . . and dream about being able to divide us. . . . Some have boasted that the time for heroic deeds has passed. . . . When the going gets a little hard, defeatists start in: "Well, we have to be careful, just in case we should think about some reforms." . . . There are fools . . . who harbor illusions and think that fifth columns can be organized here. Keep a close watch on those people . . . many of them are not raising the flag of reaction and imperialism openly; instead they say they want to "improve" the revolution. . . . Those who think they can repeat here the story of what has happened in other countries are headed for a collision . . . we will never allow anyone to play at that here, never! . . . They will be crushed by the people, the Committees for the Defense of the Revolution. . . . Serving as imperialist puppets at this time would be the same as becoming the greatest traitors in Cuban history. . . . Keep up the guard and come out resolutely against the few citizens who have lost their morale and try to pass their demoralization to the rest. We will never surrender . . . we will know how to die in battle. . . . If to crush the revolution they had to kill all the people, the people will be willing to die in support of their leaders.[101]

Conclusions

The prospects of Cuba's compensating for the loss of trade with Eastern Europe and the USSR by expanding trade with China, as well as developed and developing market economies, are not promising—at least not in near future. China cannot export to Cuba most of the capital goods, manufactures, and spare parts that Eastern Europe and the former USSR used to provide. The increase in the purchase of sugar by China is small, due to that nation's growing self-sufficiency and other factors, and it has absorbed only a tiny fraction of the sugar surplus left by Cuba's former buyers in the vanished CMEA.

Trade with Western Europe, Canada, and Japan steadily declined through the 1980s and particularly after 1986, due to Cuba's lack of saleable exports and fresh credit; in addition, the European Community is a growing net exporter of sugar. In Asia, competition from Australia, Thailand, and other closer and more efficient sugar producers presents a serious challenge to Cuba. Trade with Latin America is very small and deficitary, as many potential partners are either sugar exporters or self-sufficient. Cuba's expansion of trade in the region is also obstructed by U.S. dominance, poor competitiveness of Cuban exports, and U.S. free trade agreements with Canada and Mexico. Foreign investment has been growing in Cuba, but we lack data to measure its magnitude and economic impact. Finally, the United States is tightening the embargo on the island, and U.S. subsidiaries abroad have been prohibited from trading and investing in Cuba.

A necessary condition for Cuba's reintegration into the capitalist market is export diversification, a frustrated dream for almost 100 years of the Cuban Republic. But the potential for significantly expanding traditional and nontraditional exports is quite limited, at least for some years. Natural and technical impediments will prevent a substantial increase in sugar production well beyond the 1986–91 average output of 7.5 million tons, and even the doubtful official figure for the 1992 crop was 500,000 tons below that figure, due to domestic and external constraints.

The grandiose plans to triple nickel output have not materialized, and, after a modest increase in 1988–89, there has been a decline owing to the shutdown of a large new plant and the fuel shortage. The lack of advanced technology, the poor quality of Cuban ore, and the fuel shortage are serious obstacles. Output of tobacco leaf has oscillated with a tendency to decline, and production of the famous Havana cigars has halved—this before the major world buyer of Cuban tobacco ended its dealings, alleging a deterioration in quality. Reexports of Soviet oil, the main source of hard currency in the 1980s, ended in 1990.

The most promising sources of revenue are citrus fruits, fish/seafood, biotechnological/medical exports, and tourism. In spite of dramatic increases in domestic output and export shares (ten and seven times), citrus and fish/seafood face limitations, and output of both products significantly declined in 1989. Reportedly, biotechnical and medical exports are rapidly increasing and appear most promising; however, we lack solid data on the profitability of this industry, quality of products, and value of total exports. Although biotechnical exports to the USSR were expanding fast, Cuba must overcome fierce market competition to make this a successful source of hard currency. Finally, tourism has much potential but in 1990 yielded only 0.6 percent of GSP; optimistic plans project a four- to fivefold increase in revenue in 1991–95, but Cuba will have to improve its services and marketing to get tourists to return and to keep attracting foreign investors.

All additional annual revenue from new nontraditional exports plus tourism ($1.5 billion at best) is grossly insufficient to offset the annual losses in trade and aid resulting from the collapse of socialism (more than $6 billion). The island must develop an "export culture" to improve the quantity, assortment, quality, and stability of its exports and, to achieve that end, must make domestic management more responsive to world demand and prices.

It is improbable that in the foreseeable future Cuba can find either domestic or external sources of oil to substitute for the 45–70 percent cut in Soviet supply. Domestic oil output declined 31 percent in 1986–91, and Cuban crude is of poor quality. Despite various contracts for oil exploration and production, actual results are disappointing so far; even if large quantities of good-quality oil were found, it would take from four to six years to produce oil. Cuba's nuclear plant in Juraguá, long paralyzed or progressing very slowly, was canceled. Production of alcohol from sugar is out—prospects are poor for good sugar crops in the immediate future. And the leaders of three major oil-exporting countries in Latin America have recently stated that they do not intend to export oil to Cuba at subsidized prices.

The FP makes good sense and it is urgently needed. What is questionable is the huge size and cost of this program, its design and implementation, its unrealistic targets, and its underestimation of the severe limitations imposed by the worst crisis endured by the revolution. It is probable that the FP will increase output of some foodstuffs in some provinces and municipalities. But the overall FP targets are not feasible and cannot be met.

The question then is whether the partial gains from the FP justify such an enormous investment of capital and human resources; what damage could such an ambitious program inflict on the rest of the economy? Alas, history repeats itself, and the unthinkable scenario of 1970 is back in the revolution's theater. One important element of the plot has dramatically changed, however: in the 1990s the USSR cannot save Cuba from the crisis—in fact, the downfall of the USSR is a major cause of the current crisis—and the Cuban population, suffering more deprivation than ever before, might not accept another failure.

Presenting the FP as an ideological and political battle that will end in victory, thus proving the feasibility of socialist agriculture and solving Cuba's food problem once and for all, might win Castro time domestically and confront the world crisis of socialism externally. But the failure of this colossal program could lead to defeat on all fronts.

Despite sympathy toward modest market-oriented reform in some intellectual and technical circles in Cuba, Castro's stern opposition and the outcome of the Fourth Party Congress make that alternative politically unfeasible—at least for the near future. And yet, such reform is the only realistic alternative to overcome the current crisis. Hence, the forecast is gloomy: gradual economic deterioration and increasing frustration and popular discontent. Although there are significant differences between Cuba and the former socialist countries of East Europe, the worsening situation could eventually invite the type of radical change in Cuba that took place in those societies.

NOTES

Abbreviations used in notes:
    AEC: *Anuario Estadístico de Cuba*
    BEC: *Boletín Estadístico de Cuba*
    GWR: *Granma Weekly Review*

I greatly appreciate the bibliographical help provided by my research assistants, Ivan Brenes and Rafael Tamayo; the various versions of this chapter typed by my secretary, Mimi Ranallo; the editing by Shirley Kregar; the materials supplied by José Alonso; the financial support of Latin American Studies Association for a trip to Cuba in July 1990; and the financial support of the Mellon Foundation to conduct research in several European countries in 1990–91.

1. Miguel Figueras, interview, Havana, July 11, 1990; José Luis Rodríguez and Pedro Pablo Cuscó, interview, Havana, July 10, 1990.

2. Comité Estatal de Estadísticas, *AEC 1986* to *1989.*

3. *GWR*, January 27, 1991, p. 9; *Granma International*, May 5, 1991, p. 7; *Granma*, February 19, 1992, p. 6.

4. Ramón Sánchez Parodi, deputy prime minister, quoted by Anne Marie O'Connor, "East Bloc Upheavals Upset Castro," *Pittsburgh Post-Gazette*, January 2, 1990, p. 2; Fidel Castro, "Speech at the 30th Anniversary of the CDRs," *GWR*, October 7, 1990, p. 4, "Fidel's Closing Speech at 8th Regular Session," ibid., January 3, 1991, p. 3, and "Speech at the Inauguration of the Family Doctor Home," ibid., February 10, 1991; Michael Browning, "Cuba Boosts Ties with China," *Miami Herald*, October 17, 1991.

5. Ted Turner, interview with Fidel Castro, CNN, June 25, 1990.

6. Fidel Castro, "Discurso en la Clausura del VII Congreso del Sindicato de Trabajadores de la Educación . . . ," *Granma*, December 22, 1991.

7. Tu Guangnan, member of Beijing Latin American Institute, "Cuba Chinese Relations Today," lecture at the University of Pittsburgh, March 24, 1992; Cuban ambassador in Beijing, quoted in Browning, "Cuba Boosts Ties with China," and "Looking to the Future," *La Sociedad Económica*, Bulletin no. 13, 1992.

8. Julio Carranza, vice director of the Centro de Estudios de América (CEA), Havana, July 11, 1990; Pedro Monreal, "Cuba y la nueva economía mundial: El reto de la inserción en América Latina y el Caribe" (Havana: CEA, 1990); Carlos Rafael Rodríguez, "Cuba's Predicament: A Fate Worse than Imperialism?" *NPQ*, Winter 1991, p. 10.

9. Discussions in Havana with Cuban economists at CEA and CIEM.

10. Archibald R. M. Ritter, "The Cuban Economy in the 1990s," *Journal of Interamerican Studies and World Affairs 32*, no. 3 (Fall 1990): 137; *Financial Times*, August 7, 1990, p. 4; and "Cuba no puede pagar," *El Nuevo Herald*, October 16, 1991; "Debt for Equity Discussed," *Cuba Business*, December 1991, p. 5.

11. See Jorge Pérez-López, *The 1982 Cuban Joint Venture Law: Context, Assessment and Prospects* (University of Miami: Institute of Interamerican Studies, 1985); Comité Ejecutivo del Consejo de Ministros, *Posibilidad de negocios conjuntos con Cuba*, Havana, March 1991; "Resolución sobre el desarrollo económico," *Granma*, October 23, 1991, p. 6; Arleen Rodríguez Derivet, "Lo que no es eficiente no es socialista" (interview with Carlos Lage), *Juventud Rebelde*, January 26, 1992, pp. 6–7; Jorge Domínguez, information provided at the UCLA Seminar on Cuba, Los Angeles, February 28, 1992.

12. Business International, *Developing Business Strategies for Cuba* (New York: 1992), p. 26.

13. Alberto Arrinda Piñeiro, "Una compleja categoría económica," *Tribuna del Economista* 1, no. 4 (September 1989): 3.

14. Debate published in several issues of *Tribuna del Economista* 1, no. 3 (August 1989): 6; 1, no. 4 (September 1989): 3; 1, no. 5 (October 1989): 3; and 1, no. 11 (April 1990): 2.

15. Ibid.; J. L. Rodríguez, interview; Tania García, interview, Havana, National Bank of Cuba, July 12, 1990.

16. José Coma, "Rodríguez Vigil concluyó su visita a Cuba," *ABC* (Madrid), November 20, 1991, p. 51.

17. "Crisis at the Embassies," *Cuba Business* (August 1990), p. 1; "About Joint Ventures: Doing Business with Cuba," *GWR*, October 7, 1990, p. 8; IRELA, "Cuba: the Challenge of Change," Madrid, Dossier 27, October 1990, p. 18.

18. *El Pais* (International Edition), April 22, 1991, p. 12.

19. *El Nuevo Herald*, July 19, 1991, pp. 1A, 2A, 4A; ibid., July 20, 1991, p. 8A. The second summit was widely covered by the *Miami Herald* and *El Pais*, July 20–30, 1992); see also "Felipe González se distancia definitivamente de Castro," *La Vanguardia* (Barcelona), August 17, 1992, p. 8.

20. Rodríguez Derivet, "Lo que no es," pp. 6–7.

21. *AEC 1986* to *1989;* Peter Buzzanell, "Cuba's Sugar Industry Facing a New Order," *Sugar and Sweetener* (March 1992): p. 38.

22. John M. Kirk, "Surrogate Diplomacy," *Cuba Business,* August 1990, pp. 3, 5; Buzzanell, "Cuba's Sugar," pp. 37–39; Howard W. French, "Cuba, Long Forbidden, Wins Major Attention Abroad," *New York Times,* April 19, 1992, p. F5; Gillian Gunn, "Cuba's Search for Alternatives," *Current History* 91, no. 562 (February 1992): 60–61.

23. *Marazul Boletín,* March 1992, p. 3. The value of the annual remittance is from Jaime Suchlicki, America's Society Seminar on Cuba, New York, March 13, 1992.

24. U.S. Department of the Treasury, Office of Foreign Assets Control, "An Analysis of Licensed Trade with Cuba by Foreign Subsidiaries of U.S. Companies"; Susan Kaufman Purcell, "Collapsing Cuba," *Foreign Affairs* 17, no. 1 (1992): 144; "Second-Hand Wire," *Economist,* March 21, 1992, p. 47.

25. Business International, *Strategies for Cuba,* p. 26. See also discussion on U.S. subsidiaries on pp. 27–29.

26. Alfonso Chardy, "Phone Link May Ring Up Cash for Cuba," *Miami Herald,* February 23, 1991, pp. 1A, 18A; "Second-Hand Wire," p. 47; French, "Long-Forbidden," p. F5.

27. "Another Turn of the Screw," *Cuba Business,* August 1990, p. 8; "U.S. Subsidiary Trade with Cuba," *Cuban Business,* October 1990, p. 16; information from Florida Senator Connie Mack's office in Washington, D.C., March 1991; *Marazul Boletín,* pp. 2–3; Kaufmann Purcell, "Collapsing Cuba," p. 145.

28. For two divergent viewpoints on U.S. relations with Cuba, see Gillian Gunn, "Will Castro Fall?" *Foreign Policy* 79 (Summer 1990): 145–50; Susan Kaufman Purcell, "Cuba's Cloudy Future," *Foreign Affairs* 69, no. 3 (Summer, 1990): 113–30; and Cathy Booth, "The Man Who Would Oust Castro," *Time,* October 26, 1992, p. 56.

29. Ricardo Alarcón, "Necesidad de poner fin al bloqueo económico, comercial y financiero [del] gobierno de los Estados Unidos . . . contra Cuba," New York, Permanent Mission of Cuba to the UN, November 13, 1991; Kaufman Purcell, "Collapsing Cuba," p. 140.

30. Turner, interview.

31. Monreal, "Cuba y la nueva economía mundial," pp. 8–11; *AEC 1986* to *1989*.

32. *AEC 1989; GWR,* March 25, 1990, p. 10; Kaufman Purcell, "Cuba's Cloudy Future," pp. 120–22; Gunn, "Cuba's Search," pp. 132–50; "Plena reanudación del nexo

con Colombia," *El Nuevo Herald,* November 23, 1991, p. 3A; Buzzanell, "Cuba's Sugar," p. 38.

33. "Mexico estudia invertir en Cuba," *El Nuevo Herald,* October 16, 1991; "Letting Cuba Down Gently," *Economist,* October 12, 1991, p. 42; French, "Long Forbidden," p. F5.

34. "Declaración de la Asamblea Nacional del Poder Popular," *Granma,* December 28, 1991, p. 1.

35. Monreal, "Cuba y la nueva economía mundial," pp. 11–24. The "natural market" view is summarized by IIE, *Situación actual de la economía cubana* (Havana: JUCEPLAN, 1992), p. 12.

36. Ramón Martínez Carrera, "Cuba: Crecimiento económico e inestabilidad externa," *Economía y Desarrollo* 1 (January–February 1990): 30–35.

37. Isis Mañalich, "Lo que afecta a las exportaciones cubanas," *Tribuna del Economista* 1, no. 12 (May 1990): 10.

38. See, for instance, Claes Brundenius and Andrew Zimbalist, "Recent Studies on Cuban Economic Growth: A Review," *Comparative Economic Studies* 27, no. 1 (Spring 1985): 21–45; and for a reply, Carmelo Mesa-Lago and Jorge Pérez-López, "Imbroglios on the Cuban Economy," ibid., 75–78. The same argument was repeated by Zimbalist and Brundenius in *The Cuban Economy: Measurement and Analysis of Socialist Performance* (Baltimore: John Hopkins University Press, 1989): 143–45. See my critical review of this book in *Economic Development and Cultural Change,* 40, no. 2 (January 1992): 432–39. Finally, José Luis Rodríguez repeats these arguments in *Crítica a nuestros críticos* (Havana: Editorial Ciencias Sociales, 1988): 49–50, which are refuted in Carmelo Mesa-Lago, "Crítica a 'Crítica a nuestros críticos,' " CIEM, 1992.

39. Mañalich, "Lo que afecta," p. 10; and Angel Galicia, "¿Cultura exportadora?" *Tribuna del Economista* 1, no. 3 (August 1989): 10.

40. Peter J. Buzzanell and José F. Alonso, "Cuba's Sugar Economy. Recent Performance and Challenges for the 1990s," *Sugar and Sweetener* (June 1989): 17–28. See also *AEC 1988* and *1989;* and *GWR,* July 10, 1988, p. 4.

41. Buzzanell and Alonso, "Cuba's Sugar Economy," pp. 18–26. Also see Robert Graham, "Sugar Record in Sight," *Financial Times* (Special Supplement on Cuba), February 17, 1989, p. 36; conversation with Manuel Sánchez Pérez, Los Angeles, April 22, 1988; *GWR,* December 28, 1989, pp. 1–5.

42. *AEC 1985* to *1989;* Buzzanell, "Cuba's Sugar," pp. 159–60.

43. Rodríguez Derivet, "Lo que no es," pp. 6–7; "Looking to the Future"; "Siege Economy," *Oxford Analytica,* February 5, 1992; Buzzanel, "Cuba's Sugar," p. 32; Nicolás Rivero, "The Future for Cuban Sugar," *International Sugar and Sweetener Report,* 124, no. 10 (March 20, 1990): 161–62.

44. Pedro Monreal, conversations at a meeting on Cuba at the University of Warwick, May 11, 1989; *Tribuna del Economista* 1, no. 4 (September 1989): 6–7; "Nickel," *GWR,* January 21, 1990, p. 12; *Cuba Quarterly Situation Report,* 2d quarter III, 1990, p. 12; Archibald Ritter, conversations in Havana, July 8, 1990; "Discuten futuro del níquel," *El Nuevo Herald,* June 22, 1990, pp. 1, 4.

45. *BEC 1966* to *1971; AEC 1972* to *1989; GWR,* April 8, 1990, p. 3.

46. Ibid.; *Tribuna del Economista* 1, no. 6 (November 1989): 1.

47. *BEC 1966* to *1971; AEC 1972* to *1989;* Tim Coone, "A Fleet Near Full Capacity," *Financial Times,* February 17, 1989, p. 36.

48. Interview with a CIGB technician, Havana, July 11, 1990; "Lo que se ha logrado en el campo de investigaciones científicas," *Granma,* February 25, 1991, pp. 3–4; IIE, *Situación actual,* pp. 32–38.

49. C. R. Rodríguez, interview, Havana, July 12, 1990, and "Speech at the 45th Meeting of the CMEA," *GWR,* January 21, 1990, p. 10; Gunn, "Will Castro," p. 139; ibid., April 29, 1990, pp. 1, 3; ibid., August 3, 1990, pp. 3–5.

50. *AEC 1989;* J. L. Rodríguez, "Commentary," pp. 4–5; Miguel Figueras, quoted by Julie M. Feinsilver, "Will Cuba's Wonder Drugs Lead to Political and Economic Wonders? Capitalizing on Biotechnology and Medical Exports," *Cuban Studies* 22 (1992): 79–111.

51. Feinsilver, "Will Cuba's Wonder Drugs?" See also Richard Boudreaux, "Cuba Hopes its Doctors Can Cure the Economy," *Los Angeles Times,* February 19, 1991, p. 4.

52. Conversation with Archibald Ritter, Havana, July 11, 1990; and Castro, "Speech at the Closing Session of 5th Congress of the FMC," *GWR,* March 18, 1990, p. 2.

53. Feinsilver, "Will Cuba's Wonder Drugs?"

54. *Ibid.*; Boudreaux, "Cuba Hopes," p. 4; Susy P. de Ulises, "Biotechnology: A Change of Gene," *Prisma* (April–May 1992): p. 33.

55. Feinsilver, "Will Cuba's Wonder Drugs?"; Joel Gutiérrez, "Castro elogia droga que da vigor sexual," *El Nuevo Herald,* October 15, 1991, p. 4A.

56. *AEC 1972* to *1989;* R. Graham, "Austerity and Experiment," *Financial Times,* February 17, 1989, p. 34; *GWR,* April 29, 1988, p. 3; ibid., July 22, 1990, p. 9; Ramón Martínez Fernández, "El turismo internacional en la perspectiva económica de Cuba," *Tribuna del Economista* 1, no. 7 (December 1989): 12–13; Miguel A. Rodríguez-Espí, "The Cuban Tourist Industry," unpublished, University of Pittsburgh, December 1991; "Aumentará en un 40% la recepción de turistas," *Granma,* January 28, 1992, p. 2.

57. Ibid.; Gareth Jenkins, "Beyond Basic Needs: Cuba's Search for Stable Development in the 1990s," in *Cuba in Transition: Crisis and Transformation,* ed. Sendor Halebsky and John M. Kirk (Boulder: Westview Press, 1992): 145–46; Fidel Castro, "Discurso en la inauguración del IV Congreso del PCC," *Granma,* October 14, 1991, pp. 6–7; Business International, *Strategies for Cuba,* pp. 64–65.

58. Fidel Castro, "Speech at the Opening of Two Hotels at Varadero Beach," *GWR,* May 27, 1990, pp. 2–3.

59. Jenkins, "Beyond Basic Needs," p. 145; Rodríguez-Espí, "Cuban Tourist"; "The Self-Laceration of Cuba," *Economist,* July 28, 1990, p. 32; and my own observations on trips to Cuba in 1978, 1979, 1980, and 1990.

60. Gillian Gunn, UCLA Seminar on Cuba, February 28, 1992; Andrés M. Oppenheimer, America's Society Seminar on Cuba, March 13, 1992; Rodríguez-Espí, "Cuban Tourist."

61. Donald E. Schulz, ed., "Cuba and the Future," U.S. Army War College, January 16, 1992, p. 3; "Siege Economy."

62. *AEC 1981* to *1989; Compendio Estadístico de Energía 1989;* G. Zuikov et al., "Informe sobre la economía cubana," Miami, 1992, pp. 29–30; Rodríguez Derivet, "Lo que no es," pp. 6-7; Deborah Hargreaves, "The Coup Collapses, Soviet Energy a Pri-

ority," *Financial Times,* August 22, 1991, p. 5; José Alonso, "Programas energéticos en la URSS y sus posibles efectos en Cuba," Miami, Radio Martí, August 27, 1991, pp. 1–5.

63. José de Córdoba, "Cuba's Search for Offshore Oil to Replace Soviet Crude Supplies Appears to Falter," *Wall Street Journal,* April 15, 1992, p. A17. See also Kaufman Purcell, "Collapsing," pp. 135–36; Rodríguez Derivet, "Lo que no es," pp. 6-7; French, "Long Forbidden," p. F5; Eric Ehrmann and Christopher Barton, "Stop Propping Up the Castro Regime," *The New York Times,* December 8, 1991, p. F15; and "De Cuba" (Havana: IPS, 2 April 1992).

64. *GWR,* October 28, 1984, p. 2, ibid., March 24, 1985, p. 2; Tim Coone, "The Nuclear Future," *Financial Times,* February 17, 1989, p. 37; *Economics Press Service* 3, no. 3 (February 1990); Zuikov et al., "Informe," p. 30; Ehrman and Barton, "Stop Propping," p. F15; "Información a la población sobre medidas adicionales con motivo de la escasez de combustible y otras importaciones," *Granma,* December 20, 1991, p. 1; *Notmex,* March 24, 1992; Miami Whitefield, "Work Is Suspended on Nuclear Plant, *Miami Herald,* September 6, 1992, p. 13A.

65. "Castro's Interview for Brazilian Bandeirantes TV," São Paulo, March 15, 1990.

66. "Letting Cuba Down Gently," *Economist,* October 12, 1991, p. 42; "Cuba Seeks Barter Iranian Oil for Sugar," *Times of the Americas,* January 8, 1992, p. B1; "Conferencia de prensa del grupo de los tres," *Granma,* October 25, 1991, p. 2; "Conferencia de Prensa ofrecida por Fidel Castro," *Granma,* October 26, 1991, p. 3; Kaufman Purcell, "Collapsing," p. 140; Ehrman and Barton, "Stop Propping," p. F15.

67. Castro, "Speech at the 30th Anniversary," pp. 3–4, and "Discurso en las Conclusiones de la Asamblea Provincial del Partido en La Habana," *Granma,* February 5, 1991, pp. 3–4; discussions at a meeting on Cuba at the University of Warwick, May 11–13, 1989.

68. Castro, "Discurso en las Conclusiones de la Asamblea," pp. 3–4.

69. Sources on production goals for foodstuffs are, unless specified: Castro, "Speech at the 30th Anniversary," pp. 3–4, and "Discurso en las Conclusiones de la Asamblea," pp. 3 5; "El pais realiza un excepcional e inteligente esfuerzo" [discussions at the National Assembly], *Granma,* December 27, 1990, pp. 3–5; "Fidel at the Closing Session of 5th National Forum on Spare Parts," *GWR,* December 30, 1990, p. 2; "Fidel's Closing Speech at 8th Regular Session of National Assembly of People's Power," *GWR,* January 13, 1991, pp. 2–3; "Cuando defendemos el socialismo," *Granma,* February 19, 1991, pp. 4–5; and "Cuba: Programa Nacional de Acción," Cumbre Mundial de la Infancia, Havana, December 1991, pp. 37–50.

70. Cited in "Economy Stumbling Toward Free Market," *Pittsburgh Post-Gazette,* March 4, 1991, p. 7.

71. Castro, "Discurso en las Conclusiones de la Asamblea," p. 5 and "Fidel en la clausura de la Asamblea Provincial, en La Habana," *Granma,* February 26, 1991, p. 4.

72. "Presentación del Informe sobre el Programa Alimentario," *Granma,* December 27, 1990, p. 2; Castro, "Discurso en las Conclusiones de la Asamblea," pp. 3, 5.

73. "Economy Stumbling," p. 7; Castro, "El pais realiza," pp. 3–5, "Speech at the 30th Anniversary," p. 3, and "Discurso en las Conclusiones de la Asamblea," p. 3.

74. "Two Million Workers Mobilized," *GWR*, November 11, 1990, p. 1; "El pais realiza," p. 4; "Resumen de los debates en la Asamblea Nacional," *Granma*, December 29, 1990, p. 2; "Pleno del Comité Nacional de la FMC," *Granma*, January 24, 1991, p. 8; and Castro, "Discurso en las Conclusiones de la Asamblea," p. 3.

75. Castro, "Speech at the 30th Anniversary," pp. 3–4; "Fidel Closing Speech at 8th," pp. 2–3; "Clausuró Fidel," *Granma*, February 18, 1991, p. 1; "Lo que se ha logrado," *Granma*, February 25, 1991, p. 5; "Fidel en la Clausura de la Asamblea Provincial," p. 4; Fidel Castro, "Discurso en la inauguración del frigorífero Proeza Laboral," *Granma*, April 3, 1991, p. 5.

76. Ibid.; Castro, "Discurso en las Conclusiones de la Asamblea," pp. 4–5, and "Unicamente con la Revolución, se pueden hacer estos planes," *Granma*, February 4, 1991, pp. 4–5.

77. Most of the following analyses come from "Unicamente con la Revolución," pp. 1, 4–5. See also "Fidel Interviewed by Granma," *GWR*, October 7, 1990, p. 3; "El país realiza un excepcional," pp. 3–5; and Castro, "Discurso en las Conclusiones de la Asamblea," p. 5.

78. *Cuba Business*, October 1990: p. 3; "Pleno del Comité Nacional de la FMC," p. 8.

79. "Resumen de los debates," p. 3; "Unicamente con la Revolución," pp. 4–5; *Tribuna del Economista*, June 1989, p. 9; "Economy Stumbling," p. 7.

80. *AEC 1988;* "Presentación del informe," p. 2; "El país realiza," pp. 3–5; "Fidel at the Closing Session of 5th," p. 2; "Fidel Closing Speech at 8th," pp. 2–3; "Economy Stumbling," p. 7.

81. Ibid.; Castro, "Discurso en la inauguración del frigorífero," p. 5.

82. "Fidel Interviewed," p. 3; "Fidel Closing Speech at 8th," pp. 3 5; "Cuando defendemos el socialismo," pp. 4–5; Castro, "Discurso en las Conclusiones de la Asamblea," p. 5, and "Discurso en la inauguración del frigorífero," p. 5; "Fidel en la reunión del Comité Ejecutivo del Consejo de Ministros," *Granma*, May 18, 1991, p. 3; "Discurso en la clausura del V Congreso del Sindicato de Trabajadores Agropecuarios," *Granma*, November 26, 1991, pp. 3–5.

83. *AEC 1979* to *1989;* Castro, "Speech at the 30th Anniversary," pp. 3–4; "Fidel at Closing Session of 5th," p. 2; "Fidel Closing Speech at the 8th," pp. 2–3; "Cuando defendemos el socialismo," p. 5; Leonardo Cuesta Alvarez, "Falta pienso pero tambien organización y disciplina," *El Militante Comunista*, no.4 (April 1990): 20–25; "Economy Stumbling," p. 7; "Isla de la Juventud: De la tierra cuanto pueda dar," *Granma*, January 3, 1991, p. 3; "Cuba: Programa," p. 48.

84. "Fidel at the Meeting on Cattle Breeding," *Granma International*, June 2, 1991, p. 2; Fidel Castro, "Discurso en la inauguración del IV Congreso," and "Discurso en la Clausura del V Congreso," pp. 3–5.

85. "El pais realiza," pp. 3–4; "Resumen de los debates," pp. 2–4; Castro, "Discurso en la inauguración del frigorífico," p. 4; "A levantar parejo," *Juventud Rebelde*, March 29, 1992, p. 3.

86. Castro, "Speech at the 30th Anniversary," pp. 3–4; "Fidel Interviewed," p. 3.

87. "Fidel's Closing Speech at 8th," pp. 2–3, and Castro, "Discurso en las Conclusiones de la Asamblea," p. 5. See also "Cooperative Members and Private Farmers Taking Sure Steps," *GWR*, February 10, 1991, p. 4.

88. "Economy Stumbling," p. 7.

89. See note 80.

90. "Fidel en la Clausura de la Asamblea Provincial," p. 4; "Fidel Closing Speech at the 8th," pp. 2–3; Castro, "Discurso en las Conclusiones de la Asamblea," p. 5.

91. "Presentación del Informe sobre el Programa Alimentario," p. 2.

92. "Cooperative Members and Private Farmers," p. 4.

93. "El pais realiza," pp. 3–5; "Matanzas: Ante el reto del Período Especial," *Granma*, January 17, 1991, p. 4.

94. Rodríguez, "Commentary," p. 8.

95. F. Castro, "Discurso en la plenaria del 6° Congreso de la UJC," Havana Radio, April 4, 1992.

96. This is my interpretation of views expressed by several Cuban social scientists in two round-table discussions held in Havana in July 1990.

97. Fulton Armstrong, Conference in Washington, D.C., October 19, 1990; Eugenio Balari, quoted by Anne Marie O'Connor, "Fidel's Last Resort," *Esquire*, March 1992, p. 57.

98. See note 95.

99. C. R. Rodríguez, interview.

100. Castro, "Closing Speech at the Second National Meeting of Production Cooperatives," *GWR*, June 1, 1986, p. 3; "Speech to Close Pedagogy 90 Congress," *GWR*, February 5, 1990, p. 2; "Speech at the Session Closing the 16th Congress of the CTC," *GWR*, February 11, 1990, p. 4; "Fidel en la Clausura de la Asamblea Provincial," p. 3.

101. Castro, "Speech at the Session Closing the 16th," p. 4; "Speech at the Closing of the 5th Congress of the FMC," *GWR*, March 18, 1990, p. 11; ibid., March 25, 1990, p. 2; "Speech at the 30th Anniversary of the CDRs," pp. 1, 9; "Discurso en la Clausura del Congreso," p. 6; "Discurso en la Clausura del IV Congreso del PCC," pp. 8–10.

7

Cuba and the
Central American Connection

◇ ◇ ◇

MITCHELL A. SELIGSON

IT IS MORE than accidental that the end of the cold war coincides with the termination of the "hot wars" in Central America. The international tensions related to the East-West conflict spilled over to the Third World, and the easing of those tensions has helped bring a measure of peace to Central America. Revolutionary Cuba loomed quite large for the Central American republics throughout the cold war. For some, it was the most proximate external threat to their stability. For others, Cuba represented their closest ally in the struggle against U.S. imperialism. For Cuba, Central America presented perhaps its best opportunity to find allies in its conflict with the United States and in its effort to spread revolutionary socialism throughout the Third World.

This chapter looks at Cuba as it relates to and is perceived by Central America. First it reviews, in broad strokes, this relationship during a period of revolutionary turmoil in Central America. It then examines the policy implications of the relationship, with particular focus on the policy-relevant opinions of the mass public in Central America. The data come from a survey of more than 4,000 respondents drawn from the five Central American countries plus Panama.

Cuba's Relations with Central America: An Overview

The cold war is over, but cold war thinking in the United States is still with us. Paradoxically, while the cold war was a time of great uncertainty about the future, especially regarding the constant threat of nuclear annihilation, it was also a time of great certainty. It was certain that the Soviet Union, its allies, and communism were enemies of the United States. Identification of friend and foe was clear-cut. U.S. foreign policy was made in stark, black-and-white terms.

The end of the cold war has greatly reduced the threat of nuclear war, but it also has vastly increased the complexity of the world in which foreign policy is crafted. In Washington there has been much celebration—after all, "we won." But it is a mistake to think that the simplistic lenses that used to define the world during the cold war will provide the clear vision needed to understand the complexities of the new world order being constructed "after the fall."

Some optimistically see this new world order as wrought in the image of the United States. In military preeminence, the United States is certainly dominant. In the late 1940s the United States held an unchallenged monopoly of nuclear weapons. Today, while there are other nuclear powers, no one seriously doubts that the United States is primus inter pares. And in conventional warfare, as the war with Iraq demonstrated, no other nation can seriously challenge the United States.

But beyond the realm of military supremacy, the picture becomes far more nuanced. In the new world, friend and foe are no longer self-evident categories. It is a world exhibiting a great diversity of interests, interests that during the cold war tended to be sublimated to the larger struggle of East versus West.

Nowhere was this cold war pattern clearer than in Latin America. U.S. foreign policy there was long dominated by a national security doctrine firmly based on the East-West conflict. Other considerations, such as a defense of human rights, from time to time were added to the equation. But, as Lars Schoultz demonstrates, under this doctrine "Latin America becomes inert, a passive object of no intrinsic value, a place where the United States and the Soviet Union play out the drama of international politics. It is difficult to overemphasize how policy makers' dominant concern for security leads to this conception of Latin America."[1] The threat to U.S. security obviously came not from the Latin American military forces (whose principal threat was to the human rights of their own citizens) but, Schoultz argues, from the United States' potential loss of control over strategic raw materials, military bases, and sea lines of communication. The ultimate fear, of course, was that Soviet control over a Latin American nation would, as happened in the case of

Cuba, introduce the direct threat of Soviet nuclear missiles right in our own "backyard."

In the 1980s, the focal point of U.S. attention in this hemisphere was Central America. As President Ronald Reagan forcefully stated, "The national security of the Americas is at stake in Central America. If we cannot defend ourselves there, we cannot expect to prevail elsewhere. Our credibility would collapse, our alliances would crumble, and the safety of our homeland would be put in jeopardy."[2] As a result, the United States "drew the line" against communist aggression and funded the contras to unseat the Sandinistas in Nicaragua, while in El Salvador the State Department embarked upon its longest and most costly war— twelve years, $6 billion—since Vietnam.[3]

The concern with communist expansion in Central America was by no means misplaced. There is much evidence to support the view that by the early 1980s Central America had become a major, if not *the* major, focal point for Soviet and Cuban foreign policy in the Third World. Earlier in the cold war, Central America had been peripheral for the Soviet Union. A leading Soviet expert on Latin America, Kiva Maidanik, observes, "Nowhere have Soviet interests been fewer than with regard to Central America. The Soviet Union paid virtually no attention to this area until 1978."[4] But after the Sandinista victory and the outbreak of civil war in El Salvador, that policy was to change markedly. Maidanik argues that the Soviets saw themselves defending the sovereignty of small states against the North American goliath. Cuba's strong interest in Central America predates that of the Soviet Union. Almost from the outset of the Cuban revolution, Central America was seen as a logical area for the expansion of Cuban interests. Several factors created this perception, not the least among which was propinquity. But Central America also seemed ripe for revolution, given its poverty, large peasant populations, and extensive U.S. capital investment in the form of fruit companies that could serve as a target of social unrest. One might speculate that had it not been for Che Guevera's South American origin, his venture to create a guerrilla movement in Bolivia might well have occurred somewhere in Central America.

Cuba's interest in Central America was greatly increased by the Sandinista victory in Nicaragua. According to an extensive analysis, based on original Soviet and Cuban documents, Rodolfo Cerdas finds that "in 1982, the Communist Party Conference in Havana declared that the centre of gravity of the Latin American revolution had shifted to Central America and the Caribbean."[5] And Sergo Mikoyan, quoted by Cerdas, makes it clear that armed struggle, irresolvable by negotiation, would need to counter any bourgeois drift toward democratic transition.[6]

Whatever the degree of Soviet and Cuban involvement in Central America's struggles of the 1980s, the U.S. State Department produced a flood of reports that may have persuaded many in Central America to believe that such involvement was indeed extensive. Hence, whereas one recent study says that secret documents in the State Department's Bureau of Intelligence and Research reported only limited Soviet and Cuban interference in the region, State was saying publicly that the war in El Salvador was a "textbook case of indirect armed aggression by Communist powers through Cuba."[7] And even that analyst, sympathetic to the view that the Soviet-Cuban role was overblown, admits that both provided material assistance to the Salvadoran guerrillas.[8]

The Soviet Union's and Cuba's ability to project their power into the region was far more limited than their desire to support revolutionary struggles there. No responsible scholar has suggested that the Nicaraguan revolution of 1979 was a product of Soviet or Cuban efforts. Indeed, the revolution seemed to surprise Moscow and Havana as much as it did Washington. Soviet-line communists and the parties they represented in Nicaragua had little directly to do with the revolution and found themselves scrambling to keep up with the "objective conditions" created by the Frente Sandinista de Liberación Nacional (FSLN). Cole Blasier shows that the Soviet-line parties in both Nicaragua and El Salvador were peripheral to the main centers of revolutionary power and armed struggle.[9] Yet, once the Nicaraguan revolution occurred and civil war broke out in El Salvador, at least at the level of rhetoric and to a limited extent in terms of material support, the Soviet Union provided maximum backing to the insurgents in the early years of the Central American struggle.

Gorbachev's accession to power and his policies of perestroika and glasnost were to change the Soviet view and reduce its capabilities for international revolution. Cuba, however, remained hopeful that revolution could be spread to Central America. It invested heavily in Nicaragua and El Salvador. Ultimately, however, Cuba too recognized the difficulty of supporting revolutionary struggles in Central America.[10] The defeat of the Sandinistas in the 1990 elections, the breakdown of the Soviet Union in 1991, and the signing of the peace agreements in El Salvador in 1992 ended any hope that Central America would join Cuba in its socialism and opposition to the United States. In January 1992, Castro told an academic conference in Havana, "Times have changed, we have changed. Miliary aid outside our border is a thing of the past. The most important task is to see that the Cuban Revolution survives. Abroad we intend to live by accepted norms of international behavior."[11]

Cuba hopes to put aside the stigma of the cold war and help resolve its pressing economic difficulties by breaking out of the U.S.-imposed trade embargo. One way it has attempted to do so is to expand economic ties with its neighbors in Central America. Cuba has something to offer, by way of public health and medical technology and administration, and could benefit from basic grains produced in Central America. One indication of early success was the reopening of trade relations between Costa Rica and Cuba in 1988.[12]

While this trade could be mutually beneficial, decades of official hostility expressed by every country in the region, except Nicaragua during the ten-year rule of the Sandinistas, will constrain these efforts. But a further difficulty will be continued U.S. opposition to any measures that could strengthen the Cuban economy. From the U.S. perspective, more than thirty years of economic embargo have not toppled the Castro administration because of extensive Soviet and Eastern bloc support. But now that such support is ending, the United States sees a greater opportunity than ever before to weaken and eventually dislodge Castro from power through economic pressure. The United States would not be pleased to see an expansion of trade between Central America and Cuba at this critical juncture.

In the absence of the cold war, divergences between Central America and the United States, devoid of ideological disputes but rooted in true differences in national interest, will likely come to the fore. Trade with Cuba is only one area, but numerous other questions concerning migration, the environment, human rights, and so forth, will emerge as points of potential conflict.

This chapter attempts to project what regional relations might look like in the future by measuring Central American attitudes toward Cuba. (It would be ideal also to have the converse—data on Cuban attitudes toward Central America—but it is still impossible to conduct free and open public opinion surveys on the island.) In the following section, I argue that public opinion provides important constraints on the formulation of policy and, therefore, knowledge of popular opinion can help predict future foreign policy decisions.

Public Opinion and Foreign Policy

Political scientists have become increasingly skilled in analyzing public opinion, especially in predicting the outcome of elections or explaining why some groups of voters prefer candidate A over candidate B. But the science of public opinion analysis has been far less successful in linking mass opinions to policy outcomes. The problem is, quite simply, that once candidates are elected, their actions often vary significantly from the expectations of their supporters. Researchers wonder, therefore, about the importance of studying public opinion when its impact might be limited only to determining the outcome of elections.

The difficulty of linking public opinion to policy outcomes is perhaps greatest in the field of foreign policy. Walter Lippmann was a strong proponent of the view that the mass public was both uninterested and uninformed about foreign policy matters.[13] Many years later, poll data led Gabriel Almond to conclude that Lippmann was right: public opinion was so unstable that foreign policy makers who followed it ran the risk of making bad policy.[14] It became conventional wisdom that there are two formidable barriers to linking the views of citizens with the foreign policy decisions of elected officials. First, foreign policy is thought to be highly enigmatic, far beyond the ken of the average voter. After all, to take a stand on foreign policy, one must be knowledgeable about other states and alien cultures; further, with that knowledge one must decide how foreign policy can best take advantage of a complex, rapidly changing environment. Second, even if voters are capable of understanding complex issues, they are far more interested in local problems than in foreign policy. Voters are often intensely concerned about the quality of local schools and roads, yet fear the increased real estate taxes that may be required to pay for improvements. Of course, not all questions that stir voters' interest are local; national issues such as unemployment and inflation are also salient. But foreign policy, Almond argues, rarely touches the voter in any direct way, and therefore few decide how to vote on the basis of such issues and even fewer pressure their representatives to achieve changes in foreign policy.[15]

In recent years, however, our understanding of the relationship between public opinion and foreign policy has changed as a result of two factors, one political and the other scholarly. First, the Vietnam War demonstrated that, at least on certain foreign policy issues, public opinion can have a great influence. No one seriously disputes the view that it was the mass protests of the 1960s that brought a halt to the bombing of North Vietnam and, ultimately, President Lyndon Johnson's decision not to run for a second term. In addition, scholars made major advances in the study of public opinion on foreign policy during the 1980s. Whereas conventional wisdom held that foreign policy is so intricate that the mass public have no clear and systematic views on the subject, researchers have found that voters do indeed have rational, stable, and relatively consistent views on complex foreign policy issues.[16] Moreover, in marked contrast to the classic idea that the public's views had no structure,[17] research shows that people formulate views on specific foreign policy issues on the basis of an underlying set of beliefs—even when their information is fragmentary. We know, for example, that deeply held beliefs on militarism, communism, and xenophobia help determine how most voters feel about a variety of foreign policy issues, from defense spending to nuclear weapons and disarmament treaties.[18] These findings not only apply to citizens of the United States; similar belief systems also influence the mass public in Central America in their foreign policy views.[19]

Not only has research demonstrated that the public holds some structured, rational foreign policy beliefs, it also proves that voters' opinions influence foreign policy. Whereas the classic view held firmly that leaders can make policy, especially foreign policy, with no regard for public opinion, a study of U.S. presidential campaigns between 1952 and 1984 reveals a strong impact of popular attitudes on the outcomes.[20] Moreover, defense expenditures authorized by the U.S. Congress during the Reagan administration show a very strong influence of public opinion.[21]

Central America is now ruled by democratic regimes, and, in democracies, public opinion counts.[22] We can anticipate, therefore, that foreign policy will no longer be decided entirely by political elites in consultation with technocrats isolated from the pressure of public opinion. Leaders may enter into agreements, but masses can undo them if they find them objectionable. At one level, voters can vote out of office those whose policies differ from their own preferences. At another level, pressure groups comprised of small farmers or industrial workers, whose opinions were of little import to dictatorial regimes, can today go out on strike, block highways and ports, and seriously obstruct normal economic processes, knowing that their actions are far less likely to provoke violent reprisals from security forces. Politicians who ignore those views do so at their own peril.

What are the opinions of Central Americans toward Cuba? In this chapter, I present the results of the largest systematic effort ever undertaken to tap the attitudes of Central Americans on various aspects of foreign affairs. It gives us a firsthand look at how opinions vary—in attitudes toward Cuba, the United States, and the USSR, and toward themselves and other nations of the region. Moreover, the chapter examines differences among subsets of respondents, such as those who are more informed on public issues versus those who are less well informed. After briefly characterizing the sample, I will describe the results.

Methodology

For this study, a total of 4,180 interviews were conducted in the five Central American countries and Panama. Although it might have been desirable to interview a national probability sample, urban and rural, in each country, limited resources dictated that the sample be urban.[23] Hence, when I refer to Central American public opinion, I refer to *urban* public opinion.[24] This limitation is not serious, however, since urban populations are more likely to be more attentive to foreign policy issues for two reasons. First, they have greater access to the mass media. For the sample as a whole, 61 percent of the respondents reported regularly listening to radio news, 63 percent regularly read a newspaper, and 81 percent regularly watched TV news. In rural areas, few people have access to newspapers, and a significantly smaller proportion have access to TV than in urban areas. Second, levels of education in Central American towns and cities are far higher than in rural areas, and education is a major factor in providing access to information about complex international questions.

The samples varied in size (Guatemala, 904; El Salvador, 910; Honduras, 566; Nicaragua, 704; Costa Rica, 597; Panama, 500). These differences partly reflect the size of the populations studied, but mainly reflect the resources available to the study team in each country. To eliminate differences caused by unequal sample sizes, the entire sample was weighted so that each country represents one-sixth of all interviews.[25]

It would have been ideal to conduct each survey at precisely the same moment, but this was not possible. First, Costa Rica was established as the locus of the pilot test of survey items. That sample was polled in fall 1990. Second, funding for the surveys in Honduras, El Salvador, Nicaragua, and Panama was not confirmed until later, so those samples were interviewed during June, July, and August 1991. Finally, because funding for the Guatemala survey came last, it was conducted in February 1992. These differences in the dates of the surveys could influence some of the results. For example, the cold war ended just as the surveys were being conducted in El Salvador, Honduras, Nicaragua, and Panama, but had not yet occurred at the time of the Costa Rican survey. The Guatemala study was conducted after the breakup of the Soviet Union.

Findings

I now turn to the results. First, I will describe the popular images of Cuba and the former Soviet Union revealed by the surveys, then compare them to images of other countries (the United States, Mexico, and the nations of Central America), noting similarities and differences. I will seek to explain the origins of these perceptions by analyzing respondents' views toward communism. I then attempt to determine if these views translate into specific foreign policy perspectives regarding trade with Cuba and the Soviet Union. Finally, I analyze the underlying attitudes that explain why some Central Americans are more predisposed toward Cuba and the former Soviet Union.

Images of Cuba and Other Countries

Trustworthiness. A fundamental theme in international relations is perception; policy makers and the mass public hold beliefs, or images, about the basic characteristics of other nations. Since how other nations are perceived is a key to policy, misperceptions—erroneous images— have often been the cause of misguided foreign policy.[26] One of the most revealing images concerns trust. Nations perceived as trustworthy by the mass public are those with whom constructive international relations

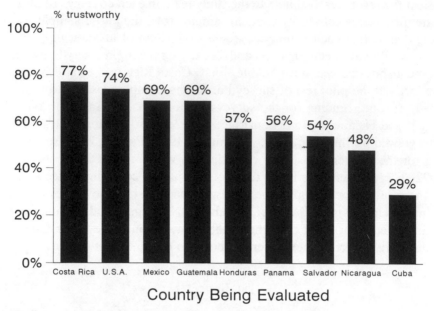

Country Being Evaluated

FIG. 7.1 **Evaluation of Trustworthiness of Other Countries**
(entire Central American sample)

may well take place. On the other hand, when another nation's actions
are viewed with mistrust, international hostility and conflict will likely
be the result.

   To assess the images of Cuba held by Central Americans, we decided
that the data would make sense only in a broadly comparative context.
We would know little, for example, if we evaluated Central Americans'
perceptions of the trustworthiness of the Cuban government without
knowing how the image of Cuba compared to those of other nations.
Similarly, it was important to distinguish among the popular attitudes in
each country, since images of Cuba could vary substantially. As a result,
we asked respondents how trustworthy was the government of each of the
other nations in the region, as well as the governments of Cuba, Mexico,
and the United States.[27]

   Figure 7.1 presents data on trust.[28] The combined responses for all
six nations reveal a dramatic difference in the perceived trustworthiness
of Cuba versus the other eight nations studied. Less than 30 percent of

respondents trusted the government of Cuba, compared to nearly half or more who believed that the governments of Honduras, Panama, El Salvador, and Nicaragua were trustworthy. Guatemala and Mexico had an even more positive image, with more than two-thirds of respondents trusting those governments. Most highly esteemed were Costa Rica and the United States, with approximately three-fourths of respondents finding them to be trustworthy.

In some respects, these findings are remarkable. The very high evaluation of the United States comes as a surprise to those who might feel that the United States' frequent political, economic, and military intervention in Central American affairs would result in a negative evaluation. Evidently this was not the case for the great majority of urban Central Americans. Less surprising is the high esteem in which Costa Rica is held. Costa Rica is known throughout the region as the most democratic and peaceful of all Central American nations. Moreover, Costa Rica's active role in agreements leading to the end of most of the region's military conflicts no doubt reinforced its positive image.

What clearly stands out in these initial results is the dramatic contrast between Cuba's image and those of the other nations in the survey. The government of Cuba was seen as trustworthy by only a small minority of urban Central Americans. These findings were complimented by others, to be discussed later.

The data in figure 7.1 present an aggregated pattern that ignores differences among individual nations. Presenting the evaluations of each nation's government would be too cumbersome for our purposes, but the survey data show that perceptions of Cuba's trustworthiness vary dramatically. Guatemalans, Salvadorans, Costa Ricans, and Panamanians overwhelmingly distrusted the Cuban government, with approximately 80 percent of each sample expressing negative views.[29] Not surprisingly, Nicaraguans were far more positive toward the government of Cuba than were citizens of any other Central American nation (51 percent), and it was similarly unsurprising that they were the least positive with respect to the United States (54 percent). Even so, mistrust of the United States by Nicaraguans was far lower than mistrust of Cubans on the part of the other Central Americans. These results, so obviously shaped by the last decade of Central American history, in which Nicaragua allied itself with Cuba and against the United States, gives one confidence that these data reflect meaningful public sentiments.

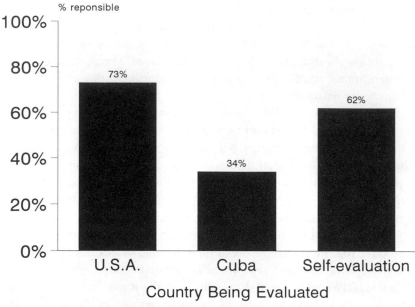

FIG. 7.2 **Evaluation of Responsibility of System of Government**
(entire Central American sample)

Responsibility of the Government System. The survey reveals a similarly negative picture of the responsibility of the Cuban government. Respondents were asked how responsible were the governments of Cuba, the United States, and their own country.[30] Figure 7.2 shows that positive ratings for the United States were more than twice as high as for Cuba, and resspondents' evaluations of their own countries were nearly as favorable. The individual countries' views on the responsibility of the Cuban government showed a pattern similar to that uncovered earlier; Nicaraguans differed from other Central Americans in being far more positive toward Cuba and more negative toward the United States.

Figure 7.3 shows that Central Americans were much more skeptical about the responsibility of the Cuban system of government than they were about the United States or their own government.[31] Nicaragua again stands out, with over half of Nicaraguans finding the Cuban government to be responsible, and precisely half finding the United States responsible. Hence, on both trustworthiness and responsibility, Nicara-

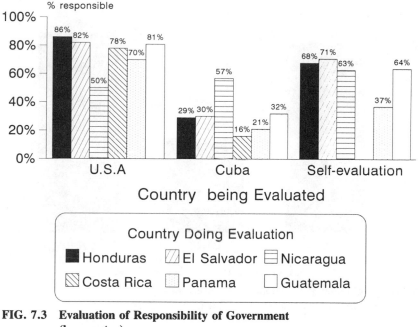

FIG. 7.3 **Evaluation of Responsibility of Government**
(by country)

guans' views on Cuba were far more positive than those of other Central Americans.

Friendliness of the Government System. A final question about Cuba concerned the "friendliness" of its government. Responses were systematically more positive than those regarding Cuba's level of responsibility and trustworthiness (see figure 7.4). Yet the same pattern was found: twice as many Central Americans saw the U.S. government as friendly than saw Cuba in this way. Figure 7.5 shows the familiar pattern: Nicaraguans were far more likely—more than three-quarters of respondents—to view the Cuban government as friendly.

Explaining the Negative Images of Cuba

We now have a clear picture of the very negative image that Central Americans, except for Nicaraguans, displayed toward Cuba. The island was considered to be governed by an untrustworthy, irresponsible, un-

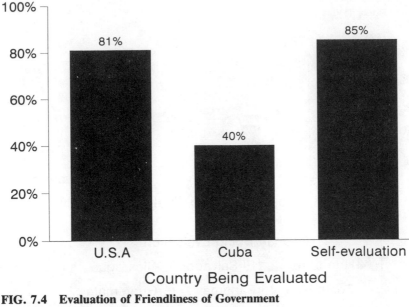

FIG. 7.4   **Evaluation of Friendliness of Government (entire Central American sample)**

friendly regime by the great majority of Central Americans interviewed. We also know that these negative images were not merely the result of a generalized xenophobia, since images of other countries, both inside and outside Central America, were far more positive than were images of Cuba.

A hypothesis that immediately comes to mind is that these negative images of Cuba are associated with attitudes toward communism. Long before the Cuban revolution, communism was an important issue throughout Central America. As early as the 1930s, when labor unions first began to gain strength in the region, governments and the Catholic church expressed fear of communist influence. In fact, many union groups were indeed linked to incipient communist parties in Central America, and the parties, in turn, had links to Moscow. Communist influence grew during World War II, when the United States and the USSR found themselves allied in the struggle against Germany. Communist political power was a major issue in Costa Rica's civil war in 1948, and the U.S. intervention in Guatemala in 1954 was justified on grounds

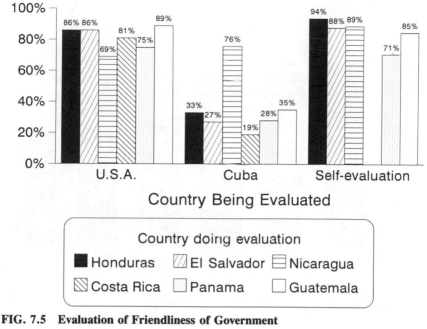

FIG. 7.5 **Evaluation of Friendliness of Government**
(by country)

of fighting communism in that country. Central America's focus on the Soviet Union as a threat shifted to Cuba, once that nation became communist. Hence, from the early 1960s on, groups representing the status quo in Central America regarded Cuba with considerable suspicion.

Fear of Communism. Three items in the Central America survey indicated a widespread popular fear of communism in Central America. We first asked, "If a Central American country were to become communist, should it be considered a great threat to the national interests and security of _____." [The name of the respondent's country was inserted.] Results are presented in figure 7.6. Between two-thirds and four-fifths of all respondents, except for Nicaraguans, saw communism in Central America as a great threat to their country. In Nicaragua, slightly less than half of respondents saw such a threat.

Preventing the rise of communism in Central America also concerned the great majority of respondents. They were asked to what extent

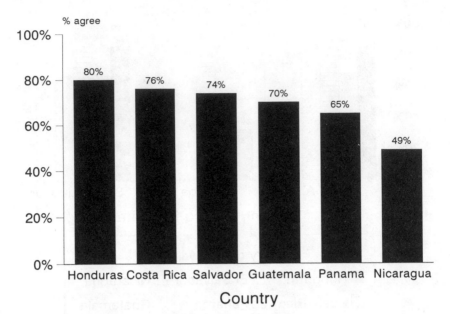

% agree

**FIG. 7.6 Communism Is a Great Threat to Our Nation
(by country)**

they agreed with the following statements: "It is extremely important for
_____ [respondent's country filled in] to do every-
thing possible to prevent the expansion of communism to other Central
American countries." As shown in figure 7.7, majorities in each country,
including Nicaragua, expressed an anticommunist bias, with the highest
level in Costa Rica, where 85 percent of respondents felt this fear.

The final item evaluating communism provoked a somewhat more
muted response. Those interviewed were asked to what extent they
agreed with the following: "Communism could be an acceptable form of
government for some countries of the world." In this item, the threat was
less direct, since the focus was shifted from Central America to somewhere else. Majorities in each country except Nicaragua found communism unacceptable anywhere in the world, as shown in figure 7.8. The
relatively low level of fear in El Salvador is somewhat surprising, but
perhaps shows the effect of FMLN propaganda in which communism is
portrayed as being a legitimate solution.

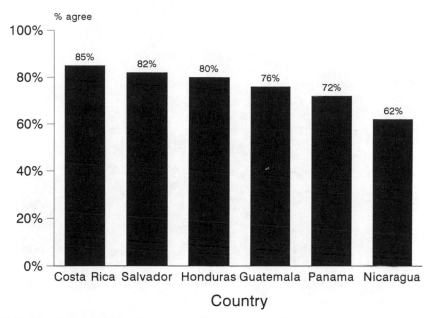

% agree

FIG. 7.7 **It Is Important to Prevent Communism in Central America (by country)**

The Cuban Threat. The survey then sought to determine, in light of the fear of communism, to what extent Cuba was seen as a threat. Respondents were asked whether they agreed with the statement, "Cuba is a great threat for the stability of Central America." Figure 7.9 shows that in every country except Nicaragua, majorities agreed that Cuba represented a menace. While these findings are consistent with those presented above, they also reveal that significant numbers of Central Americans did not feel threatened by Cuba. In Nicaragua, of course, nearly two-thirds of those interviewed did not. In Panama and Guatemala, only a slight majority felt that Cuba was a threat. This question was not asked in Costa Rica.

Policy-Relevant Attitudes: Masses and Elites

We now have a broad picture of attitudes toward Cuba on the part of the Central American public interviewed in our survey: they were quite negative for all countries except Nicaragua.

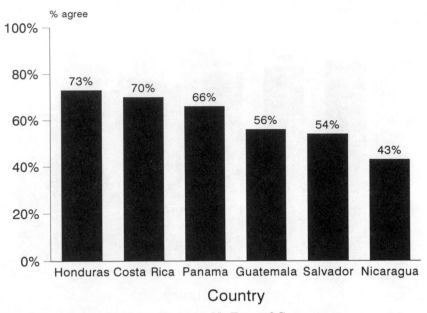

FIG. 7.8   **Communism Is an Unacceptable Form of Government
(by country)**

Many of these attitudes also prevail in the United States, as numerous opinion polls have demonstrated. These views provide strong support for the U.S. State Department's consistently tough policy toward Cuba. Aimed at the isolation of Cuba, U.S. policy uses a total trade embargo as a means to achieve that goal.

Commercial Ties with Cuba and the USSR.   Do most Central Americans support a similar policy toward Cuba? No. For the six countries in the study, more than half (57 percent) favored commercial ties with Cuba. Figure 7.10 shows that such support varied from country to country and was highest, not surprisingly, in Nicaragua. In other countries, majorities in Honduras and El Salvador supported trade with Cuba, whereas slim majorities opposed it in Costa Rica and Panama.

Trade with the Soviet Union, with its long history of backing radical movements in Central America, received much stronger support from Central Americans. As shown in figure 7.11, two-thirds or more of respondents favored such trade. This more positive view is possibly related

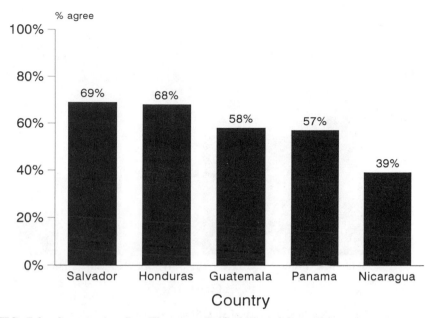

% agree

FIG. 7.9 **Communism Is a Threat to the Stability of Central America (by country)**

to the perception that the USSR, being more advanced economically than Cuba, might have more to offer. Another explanation is that despite Soviet aid to radical movements in Central America, its great distance makes it less of a threat. Unfortunately, the survey did not allow us to test these competing explanations.

Whatever the reasons for the more positive views toward trade with the USSR versus Cuba, there seems to be a strong dose of pragmatism among the mass public in Central America that allows people to overcome their fears and suspicions of communism and to opt for commercial ties with communist countries. In the United States, on the other hand, the cold war mentality of "evil empire" thinking produces popular support for the official policy of isolating Cuba. Hence, in the United States, mass and elite thinking are consonant.

Elite Perspectives. There is some evidence that in Central America elite thinking is even more tolerant of pragmatic polices, including trade with Cuba, than in the United States. As part of the larger survey, small

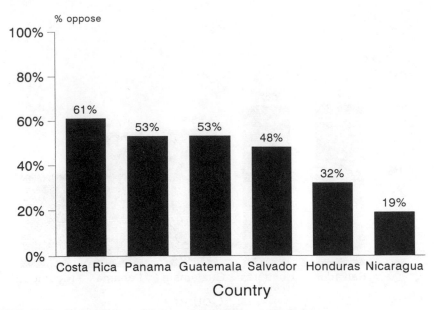

FIG. 7.10   Opposition to Commercial Relations with Cuba
(by country)

surveys were carried out among leaders in El Salvador, Honduras, and Panama. The largest was conducted in El Salvador, where sixty-three legislators, comprising 80 percent of the members of the Asemblea Legislativa, were asked many of the same items that were used in the mass sample. Even though 63 percent of Salvadoran legislators believed that communism was an unacceptable form of government, compared to 54 percent of the mass public, only 25 percent of the legislators opposed commercial ties with Cuba, compared to 48 percent of the mass public. The same pattern emerged in elite attitudes toward trade with the Soviet Union. Only 5 percent of Salvadoran legislators opposed such trade, compared to 37 percent of the mass public. A smaller sample in Honduras produced a similar pattern.[32] Only 17 percent of Honduran leaders believed that communism was acceptable, compared to 27 percent of the mass sample. Yet 82 percent of the elites versus 68 percent of the mass public supported commercial ties with Cuba. A sample of twenty-nine Panamanian leaders revealed similar findings. Although elite and mass

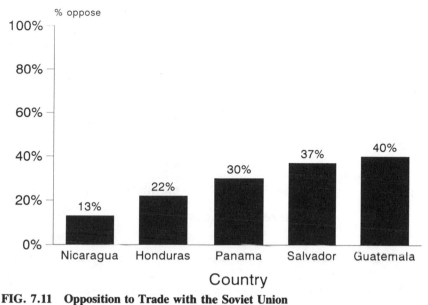

FIG. 7.11   **Opposition to Trade with the Soviet Union**
(by country)

opinion on the acceptability of communism were nearly identical (35 percent of the elite versus 34 percent of the public), elites were much more favorably disposed to trade with Cuba (93 percent versus 48 percent of the mass public). Indeed, all Panamanian leaders favored trade with the Soviet Union. In sum, although mass and elite opinion show considerable parallels, in each country political elites were more apt to favor trade ties with Cuba.

These comparisons suggest that characteristics of subsets of the mass samples may help explain why some respondents were more predisposed toward Cuba. One factor may be access to information. Elite groups are more informed about all subjects, including politics. This suggests that attitudes toward Cuba among the informed public may resemble those of their leaders.

To explore this hypothesis, we constructed an index of respondents' political knowledge.[33] That information was then associated with some of the key variables already examined. In figures 7.12 and 7.13, respondents' attitudes toward the degree of responsiblity and friendliness of the

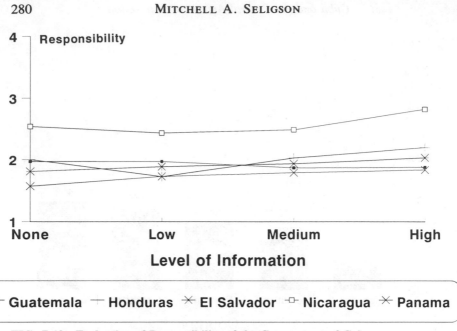

FIG. 7.12 **Evaluation of Responsibility of the Government of Cuba
(controlled for level of information)**

Cuba government are controlled by their level of information. Although the pattern is not dramatic, higher levels of information are clearly related to a more positive image of Cuba.

Explaining Differences Between Public Opinion in the United States and Central America

This analysis of both mass and elite views in Central America suggests a paradox. Even though for over a decade Central America has been engaged in civil war and revolutions in which communist influence has been a central issue and even though Cuba and the Soviet Union provided material and moral support to the Sandinistas in Nicaragua and to the FMLN in El Salvador,[34] pragmatic policies had much stronger support in the region than in the United States. Obviously, trade with Cuba is of little consequence for the United States, and therefore the embargo poses no economic threat. But the same can be said for Central American nations, the great bulk of whose trade is with the United States and Western Europe. Central America's largest trading partner beyond those ma-

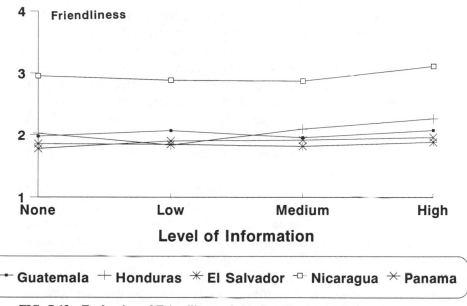

FIG. 7.13 **Evaluation of Friendliness of the Government of Cuba (controlled for level of information)**

jor industrial powers is Mexico, but even there, total exports for all of Central America for 1989 was only $55 million, amounting to less than 1 percent of regional exports and about 7 percent of imports.[35] Trade with the Caribbean community (CARICOM) was about 1 percent of exports and imports. The potential for significant trade with Cuba, a country whose major export, sugar, is also a significant Central American export commodity, is very limited indeed. Even so, Central American masses and leaders favored trade with Cuba and overwhelmingly supported trade with the Soviet Union.

The explanation for this paradox, I would argue, is that Central Americans do not view the world in the same unidimensional fashion that has been commonplace in the United States since the onset of the cold war. Central Americans have more than one focus in their attention to international affairs. On the one hand, they certainly have been concerned with threats of communist intervention—threats that were no doubt more keenly felt by the average citizen there than in the United States. At the same time, the United States, too, was a source of concern for some Central Americans. After all, no country has more frequently violated Central America's sovereignty than the United States. One only need recall the sponsorship of the armed intervention in Guatemala in 1954, support for the contra war in Nicaragua, and the 1989 U.S. invasion of Panama to affirm this fact. Of course, U.S. intervention is probably viewed favorably by many Central Americans, given the positive images of the United States described earlier. The ability of Central Americans to view both the positive and negative aspects of intervention allows them to see the world order as more complex than it is for the average U.S. citizen.

One could pursue this interpretation too far, forgetting that not all Central Americans favor trade with Cuba. Indeed, as figure 7.10 shows, whereas four-fifths of Nicaraguans favored such trade, nearly two-thirds of Costa Ricans opposed it, with other countries of the region falling somewhere in between. Indeed, the division of opinion in the region is even greater than figure 7.10 implies, because that figure (like the others) clusters all those who favored (or opposed) a given position into one category and does not distinguish by intensity of opinion. For example, 61 percent of Costa Ricans opposed trade with Cuba, but it is important to observe that fully 41 percent of all Costa Ricans stated that they *strongly* opposed such trade. At the same time, whereas most Nicaraguans supported trade with Cuba, 14 percent *strongly* opposed it, while 57 percent *strongly* favored it. By measuring intensity of opinion, one can better determine what characteristics led some respondents to favor trade with Cuba and others to oppose it.

To explore the factors associated with supporting trade with Cuba, we used multiple regression analysis, with three sets of variables: demographic, socioeconomic, and attitudinal. The basic demographic characteristics were sex and age. A positive coefficient indicates that more males favored trade with Cuba than females. Socioeconomic variables included income, education, and the already discussed scale measuring how informed respondents were about world and national politics. Items about attitudes included religiosity, system support, democratic norms and leftist ideology. Religiosity was measured by how often respondents attended church.[36] System support was measured by five items that measured belief in the legitimacy of one's system of government.[37] Political tolerance was gauged by four items focusing on how far respondents were willing to extend key civil liberties to the opposition.[38]

Support for democratic norms was measured by five items measuring the extent to which respondents advocated either conventional or violent means of expressing political demands. Finally, leftist ideology was measured by respondents' self-identification on a ten-point left-right ideology scale. The regression analyses are presented in table 7.1.

Some clear patterns emerged. First, demographic and socioeconomic factors were not consistent (significant) predictors of support for trade with Cuba. Only in Guatemala was education the strongest predictor, and it was of no significance in Honduras, Nicaragua, Costa Rica, and Panama. Age played a role only in Costa Rica, where older respondents were slightly less apt to support trade with Cuba.[39] Sex differences were significant in El Salvador, Costa Rica, and Panama, with fewer females supporting trade with Cuba than males. Access to information played a role in all but Nicaragua and Guatemala, but in both countries, the simple correlation coefficients were also significant between level of information and support for trade with Cuba. In those two countries, the other variables played a greater role, and hence level of information receded in importance. This means that in all countries the more informed citizens were more likely to favor trade with Cuba. This pattern emerges clearly in figure 7.14.

Attitudes are the most consistent indicators of favoring trade with Cuba. Respondents who were more predisposed toward political participation (both democratic and violent) most consistently supported trade with Cuba. Similarly, leftist ideology and political tolerance played a role. Low levels of support for the system were also associated with greater support for Cuban trade.

The portrait that emerges from this analysis is that Central America's more informed, civil-libertarian, and left-leaning citizens were more likely to support trade with Cuba than those who were less informed, less politically tolerant, and more right-wing.

Conclusions

This chapter shows that since Castro fought his revolution, Cuba has been highly relevant for Central America. Leftists of all varieties have sought Cuba's support for their programs. In Nicaragua and El Salvador, such support took both material and moral forms. For some Central Americans—those seeking radical changes in their society—Cuba has

TABLE 7.1
Regressions of Support for Trade with Cuba on SES, Demographic Characteristics, and Attitudes
(Beta weights of significant predictors)

Predictors	Guatemala	El Salvador	Honduras	Nicaragua	Costa Rica	Panama
Demographic factors						
Sex		.15			.16	.09
Age					-.10	
SES: Socioeconomic status Income	.10					
Education	.23	.13				
Information		.23	.29		.13	.15
Attitudes: Religiosity						-.22
System Support		-.15	-.20			-.09
Tolerance			.19			.34
Democratic Participation	.11	.14	.29	.35		
Violent participation	.09	.09	.39	.12	.13	.17
Leftist Ideology	.14			.17	.23	.14
R^2	.11	.14	.33	.16	.12	.24
Minimum N	516	514	507	419	400	453

Source: University of Pittsburgh Central American Public Opinion Project.

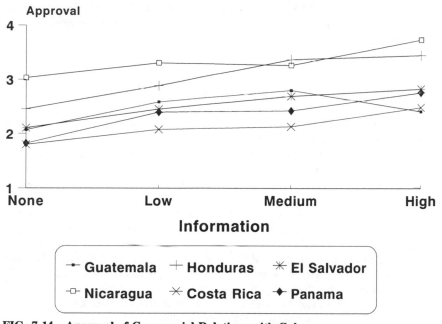

FIG. 7.14 Approval of Commercial Relations with Cuba
(controlled for level of information)

been viewed as a friend. But those who would defend the status quo have viewed Cuba with suspicion and even fear. The majority of citizens in all countries in the region fear Cuba, with the exception of Nicaragua.

The end of the cold war, coupled with the Sandinista defeat in Nicaragua and the cessation of civil war in El Salvador, has radically changed the face of Central America. Cuba's capacity to influence events in the region has greatly diminished, partly because it now must concentrate all its efforts on the survival of its own revolution, and partly because radical groups in Central America are not nearly as prominent as they were only a few years ago.

One can assume that in this new enviroment, fears of Cuba will diminish throughout the region. Yet, despite past fears, Central Americans express a rather pragmatic view of foreign policy. Even in the one survey we conducted after the end of the cold war (in Guatemala), fear of Cuba was still great; yet many Central Americans are willing to trade with Cuba. As democracy develops in the region, mass attitudes will likely carry more weight. As Central America struggles to solve its economic problems, Cuba may come to play a role, albeit in a minor way, in that struggle.

NOTES

I would like to thank Rodolfo Cerdas and Richard Fagen for their helpful comments, and Carmelo Mesa-Lago for his numerous suggestions.

1. Lars Schoultz, *National Security and United States Policy Toward Latin America* (Princeton: Princeton University Press, 1987), p. 325.

2. Ronald Reagan, address to a joint session of Congress in April 1983, quoted in ibid., p. 269.

3. Benjamin C. Schwarz, *American Counterinsurgency Doctrine and El Salvador: The Frustration of Reform and the Illusions of Nation Building* (Santa Monica: Rand, 1991), p. 1.

4. Kiva Maidanik, "On the *Real* Soviet Policy Toward Central America, Past and Present," *The Russians Aren't Coming: New Soviet Policy in Latin America*, ed. Wayne S. Smith, (Boulder: Lynne Reinner), 1992, pp. 90–91.

5. Rodolfo Cerdas Cruz, "New Directions in Soviet Policy towards Latin America," *Journal of Latin American Studies* 21 (1) (February 1989): 7.

6. Ibid., pp. 7–8. Cerdas bases his conclusions upon Mikoyan's papers, "Las particularidades de la revolución en Nicaragua y sus tareas desde el punto de vista de la teoría y prática del movimiento liberador," *América Latina* (Moscow), no. 3 (1980): 103; and Sergo Mikoyan, "La creatividad revolucionaria abre el camino hacia la victoria," *América Latina*, no. 2 (1980): 4.

7. U.S. State Department, white paper, quoted by Donna Rich-Kaplowitz, "The U.S. Response to Soviet and Cuban Policies in Central America," in *The Russians Aren't Coming*, ed. Smith, p. 106.

8. Ibid., p. 107.

9. Cole Blasier, "The Soviet Union," in *Confronting Revolution: Security Through Diplomacy in Central America*, ed. Morris J. Blachman, William M. Leogrande, and Kenneth Sharpe (New York: Pantheon Books, 1986), p. 268.

10. Rodolfo Cerdas Cruz, "Perestroika y revolución: los cambios en la política soviética hacia América Central," *Anuario de estudios Centroamericanos* 15, no. 2 (1989): 5–24.

11. Fidel Castro, quoted by Anthony Lukas, "Fidel Castro's Theater of Now," *New York Times*, January 20, 1992, p. A15.

12. Cerdas, "New Directions," p. 13.

13. Walter Lippmann, *Public Opinion* (New York: Harcourt, Brace, 1922), and *The Phantom Public* (New York: Harcourt Brace, 1925).

14. Gabriel Almond, *The American People and Foreign Policy* (New York: Praeger, 1950).

15. The classic statement is found in Warren E. Miller and Donald E. Stokes, "Constituency Influence in Congress," *American Political Science Review* 57 (1963): 45–56.

16. The most important are Benjamin I. Page and Robert Y. Shapiro, "Changes in Americans' Policy Preferences, 1935–1979," *Public Opinion Quarterly* 46 (1982): 24–42; Robert Y. Shapiro and Benjamin I. Page, "Foreign Policy and the Rational Public," *Journal of Conflict Resolution* 32 (1988): 211–47.

17. Philip E. Converse found that Americans did not hold views with any ideological coherence. "The Nature of Belief Systems in Mass Publics," in *Ideology and Discontent*, ed. David E. Apter (New York: Free Press, 1964).

18. Jon Hurwitz and Mark Peffley, "How are Foreign Policy Attitudes Structured? A Hierarchical Model," *American Political Science Review* 81 (1987): 1100–20; Mark A. Peffley and Jon Hurwitz, "A Hierarchical Model of Attitude Constraint," *American Journal of Political Science* 29 (1985): 871–90.

19. Jon Hurwitz, Mark Peffley, and Mitchell A. Seligson, "Foreign Policy Belief Systems in Comparative Perspective: The United States and Costa Rica," *International Studies Quarterly*, September 1993.

20. John H. Aldrich, John L. Sullivan, and Eugene Borgida, "Foreign Affairs and Issue Voting: Do Presidential Candidates 'Waltz Before a Blind Audience'?" *American Political Science Review* 83 (1989): 123–41.

21. Larry M. Bartels, "Constituency Opinion and Congressional Policy Making: The Reagan Defense Buildup," *American Political Science Review* 85 (1991): 457–74.

22. There is good reason to be skeptical about the degree of democracy in some of the countries in the region, as human rights violations and military control over key policy areas continue. Nonetheless, elections have become the regularized mechanism for the selection of rulers and the peaceful transfer of power throughout Central America. See John A. Booth and Mitchell A. Seligson, eds., *Elections and Democracy in Central America* (Chapel Hill: University of North Carolina Press, 1989).

23. This study is based on the Central American Pubic Opinion Project of the University of Pittsburgh, conceived in 1989 to tap the opinion of Central Americans on a variety of issues, including attitudes toward Cuba. The study received support from the Andrew Mellon Foundation, the Tinker Foundation, Inc., the Howard Heinz Endowment, the University of Pittsburgh's Central Research Small Grant Fund, the North-South Center at the University of Miami, and the Instituto de Estudios Latinamericanos (IDELA). Collaborating institutions in Central America were: Guatemala—Asociación de Investigación y Estudios Sociales (ASIES); El Salvador—Instituto de Estudios Latinoamericanos (IDELA); Honduras—Centro de Estudio y Promoción del Desarrollo (CEPROD) and the Centro de Documentación de Honduras (EDOH); Nicaragua—Centro de Estudios Internacionales (CEI) and the Escuela de Sociología, Universidad Centroamericana (UCA); Costa Rica—Universidad de Costa Rica; Panama—Centro de Estudios Latinamericanos "Justo Arosemena" (CELA). Collaborating doctoral students in political science at the University of Pittsburgh were Ricardo Córdova (El Salvador), Annabelle Conroy (Honduras), Orlando Pérez (Panama), and Andrew Stein (Nicaragua). Collaborating faculty were John Booth, University of North Texas (Nicaragua and Guatemala), and Jon Hurwitz, University of Pittsburgh (Costa Rica).

24. The sample was of a multistage stratified design. The first level of stratification was the most obvious; we divided the entire population to be studied into the six nations of the region. Hence, each country represents a stratum in the design. Within each country, the urban area was defined. We sought to narrow our definition of *urban* to include the areas of major population agglomeration. In Guatemala, this meant Guatemala City, as well as eleven other cities, including Escuintla, Quetzaltenango, and Chimaltenango. In El Salvador, it meant greater metropolitan San Salvador, including the city of San Salvador (divided into fourteen zones) and the eight surrounding *municipios:* Soyapango, Cuscatancingo, Ciudad Delgado, Mejicanos, Nueva San Salvador, San Marcos, Ilopango, and Antiguo Cuscatlán. In Honduras, it meant the nation's two large metropolitan areas, Tegucigalpa (the capital) and San Pedro Sula. In Nicaragua, this definition included Managua (the capital) and the regional cities of Leon, Granada, and Masaya. In Costa Rica, the sample covered the greater metropolitan region, incorporating San José (the capital) and the provincial capitals of the *meseta central*—Cartago, Heredia, and Alajuela. Finally, the Panama sample was confined to the metropolitan Panama City area.

25. Country sample designs were of area probability design. In each country, the most recent population census data were used to stratify the urban areas into lower, middle, and upper socioeconomic status (SES). The sample size assigned to each stratum was based upon these SES estimates. Within each stratum, census maps were used to select, at random, an appropriate number of political subdivisions (for example, districts) and, within each subdivision, the census maps were used to select an appropriate number of segments from which to draw the interviews.

26. For the classical elaboration of this theory, see Richard W. Cottam, *Foreign Policy Motivation: A General Theory and a Case Study* (Pittsburgh: University of Pittsburgh Press, 1977), pp. 54–92. For an updated view of this perspective, see Richard K. Herrmann, "Perceptions and Foreign Policy Analysis," in *Foreign Policy Decision Making: Perception, Cognition and Artificial Intelligence,* ed. Donald A. Sylvan and Steve Chans (New York: Praeger, 1984).

27. Over 93 percent of the respondents gave an opinion for each of the countries, with fewer than 3 percent not responding in their evaluation of the U.S. government.

28. The respondents were asked to choose among "very trustworthy," "somewhat trustworthy," "little trustworthy," and "not at all trustworthy." For simplicity of presentation, figure 7.1 divides the responses into the two positive options versus the two negative options.

29. Hondurans were found to have surprisingly positive views toward Cuba—surprising because Honduras is considered to be a conservative nation with little that would bind it to Cuba. Closer examination reveals, however, that Hondurans were also far more positive toward the United States and Mexico than were the people of any other nation in the region, indicating that for this item, Hondurans used a different "metric" than did respondents in other nations. If one corrects for this overly positive evaluation by subtracting from the scores for each nation their overall mean score for all nations, then one finds that Hondurans, too, gave a negative evaluation of Cuba, with El Salvador giving an even more negative score. Even Nicaragua's scores are negative, but only slightly so. Hence, the anomaly of Hondurans' highly positive rating is explained by the differences in the metric used rather than any substantive disparities.

30. The question asked was: "Do you think that the government of Cuba is very responsible, somewhat responsible, a little irresponsible, or very irresponsible?" For simplicity of presentation, the chart shows only the overall percentage evaluation of the nation.

31. Note that the Costa Rican survey did not include a self-evaluation item on this dimension.

32. The Honduran sample was comprised of only eighteen respondents.

33. Respondents were asked if they could identify the leader of the Soviet Union, the U.S. secretary of state, and the number of representatives in their national legislature. In the case of the Guatemala survey, which took place after the collapse of the Soviet Union, we accepted Yeltsin or Gorbachov as the leader of "Russia, the former Soviet Union."

34. It is unclear whether such support was also provided to guerrilla groups in Guatemala and Honduras. No doubt, as researchers gain access to security files in the former Soviet Union (and perhaps, one day to Castro's Cuba), this issue will become clearer.

35. "La Cooperación del Banco Nacional de Comercio Exterior con Centroamerica," *Revista de Comercio Exterior,* supplement (April 1991): 5.

36. Several other items in the questionnaire measured religiosity, such as a scale of religious fundamentalism, but the item used here seemed to work the best.

37. This measure has been labeled "political support-alienation." Its five-item administration in this survey included pride in the system, belief in the fairness of trials, respect for the system, degree to which the system protects basic rights, and belief in the need to support the system. Further discussion of this scale is contained in Mitchell A. Seligson, "On the Measurement of Diffuse Support: Some Evidence from Mexico," *Social Indicators Research* 12 (January 1983): 1–24.

38. These liberties include the right to vote, run for office, and exercise free speech. The items are discussed in Mitchell A. Seligson and John A. Booth, "The Political Culture of Authoritarianism in Mexico: A Reevaluation," *Latin American Research Review* 19, no. 1 (January 1984): 106–24.

39. The negative sign of the beta weight shows that greater age is associated with lower support for trade with Cuba.

8

The Impact of the Collapse of Communism and the Cuban Crisis on the South American Left

◆ ◆ ◆

SILVIA BORZUTZKY AND ALDO VACS

WHEN MIKHAIL GORBACHEV began to implement perestroika, glasnost, and the foreign policies of "new thinking," he did not imagine the impact they would have on leftist parties all over the world. Given the scope and depth of the problems he had to face, it is safe to assume that the Latin American Left ranked among the least important political issues on his agenda. However, these reforms and the eventual collapse of socialism in Eastern Europe and the Soviet Union became life-and-death issues for the South American Left. This chapter is a preliminary attempt to assess the impact of those changes, and of the antimarket economic reforms and subsequent crisis in Cuba, on the Left in countries of the Southern Cone: Argentina, Chile, Uruguay, and Brazil. We focus on the traditional communist and socialist parties, not on ultraleftist groups or paramilitary organizations. The chapter also outlines the response of the Left to those changes.

In our study of the South American Left, it is essential to examine not only the content of the Soviet reforms but also their timing, since they came in the wake of more than a decade of violent repression under bureaucratic-authoritarian regimes. Thus, by 1986 the Southern Cone leftist parties had to face two fundamental problems: the domestic need to build or rebuild their political structures and the international impact of the economic and political reforms launched by Gorbachev. The disappearance of the international communist system on which these parties depended ideologically, organizationally, and financially was a major blow. These parties' ability to respond to these processes reflected their

291

degree of ideological flexibility vis-à-vis their commitment to Marxist-Leninist ideology.

Thus, while the more dogmatic communist parties in Latin America have had a hard time finding answers to these problems, the more flexible socialist parties have adapted to new conditions by redefining their relationship with Marxism and by "renovating" their ideological and practical positions. As one observer notes, "If revolution was the catchword of the 1960s, 'renovation' appears to be the dominant theme of the new political era as the left struggles to articulate a socialist alternative to Latin America's crisis-ridden but increasingly entrenched capitalist system."[1]

New Thinking, Glasnost, and Perestroika

The leaders who came to power in the Soviet Union in 1985 inherited a country in crisis. Soviet society was chronically ill, and the illness had produced a systemic crisis that paralyzed the nation's political and economic systems. The sick body could be cured only by major political and economic reforms. In the political arena, Gorbachev's vision involved the democratization of Soviet life, decentralization, changing the political orientation of the Soviet bureaucracy, and greater respect for the rule of law. His economic reforms moved toward some form of "market socialism" to cope with economic stagnation.[2] The "new thinking" in foreign affairs, in turn, allowed Gorbachev to rebuild the USSR's relationship with the major Western countries, particularly the United States and Western Europe, replacing the traditional confrontation with the United States with cooperation while he moved toward eliminating areas of conflict in the Third World. Changes in Soviet foreign policy led to reduced military expenditures and access to Western credits and technology.

The new Soviet approach to international relations emphasized the need to rise above ideological disagreements and stressed the advantages of diplomacy over the threat of military force to resolve international problems.[3] International security was defined as "indivisible," a common good to be placed above ideological disagreements. The adoption of the notion of global interdependence was accompanied by a rejection of confrontational, bipolar views and by a new emphasis on multipolarity and diversity that would force the superpowers to forsake their imperial ambitions.[4] The arms buildup and Third World military commitments of the Brezhnev era were seen as wasteful and counterproductive: they escalated the arms race, drained off scarce resources, and limited the USSR's chances of obtaining foreign capital and technology from Western developed countries without securing well-defined strategic or political advantages. It was considered appropriate to remind even socialist-oriented countries that they should build socialism through their own efforts and with only limited Soviet support.[5] This reinforced the trend toward establishing cooperative relations with those Third World countries that, irrespective of their socioeconomic and political systems, could set up mutually beneficial economic and diplomatic links with the USSR.

Gorbachev emphasized that the USSR did not want to interfere in the internal affairs of Latin American countries to promote revolutionary change. He stated:

> We do sympathize with the Latin American countries in their efforts to consolidate their independence in every sphere and cast off all neocolonialist fetters, and we have never made any secret of this. We much appreciate the energetic foreign policies of Mexico and Argentina, their responsible stances on disarmament and international security, and their contribution to the initiatives of the Six. We support the peacemaking efforts of Contadora Group, initiatives by Central American heads of state, and the Guatemala City accord. We welcome the democratic changes in many Latin American countries, and appreciate the growing consolidation of the countries of the continent which will help preserve and strengthen their national sovereignty.
>
> At the same time, I would like to emphasize once again that we do not seek any advantages in Latin America. We don't want either its raw materials or its cheap labor. We are not going to exploit anti-U.S. attitudes, let alone fuel them, nor do we intend to erode the traditional links between Latin America and the United States. That would be adventurism, not sound politics, and we are realists, not reckless adventurers. But our sympathies always lie with nations fighting for freedom and independence. Let there be no misunderstanding on that score.[6]

In practice, this formulation led to attempts to develop and strengthen diplomatic relations with the largest countries in South America (Argentina, Brazil, and Peru). The relative autonomy of these countries' foreign policies and their agreements with the USSR on issues such as international security, regional peace, and nuclear disarmament aided this process. This relative autonomy had an added advantage from the Soviet

perspective: foreign policy initiatives taken by these intermediate powers, even if they clashed with U.S. views, could not be attributed to
Soviet influence, thus reducing the chances of a rise in superpower tensions. Moreover, their regional importance was expected to increase the
changes of establishing new diplomatic agreements between the USSR
and other countries in Latin America.

Reinforcing this trend, the "new thinking" also led to Soviet initiatives aimed at expanding and diversifying economic relations with Latin
American countries whose economies were seen as complementing the
USSR's, while emphasizing the need to eliminate persistent trade deficits with some of them. The definition of a *complementary* economy
was expanded to cover not only raw materials and primary products
needed by the USSR and the Soviets' interest in selling its manufactured
goods, but also to include mutually profitable scientific-technological
exchanges. Thus, also from an economic perspective, the new Soviet approach favored strengthening ties with countries in the region that would
be best able to engage in trade relations and scientific-technological
cooperation.

As the Soviet approach to Latin America under Gorbachev became
ever more pragmatic and nonideological, it favored opening new diplomatic relations—and deepening existing ones—with all Latin American
governments, regardless of political orientation. Nations without diplomatic ties with the USSR included Honduras, Paraguay, El Salvador, and
Belize, as well as Chile, which had such relations in the past before
breaking them off.[7]

At the same time, to dispel any remaining misgivings, the Soviet
government further distanced itself from the pro-Moscow communist
parties in the region by stressing the diversity and decentralization of the
international communist movement, the USSR's respect for other countries' sovereignty, and its refusal to interfere in their domestic affairs.

The new Soviet strategy also attempted to reduce the burden of economic and military aid to Cuba and Nicaragua. Without completely
abandoning these allies, Gorbachev made it clear that Soviet priorities had changed and that the political considerations that had motivated
past largess had been replaced by a need to gradually eliminate aid
and subsidies. Proclamations of solidarity with these revolutionary governments was accompanied by suggestions that they should expand their

economic relations and avoid actions that could threaten the emerging international detente.

To reduce tensions with the United States—a basic element of Gorbachev's foreign policy strategy—the USSR had to discourage Cuban activities that could obstruct superpower cooperation. The Soviet economic crisis demanded that the USSR reduce its burden of economic and military aid to Cuba and recommend changes in the Castro government's inefficient economic policies and costly military initiatives. Having abandoned a confrontational approach in foreign relations in favor of interdependence, the Soviet Union reassessed its "international socialist duties" and how to fulfill these obligations.

Gorbachev's visit to Cuba in April 1989 highlighted some of the controversial aspects of the Soviet-Cuban relationship.[8] In his speech before the Cuban National Assembly, Gorbachev indicated a growing inclination to reestablish Soviet economic relations with Cuba on stricter criteria of rationality and reciprocity.

The South American Communist Parties and the Cold War

For sixty or seventy years, the South American Left, particularly the communist parties, relied heavily on the internationalism of their ideology and on Soviet aid in building and maintaining power at the local level. The parties' international character provided not only an ideological context, but also financial and organizational support. From the beginning, the history of these parties was intimately linked to world events such as the Bolshevik revolution and the creation of the Third International in 1919. Lenin's death and the ensuing power struggle produced internal divisions in the Latin American parties between pro- and anti-Stalinist factions—struggles that ended with their adoption of the Stalinist discourse, including the notions of capitalist encirclement and inevitability of war. This approach led to denunciations of the U.S. presence in South America and anti-imperialist positions. Throughout the 1930s and the 1940s, the parties followed the swings in Stalin's foreign policy, often paying a high political price for their loyalty to Moscow.[9]

By 1947 the defining strategic issue both at the international and the domestic level was the cold war and the division of the world into two camps. Each superpower perceived the other as aggressive and pursued defensive policies that were seen as expansionist by the other side. Each established an area of influence, and the international political system was perceived as a zero-sum game. Latin America remained within the sphere of the United States, which had the power to influence the actions of the region's major political actors, including the military. The United States secured the support of regional governments by creating a political and defense system geared to fight communism and by keeping Latin America firmly within the range of U.S. economic influence.

The special relationship between the United States and Latin America was established formally in the Rio Treaty and the Organization of American States charter, which in practice allowed the United States to intervene in Latin American affairs to maintain hemispheric peace and security. In 1950 Assistant Secretary of State Edward Miller laid down the Miller Doctrine, which justified collective intervention in case of communist political aggression against the hemisphere and unilateral U.S. action if necessary.[10] The Monroe Doctrine was reinterpreted according to cold war logic, and the principles established in the Miller Doctrine remained central to U.S. foreign policy toward Latin America until the end of the 1980s.

On the Soviet side, Stalin defined the issue in terms of capitalist encirclement and moved to establish firm control of Eastern Europe and the international communist system. The Latin American communist parties, an integral part of this system, showed their loyalty to Moscow by supporting Soviet control of Eastern Europe and condemning the United States as an imperialist, expansionist power. Thus, while at the local level the parties favored revolutionary ideas, at the international level they argued for the liberation of Latin America from the imperialist domination of the United States.

The adoption of the "peaceful road" policy by the Twentieth Congress of the Soviet Communist party (CPSU) opened up a new era for communist parties throughout the world. According to the new policy, the parties emphasized political action instead of revolutionary policies. Such an emphasis remained the basic strategy of South American communist parties even after this policy was challenged by the Chinese and Cuban revolutions. In fact, the Cuban revolution had challenged the most basic principles of the peaceful road policy, and it triumphed in spite of the lack of support from Cuba's Popular Socialist party, the official name of the Cuban Communisty party. It owed its success to the actions of

Fidel Castro and the 26 of July Movement and Ernesto (Che) Guevara's views about revolution.

In the 1960s, as a result of the triumph of the Cuban revolution, the initiative within the South American Left passed to guerrilla groups that, inspired by Guevara, argued for a Latin American revolution. Guevara's theory of *foquismo* held that a small group of guerrilla fighters could create the conditions for a massive peasant uprising even if so-called objective economic conditions required for a socialist revolution had not been achieved.[11] The new Left supported by Castro also emphasized nationalism and anti-imperialist struggle, the need for indigenous responses to Latin America's political and economic problems, and a new altruistic, idealistic citizen. The United States, for its part, saw the Cuban revolution and guerrilla movements as major threats to its security. Although the U.S. response to events in Cuba did not bring about the end of the Castro regime, it certainly affected the course of the revolution and of the Cuban-Soviet relationship. The U.S. counterinsurgency policy, on the other hand, was effective in controlling and defeating guerrilla movements throughout the region.

By the end of the 1960s, with the death of Guevara and the failure of regional guerrilla movements, the communist parties reaffirmed their commitment to the USSR and the peaceful road to socialism. But the Cuban experience had become part of the region's political history, reinforcing cold war competition and redefining U.S. policies toward Latin America. The United States, determined to prevent the appearance of new leftist regimes, viewed its policies toward the region through an East-West prism. Thus, while the peaceful road principle guided the behavior of the communist parties, U.S. responses to leftist regimes and movements in the region were shaped by a bipolar, military approach. The counterinsurgency policies of the Kennedy and Johnson administrations and U.S. intervention in the Dominican Republic were major trademarks of this policy. The South American leftist parties maintained a strong anti-imperialist discourse that was highly critical of U.S. policies in the region, and the communist parties pursued a two-pronged policy that supported working-class demands for short-run improvements in their socioeconomic condition while proclaiming the peaceful transition to socialism in the long run.

The contradictions between supporting both the peaceful road and anti-imperialist discourse were clearly reflected in the conflicts under the

Allende regime and in the contrast between Soviet and U.S. policies in Chile. At the domestic level, the discrepancy between the peaceful road and armed struggle were reflected in the clash between socialists and communists, the main partners in the Popular Unity coalition, over the parties' divergent strategies. The communist strategy was to consolidate first and advance later, while the socialists argued for just the opposite. In practice, these strategic and ideological differences led to different approaches to Chile's political institutions, the problem of political violence, and the pace and depth of economic reform. In the long run, the conflict not only affected these policies, but also paralyzed the Allende administration.[12]

At the international level, while the United States perceived Chile's regime as just another form of communism that threatened U.S. influence in the region—according to Richard Nixon, together with Cuba, it would engulf Latin America in "a red sandwich"[13]—the Soviet Union saw Allende's victory as confirming the viability of the peaceful road policy; the Soviets hailed his election as a truly outstanding event. However, in practice the USSR did not show any real financial or military commitment to the Popular Unity government. What General Secretary Brezhnev wanted was to develop and maintain a spirit of detente with the United States and Western Europe. From the Soviet standpoint, writes Nicola Miller, "the prestige to be won among the world's left-wing forces by supporting Allende simply did not compare with the potential political and economic benefits of peaceful coexistence with the United States, and Moscow was wary of overplaying its hand in a country that Washington considered as within its area of influence."[14]

Moreover, the high cost of the Soviet-Cuban relationship, discussed in chapters 3 and 4, forced the USSR to assess its involvement in the Third World and to conclude that it should aid developing countries only if such aid did not impede the progress of the socialist community.[15] Clearly, while communist parties in South America depended on ideas and support from Moscow, they were not essential to the Soviet policy design. On the contrary, Moscow was fairly insensitive to the effects of its policies on those parties. Brezhnev's unconcern over the impact of his policies in Chile or in Nicaragua was repeated on a much larger scale by Gorbachev in the late 1980s.

Cuba's foreign policy had been changing since the late 1960s. The death of Guevara, the deterioration of the Cuban economy, and Cuba's subsequent rapprochement with the USSR led to a normalization of Cuba's relations with Latin America and the acceptance of both democratic and military regimes throughout the region. After Allende's election, Castro acknowledged that there might be various roads to socialism. In his visit to Chile in 1971 he stated that what was taking place in Chile was a revolutionary process—which according to him was different from a revolution—in which the revolutionaries were trying to carry out changes peacefully.[16] However, the overthrow of Allende's regime led him to argue anew that armed revolution was the only road to socialism; but, in partial compromise with the Soviet position (and in view of his own limitations), he argued that revolution should be the result of indigenous processes, not the result of external actions.[17]

In South America in the early 1970s, the traditional Left was comprised of communist and socialist parties, the latter following Marxist principles more loosely than their communist counterparts. What is more important, the socialists were not dependent on Moscow for ideological and programmatic guidance and financial support. What Jobet argued in 1971 regarding the Chilean socialists explains the survival of socialist parties despite the current crisis. For the Chilean socialist, writes Jobet, in an assessment that also applies to socialists in most Latin American countries, Marxism is a flexible doctrine; "it is neither the schematic codification of dogmas nor a bunch of citations of the classics interpreted in an opportunistic fashion by those who are permanently serving foreign policies instead of serving the interests of Chilean workers."[18] Socialists stressed instead a regional and nationalist perspective, highlighting the importance of Latin American revolutionary movements and processes, including Peru's American Popular Revolutionary Alliance (APRA), Bolivia's Revolutionary Nationalist Movement (MNR), and the Mexican and Cuban revolutions.[19] The parties showed their independence from the Soviet Union—energetically condemning the Molotov-Ribbentrop Pact and the Soviet invasion of Czechoslovakia, for example.[20]

The Cuban revolution had a different impact on Latin American socialists. Because of their independent line and emphasis on nationalism and indigenous change, they more than the communists held the pro-Cuban banners. Cuba's revolution played a central role in the praxis of socialist parties, not only providing a concrete experience of a nationalist, anti-imperialist revolution, but also modifying their ideological position on revolutionary processes. By the early 1960s socialists were questioning the peaceful road policy, proposing that different forms of struggle should be used and combined according to national or local conditions.[21] But, instead of fighting in the mountains of South America, the socialists continued to struggle in the chambers of Congress as long as Congress remained open.

Bureaucratic-Authoritarian Regimes and the Left in the 1980s

The military regimes that came to power in Brazil and the Southern Cone countries in the 1960s and 1970s shared a number of characteristics, structuring a new and different form of military regime that Guillermo O'Donnell labeled *bureaucratic-authoritarian*.[22] These regimes appeared in response to similar processes, followed comparable political and economic policies, and repressed the Left.

Argentina

In Argentina the military government that came to power in March 1976 initially favored closer economic and diplomatic relations with the USSR.[23] The Argentine Communist party (PCA), though limited by some repressive measures, was not outlawed but only ordered to "suspend" its activities. The party defended the "moderate" sectors of the armed forces, praised their liberal disposition, and commended the move to establish closer ties with the socialist countries. Friendly Soviet-Argentine relations reached a climax in 1980 when Argentina's military government refused to join the grain sales embargo against the USSR following the invasion of Afghanistan, a move praised both by the Soviet government and the PCA as a demonstration of independence from the United States.

Brazil

The military government that took power in a 1964 coup unleashed a wave of repression against the Brazilian Communist party (PCB), while a noticeable chill developed in Brazil's relations with the USSR. In the name of "national security," the military regime embraced a strongly anticommunist doctrine that called for suppression of Marxist groups, closer relations with the United States, consistent anti-Cuban and anti-Soviet positions in the diplomatic arena, and support for similarly oriented military governments in Latin America. Members of the PCB were jailed, tortured, and killed, and repression increased as splinter groups that disagreed with the peaceful road tactics supported by party leaders began to look toward the Cuban revolution as a model and engage in armed resistance. Diplomatic relations with the USSR were maintained, but at a very low level; the Brazilian government denounced the Castroite-Soviet influence behind subversive groups, and the Soviet press depicted Brazil's regime as a reactionary, subimperialist government whose economic accomplishments were achieved by the super-exploitation of the working class.[24]

In 1974 General Ernesto Geisel introduced a foreign policy of "responsible pragmatism" that ended Brazil's automatic alignment with the United States and called for more diversified external relations, including closer ties with socialist and nonaligned countries. At the domestic level, the process of gradual political liberalization (*apertura*) did not result in the legalization of the PCB, but anticommunist repression subsided and the party was able to engage in political activities by supporting the opposition Partido do Movimento Democratico Brasileiro (MDB) and even electing some of its members to Congress under the MDB's ticket.

At the same time, the Soviet Union carefully avoided any hint of interference in Brazil's domestic affairs, merely stating its support for the process of political liberalization. After the PCB split in two factions—a larger "Eurocommunist" organization headed by Giocondo Dias and a smaller pro-Soviet group led by Luiz Carlos Prestes after his return from Moscow in 1980—the CPSU refused to take sides in the dispute. It maintained low-profile contacts with both factions, emphasizing the role played by the communists in the transition to democracy and their support for the Democratic Alliance ticket that in 1985 helped to elect the first civilian administration since 1964.[25]

Chile

Communists and socialists alike bore the brunt of General Pinochet's repressive policies. Chile and the USSR broke diplomatic relations; both leftist parties were outlawed and their leaders were either killed or forced into political exile. A major event in the history of the Latin American Left occurred in 1981 when Chile's Communist party abandoned the peaceful road and embraced popular rebellion instead. Here again one sees the impact of both domestic and international dynamics. As Luis Corvalán, general secretary of the party, argued in 1982, "We are not going to wait until the required conditions are one hundred percent developed. We believe that the struggle will allow us to create those conditions. We believe that the most profound and solid unity is the one created in the course of the struggle as in Cuba and Nicaragua, El Salvador and Guatemala."[26] Asserting the right to rebel, the party accepted the use of force as one more instrument in its struggle against a regime that was itself guilty of violence and terrorism.

Advocacy of violent methods and popular insurrection also entered the political debate in Chile during its transition toward democracy. The Manuel Rodríguez Patriotic Front (FPMR), officially established in 1983, made clear the party's commitment to armed struggle and indicated that the party was following the path of Castro and the Sandinistas. The FPMR proposed a direct confrontation with the military regime and a popular rebellion in which the FPMR would act as the central revolutionary organization. However, party leaders failed to understand that political and economic conditions in Chile in the 1980s were totally different from those in Cuba in 1959 or in Nicaragua in 1978 and that the Pinochet regime represented a different form of authoritarianism. In the long run, the party's policy change complicated the process of political transition both for the party and for the society at large, and it failed to topple the Pinochet regime. Moreover, the party had difficulty adapting to the new strategy, which was not supported by most members. The FPMR did not influence the political transition and, after 1988, the party confronted both an entirely different political environment and an armed group within its own ranks.

In the meantime, the USSR and the United States had become embroiled in a new cold war that intensified the arms race and led to new conflicts in several areas of the world. The USSR maintained partial control of the international communist system, reaffirming the principles of the peaceful road. By and large, Latin American communists remained loyal to the USSR, while the USSR continued to give South America low priority. The Chilean party, despite its advocacy of popular rebellion, remained faithful to Moscow's foreign policy by supporting the USSR's invasion of Afghanistan in 1979, arguing that it was a sign of fraternal and generous help to the people of that country.[27]

Uruguay

As Charles Gillespie argues, Uruguay's democratic regime did not break down in a single event but rather was eroded over a period of about six years, beginning with the December 1967 executive order banning the Socialist party of Uruguay, which had advocated guerrilla warfare for national liberation. The process ended in 1973 when military leaders rebelled against President Juan María Bordaberry and forced him to accept the creation of a National Security Council to oversee his actions. The military later closed the Congress, dissolved the National Confederation of Workers (CNT), banned most of the parties of the Broad Front, and arrested their leaders, including Liber Seregni, a retired general.[28] As elsewhere in South America, the military justified its actions by arguing that the country was in crisis, suffering from economic instability, labor-industrial strife, ideological extremism, and mounting violence. However, in this case not only right and center politicians were tempted by the idea of a military coup; even "the left was seduced by the chimera of a progressive Peruvian-style coup,"[29] and the Broad Front leader General Liber Seregni endorsed the military's actions in February 1973.

Uruguay's Broad Front, founded in 1971, was comprised of about ten political groups, including the communist and the socialist parties. In spite of the repression unleashed by the military, the Broad Front managed to maintain a low level of clandestine activity. Throughout the period, the Left had to contend with a major political issue: the failure of both the guerrilla and the electoral strategies. Just as with Chile's Popular Unity coalition, the communists represented a moderating force, criticizing both the terrorists' adventurism and the socialists' ultraleftism. The discussion led to a rehabilitation of bourgeois democracy as a central principle in communist and socialist ideology in the postauthoritarian period.[30]

During the transition to democracy, military leaders and their allies argued that the Left should never be allowed to operate again. However in March 1989 the military released Liber Seregni from prison. Although he was banned from politics, the action indicated a softening on the part of the military hard-liners; moreover, Seregni called for peace and conciliation between former enemies. With the support of the communists, Seregni was determined to integrate the Left into Uruguay's new political system by transforming it into a democratic force.

Despite many handicaps in the 1989 election (including the Left's late rehabilitation and the denial of political rights to many supporters), the Broad Front was able to revitalize its political base by presenting a moderated position. This new position was not the result of ideological changes at the grass-roots level, but of decisions made by national leaders.[31] By 1985 Rodney Arismendi, general secretary of the Communist party of Uruguay (PCU), argued for a Uruguayan road to socialism that emphasized the role of the Broad Front in the transition and the development and consolidation of democratic institutions.[32]

The Impact of Military Regimes on the Socialist Parties in the Southern Cone Countries

During the period of military rule, the evolution of the socialist parties's political role in Chile and Uruguay shared some common features. In Argentina and Brazil, socialist organizations had existed since the late nineteenth century, but their political impact was limited by the presence of very strong populist movements such as Peronism and the Getulio Vargas movement.

The position of Chile's socialist party underwent a major transformation under military rule. While the communists tended to support armed struggle, the divided socialists moved in an opposite direction, emphasizing the construction of a multiclass alliance and adopting Gramscian principles. Of all the factions of the early 1980s, followers of former senator Carlos Altamirano took the lead in this ideological transformation. His group helped to unify the socialist party, as well as to form a broad alliance between the socialists and other parties. In Altamirano's words, "The essential goal is to transform socialism into a great national political force, and this is not going to be accomplished by using the flags of a class-based reductionism."[33] The socialists were clearly abandoning some Marxist-Leninist principles, acquiring in the process strategic flexibility that facilitated their political renovation. Their strategy both unified the party and reintegrated it into the political system, while the communists remained isolated and divided.

In Uruguay too the military regime had a different impact on the socialists than on the communists. The socialist party avoided internal schisms under military rule and reemerged, with a more moderate platform, with stronger popular support than it had before the elections. In brief, both the Chilean and the Uruguayan socialists, as well as the PCU, emerged from the miliary period convinced that only the democratic road and strong democratic institutions could guarantee their survival and growth, that democratic institutions mattered not only for the parties, but also for the protection of individual rights. Thus, the parties' redefinition of themselves included acknowledging the importance of human rights and defending political institutions that protected those rights.

The Post-1985 Years: Gorbachev, Castro, and the Transition to Democracy in the Southern Cone

Gorbachev's reforms in the USSR were prompted by the failure of "real socialism," namely the Soviet interpretation of Marxist-Leninist ideology and its application in the former socialist camp. The system failed not only to promote economic efficiency and competitiveness, but also to fulfill the socialist dream of creating a freer, more egalitarian society than those of capitalist democracies. This failure, in turn, led to a reassessment of the basic economic and political logic of the system, as well as the USSR's international role.

Simultaneously, as South America began to move toward democracy, the Left was reincorporated into the political arena. It is significant that this process took place amid a persistent economic crisis and in an economic environment created by the military regimes' neoliberal fiscal policies. Thus, leftist parties had to confront domestic economic and political challenges as well as a changed international system.

In analyzing the impact of the reforms in the USSR on the Left, one must distinguish again between communists and socialists. The effect of these reforms among communist parties has been devastating; having lost their identity and their model, they now question their programs and their future. Communists must rethink their approach toward what they have always defined as bourgeois democracy and capitalism. The new assessment has to incorporate not only the transformations taking place in the dissolved Soviet bloc but also their own experiences under both democratic and authoritarian regimes, and the political and economic changes taking place in Cuba. The socialist parties, on the other hand, by redefining their ideological framework and their programs, have undergone political renovation.

Communist Parties

In ideological terms, Gorbachev's reforms and the rise of Cuba's counter reform had mixed consequences in Argentina and Brazil, creating tremendous disarray among the leftist forces, especially the communist parties. When Gorbachev made it clear in 1986 that the Soviet government and the Soviet Communist party were not interested in interfering in the internal affairs of countries with which the USSR maintained normal diplomatic relations, South American communist parties were for the first time forced to design their own political strategies according to an autonomous diagnosis of the domestic and international circumstances affecting each country. The pro-Soviet communist parties in Argentina and Brazil, which had always followed the vagaries of Soviet strategic and tactical decisions, were now forced to reassess their domestic and international positions. The internal debate and the attempts to follow an independent course resulted, in most cases, in acute factional struggles and organizational splits.

In Argentina, the PCA entered a period of ideological and organizational turmoil made worse by criticisms of the party's support of the military regime and its ill-fated alliance with the Peronists that brought catastrophic defeat in the 1983 elections for Congress.[34] Partially recovering, the PCA elected a younger, less moderate leadership and moved to the left, establishing an electoral alliance, Frente del Pueblo (FREPU, People's Front), with the Trotskyist-led Movimiento al Socialismo (MAS, Movement toward Socialism).[35] This new coalition was not electorally successful (it obtained only 2 percent of the votes in the 1985 congressional elections), but the PCA continued to denounce the Radical (social democratic) government of President Raúl Alfonsín, hoping to increase its electoral strength as low- and middle-income sectors of the population became disenchanted with the administration's policies.

The PCA's leftward turn was accompanied by a new endorsement of the Cuban experience as a model for the socialist transformation of Latin American society and unprecedented praise for Che Guevara and his revolutionary ideals. The new PCA leaders began to travel frequently to Havana, where they established closer ties with the Cuban Communist party and Fidel Castro.[36] This led to a more favorable assessment of the guerrilla organizations that had been active in Argentina in the 1960s and 1970s, which were now described as "revolutionary" (though misguided) and no longer as "petit-bourgeois adventurists." Finally, the turn toward more radical positions culminated in the Sixteenth Congress of the PCA where the revolutionary example of Cuba was exalted, the possibility of armed struggle vindicated, and the Alfonsín administration denounced as opportunistic and weak in relation to U.S. imperialism.[37] In turn, Alfonsín accused the party of promoting violence and trying to destabilize the nascent Argentine democracy.

Faced with this growing feud, the Soviet government and the CPSU, wishing to preserve cordial relations with the Alfonsín administration, did not support the PCA. The PCA continued to praise the Cuban model and to reject Soviet ideological and political shifts as contrary to Marxist-Leninist ideas and methods. In 1990, as reported by Yevgueni Lisov, Russian assistant attorney general, the CPSU terminated economic aid to the PCA, which between 1981 and 1990 had totaled $4.65 million.[38] In early 1991, the PCA's internal conflicts resulted in the consolidation of diverse internal factions, some of them devoted to defending Marxist-Leninist orthodoxy and the Cuban experience, while others called for redirecting party ideology toward democratic socialism and making its structure more democratic.

In Brazil, the PCB had split into reformist and orthodox factions before the rise of Gorbachev, with the Eurocommunist (reformist) group gaining control over the party organization. In July 1985 the PCB was legalized; it participated in the November municipal elections in an alliance with the majoritarian PMDB, electing close to a hundred council members and seven mayors. At the same time, ten federal deputies elected on the PMDB ticket publicly disclosed their membership in the party. The PCB thenceforth adopted very moderate positions, supporting José Sarney's economic and social policies and trying to present itself as an alternative to the populist Left—led by Leonel Brizola—and the radical Left—gathered under the banner of the Partido dos Trabalhadores (PT, Workers' party).

The USSR and the CPSU maintained relations with the Eurocommunist leadership of the PCB, as well as with the more orthodox faction led by Luiz Carlos Prestes, but tried to avoid any appearance of interfering in domestic Brazilian affairs. According to Anatoly Smirnov, former head of the CPSU's International Department, by 1987 Soviet aid to the PCB—$300,000 annually since 1973—was terminated.[39] In 1989, the PCB's presidential candidate, Roberto Freire, obtained only 1 percent of the votes in the first round, and the party supported the PT candidate, Luiz Inacio da Silva (Lula), in the second balloting. In the 1990 congressional elections, the PCB elected five deputies, Freire among them, who soon became the leader of the party.

In Chile, perestroika and glasnost were seen as peculiar to the USSR and not a major threat to the survival of communism. In fact, even up to mid-1989 the response to these reforms indicates that they were seen as a reinterpretation of traditional dogma. For instance, in the Fifteenth Congress of the Communist party of Chile held in 1989, perestroika was defined as "a revolution within the revolution" and as a "vigorous return to Leninist ideas designed to correct the mistakes of the Stalinist period and of years of stagnation."[40] By 1989, changes in Chile's internal political situation and the proximity of the presidential elections should have forced the party to redefine its political strategy vis-à-vis popular rebellion and the process of transition, but it did not, generating divisions within the party. According to one critic, "The strategy of popular rebellion demonstrated that the incomprehension of the changes in Chile's political situation after 1986 separated the party from popular sentiment and from other democratic sectors in Chilean society."[41]

In 1990, after the collapse of the East European regimes, the national conference of the Chilean party interpreted the reforms in the former USSR as produced by the failure of one form of socialism—bureaucratic (real) socialism—and declared that the party would support a process leading to "more socialism and more democracy."[42] However, at the same conference party leaders reaffirmed the principles of democratic centralism, class struggle, and popular rebellion. (By 1990 the policy of popular rebellion was one of the strategies that the party *could* pursue in order to achieve its goals.)[43] These decisions led to the formation of a dissident group that questioned the viability of these traditional Marxist principles. They also argued that Gorbachev's reforms involved a departure from Marxism and called for similar reforms in the Chilean Communist party. The party's General Secretary Volodia Teitelboim responded by arguing that perestroika was a Soviet phenomenon and it was not going to take place in Chile.[44] But Teitelboim has been proven wrong; the dissidents launched a process of ideological renovation that favors the development of a more flexible theoretical foundation inspired by Gramsci's views, leading to a more democratic vision of socialism and an emphasis on hegemony and consensus rather than the dictatorship of the proletariat.[45]

Substantive criticism of the party's responses to both internal and external change led to a challenge to the very structure and organization of the party: the notion of democratic centralism. In one critic's words, "For decades we constituted a section of the central committee of the Communist International, which functioned in Moscow. Our program, structure, and leaders had to be approved by the Executive Committee of the Communist International."[46] There is little doubt that in the past the party had adopted not only Leninist practices, but also some Stalinist characteristics, and its members had grown used to blindly following the policies of the leadership. According to Gladys Marín, a former deputy and party leader, "Discussion is something new within our party, and within other communist parties as well."[47]

By mid-1991 the party's mainstream not only had failed to reform its structures, but also continued to misinterpret the nature and extent of the reforms taking place in the USSR, arguing that Gorbachev was not renouncing Marxist-Leninist ideas and that the Communist party of Chile would continue to be founded on the ideas of Marx, Engels, and Lenin.[48] Among former communists today, one sees three divisions: those who stayed in the party and supported the policies of the current leadership; those who abandoned the party because of disagreements with the leadership and formed the PDI, or Participación Democrática de Izquierda (Leftist Democratic Participation); and those who were expelled from the party because of disagreements with the leadership.

In 1992, a new leftist front was created. The MIDA, or Movimiento de Izquierda Democrático Allendista (Allendista Leftist Democratic Movement), was organized around the Communist party and designed to enhance the party's position in the 1992 municipal elections.[49] Lacking in this new political structure was any redefinition of the communists' identity and discourse, not to mention a popular foundation. Although it was apparently created to end the party's political isolation, it will likely fail because it is the invention of political elites from various small parties with little support and without a real program or base. Other parties joining the MIDA include the former MIR (Leftist Revolutionary Movement), the Workers Action Communist party (which followed the Albanian line), the Manuel Rodríguez Patriotic Movement, and a few marginal socialist groups.

Communists in Uruguay also reacted very slowly and with much difficulty to the changes in the USSR, due to the party's trust in the USSR and its blind belief in Marxist dogma. In the eyes of one analyst, "These dogmas functioned as self-censorship, creating cognitive discordances that blocked the individuals' ability to think. . . . There are, also, mechanisms of idealization that do not leave any room to analyze mistakes or defeats; . . . [defeats] are the result not of one's failure but of the actions of the enemy."[50] For instance, as late as 1988, Rodrigo Arocena, general secretary of the PCU, sent a telegram to the Polish workers emphasizing the working-class nature of the Polish state.[51]

In 1990 the Twenty-second Congress of the Uruguayan party adopted a set of policies calling for renovation, including the abandonment of such concepts as the dictatorship of the proletariat and the armed struggle. The reforms did not take place, however, because control of the party remained in the hands of the traditional leaders.[52] Some Uruguayan communists now question their loyalty to Marx and Lenin; two groups are in conflict: the *históricos,* identified with the traditional communist stand, and the *renovadores,* who call for an open social-democratic front.[53] A total rupture took place in April 1992, when fourteen members of the central committee resigned, including Jaime Pérez, general secretary of the party.[54]

Socialist Parties

Although the reverberations of the Soviet collapse and the Cuban counter reform are most obvious in the case of the communist parties, these developments have also had a significant impact on other segments of the South American Left. Among socialist parties and groups, greater ideological and organizational flexibility, as well as opposition to the Soviet model, have eased their accommodation to new circumstances. Cuba's economic, social, and political problems have reinforced the pragmatism of most South American socialists. Accepting the impossibility of a radical socialist transformation, they concentrate their efforts on gradual reform—introducing marginal changes in social policy while promoting an orderly political enfranchisement of low-income groups, but only under conditions that do not threaten existing liberal democracies.

Most socialists emphasize their longstanding disagreement with Leninist-Stalinist methods and ideas. They argue for programmatic renovation, stressing the pluralistic democratic features of their ideology while abandoning or minimizing traditional Marxist calls for radical and total socioeconomic transformation of the capitalist system. The new model does not aim to build a working-class revolutionary party; it appears to follow the example of West European social democratic parties (Spanish, Portuguese, Italian) that have become catchall organizations with limited reformist goals.

In Chile, as we have argued, the socialists' ideological renovation had begun before Gorbachev came to power. They had to deal with their own political fragmentation, with the need to establish a broad alliance to facilitate the transition to democracy and to reexamine Marxist doctrine. The discussion started a process that culminated in abandoning Leninism and accepting pluralist democracy as a central socialist goal. In their search for a more flexible form of Marxism, some socialist leaders began to adopt Gramsci's concept of the "historical bloc," which focuses on the need to build grass-roots organizations that in turn would create new forms of political participation and a more egalitarian society.

Others have gone one step further and have proposed a total elimination of Marxism from party ideology and a more flexible approach to market-oriented economic policies.[55] Jorge Arrate, current president of Chile's Socialist party, defines the renovation as a new formulation of the socialist idea. "It involves a process of self-criticism of the past and the establishment of an antidogmatic and democratic ideology . . . that reaffirms the existence of our own road."[56] In a 1992 interview, Enrique Correa, minister of government in the Aylwin administration and Socialist party leader, argued that what is left of socialist ideology is a passion to balance liberty and equality, and that the real breakthrough in Chilean politics would take place when the socialists cut, definitively, the umbilical cord that ties them to the past.[57] He argues also that after the fall of the Berlin Wall the only viable Left is the social democratic Left. After praising the policies of Felipe González in Spain and François Mitterrand in France, he concludes,

> Once the country achieves economic development and equity [people] would understand the political courage of the socialists as they travel through uncharted lands. This new leftist approach involves a new way of being leftist that involves moderation, democracy, trust in the rules of the market, an active role of the state in protecting social equity, and abandoning statism and economic centralization.[58]

In Uruguay socialists have experienced a similar phenomenon. Thus, at the last Extraordinary Party Congress of November 1991, the party's Central Committee proposed to adopt a new political line that eliminated not only the party's traditional Marxist-Leninist foundations, but even references to José Mariátegui and Salvador Allende. It is now defined as a working-class party that favors the establishment of a new democracy based on pluralism and political competition.[59]

In conclusion, it is clear that while Latin America's communist parties in recent years have lived in a state of permanent denial that prevents them from appreciating political realities both at home and abroad, socialist parties have undergone ideological renovation. Central to the new socialist approach are not only traditional concerns with social equity and working-class issues, but also a respect for democracy and a determination to preserve democratic institutions, accepting the market as the basic regulator of economic activity, and a renewed concern with human rights issues arising from party members' experience under the military regimes.

Speculations About the Future: The Divergent Paths of the South American Left

As we ponder the future of the Left in South America, we should discuss three sets of issues: first, the impact of the collapse of the Soviet bloc on the future of these parties, particularly the communists; second, the effect on the Left of Castro's Rectification Process and Cuba's political and economic crisis; and finally, the place of these parties in their countries' political and economic landscape.

Communist parties have reacted only belatedly, if at all, to events in the Soviet Union after the foiled coup of August 1991. It is not a question of interpreting Gorbachev's reforms, but of the disappearance of the Soviet Union and its replacement by a loosely formed Commonwealth of Independent States (CIS) under Boris Yeltsin's troubled leadership. Maybe Latin American communists should emulate their Italian counterparts and dissolve themselves. As one analyst argues, "The choice [for Italian communists] was between sliding back from the precipice or leaping into it,"[60] but in fact this strategy did not save the party from divisions and conflict, since Occheto (the general secretary) failed to unify the party behind him. South American communists have chosen to slide into the chasm.

The disintegration of the USSR was accompanied by the elimination of the CPSU and the rejection of communist ideology. In September 1991, Boris Yeltsin said:

> Communist expansionism did not bring happiness to the peoples of the countries that fell into its sphere of influence. On the contrary, the communist idea has found itself downcast for many long years, while the people's humanist potential has been seriously undermined. In the end, violence to man and his spirit and to social groups and peoples, to the whole of society, could not lead and did not lead to liberation.[61]

The defection of the former Soviet leadership helped to cast Cuba in its new role as the last bastion of Marxist-Leninist orthodoxy. Cuba reasserted its commitment to communist ideology and to the party in the Fourth Party Congress. In the words of Fidel Castro, regarding an expansion of the party's membership:

> This [debate] is essential under the circumstances in which we are living, that of a special period, in which we have to fulfill the slogan of saving the fatherland, the revolution, and socialism. . . . Of course, it is important to know about the influencing role of the party; it is a sacred and essential thing. I mention this because of what happened in the Soviet Union, where the party was dissolved through a presidential decree. . . . The revolution is not conceived without the party. Power is not conceived without the party. Socialism is not conceived without the party.[62]

As expected, the controversy between Soviet and Cuban leaders exacerbated internal tensions in Argentina's and Brazil's communist parties and exacerbated their internal disarray: some groups decided to discard the ideological and organizational Marxist-Leninist tradition, while others supported Cuba's orthodox approach.

In Argentina, the PCA had split into factions by the end of 1990, with some groups calling for the abolition of the party to make way for a broader leftist democratic force and others wanting to maintain the party's existing organization and ideology and expressing solidarity with the Cuban model. As the latter group prevailed, the former (including some members of the PCA's central committee) resigned, denouncing the lack of internal democracy and the refusal of orthodox members to modernize the party. The failed coup in the USSR led to new problems; PCA leaders refused to condemn the putsch, a position harshly criticized by some

party members and by the PCA's electoral allies, including the Movimiento al Socialismo (MAS).[63] The Cuban issue also generated deep
divisions in the Left, which became clear in 1992 during the May Day
demonstration organized by the leftist parties in Plaza de Mayo. Luis
Zamora, a leader of the MAS, criticized Cuba's "single party regime"
and was attacked by members of the PCA, who threw coins at Zamora
and engaged in a brawl with MAS militants while voicing their support
for Castro's government.[64]

In Brazil, the coup also aggravated the PCB's internal dissension as
members of the orthodox faction criticized the vehement condemnation
of the putsch by the party's president, Roberto Freire, and submitted
their resignations.[65] In August 1991, Juliano Siqueira, a member of the
PCB central committee sympathetic to Cuba, announced his intention
to leave the party with these words: "I believe that currently the only
things the PCB has in common with communism are the party name and
flag. The PCB has become a social democratic party and the Marxist-
Leninist theory supporters can only be members of parties that support
class struggle."[66]

In January 1992, the split was made final when orthodox groups, dissatisfied with the decisions made by the Tenth Congress of the PCB to
abandon Marxism-Leninism and to change the party's name to Partido
Popular Socialista (PPS, People's Socialist party), resolved to create a
new organization. Under the leadership of Horacio Macedo, Ivan Pin-
heiro, and Oscar Niemeyer, it would keep the Communist party name
and symbols, advocate Marxist-Leninist revolutionary methods and programs, and defend Cuba's revolutionary example.[67] Meanwhile, Roberto
Freire, the leader of the newly created PPS, supported the democratic
option and criticized Castro's intransigence:

> This is a process of continuity and change. Some communist parties were dis-
> banded while others have been renewed and are treading the path of the so-called
> Democratic Left. . . . The new thing is socialism with democracy and free-
> dom. . . . Fidel will have to open the country, both politically and economically
> speaking. I hope he is able to accomplish the perestroika that Gorbachev was
> unable to accomplish.[68]

It is obvious that without Soviet support and torn by internal disarray,
the Argentine and Brazilian communist parties have lost most of their
former (modest) political influence. Centrist and conservative adminis-

trations and parties have no reason to fear them, nor any reason to invoke the specter of communism for ulterior purposes as in the past (such as to obtain U.S. support or to justify political repression). However, from the perspective of these same groups, the decline of the pro-Soviet communist parties that were characterized by pragmatism and moderation might not be a blessing: their collapse might invite the rise of more radical, less predictable leftist organizations whose ability to influence and mobilize the population had been inhibited by the presence of relatively well-organized orthodox communist groups.

In Chile and Uruguay there was a deepening of divisions that had already begun. This culminated with the fracturing of both communist parties in early 1992 and their marginalization from national politics. Cuba's political and economic reforms seemed to have had less impact on these two parties than on their counterparts in Argentina and Brazil.

Castro's is now the only Marxist-Leninist regime left in the Western world, and the question is whether he or his regime can provide the model and support needed by the South American leftist parties. What is important is that Castro's influence has always been much greater over socialists and guerrilla groups than traditional communist parties because of his conflicts with the USSR, his emphasis on regional political and economic issues, and his support of violent revolution. Thus, in spite of his charisma, Castro does not have the influence over the Latin American communist parties that the Soviet Union once had, and he now lacks the structural, financial, and organizational capability to replace the former Soviet Union. What the leftist parties need besides new ideological foundations is an influx of financial and organizational assistance. Given Cuba's deep economic crisis, it is unlikely that Castro could provide such aid.

Clearly, much of the appeal of the Cuban revolution for the Latin American Left during the past thirty-four years was the result of a convergence of personal, policy-oriented, and international factors, and these sources of appeal have either drastically changed or eroded. At the personal level, Castro's charisma provided Latin American leftists with a popular, regional leader who could challenge not only one but both superpowers. From a policy standpoint, the popularity of Castro and his revolution were enhanced by the success of socioeconomic policies that brought considerable social equity to Cuban society. Finally, Castro's success was grounded in a bipolar international system that not only assured him Soviet support but also enabled him to brandish the banner of Latin American anti-imperialism. By 1992, Castro's charisma has clearly declined, the economic crisis has eroded Cuba's socioeconomic gains, and the bipolar system has disappeared—the United States has no ideological or military rival.

Moreover, the centralization of political and economic power that is the trademark of Cuba's Rectification Process is too close to Stalinism and to the failed policies of Eastern Europe to solve the complex domestic and international economic issues faced by Latin American countries: trade relations, debt problems, budget equilibrium, inflation, regional integration, and popular demands. For instance, Cuba's Fourth Party Congress, held in October 1991, called for reorganizing the central administration "with the goal of guaranteeing the necessary centralization of decision making."[69] At the same time, Castro is apparently determined to preserve the political status quo and to prevent political change.[70]

Events in the Eastern bloc and Cuba's economic problems have led to increasing political discontent and the apparent growth of a political opposition. Castro's response, by and large, has been to intensify repression, as in the case of human rights activist Maria Elena Cruz Varela, the organization of peasant vigilante brigades to preserve order in the countryside, and using "so-called rapid-deployment forces modeled after former Panamanian dictator Manuel Noriega's 'dignity battalions' and the Sandinistas' infamous 'turbas,' to harass and beat up people whose crime is to support human rights and democracy."[71]

At the international level, Castro's confrontational stance is also outmoded. Maybe he can argue that the choice is "socialism or death," but for most leaders and militants of the traditional South American Left, the choices are quite varied and there is no need to challenge U.S. power in the hemisphere, given the disappearance of the Soviet bloc and existing economic ties between the United States and South America.[72]

Castro, the Cuban Communist party, and the entire population and economy clearly face enormous challenges that reduce Cuba's capacity to project its influence on the South American Left. This decline of influence—manifested in the rejection of the Cuban model by the renovated Left—is counterbalanced by gains among the ranks of the more radical Left. The collapse of the USSR and Eastern Europe give the Cuban regime an opportunity to project a new image as an uncontested champion of Marxist-Leninist orthodoxy and revolutionary socialism, as a nationalistic actor no longer dependent on the USSR, as the main challenger to U.S. hegemony, and as the main opponent to the hemisphere's general acceptance of the neoliberal free market model.[73]

In this context, it would be premature to announce the demise of Cuba's influence on the South American Left. The more radical sectors of the Left may defend Cuba—albeit recognizing its shortcomings in economic policies, democratic participation, and human rights—as the last example of revolutionary ideals and practices in the Americas, and they could gravitate toward Castro and the Cuban Communist party.

In turn, the Cuban leadership will do whatever is necessary to maintain and strengthen this solidarity. An interesting example of this new approach is the resolution approved by the Fourth Party Congress to admit religious believers into the party. This will facilitate closer relations with South American grass-roots groups such as the church-sponsored *comunidades eclesiásticas de base*.

While in Argentina, and to a lesser extent in Brazil, factions of the communist parties have turned to the left, in Chile and Uruguay they are divided and unable to find a political line. For the renovated socialists, on the other hand, Castro is a remnant of the past—or, in the words of Carlos Altamirano, "The period of the great wars . . . of the great Leninist revolutions . . . and the great nationalist revolutions in the Third World is over. . . . The confrontational stage is being replaced by a period of cooperation."[74] Castro just does not fit into this new world order.

Is there a role for the Left in South American politics? It seems that in spite of the disappearance of communism from the Soviet Union and Eastern Europe, leftist parties (not necessarily communists) will still have a place in the region's political systems. During the 1980s, South America experienced two crucial processes: democratization and a severe economic crisis. As the poor regain the right to vote and to participate in politics, one might expect to see a need for parties representing their views and pressure on politicians to address their needs, as well as environmental problems, human rights, and women's rights. The remnants of the traditional communist parties will have difficulty dealing with these issues, and the renovated socialists are already developing a pragmatic, nontheoretical socioeconomic agenda oriented toward specific issues. Can the nontraditional Left, or groups formed by dissident communists and socialists, gain the support of population sectors that are (or soon will be) disenchanted with the programs of renovated leftist groups or of liberal democratic regimes?

Changes in the Left could produce changes in Latin America's political cycles, which in the past have pushed countries from democracy to authoritarianism and vice versa. Two scenarios are possible: either the Left becomes so fragmented that it in fact disappears as a major political actor, or its fragmentation could encourage the rise or strengthening of more radical and less predictable organizations capable of influencing and mobilizing low-income groups because of the disappearance of the reformist orthodox parties.

It is important to note that although Marxism might have faded, the issues that Marxism dealt with and the leftist parties addressed have not. As Richard Rorty suggests, maybe it is time to start talking not in large theoretical terms, but in fairly concrete practical terms. Those in South America concerned with social equity should talk about "greed and selfishness rather than about bourgeois ideology, about starvation wages and layoffs rather than about the commodification of labor, and about differential per-pupil expenditure and differential access to health care rather than about the division of society into classes."[75]

NOTES

1. Kenneth Roberts, "Renovation in the Revolution? Dictatorship, Democracy, and the Evolution of the Left in Chile," presented at the XVI Congress of the Latin American Studies Association, Washington, D.C., April 1991, p. 1.

2. Seweryn Bialer, "Gorbachev's Program of Change: Sources, Significance, Prospects," in *Gorbachev's Russian and American Foreign Policy*, ed. S. Bialer and M. Mandelbaum (Boulder: Westview, 1987), pp. 254–55, 369; and "Domestic and International Factors in the Formation of Gorbachev's Reforms," in *The Soviet System in Crisis: A Reader of Western and Soviet Views*, ed. A. Dallin and G. W. Lapidus (Boulder: Westview, 1991).

3. Mikhail S. Gorbachev, *Perestroika: New Thinking for Our Country and the World* (New York: Harper and Row, 1987); Sylvia Goodby, *Gorbachev and the Decline of Ideology in Soviet Foreign Policy* (Boulder: Westview, 1989).

4. Irina Zorina, "Nuevos enfoques en la política exterior de la URSS hacia el 'Tercer Mundo', América Latina y los países del Cono Sur," in *Nuevos Rumbos en la relación Unión Soviética/América Latina*, ed. Roberto Russell (Buenos Aires: FLASCO–Grupo Editor Latinoamericano, Colección Estudios Internacionales, 1990), pp. 121–22.

5. See Eusebio Mujal León, "La URSS y América Latina: Una relación en vias de desarrollo," in *Nuevos Rumbos*, ed. Roberto Russell, p. 134.

6. Gorbachev, *Perestroika*, p. 188.

7. See Serguei Iskenderov, "La política de la Unión Soviética respecto a América Latina, hoy," interview with Yuri Pavlov, chief of the Latin American Department of the Soviet Foreign Relations Ministry, *Noticias de la Unión Soviética* 10, no. 375 (July 26, 1989): 2–3; and ibid., no. 376 (August 3, 1989): 2–3.

8. On Gorbachev's visit to Cuba, see Agencia de Prensa Novosti, "Mijail Gorbachov comenzó su visita a Cuba," *Noticias de la Unión Soviética* 10, no. 307 (April 3, 1989): 1–2; "Gorbachov en La Habana: Una visita histórica," *URSS: Documentos, materiales, información*, Sección de prensa de la embajada de la URSS, Argentina (5 April 1989); and "'Un acontecimiento muy significativo: Hemos abordado todas las cuestiones de la política mundial' dijo Gorbachov al término de su visita a Cuba," *Noticias de la Unión Soviética*, 10, no. 309 (April 6, 1989): 1–2.

9. Boris Yopo, "Las relaciones internacionales del Partido Comunista" in *El Partido Comunista en Chile*, ed. Augusto Varas (Santiago: CESOC-FLACSO, 1988), pp. 373–402; G. Caetano and J. P. Rilla, "La izquierda uruguaya y el 'socialismo real': Visión histórica de algunas trayectorias," in *La herencia del socialismo real*, ed. Hugo Achugar (Montevideo: Fesur, 1991), pp. 9–59; Oscar Arévalo, *El Partido Comunista* (Buenos Aires: Centro Editor de América Latina, 1983); Ronald Chilcote, *The Brazilian Communist Party: Conflict and Integration, 1922–1972* (New York: Oxford University Press, 1974).

10. Walter LaFeber, *Inevitable Revolutions: The United States in Central America* (New York: Norton, 1984), pp. 93–98.

11. Guevara's ideas are discussed in *Ché Guevara Speaks: Selected Speeches and Writings* (New York: Merit, 1967) and by Regis Debrais in *A Critique of Arms* (New York: Penguin, 1977).

12. For an analysis, see Silvia Borzutzky, "Chilean Politics and Social Security Policies," Ph.D. diss., University of Pittsburgh, 1983, pp. 201–10.

13. Cited by Nathaniel Davis, *The Last Two Years of Salvador Allende* (Ithaca: Cornell University Press, 1985), p. 6.

14. Nicola Miller, *Soviet Relations with Latin America, 1959-1987* (Cambridge: Cambridge University Press, 1989), pp. 130–31.

15. Ibid., p. 131.

16. Carmelo Mesa-Lago, *Cuba in the 1970s: Pragmatism and Institutionalization* (Albuquerque: New Mexico University Press, 1978), pp. 128–29.

17. Fidel Castro, Speech, *Time*, February 11, 1974, pp. 37–38; see Mesa-Lago, *Cuba in the 1970s*, chap. 4.

18. Julio César Jobet, *El Partido Socialista de Chile* (Santiago: PLA, 1971), p. 48.

19. Tomás Moulian, *Democracia y socialismo en Chile* (Santiago: FLACSO, 1983), p. 85.

20. Caetano and Rilla, "La izquierda uruguaya," pp. 48–51; Jobet, *El partido*, p. 143.

21. Caetano and Rilla, "La izquierda uruguaya," p. 52; Moulian, *Democracia*, p. 89.

320   SILVIA BORZUTZKY AND ALDO VACS

22. Guillermo O'Donnell, *Modernization and Bureaucratic Authoritarianism* (Berkeley: Institute of International Studies, University of California, 1973).

23. Aldo C. Vacs, *Discreet Partners: Argentina and the USSR since 1917* (Pittsburgh: University of Pittsburgh Press, 1984), pp. 41–65, 71–90.

24. On the Brazilian "national security doctrine," see Maria Helena Moreira Alves, *State and Opposition in Military Brazil* (Austin: University of Texas Press, 1985). On the Soviet characterization of the Brazilian military regime, see, for instance, the debate on Latin American authoritarian regimes in "En torno al problema de los regimenes autoritarios de derecha contemporaneos," *América Latina* 3 (1976): 76–155.

25. On the evolution of the PCB's internal dispute and its electoral role, see the articles on Brazil published between 1981 and 1986 in Richard F. Staar, ed., *Yearbook on International Communist Affairs* (Stanford: Hoover Institution Press).

26. Luis Corvalán, "Rebelión Popular: Camino de nuestro partido" (Santiago: mimeographed, 1982), quoted by Yopo, "Las relaciones," p. 391.

27. Yopo, "Las relaciones," p. 389.

28. Charles G. Gillespie, *Negotiating Democracy: Politicians and Generals in Uruguay* (Cambridge: Cambridge University Press, 1991), pp. 33–34.

29. Ibid., p. 44.

30. Ibid., p. 63.

31. PCU, *Congresos y Documentos del Partido Comunista de Uruguay* (Montevideo: Comisión Nacional de Propaganda del PCU de Uruguay, 1988), pp. 233–87.

32. PCU, *Congresos*, p. 303.

33. Patricia Politzer, *Altamirano* (Buenos Aires: Grupo Editorial Zeta, 1989), p. 117.

34. For analyses of the evolution of the CPA's positions and internal debates, see, for instance, Oscar Arévalo, *El Partido Comunista* (Buenos Aires: Centro Editor de América Latina, 1983); and Ricardo Falcón and Hugo Quiroga, *Contribución al estudio de la evolución ideológica del Partido Comunista Argentino (1960-1984)*, unpublished manuscript, Buenos Aires, September 1985.

35. On the internal changes and the more radical positions adopted by the CPA in 1985, see Maria Seoane, "Autocrítica comunista: El puntapié inicial," *El Periodista de Buenos Aires* 68 (December 27, 1985–January 6, 1986), p. 4; and Patricio Echegaray (secretary general of the CPA), "Queremos cambiar el poder, no voltear el gobierno," ibid., 79 (March 14-20, 1986), p. 40.

36. See Joaquín Morales Solá, *Asalto a la ilusión: Historia secreta del poder en la Argentina desde 1983* (Buenos Aires: Planeta Espejo de la Argentina, 1991), pp. 231–32.

37. Ibid., pp. 234–35.

38. Foreign Broadcast Information Service (hereafter FBIS), Latin America (19 February 1992), p. 29. This charge was denounced as a lie by the PCA press secretary, Oscar Laborda, who added that the PCA was financed by its members and followers and that it was "ridiculous to charge us with having received funds up to 1991, because in 1983 our party began a revision process that, as of 1986, resulted in the distancing of the two parties."

39. See James Brooke, "Hammer-and-Sickle Falls out of Fashion in Brazil," *New York Times*, January 28, 1992, p. A6.

40. *Informe del Comité Central al XV Congreso Nacional del Partido Comunista,* May 1989, p. 24, published in *El Siglo,* supplement.

41. Luis Guastavino, "A la Conferencia Nacional del Partido," May 1990, pp. 8–9, quoted by Roberts, "Renovation," p. 23.

42. *Conferencia Nacional,* Partido Comunista de Chile, published in *El Siglo,* June 3–9, 1990 (separata).

43. Ibid.

44. *El Siglo,* (separata).

45. Roberts, "Renovation," p. 15.

46. Guastavino, "Conferencia," p. 3, quoted by Roberts, "Renovation," p. 28.

47. *El Siglo,* May 27–June 2, 1990 (separata).

48. *Análisis,* August 5–11, 1991, p. 40.

49. *Análisis,* December 23, 1991–January 5, 1992, pp. 10–11.

50. Manuel Laguarda, "Asumir la crisis del socialismo real," quoted in Achugar, *La herencia,* pp. 175–76.

51. Ibid., p. 178.

52. *La República,* April 5, 1992, pp. 2–3.

53. *Búsqueda,* December 5, 1991, p. 9.

54. *La República,* April 5, 1992, pp. 2–3.

55. The process of socialist renovation has been analyzed by Ignacio Walker, *Socialismo y democracia: Chile y Europa en perspectiva comparada* (Santiago: CIEPLAN-Hachette, 1990); Carlos Bascuñan Edwards, *La izquierda sin Allende* (Santiago: Planeta, Espejo de Chile, 1990); Alexis Guardia, *Chile, país centauro: Perfil del socialismo renovado* (Santiago: Ediciones BAT, 1990); Jorge Arrate, *La fuerza democrática de la idea socialista* (Barcelona: Ediciones Documentas, 1985).

56. Arrate, *La fuerza,* chap. 10.

57. *El Mercurio* (international edition), interview with Enrique Correa, January 30–February 5, 1992, p. 6.

58. Ibid.

59. *La República,* 16 November 1991, p. 10.

60. Martin J. Bull, "Whatever Happened to Italian Communism? Explaining the Dissolution of the Largest Communist Party in the West," *West European Politics* 14, no. 4 (October 1991): 116.

61. FBIS, Soviet Union, 12 September 1991, p. 1.

62. FBIS, Latin America, 15 October 1991, p. 32.

63. FBIS, Latin America, 22 August 1991, p. 32.

64. *Clarín* (international edition), April 23–May 4, 1992), p. 5.

65. See FBIS, Latin America, August 21, 1991, p. 19; ibid., August 22, 1991, p. 38.

66. FBIS, Latin America, August 22, 1991, p. 38.

67. See FBIS, Latin America, January 24, 1992, pp. 35–37; and Brooke, "Hammer-and-Sickle."

68. FBIS, Latin America, January 24, 1992, pp. 35–36.

69. "Resolution on the Country's Economic Development," Fourth Congress of the Cuban Communist Party, *Granma International,* October 27, 1991.

70. A.R.M. Ritter, "Prospects for Economic and Political Change in Cuba in the 1990s," Development Studies Working Paper Series, Norman Paterson School of International Affairs, Carleton University, Ottawa, April 1991.

71. Susan Kaufman Purcell, "Collapsing Cuba," *Foreign Affairs* 17, no. 1 (special edition: "America and the World 1991/92"): 139.

72. For an analysis of the impact of the end of the cold war, see Wayne S. Smith, ed., *The Russians Aren't Coming: New Soviet Policy in Latin America* (Boulder and London: Lynne Rienner, 1992).

73. See FBIS, Latin America, October 15, 1991, pp. 27–28.

74. Politzer, *Altamirano*, p. 164.

75. Richard Rorty, "The Intellectuals and the End of Socialism," *Yale Review* 80, nos. 1–2 (April 1992): 5.

9

A Strategy for the Economic Transformation of Cuba Based on the East European Experience

❖ ❖ ❖

JAN SVEJNAR AND JORGE PÉREZ-LÓPEZ

THIS CHAPTER examines the lessons for Cuba from the transition strategies and policies pursued by the transforming socialist economies, with a special emphasis on countries in Central and East Europe (CEE). Their experiences are relevant for Cuba because the Cuban economy is systemically very similar to those in most CEE countries until 1990. Moreover, certain features of the Cuban economy in the 1990s (such as a growing budget deficit, a high foreign debt) parallel conditions in Yugoslavia, Poland, and the Soviet Union before the loss of macroeconomic control, the onset of hyperinflation, and the introduction of stabilization measures at the start of the transition. Finally, like the East European countries, Cuba has suffered a major external shock as a result of the disintegration of the Council for Mutual Economic Assistance (CMEA) and the collapse of the Soviet market in the early 1990s.

We begin by summarizing the initial economic conditions of the command economies, the main policy changes made in the early stages of the transition, and obstacles to change. Then we draw lessons from the East European experience for designing an optimal transition strategy for Cuba.[1] Since the timing of any future Cuban transformation is uncertain, this section presents principal elements rather than a full-fledged framework for a transition strategy.[2] Section 4 concludes with lessons from the East European experience for potential change in Cuba.

323

Economic Conditions Before 1990 and Recent Developments

Before the transformation began, the socialist economies shared a number of similarities that to a large extent determined their economic outcomes.[3] Most important were: the limited existence and functioning of domestic markets; an openness to regulated trade within the CMEA, together with isolation from other international markets; centrally controlled prices; perverse economic incentives that encouraged inefficiency; policy imperatives such as the maintenance of full employment irrespective of labor productivity in a given use; ill-defined property rights within the state or social ownership system; and the virtual absence of institutions essential to market-related activities such as banking, accounting, auditing and taxation. These common conditions resulted in misallocated resources, little incentive to innovate and maintain infrastructure and capital equipment, low incomes and productivity, and macroeconomic instability.

On the positive side, the transforming CEE economies, like Cuba, developed a relatively solid and broad skilled work force.[4] Some also have potentially good access to foreign aid.

In recent years, the CEE countries have undergone major transformations, although they differ in the changes they have emphasized and the speed of implementation. In this section we summarize the main economic policy initiatives undertaken so far and focus on common patterns across countries. What we lose in detail we gain in simplicity and analytical power.

Macroeconomic Stabilization

The principal goal of the changes was to stabilize the economies and create institutions for maintaining macroeconomic stability. This goal arose from the realization that the communist system resulted in a situation that was unstable absent central controls. Indeed, all the socialist countries shared these controls, which significantly limited the use of standard macroeconomic policies to attain stability.

Within the framework of centrally set prices and wages, money was used to facilitate consumer transactions under hard budget constraints. However, on the enterprise side, given the centrality of quantity planning, money was a passive instrument enabling command transactions to take place under soft budget constraints. Monetary policy, thus subordinated to the system of quantitative allocations, did not play an independent role. As the system began to disintegrate, monetary policy was used in several socialist economies to delay the downfall of the system. In Poland, Yugoslavia, and the Soviet Union, for example, an expansive monetary policy—excessive printing of money—was used to avoid fiscal problems at the government and enterprise level, which resulted in hyperinflation. The more conservative governments of Czechoslovakia and East Germany, in contrast, did not resort to excessive printing of currency.

Many economists also argue that the socialist economies suffered from a monetary overhang in that consumers held extra savings or money balances because they could not find enough goods and services to purchase. The significance of this phenomenon has been disputed, as very active black markets provided goods and services at market clearing prices. The debate has real significance for designing an appropriate stabilization program because monetary overhang could add to inflationary pressures, once prices are liberalized.

Fiscal balance was traditionally maintained through centrally controlled wages and prices, confiscation of profits,[5] and a residual determination of subsidies to loss-making firms. As the system began to collapse, most governments started running budget deficits in an attempt to maintain subsidies on socially sensitive goods and services. In the case of Poland, for instance, the estimated 1989 budget deficit was 5–7 percent of GDP.[6] Another sign of increasing fiscal stress was the gradual and significant reduction in investment in infrastructure.

Some socialist countries also accumulated considerable foreign debt. In 1990 the ratio between external debt and gross domestic product (GDP) in Bulgaria, Poland, and Hungary stood at 50 percent, 65 percent, and 80 percent, respectively. By contrast, figures for Czechoslovakia (19 percent) and Romania (3 percent) were much lower.[7]

In an attempt to cope with these problems, most Central and East European countries adopted heterodox macroeconomic programs with the assistance of the International Monetary Fund. The programs relied on the imposition of three nominal anchors—restrictive monetary and fiscal policies, a fixed exchange rate, and wage bill controls—together with the creation of standard institutions such as an independent central bank, an auditing system, and an effective tax office.

Microeconomic Policies

On the microeconomic front, the reforming governments adopted two types of measures: some to reallocate resources and others to enhance their efficient use given their allocation. The former measures have received considerable attention because labor is historically immobile and capital appears to be seriously misallocated. Yet the latter measures are also extremely important in the short term, as leaders decide how best to use labor under the existing capital structure.

Regarding measures to improve the use of resources, one must distinguish between internal reforms that can be imposed by a firm's management (such as improved incentives to productivity) and institutional reforms that require government action (for example, introducing competition or a legal system). Internal reforms can be decentralized; however, economywide uniformity is important to institutional reforms but requires competent policy decisions on the part of the government.

Price Liberalization.   Virtually all transforming economies have undertaken a sweeping liberalization of prices. Most producer and consumer prices have been freed, although prices of basic commodities (such as bread and apartment rentals), as well as some industrial commodities, continue to be controlled in some countries. Price liberalization has definitely provided better signals to producers and consumers and has led to more efficient allocation and use of resources.

Privatization.   All governments have moved forcefully to privatize small enterprises, most often by auction and direct sale. As with any new large-scale program, privatization first encountered organizational difficulties. However, after initial problems it has proceeded quite smoothly in Czechoslovakia, Hungary, and Poland, where most small firms were privatized in the first two years of the transformation. Indeed, tens of thousands of outlets and small establishments have been privatized in each country, and the "small privatization" process continues, with immense gains in efficiency through a better use of resources. In some cases (for example, Czechoslovakia), the reallocation of resources has been limited, as the government stipulated that privatized stores should carry on the same type of business for several more years.

The privatization of medium-sized and large enterprises has been the pivotal, yet the most difficult and frustrating, aspect of the transformation to a market economy. Most observers agree that the success of the entire transition hinges on successful privatization, but no one has come up with an appealing scheme for achieving this goal *well* in a short period. The problem is so daunting that all countries except Czechoslovakia and the former German Democratic Republic have slowed their privatization efforts. Hence most large and medium-sized firms remain state-owned, and their commercialization (that is, their reorientation toward marketlike behavior through greater autonomy from central ministries and tighter supervision and control by boards of directors) has so far been more de facto than de jure. Since the issue is so important, we briefly sketch the problems encountered in Hungary and Poland and provide a more detailed assessment of rapidly privatizing Czechoslovakia.

In 1989 Hungary proclaimed a five-year goal of privatizing about 50 percent of its medium-sized and large firms. It went furthest in the early phase, privatizing about 10 percent of such firms by the end of 1990. Much of this was spontaneous (self-) privatization whereby those in control of enterprises (often members of the old communist elite) transferred productive state assets into new private firms. This not only weakened the remaining state enterprises, but also provoked substantial public disapproval. In 1990, the process was greatly centralized and slowed down when a State Property Agency was formed to oversee all privatization. Reportedly, only about 300 enterprises were privatized in 1991, after which time Hungary became the prototype of slow and cautious, but solidly executed, privatization. By the second half of 1991, the process was again restructured to speed the pace.[8]

After much debate, in early 1990 the Polish government proclaimed the goal of privatizing 400 large and medium-sized firms (out of about 5,000) by creating twenty or so mutual funds, administered by Western experts, to control and manage them. A majority of the shares in these funds were to be distributed to all adult Polish citizens. But the number of firms to be included in the scheme has been reduced, and since the 1991 parliamentary elections the new government has delayed the entire process. Apparently, some of the same concerns raised by spontaneous privatization in Hungary have delayed large-scale privatization in Poland.

Czechoslovakia's privatization program is the only one (apart from the West German-sponsored program in the former GDR) that is seriously moving ahead. The program's ambitious goal of privatizing about 6,000 firms enjoys general approval among the population. The program has two phases. The first, carried out in 1992, privatized about 3,000 firms on the basis of plans selected from a number of competing proposals submitted by the Czech and Slovak privatization ministries as well as the Federal Ministry of Finance.

Privatization projects could be drafted by any individual or group, domestic or foreign, and may choose from various methods: direct sale to an individual, sale to a private firm (domestic or foreign), or distributing shares to citizens at large through an elaborate system of vouchers. Under the voucher system, each citizen who was a permanent resident of Czechoslovakia could purchase a voucher book with 1,000 investment "points" for 1,000 Korunas (Kcs) (somewhat less than one-third of the average monthly wage). About 8.5 million adults (that is, most of those who are eligible) purchased voucher books. During the first wave of privatization, voucher holders used the points to bid for shares of the 3000 or so companies being prizatized. Voucher holders could allocate part or all of their points to one or several of the 434 privately formed Investment Privatization Funds (IPFs), or they could bid directly for enterprise shares with their points.

The process of converting points into shares will consisted of rounds in which the bidders (individuals and IPFs) knew the calling price of a share (in terms of points) in each enterprise and submitted written bids. In each round, shares were exchanged for points if the supply of shares exceeded demand. When demand exceeded supply, points were returned, the price of shares was raised by the government, and a new round of bidding took place. The government hopes that the process will succeed and that many state enterprises will rapidly improve their economic performance and stop relying on government subsidies.

However, there are dangers: the cumbersome and risky process of distributing shares to citizens, the unregulated nature of the IPFs, potential conflicts of interest for many government officials, and too rapid approval of many projects invited corruption and caused genuine economic problems. For example, converting points into shares is a clumsy disequilibrium process whereby most transactions take place in a situation of excess supply. It contains a significant gaming element, as points are returned to those bidding for firms whose share prices are below equilibrium in a given round. Individuals and IPFs that do not succeed in converting points into shares thus forgo other opportunities in firms with excess supply.

Czechoslovakia's government indicated that enterprises whose share prices were bid up above 1,000 points could be taken out of the first wave of privatization. Individuals and IPFs that go through several rounds of bidding may thus forgo numerous other chances and end up being unable to purchase even a fraction of a share in their desired firm. This regulation, which amounts to reducing supply when demand is very high, may also destabilize the entire process. Without going through a formal proof, one can imagine the cascade as the "best" firms are withdrawn, investors bid up the prices of the next most attractive group of firms above 1,000 points, and the pattern intensifies as fewer and fewer firms remain in the game. Government officials seemed unaware of or undisturbed by this aspect of the process when one of the authors brought it to their attention in mid-January 1992.

Investment Privatization Funds (IPFs) are still virtually unregulated. Requirements for starting such a fund was the deposit of 100,000 Kcs (about $3,300), proof of having a net worth of at least 1 million Kcs (about $33,000) somewhere in the world, and a signed declaration of willingness to obey a law (yet to be passed) regulating IPFs. With threshold conditions so low, 434 IPFs quickly emerged, some affiliated with reputable organizations (for example, banks) and others representing fly-by-night organizations. IPFs immediately started to compete for voucher books, and in January 1992 a number of IPFs formally offered to pay fixed multiples of the purchase value of the voucher books (1,000 Kcs). In particular, each IPF promised to pay its clients in exactly one year a guaranteed sum (usually 10,000–15,000 Kcs) for the shares held for them by the IPF. These offers were important because they stimulated most Czechoslovaks to buy voucher books. Within a matter of weeks, the number of individuals holding voucher books increased from 1.5 million to 8.5 million.

The mass purchase of vouchers increased the effective demand for shares and, with a fixed number of firms tentatively slated for privatization, it greatly reduced the value of each voucher book. The promise of an attractive payout by some IPFs after one year also spurred the number of registrations in these IPFs and created a significant danger of a run on the unregulated funds in a year's time. Meanwhile, the funds realized that each voucher book was worth considerably less than was expected with 1.5 million registrants, and some withdrew from the game. The most recent event was the drafting of a regulatory law requiring IPFs to follow certain regulatory procedures. Some funds reacted by rescinding their offer of a fixed payout or stopped operating altogether, while others conformed.

The privatization ministries responded by attempting to increase the proportion of shares slated for voucher privatization in individual projects. While this move was meant to increase the supply of shares for voucher privatization, the important side effect—giving greater importance to voucher holders than to other owners—was to disperse the ownership of many firms. Thus the problem of dispersed ownership and inadequate corporate governance, inherent in the voucher privatization method, was exacerbated.

Other potential problems are conflicts of interest and use of inside information. In particular, it is rumored that privatization officials or their close relatives have either established IPFs or serve on their boards of directors.

The Czechoslovak privatization process is clearly a major experiment. Before passing judgment, one should remember that, except for the GDR, Czechoslovakia has embarked on the most ambitious project of large-scale privatization in Eastern Europe and that similar schemes are currently being introduced in Romania, the Ukraine, and Russia.

Banking and Capital Markets

A major challenge for all the transforming economies has been to create a functioning banking sector and to set up capital markets in general. The communist system ignored the importance of a capital market; the central bank and its branch offices fulfilled the role of both central and commercial banks. There were no bond markets, so government deficits automatically resulted in increased money supply. In most countries, investment funds were divided centrally among firms, and the taxing away (confiscation) of profits of moneymaking firms enabled the government to subsidize loss-making firms. Once established, firms were rarely closed down.

All Central and East European economies have attempted to convert the traditional "monobank" system into one with an autonomous central bank and a competitive commercial bank sector. The attempt has succeeded on paper, but in practice has so far been a resounding failure. The newly created commercial banks have usually rapidly emerged from branches of the former central bank, but this transformation has been more de jure than de facto. The commercial banks are undercapitalized, they lack capable professional staff (including loan officers), and the bulk of their assets has been loaned to bankrupt enterprises. The banks provide poor financial services, and their loan activity is frequently oriented toward state enterprises at the expense of new private firms.

An important policy issue that has not been adequately handled is whether state enterprises should be made to pay off debts accumulated under the previous system. What is becoming clear is that if the government does not assume the debt or fails to offer banks and enterprises some other form of bailout, many will be insolvent and even potentially viable enterprises will be forced to close down.[9]

The Western banks that have set up subsidiaries or branch offices in Eastern Europe have so far dealt primarily with joint ventures between local and Western firms. Their financing of domestic firms has been very limited. Excessive regulation, uncertainty, and inability to enter the deposit market have apparently been principal factors hindering the expansion of foreign banks in these economies.

Enterprises must look for credit to soften the impact of new economic policies and external shocks. Since credit through the banking system has been limited by restrictive macroeconomic policies, firms increasingly borrow from other enterprises. Carried out on a massive scale, this practice could threaten the transformation process and mean insolvency for many unprofitable state enterprises. Expecting across-the-board government intervention, even efficient firms are induced to enter the mutual borrowing scheme, often forcing the government and the central bank to abandon restrictive stabilization policies and bail them out. The Polish and Yugoslav economies experienced this phenomenon, and the resulting hyperinflation, in the mid- to late 1980s.

Foreign Trade and the Council for Mutual Economic Assistance (CMEA)

Under previous regimes, foreign trade was carried out almost exclusively through foreign trade organizations (state trading companies). This monopoly over foreign trade has been reduced or eliminated in virtually all the transforming economics, and enterprises have been encouraged to seek export markets. Most countries have also opened up to the world by replacing quantitative trade restrictions with relatively uniform and low tariffs. However, many state enterprises have not yet succeeded in penetrating and getting established in new markets.

Since the East European countries had traded largely with each other, CMEA members experienced a major shock when they dissolved that organization and severed their close trade relationship. The first shock came in 1990 when Germany was reunited, removing the GDR from the CMEA. The second shock came when the CMEA was itself disbanded and the Soviet Union began to disintegrate in 1991. Finally, the terms of trade moved against the CEE countries and Cuba on January 1, 1991, when much of the world's trade with the Soviet Union began to be conducted on a hard-currency basis.

Since the division of labor within the CMEA was not necessarily based on comparative advantage, since trade gains were unfairly distributed, and since the accounting system was extremely cumbersome, it is not surprising that member countries quickly moved to abolish the trading scheme. However, impulsively doing away with the system without constructing a superior alternative (for example, a free trade area) was one of the most costly policy blunders during the transition.

Labor

The labor market, which had been severely regulated in all CEE economies, continues to be regulated during the transition.[10] The heterodox macroeconomic stabilization policies that rely on wage (bill) controls as one of the three nominal anchors have had three main effects: (1) a dramatic fall in real wages; (2) a slower rise in unemployment than might otherwise have occurred; and (3) the perpetuation, and possible exacerbation, of labor market distortions.[11]

As can be seen from table 9.1, in 1990 and 1991 real earnings fell dramatically in all CEE countries, except for Hungary (where some declines had already occurred in the late 1980s). The decline is as severe as the worst fall in real wages observed in developing countries during the stabilizations and structural adjustments of the 1980s. Table 9.1 also shows that, as late as the end of 1989, unemployment was unknown in most of the transforming economies, but by the end of 1991 it was a serious problem, despite the dramatic drop in wages. Indeed, by the end of 1991, the unemployment rate exceeded 10 percent in Bulgaria, Poland, and Slovakia (within the CSFR) and it exceeded 8 percent in Hungary. The situation in 1991 was of course just the tip of the iceberg, and higher unemployment rates are expected throughout the region.

TABLE 9.1
Wages and Unemployment in Selected Transforming Economies

	REAL EARNINGS *(percent change from previous year)*				
	Bulgaria	*CSFR*	*Hungary*	*Poland*	*Romania*
1989	2.3	1.0	0.9		2.4
1990	−2.8	−12.5	−5.1	−37.2	4.6
1991	−33.8	−26.0	−5.8	−8.4	−24.9
	UNEMPLOYMENT RATE *(end-of-year data)*				
	Bulgaria	*CSFR*	*Hungary*	*Poland*	*Romania*
1989	—	—	0.5	—	—
1990	1.5	1.0	2.0	6.3	1.0
1991	10.5	6.0	8.0	11.4	2.2

Source: Various Government and World Bank data.
a. Real wages for employees

A major problem plaguing the transforming economies is labor redundancy. Estimates of overemployment before the transition ranged from 15 percent to 30 percent, and the situation was further aggravated during the transition. The number of jobs declined much less than output, and enterprises have thus continued to hoard labor. Indeed, many firms apparently respond to declining demand for their products by introducing a hiring freeze and dismissing employees on fixed-term contracts (especially retirees and foreign workers). Only later do they start laying off regular employees. The transition thus appears to have an asymmetric effect on the employment of various groups. In the early stages, the major impact seems to be concentrated on young workers, women, and minorities.

Another problem experienced by the state-owned enterprises operating under the wage (bill) controls is brain drain. In particular, these firms find it difficult to attract and keep competent managers, technical personnel, and skilled workers. From a social welfare standpoint, the brain drain is inefficient if the productivity of the quitting employee is lower outside of the firm. This is especially true for firms with valuable capital and in which workers have firm-specific skills.

Because the East European economies are resource-poor and a well-trained work force is their major asset, continued regulation of the labor market prevents state firms from motivating employees to perform more and better work. A preferable strategy would be to allow firms to pay higher wages if they can operate without subsidies and pay profit taxes as well as a preannounced rate of return on capital.

Industrial relations have also taken on new patterns as trade unions representing workers' interests have emerged in all CEE countries. Compared to the artificial 100 percent rate under communism, union membership has diminished significantly. New trade unions have had a hard time competing for members. Negotiations are usually carried out at the national level in a tripartite (government-labor-employer) setting. In view of the unions' fragmentation and legitimacy problems, many governments have not treated labor as a full-fledged partner in the negotiations. This is unfortunate, because although the unions have generally tolerated transition policies, they could become formidable adversaries if they decided to oppose the government in a worsening economic situation.

A related issue is worker participation in management. Participatory schemes were introduced in Czechoslovakia, Hungary, and Poland in the 1980s, although on a lesser scale than in Yugoslavia. The participatory institutions became significant in Hungary and Poland (but not in Czechoslovakia) after the disintegration of the communist regimes in the late 1980s. Many government officials and economic observers assume that employee participation in management, capital ownership, and profits is economically inefficient. However, as recent studies indicate,[12] the economic effect of various forms of participation tends to be non-negative and is often positive.

The Social Safety Net

All CEE countries have established or reactivated unemployment and social security benefits, as well as a host of active labor market policies such as job retraining and public works programs. Funds for these programs were available when the transition started, but the situation is becoming more difficult with the continued rise in unemployment.

At the end of 1991, Czechoslovakia and Poland, for instance, reduced unemployment benefits and cut the coverage period from one year to six months. Other CEE countries are facing similar pressures and are likely to follow suit. Retraining workers has been slow, and expenditures on active labor market policies are generally being marginalized as preoccupation with income support takes on a new urgency.

Obstacles to Transformation

Major barriers to the transformation appear to be the absense of a simple and consistent legislative framework for a market economy, the lack of institutions conducive to market activities (for example, tax, privatization, and auditing agencies), the bureaucratic, antimarket attitudes of many government officials, the shortage of physical and financial capital, and ignorance of how a market economy functions.

Especially troublesome is the slow evolution of the private sector. As China's experience indicates, this sector is crucial for economic transformation because it provides an engine of growth and dynamism; once firmly established, it forces the state sector to improve efficiency as well. In Eastern Europe, the sluggish growth of the private sector can be largely attributed to underdeveloped financial markets, the limited collateral of the new entrepreneurs, and the high interest rates that have accompanied restrictive macroeconomic policies.

An important lesson from the CEE experience is, therefore, that encouraging the development of a well-functioning market is more like nurturing a greenhouse plant than the rapid growth of weeds. Considerable guidance and assistance from the government is needed to carry out a successful transformation.

Implications for Economic Transition in Cuba

Given the systemic similarities between the CEE countries and Cuba, the experiences in countries undergoing a transition are relevant for designing an effective strategy for Cuba. However, there are vast differences between conditions in today's Cuba and in the East European nations before the transition.[13] As Janos Kornai puts it in *The Road to a Free Economy,*

> A rather common mistake is to oversimplify and suggest that others imitate one's example. Visitors arrive in Eastern Europe laden with ready-made recipes promising instant success. "Just do what we do at home and everything will be all right." Maybe so—but maybe not. This book repeatedly reminds the reader that we have to keep in mind the peculiar *initial conditions* of the transformation.[14]

Some unique features of the Cuban economy are relevant to this analysis.

Degree of Collectivization

State ownership of the means of production is more extensive in contemporary Cuba than it was in Eastern Europe—and probably higher than in all other centrally planned economies, with the possible exception of North Korea. Comparable statistics on collectivization in socialist nations are not available. Table 9.2 presents some figures that, although not strictly comparable in coverage or time period, suggest that state control of the economy is substantially higher in today's Cuba than it has been elsewhere.

This difference is most marked in agriculture. For the four European socialist countries listed in table 9.2, the proportion of public ownership of the agricultural sector ranged from 6 percent in Bulgaria to 17 percent in the GDR, while in Cuba in 1988 it reached 92 percent. Two other features of Cuban agriculture are also relevant: (1) the collectivization rate has been rising (for example, it was 37 percent in 1961 and 70 percent in 1968);[15] and (2) the cooperative (*kolkhozy*) sector is very small compared to state farms; in 1988, cooperatives controlled 12 percent of agricultural land, compared to 80 percent for the state farms.[16]

TABLE 9.2
Nationalization Ratios for Major Economic Sectors (in percent)

	Bulgaria 1956	Poland 1960	Soviet Union 1959	GDR 1964	Cuba 1988
Industry	85	83	93	94	100
Construction	96	90	100	67	100
Transportation	100	96	100	96	100[a]
Commerce and finance	96	53	92	95	100
Agriculture	6	8	14	17	92

Sources: Bulgaria, Poland, Soviet Union, GDR: Frederic L. Pryor, *A Guidebook to the Comparative Study of Economic Systems* (Englewood Cliffs: Prentice Hall, 1985), p. 275. Cuba: José Luis Rodríguez, *Estrategia del desarrollo económico en Cuba* (Havana: Editorial de Ciencias Sociales, 1990), p. 61.

Note: These figures are not strictly comparable, but provide some rough notion of the importance of the state sector in each of the countries. Thus, they should not be considered as point estimates, but rather as indicators of the order of magnitude of collectivization. Data for Bulgaria, Poland, Soviet Union, and GDR refer to the "nationalization ratio," or the ratio of the economically active population in publicly owned enterprises to the total economically active population in the corresponding branch or sector. Data for Cuba are based on the percentage of state ownership of production units.

a. Excludes a small number of private workers in cargo handling activities.

Extent of Market Transactions

A corollary to the previous proposition is that the private sector in the Cuban economy is very small and weak. According to official statistics,[17] 94.1 percent of the economically active population was employed by the state in 1989; nonstate agricultural workers represented 4.8 percent of the economically active population (two-thirds were small farmers and one-third cooperative members); and private salaried workers and the self-employed accounted for 0.4 and 0.7 percent, respectively.

Considering the very small share of nonstate employment, it stands to reason that the number of market transactions in Cuba is minuscule, except for second-economy transactions. This contrasts with the CEE nations (for example, Czechoslovakia, Hungary, Poland), in which some promarket climate survived, despite centralized management of the economy, as a result of frequent contacts between their populations and the West European countries.[18]

In fact, since 1986, when the Rectification Process (RP) began, Cuba has reduced—virtually eliminated—legal market behavior. Among the first concrete actions taken under the RP were elimination of the peasant free markets and artisan markets that had existed since the early 1980s and severe restriction of self-employment in service occupations.[19] Recently, Cuba has also stepped up the enforcement of anti–black market regulations.

Previous Experimentation with Economic Reforms

The history of reform efforts by centrally planned economies is long and well documented.[20] It is fair to say that by the time they began to undertake comprehensive, market-oriented reforms in 1989–90, at least Czechoslovakia, Poland, and Hungary had already accumulated much experience with partial reforms and, in the interim, had adopted elements of market behavior in important segments of the economy. Hungary, in particular, could build on a solid record of privatization—decentralized management of state enterprises and liberalization of the financial sector and foreign investment—that earned its system the sobriquet of "goulash communism."

There are no reform parallels in socialist Cuba. After experimenting with alternative socialist economic models, including a radical

Mao-Guevarist model that emphasized extreme centralization, moral incentives,and elimination of financial controls, in the 1970s Cuba began to adopt the then prevalent Soviet economic model (before perestroika). The Economic Planning and Management System (SDPE), first implemented in the mid-1970s, introduced certain market-oriented instruments such as credit, interest, budgets, monetary controls, and taxes within a central planning framework.[21]

Whatever progress was made by socialist Cuba in rationalizing its economy in adopting the SDPE was reversed in the mid-1980s, first with the emasculation of the Central Planning Board (JUCEPLAN) and the normal process of developing the central plan, and then with the RP, the only case of antimarket economic reform in the contemporary socialist world (see chapter 6). If gradual experimentation with market-oriented reforms laid the groundwork in the CEE nations for the broad-gauged systemic changes that began in 1989–90,[22] it is fair to say that Cuba's resistance to perestroika and any form of market-oriented reform leave it much less prepared for such events.

Isolation from World Markets

Over the last thirty years, the Cuban economy has been largely isolated from world markets. In the 1980s, only about 15 percent of Cuba's foreign trade was conducted with capitalist or developing countries (table 9.3), a much lower share than for the CEE nations. The bulk of Cuban foreign trade was conducted with the Soviet Union and other CMEA members. This is consistent with the finding by some analysts that a larger share of the exports of the less centralized centrally planned economies went to Western markets and were thus subject to global competition and international standards.[23]

Several factors are responsible for Cuba's relative isolation from world markets, among them: (1) the sale of key exports (sugar, nickel) on preferential terms to CMEA members; (2) the shortage of hard currency and the system of barter exchange with other CMEA nations; and (3) overdependence on sugar as Cuba's main stock in trade and the failure to diversify exports to Western markets.

Upon joining the CMEA in 1972, Cuba accepted the role of raw material supplier within the socialist community. This meant that Cuba had preferential access to other CMEA markets for its raw material exports— sugar, nickel, citrus—so long as it imported goods from those nations. It

TABLE 9.3
Distribution of Cuban Merchandise Trade by Groups of Partner Countries
(in percent)

	1985	1986	1987	1988	1989
Exports	100.0	100.0	100.0	100.0	100.0
USSR and the East bloc	86.0	86.9	83.4	81.8	75.3
Other socialist countries	3.0	1.4	5.4	4.5	4.5
Capitalist countries	8.2	8.7	8.4	10.5	13.5
Developing countries	2.8	3.0	2.8	3.2	6.7
Imports	100.0	100.0	100.0	100.0	100.0
USSR and the East bloc	80.5	82.5	86.8	84.6	80.8
Other socialist countries	3.8	2.3	1.0	2.8	4.5
Capitalist countries	11.3	11.7	8.3	7.9	8.3
Developing countries	4.4	3.5	3.9	4.7	6.4

Sources: Calculated from data in Comité Estatal de Estadísticas, *Anuario estadístico de Cuba, 1989.*
Note: The East bloc nations are Bulgaria, Czechoslovakia, German Democratic Republic, Hungary, Poland, and Romania.

also meant that Cuba invested heavily, often using grants or loans from CMEA countries, in modernizing and expanding the production of sugar, nickel, and citrus. As a result, despite official rhetoric, a case can be made that there has been little diversification of Cuban exports in the last thirty years and that Cuba remains a raw commodity exporter, vulnerable to fluctuations in commodity prices in the world market.

The Cuban economy depends heavily on the production and export of a handful of basic commodities, in particular raw sugar. This overreliance on sugar and the relatively poor world market prospects for this commodity present serious challenges to reformers, as the notoriously volatile world market will make it difficult to generate revenue by exporting sugar.

Transition Strategy

The experience of the CEE nations suggests a number of policy elements that should be part of an effective transition strategy for Cuba. These are: (1) macro stabilization policies; (2) new legal frameworks and institutions; (3) freeing prices and opening up the economy; (4) creating economic incentives, the right to own property, and privatization; (5) labor market and wage controls; and (6) a social safety net. In addition, Cuba will need a strategy for obtaining external support.

Macro Stabilization Policy

Since collapsing communist governments frequently turn to budgetary deficits and monetary expansion (printing of money) as policies of last resort, macroeconomic stabilization is likely to be Cuba's first priority. As Czechoslovakia's experience indicates, stabilization is an important element of the overall package even when a transforming economy starts relatively close to a stable equilibrium.

Depending on how unstable an economy is when the transition begins, a stabilization program may use one or more nominal anchors. In Central and Eastern Europe, stabilization programs were cautious, relying on three anchors rather than just one—as would be suggested by classic theory. Authorities thus preferred to achieve stability even at the risk of creating or maintaining possibly unnecessary distortions. The stabilization was successful in the short run, especially in Czechoslovakia, Hungary, and Poland, where monthly inflation was reduced to less than 3 percent within six months. Nevertheless, the experience of developing economies suggests that initial macro stability may easily unravel if not accompanied by sufficient microeconomic change. The delays encountered in East Europe with privatization and problems associated with budget deficits indicate that this danger is real. This is especially so because the other short-term outcomes have been declining production in the formal (statistically recorded) sector, slow restructuring and reorientation of the large state enterprises, and only limited emergence of sizable new firms.

The Cuban economy is currently afflicted by severe destabilizing factors, both internal and external. Internal disequilibria are manifested in a growing budget deficit, estimated at nearly 8 percent of the global social product in 1990,[24] partly the result of "soft" budget constraints on state enterprises, and sharply reduced supplies of consumer goods under the rationing system. External disquilibria, in turn, are manifested in growing trade deficits and a very large foreign debt.

The severe macroeconomic disequilibrium in Cuba resembles the situation in Poland and Yugoslavia prior to their transition. Unless macroeconomic equilibrium can be achieved, or approached, it is impossible to achieve structural reforms leading to a market system.

In 1987, the Cuban government spent nearly 678 million pesos on price subsidies, 90 percent of which were for basic foodstuffs;[25] these subsidies represented 5.7 percent of overall state budgeted expenditures. Because Cuba has steadfastly maintained fixed prices, there is great pent-up demand for goods and services and the potential for severe inflation. In this regard, Cuba recalls communist Czechoslovakia, whose government maintained official prices largely unchanged. In contrast, Poland and Hungary effected comprehensive price reforms even before starting their transition to a market economy.

There is also evidence that Cuba suffers from severe monetary overhang—the amount of currency consumers have in hand because of the lack of goods to purchase with their wages and salaries. First, press reports suggest that black market activities have substantially increased, with unofficial prices several hundred percent higher than official prices. A recent report indicates that for rationed commodities such as eggs and coffee, black market prices exceeded official prices by 300–8,233 percent.[26] Second, according to official statistics,[27] liquidity rose substantially in 1988 and 1989 (to 4.0 and 4.4 percent of population income, respectively), after a much smaller increase in 1986 (0.8 percent of population income) and a contraction in 1987.

Finally, the Cuban economy also faces a substantial external debt and severe debt servicing problems, particularly when the hard-currency debt, plus the debt accumulated with the Soviet Union and East European nations, are taken into account. Indicators of Cuba's indebtedness and ability to repay (table 9.4) suggest that its per capita debt in 1990 was substantially higher than that of Hungary—the highest per capita debtor within the CEE nations—while its debt service ratios were more demanding than those for Poland and Yugoslavia.

Considering the severity of macroeconomic imbalance, designers of a macro stabilization strategy for Cuba might want to err on the side of caution and use multiple anchors to prevent inflation from unraveling whatever fiscal and monetary disciplines might be introduced in some areas.

A New Legal Framework and Institutions

A second priority is to create a simple, transparent, and consistent legal framework for a market economy. A fundamental lesson drawn from the experiences of the transforming socialist nations, as well as of other developing countries, is that such a framework is essential for the effective functioning of a market economy. The CEE countries are still

TABLE 9.4
External Debt of the CEE Countries and Cuba, 1990

	Net debt (billion dollars)	Debt per capita (dollars)	Debt as a % of exports	Debt as a % of GNP
Bulgaria	9.8	1,090	126	20
Czechoslovakia	6.3	400	62	5
Hungary	20.3	1,910	244	36
Poland	41.8	1,100	314	28
Romania	1.3	60	23	2
Yugoslavia[a]	15.6	660	84	34
Cuba[a]—Total	32.0	3,040	593	117[b]
Cuba[a]—Hard currency	6.2	590	115	23[b]

Sources: CEE Countries: John Williamson, *The Economic Opening of Eastern Europe* (Washington, D.C.: Institute for International Economics, 1991), p. 12. Cuba: Based on estimates in Jorge F. Pérez-López, "Economic Reform in Cuba: Lessons from Eastern Europe and the Soviet Union," mimeographed, 1990; and data from Comisión Económica para América Latina y el Caribe, *Cuba— Estudio económico para América Latina y el Caribe 1989* (Santiago de Chile, 1990).
Note: Figures may not be comparable across countries. For Cuba, the larger debt estimate is for total debt, including debt to Western countries, the Soviet Union, and Eastern Europe. The lower estimate is for hard-currency debt only. For CEE countries, debt figures may only be hard currency.
    a. 1989.
    b. Debt as a percent of global social product.

struggling to transform the communist legal system, with the outcome being an incomplete and sometimes inconsistent legal framework.[28]

Interestingly, none of the CEE countries that are striving to join the European Community has chosen to adopt a legal framework from a West European country or from the 1992 European Community framework. Since writing and calibrating new laws is a difficult and time-consuming task, Cuba might wish to consider adopting, early in its transition, portions of well-designed legal systems taken from other Latin American countries. The move would greatly strengthen the government's credibility, encourage foreign investment, and speed up the creation of well-functioning markets. From an economic standpoint, a key focus should be to set up a consistent commercial code as well as tax and bankruptcy laws.

Another prerequisite for successfully launching the transition is to establish key institutions conducive to macroeconomic stability and a functioning market system. Regarding monetary policy, Cuba's National Bank must be converted into an independent central bank, and the nation must have a competitive system of adequately capitalized, autonomous commercial banks. An independent, professional, well-staffed central bank is the best guarantor of a stable monetary policy and is crucial to a successful transition. A competitive system of commercial banking is indispensable for transforming state-owned enterprises and encouraging the rapid expansion of the private sector. In Eastern Europe, the commercial banks that were spun off the central banks continue to be over-regulated and underdeveloped, and the number of domestic and foreign banks with significant operations remains small. The influx of Western financial capital has been cautious and domestic banks frequently maintain large spreads between deposit and lending rates, and they continue to focus on their state-enterprise clients (debtors).

An especially critical problem in the transforming East European economies is the (understandable) unwillingness of banks to lend to new entrepreneurs who lack adequate collateral and business experience. This would seem to justify government intervention to encourage the development of the private sector—for example, through credit insurance. In addition to an economic rationale for such measures, there are political grounds, since the previous government prevented entrepreneurs from accumulating capital and establishing reputations in private-sector activities. The important lesson for Cuba in this context is that the ability to attract foreign capital and stimulate private-sector growth crucially depends on the government's financial-sector policies.

Other vital institutions that must be set up at the very start of the process are a central tax office and institutions for the transfer of standard accounting, auditing, and other information systems. A well-functioning tax office is essential because during the transformation the government loses its traditional sources of revenue (especially the confiscatory tax on enterprise surplus) and faces additional social and other expenditures associated with the transition.[29] Introducing audit and accounting institutions will stimulate the transition and deter large-scale corruption and illegal transfers of property, thus enhancing the legitimacy of the transformation.

Liberalizing Prices and Opening up the Economy

Once the new legal and institutional framework is at least partially in place, it is sensible to free the prices of most tradable commodities and open up the economy to trade by making the peso convertible at least for current account transactions and establishing a competitive exchange rate. While it may make sense to keep the prices of basic commodities temporarily under control for social reasons, liberalizing prices of other commodities is desirable because it brings about the adjustment of relative prices to scarcity-reflecting values.

To ensure that the prices send relatively undistorted signals, a small economy like Cuba must liberalize trade. The Cuban economy, with its great openness, must move rapidly to reform its external sector to permit the freer flow of goods and services. Since complete trade liberalization might require costly adjustments, a reasonable approach that worked well in Eastern Europe (as well as in other countries) is to eliminate all quantitative restrictions and to impose a uniform, and gradually declining, tariff on imports. A uniform tariff of 30 percent, for example, would protect domestic producers who need time to adjust, but would also send a clear signal about relative prices on the world markets. The fact that the tariff would gradually decrease according to a clear, preannounced schedule would give producers a strong incentive to improve efficiency and adjust to the market system.

Liberalizing trade and eliminating the state monopoly over exports and imports will very likely mean, at first, substantially increased imports and a deteriorating balance of payments. In the short term, external financing from organizations such as the International Monetary Fund (IMF) would be critical in addressing these difficulties. However, Cuba is not eligible for such assistance because, although it was a founding member of the IMF and participated in the Bretton Woods Conference, it is no longer a member of the IMF, having withdrawn from that organization in 1964.[30] Thus the Cuban situation differs from that of Hungary and Poland, both IMF members prior to undertaking drastic reforms; instead, it resembles former nonmember Czechoslovakia, which joined the IMF in 1945 but withdrew in 1954. Czechoslovakia was rapidly allowed to rejoin: it applied for admission in January 1990 and was readmitted in September 1990.[31]

Critical to improving Cuba's trade balance over the medium term will be the ability to establish prices for Cuban goods that will make them competitive in world markets. Among the many variables that affect competitiveness, the exchange rate is probably the single most important. Cuba's peso is not convertible internationally and is significantly overvalued.[32] Achieving a value for the peso that will make Cuban goods competitive and ensuring the peso's convertibility will be important tasks for designers of Cuba's transition strategies.

Because of the historic closeness between the Cuban and U.S. economies up to 1959—a connection that will likely be restored after the transition—Cuba may have some options regarding exchange rate policies that were not available to East European countries. A key element of Poland's stabilization strategy, and one that required massive external hard-currency resources, was to make the zloty convertible.[33] Cuba might attempt to allow market forces to determine the value of the peso by first letting it float during transition and then pegging it to the U.S. dollar.[34] Pegging to the U.S. dollar at a fixed rate would be a strategy somewhat like that chosen by Germany, whereby a fixed rate of exchange was set between the East German mark and the deutsche mark. Exchange rate policies that imply giving up some sovereignty (for example, in the form of domestic monetary policy) are politically difficult and may not be feasible even if they are appropriate from a purely economic standpoint.

Incentives, Property Rights, and Privatization

Price and trade liberalization are conducive to efficient reallocation of resources. To make this reallocation effective and to improve production efficiency, economic agents must be given appropriate incentives. In a transforming socialist economy, this means that property rights must be clearly assigned and salaries of enterprise managers should be linked to performance. Privatizing economic activities is viewed as an effective solution to the problem, and the experience of Central and East European countries indicates that privatization of small and medium-sized enterprises encourages efficiency and results in welfare gains. Although there is no solid evidence to prove it yet, it is widely believed that privatizing large firms would produce similar results. A major problem that will face Cuba is that privatizating large state enterprises and farms is difficult and complex. Strategies designed in haste could lead to massive failures, possibly requiring government intervention to prevent bankruptcies, as occurred in Chile in the early 1980s.[35]

It is also important that privatization should not be viewed by the population as an unjust enrichment of a few individuals who happen to be advantageously poised, perhaps as a result of their advancement under the previous regime. Thus the policy challenge for Cuba will be to design a scheme that is both fair and economically efficient. The very high concentration of resources in government hands highlights the critical importance of privatization for Cuba's economic transformation. Clearly, the state must devise a way to turn over some, or all, of the productive assets it controls to the public before restructuring its economy. How should privatization be carried out?

Blanchard et al. make the useful point that there is no unique path to privatization, nor is there any best structure of ownership, as illustrated by the diversity of property ownership and management arrangements across market economies.[36] Various schemes that may be relevant to the Cuban situation have been experimented with in Eastern Europe (discussed above) and in Latin America.[37]

In addition to the panoply of privatization-related issues that must be examined by strategists plotting Cuba's transition to a market economy, there are two other factors: (1) how to create a system that optimizes the contribution of foreign investors, in particular the Cuban community abroad; and (2) whether there should be some compensation for assets taken over by the socialist government and how such claims should be paid. This last consideration is particularly important in the sugar industry, where 148 of the 156 sugar mills in operation in the late 1980s were built *before* the 1959 revolution and nationalized between 1960 and 1962. To further complicate matters, some of the nationalized sugar mills have been thoroughly overhauled and equipped with modern machinery and equipment.[38]

Labor Market and Wage Controls

As mentioned above, in the short term serious distortions in the transformating East European economies stem from labor market regulations. In order for Cuba to accomplish a speedier and more efficient transformation, it may be desirable for decision makers to impose strict controls on taxes and subsidies for state-owned units, but allow for a relatively free wage determination.

An effective labor policy vis-à-vis the state enterprises is also important since many firms are likely to remain in state hands for some time during the transformation. This policy should include strong incentives for managers and workers that link their pay to the firm's economic performance. Once the economy is open to trade and prices are liberalized, the remuneration of managers and other key employees in the tradable goods sector should reflect the profitability of the enterprise. Timely action in this area might give Cuba an advantage over its East European counterparts.

An issue that may emerge in Cuba, and one that has caused a major policy debate in Eastern Europe, is the impact of worker participation in management. Evidence from both Eastern and Western Europe suggests that this system may have positive rather than negative effects, as is often assumed.[39]

Social Problems

Unemployment, open poverty, and rising crime rates are relatively new phenomena in socialist economies that can exacerbate social tensions during the transition. The European experience suggests that the severe impact of rising prices (after price liberalization) of consumer goods on low- and fixed-income households can generate strong domestic opposition to reforms. At the same time, the government should give serious attention to creating an effective social safety net, especially for those entering the labor force and laid off workers—those most adversely affected by the transition.

A special challenge to reformers will be to design an adequate social safety net to assure that all citizens have access to minimum levels of consumer goods and services and training opportunities. As Campbell points out reformers face a dilemma:

> There seems to be general agreement that the government must provide some protection and compensation to people threatened by the twin forces of unemployment and inflation. Unfortunately, there is an inescapable conflict here—all the devices for providing a safety net are likely to slow the adjustments that reform is intended to force. Subsidies or tax relief that would cushion enterprises against losses and enable them to avoid major layoffs of employees prevents precisely what *must* happen to make the economy more competitive. Indexing wages of certain categories of workers, or indexing pension payments so that inflation would not impose hardship on pensioners, or promising compensation to particular groups who will suffer from a jump in consumer-goods prices requires either inflationary budget deficits and money creation, or tax increases that will exacerbate the costs of adjustment felt by others.[40]

The extensive social welfare system in contemporary Cuba (education, health care, social security, day care)—probably the most comprehensive and costly among all socialist nations—creates a singular challenge for policy makers during the transition. On the one hand, maintaining the system, which is highly valued by the population, would severely burden the state budget and threaten the ability to impose financial controls. Yet eliminating or significantly trimming the system would impose hardships on some groups and give rise to discontent.

A middle-of-the-road approach might be to take certain actions to contain or reduce expenditures while maintaining basic services for the neediest segments of the population. For instance, the retirement age in Cuba is very low in relation to life expectancy and could probably be raised. Similarly, those who use the health system make no contribution to costs; over time, a system of partial cost recovery could be introduced.

External Assistance

Cuba's successful transition from a centrally planned, communist system to one based on democratic principles and market forces is of considerable strategic importance for the United States and Western democracies. If properly designed and executed, Cuba's transition could be supported by foreign assistance that could ease many of the problems encountered by the CEE countries.

Substantial assistance from abroad would permit Cuba to enjoy some of the benefits that the GDR derived from West Germany's support, while avoiding some of the problems the GDR experienced. Cuba could use external resources to modernize its infrastructure, and thus attract private investment, while averting the overvaluation of the exchange rate and wages that accompanied German reunification and contributed to the declining competitiveness and eventual demise of the East German economy.

As Mesa-Lago points out in chapter 6, export diversification is imperative for Cuba's reentry into the world economy. Redirecting trade toward the North American market is also crucial. Among the most constructive ways in which the United States and other Western democracies could help Cuba in its transition would be to give Cuban goods greater access to their markets. This is especially important for sugar, since in the short term Cuba has few other export options, and trade in this commodity tends to be heavily regulated.

Another potential advantage for Cuba is that it has a sizable emigre population with market-related human capital and skills that are normally in short supply during the transition. If allowed to participate in the transformation, these individuals could greatly speed up the process. They could also serve as a powerful lobby in securing foreign assistance for Cuba during the transition.

Conclusions

The experiences of the CEE countries in transforming their economies deserve careful analysis by experts designing a transition strategy for Cuba. Because of the many systemic and other similarities between the Cuban and the East European economies, many effective transition policies for Cuba can be guided by the European experience. But there are also significant differences that must be heeded.

To summarize: the experience of the CEE nations suggests that an effective transition strategy for Cuba should contain the following elements: (1) macro stabilization policies; (2) new legal frameworks and institutions; (3) freeing prices and opening up the economy; (4) creating economic incentives, the right to own property, and privatization; (5) freeing the labor market and reducing wage controls; and (6) a social safety net. In addition, Cuba will need a strategy for obtaining external support.

A coherent theoretical framework for transforming a centrally planned economy to a market system has yet to be developed. Nevertheless, the experiences of the trailblazers provide a body of knowledge from which Cuba could benefit, at least by avoiding some of the mistakes made by others.

NOTES

1. This chapter does not attempt to lay out a transition strategy such as that outlined in Jan Svejnar, "A Framework for the Economic Transition of Czechoslovakia," *Plan-Econ Report* 52 (December 29, 1989).

2. For a fuller picture, see Jorge F. Pérez-López, "Economic Reform in Cuba: Lessons from Eastern Europe and the Soviet Union," mimeographed, June 1990; Ernesto Hernández-Catá, "Long-Term Objectives and Transitional Policies: A Reflection on Pazos' 'Economic Problems of Cuba,' " in *Cuba in Transition: Papers and Proceedings of the First Annual Meeting of the Association for the Study of the Cuban Economy,* ed. George P. Montalván and Joaquín R. Pujol (Miami: Latin American and Caribbean Center, Florida International University, 1992); and Rolando H. Castañeda, "Cuba: Una opción por la libertad, el desarrollo y la paz social," in ibid.

3. See Jan Svejnar, "Microeconomic Issues in the Transition to Market Economies," *Journal of Economic Perspectives* 5, no. 4 (Fall 1991): 123–38.

4. See Alan Gelb and Cheryl Gray, "The Transformation of Economies in Central and Eastern Europe: Issues, Progress, and Prospects," mimeographed, World Bank, 1991.

5. V. Tanzi, "Tax Reform in Economies in Transition: A Brief Introduction to the Main Issues," IMF Working Paper 91/23, March 1991. According to Tanzi, confiscation of profits yielded revenue equal to 10–20 percent of GDP.

6. See Michael Bruno, "Stabilization and Reform in Eastern Europe: A Preliminary Evaluation," mimeographed, February 1992.

7. Ibid.

8. See Kemal Dervis and Timothy Condon, "Hungary: An Emerging Gradualist Success Story?" presented at the Conference on Transition in Eastern Europe, National Bureau of Economic Research, February 22–26, 1992, Cambridge, Mass.

9. On this point, see also L. Brainard, "Reform in Eastern Europe: Creating a Capital Market," *Economic Review* (January–February 1991): 49–58.

10. See, for example, Svejnar, "Microeconomic Issues in the Transition to a Market Economy"; Svejnar, "Labor Markets in Transitional Economies," presented at the World Bank Annual Conference on Development Economics, April 30–May 1, 1992; and Richard Freeman, "What Director for Labor Market Institutions in Eastern and Central Euorpe?" presented at the NBER Conference on the Transition in Eastern Europe, February 26–29, 1992, Cambridge, Mass.

11. See Svejnar, "Labor Markets in Transitional Economies."

12. See Alan Blinder, *Paying for Productivity* (Washington, D.C.: Brookings, 1990).

13. See, for example, Stanley Fisher and Alan Gelb, "The Process of Socialist Economic Transformation," *Journal of Economic Perspectives* 5 (Fall 1991): 92–93.

14. Janos Kornai, *The Road to a Free Economy. Shifting from a Socialist System: The Case of Hungary* (New York: Norton, 1990), 20.

15. Carmelo Mesa-Lago, "Ideological Radicalization and Economic Policy in Cuba," *Studies in Comparative International Development* 5 (1970): 204.

16. Carmelo Mesa-Lago, "Cuba's Economic Counter-Reform (*Rectificación*): Causes, Policies and Effects," *Journal of Communist Studies* 5, no. 4 (December 1989): 105.

17. Comité Estatal de Estadísticas, *Anuario estadístico de Cuba 1989* (Havana), p. 111.

18. Jaroslav Fingerland, "Central and East European versus Soviet Economic Reforms: A Comparison," in North Atlantic Treaty Organization, Economics Directorate, *The Soviet Economy Under Gorbachev* (Brussels: NATO, 1991), pp. 206–07.

19. Mesa-Lago, "Cuba's Economic Counter-Reform," pp. 105–09.

20. See, for example, J. Wilczynski, *Socialist Economic Development and Reforms* (New York: Praeger, 1972); Paul Hare, "Economic Reform in Eastern Europe," *Journal of Economic Surveys* 1 (1987): 25–58; and Robert Campbell, *The Socialist Economies in Transition : A Primer on Semi-Reformed Systems* (Bloomington: Indiana University Press, 1991).

21. See, for example, Carmelo Mesa-Lago, *The Economy of Socialist Cuba: A Two-Decade Appraisal* (Albuquerque: University of New Mexico Press, 1981), esp. pp. 10–29.

22. This point is made by Kornai, *The Road to a Free Economy,* p. 15.

23. Stanley Fisher and Alan Gelb, "The Process of Socialist Economic Transformation," p. 93.

24. Estimated from data in table 5.7, this volume. The ratio has been estimated from the ex ante (anticipated) budget deficit and the official value of the global social product. On budget issues in Cuba, see Jorge F. Pérez-López, *The Cuban State Budget: Concepts and Measurement* (Coral Gables: North-South Center, University of Miami, 1992).

25. Eugenio R. Balari, "The Supply of Consumer Goods in Cuba," in *Transformation and Struggle: Cuba Faces the 1990s,* ed. Sandor Halebsky and John M. Kirk (New York: Praeger, 1990), p. 164.

26. "Cuban Black Marketeers Prefer Yankee Dollar," *Sun Sentinel* (Orlando, Fla.), April 12, 1992, p. 16A.

27. Comisión Económica para América Latina y el Caribe, *Cuba—Estudio económico de América Latina y el Caribe 1989* (Santiago de Chile: CEPAL, 1990), p. 33. See also chapter 5, this volume, on excess money in circulation.

28. Cheryl W. Gray, "Tax Systems in the Reforming Socialist Economies of Europe," World Bank Working Paper 501, Policy Research and External Affairs, Socialistic Economies, Country Economics Dept., September 1990.

29. Ronald McKinnon, *The Order of Economic Liberalization: Financial Control in the Transition to a Market Economy* (Baltimore: Johns Hopkins University Press, 1991).

30. See Joaquín R. Pujol, "Membership Requirements in the IMF: Possible Implications for Cuba," in Montalván and Pujol, *Cuba in Transition.*

31. Ibid.

32. Although the official exchange rate has the peso at par with the dollar, the black market rate is 8 Cuban pesos to the dollar or even higher.

33. See, for example, Jeffrey Sachs, "Building a Market Economy in Poland," *Scientific American* (March 1992): 36–37.

34. See, for example, Hernández-Catá, "Long-Term Objectives."

35. See, for example, Rolf Luders, "Chile's Massive SOE Divestiture Program, 1975–1990: Failures and Successes," presented at the World Bank Conference on Privatization and Ownership Changes in East and Central Europe, Washington, D.C., June 13–14, 1990.

36. Olivier Blanchard, Rudiger Dornbusch, Paul Krugman, Richard Layard, and Lawrence Summers, *Reform in Eastern Europe* (Cambridge: MIT Press, 1991), p. 31.

37. See, for example, William Glade, ed., *Privatization of Public Enterprises in Latin America* (San Francisco: ICS Press, 1991).

38. See Jorge F. Pérez-López, *The Economics of Cuban Sugar* (Pittsburgh: University of Pittsburgh Press, 1991), esp. pp. 37–43; and Nicolás Rivero, "The Future for Cuban Sugar," *F.O. Licht's International Sugar and Sweetener Report* 124, no. 10 (March 20, 1992): 158–59.

39. See, for example, J. Prasnikar and J. Svejnar, "Workers' Participation in Management vs. Social Ownership and Government Policies: Yugoslav Lessons for Transforming Socialist Economies," *Comparative Economic Studies* 33, no. 4 (Winter 1991); and S. Estrin, D. Jones, and J. Svejnar, "The Productivity Effects of Worker Participation: Producer Cooperatives in Western Economies," *Journal of Comparative Economics* 11, no. 1 (March 1987): 40–61.

40. Campbell, *The Socialist Economies in Transition,* p. 221.

10

Analogies Between
East European Socialist Regimes and Cuba:
Scenarios for the Future

◇ ◇ ◇

CARMELO MESA-LAGO AND HORST FABIAN

THIS CHAPTER looks at both the past and the future. It discusses whether the factors that led to the downfall of socialism in Eastern Europe—including the USSR—are present in Cuba, then explores potential politico-economic scenarios in Cuba, ranging from continuing the status quo to a breakdown of the regime. The authors do not always agree in their assessments, their divergences reflecting both the complexity of the problem and different approaches. The authors' differences are specified; otherwise, the chapter reflects shared views and conclusions.[1]

Similarities and Differences Between Eastern Europe and Cuba and Factors Leading to Change

Socialism in Eastern Europe and Cuba shared common features, internal and external, political and economic. But there are some Cuban peculiarities worth mentioning. Domestic political regimes in Eastern Europe were characterized by a monopoly of the communist party, with all state powers subordinated to the party leadership and practical prohibition of opposition parties, contending ideologies, and organized groups. In Cuba, Castro has been a charismatic leader exerting complete dominance for thirty-four years; such a long tenure has been rare in Eastern Europe. Castro has been bigger than the Communist party—in fact, in the 1960s he delayed its reorganization and denounced its interference in administrative affairs. He probably has amassed more power than any other world socialist leader except for Stalin, Mao, and Kim Il Sung.

The economies of all these countries were characterized by collective ownership of the means of production, with tiny and tightly controlled market activity, inefficient management, and low capital and labor productivity, slowed economic growth, and industrialization favored over agriculture. Cuba diverges in this last feature: it followed Soviet-style industrialization in 1959–64, but returned top priority to sugar production in 1965–70, then moved to a more balanced economy in 1971–85, and has emphasized agriculture (along with selected service and industrial lines) since 1989. Partly due to these zigzags in development strategy, Cuba is less economically developed than most of the East European countries. Furthermore, Cuba's economic growth rate in the 1960s and 1970s was lower than that of Eastern Europe (but higher in 1981–85), while consumer goods have been consistently scarcer on the island. Conversely, Cuban records on distribution and social services (particularly health care and education) compare favorably with those in Eastern Europe.

Externally induced components of socialism were crucial in shaping the regimes. The East European states replicated the Soviet model and acquiesced to the security and economic interests of the USSR, which usually dominated their domestic communist parties. The Warsaw Pact—controlled by Moscow—provided a protective military umbrella against the West, but was also used to crush any attempt to change the communist regimes of member countries. Cuba briefly tried the Soviet model of economic organization in 1961–65 and longer in 1976–85, but experimented with opposite radical-idealistic variants in 1966–70 (Maoism-Guevarism-Castroism) and since 1986 (the Rectification Process).

The Soviet model of orthodox political organization largely followed the same cycles in Cuba. For instance, the party did matter from the early 1970s to the mid-1980s, but since then its role has declined along with the overall process of deinstitutionalization. The island did not belong to the Warsaw Pact and was too far from the USSR to be threatened by military occupation or control. Cuba usually voted along with the USSR and Eastern Europe in the United Nations and other international forums, it supported the Soviet invasions of Czechoslovakia and Afghanistan (the latter at considerable political cost), and it collaborated with the USSR in military affairs and in some subversive activities in Latin America, Africa, and elsewhere (see chapter 3).

But Castro played a key role in the nonaligned movement and confronted the Russians on several occasions—as, for example, the deployment of Soviet missiles in Cuba in 1962, the fight with the pro-Soviet communist parties in Latin America in the 1960s (see chapter 8), purging the pro-Soviet Cuban communists in 1968, claiming (in the late 1960s) that Cuba was more advanced in building socialism than the USSR, and applying models of economic organization closer to those of Mao's China than of the USSR.

The East European countries and Cuba were integrated with the Soviet economy through the Moscow-controlled Council for Mutual Economic Assistance (CMEA) and bilateral trade and aid agreements signed with the USSR. These mechanisms forged a socialist international market that effectively isolated its members from the world capitalist market and competition, with negative effects on efficiency and productivity. Soviet price subsidies and loans to these countries avoided or delayed the painful adjustments demanded by the energy crises of the 1970s.

But some East European countries (Poland, Hungary, Romania, the GDR—with the FRG) had significantly expanded economic links with the West and the world capitalist market. Conversely, Cuba's economic relations with the market economies were considerably less developed, particularly in the 1980s. Finally, Cuba's dependence on Soviet trade and aid was the highest among CMEA countries because of its concentration on the export of one product. In summary, by the end of the 1980s, Cuba (except for Romania) was the most politically independent country in the Soviet camp, but was the most economically dependent on the USSR (and the CMEA). In addition, Cuba was one of the least developed and industrialized countries of that group of nations and was among those with the least economic links to the world capitalist market.

Underlying Factors Leading to the Collapse of Socialism

As Linden shows in chapter 2, a unique combination of underlying and proximate factors precipitated the downfall of socialism in Eastern Europe. Some of these factors are present in Cuba; others are not.

Lack of Political Legitimacy. Socialism in the East European regimes (excluding Yugoslavia) was imposed by the Soviet Union, working through relatively weak communist parties, and these nations were largely dominated by Moscow thereafter. Their populations viewed the Soviet Union with suspicion and fear because of past experience—it had seized their territory, had threatened or actually intervened in their affairs—or because people blamed the USSR for the communist regimes' policies. Therefore these regimes lacked political legitimacy and suffered from a moral crisis; only through repression, often exercised jointly with the USSR, could their leaders maintain control. Charismatic leaders who did appear usually favored throwing off some degree of Soviet rule, such as Imre Nagy in Hungary, Alexander Dubcek in Czechoslovakia, and even, when he denounced the invasion of Czechoslovakia, Nicolae Ceausescu in Romania.

The Cuban regime, on the other hand, was the product of a genuine popular revolution that enjoyed almost universal support, at least in its early years. And Castro's charisma and style of governing—constantly in touch with the masses—provided the cement that bound the regime together. In this sense, Cuba still has more in common with the USSR under Lenin, China under Mao, and Yugoslavia under Tito than with the East European socialist regimes. Even more, despite his enormous power and privileges, Castro has not gone to the extremes of the personality cult reached by Mao and the extravagance of Ceausescu. Although Castro's charisma and the massive support for his revolution have eroded considerably, he can still count on the loyalty of a significant portion of the population (now probably a minority, but this is difficult to assess due to the lack of fully free opinion surveys and elections).

Yet the execution of General Arnaldo Ochoa and imprisonment of several top Cuban officials in 1989, as well as public denunciation of widespread corruption since 1986, are symptoms of a widening moral crisis within the Cuban regime and its leadership, which has experienced very little turnover in three decades. At least until late 1991, the Cuban people did not see the USSR as an enemy but as a political ally and generous supporter; this view was constantly reinforced by Castro and the news media, particularly in the 1970s and most of the 1980s. The USSR did not dominate Cuba politically—we have noted that it was the most politically independent nation within the Soviet camp—but did exercise considerable influence due to Cuba's economic dependency. Cuban leaders deny this, portraying the advantageous trade and aid conditions with the Soviets as proof of socialist solidarity among equal states. Finally, the revolution's archenemy has been the United States: for more than three decades, Cuban leaders have used the U.S. embargo and other hostile policies as a scapegoat to hide their own mistakes and to force popular loyalty to the revolution and to Castro.

Old and New Alienated Groups. In the USSR and Eastern Europe, rapid and usually violent land collectivization generated wide resentment among peasants, many of whom died as a result or went to the cities and struggled for survival there. The repression of the church also created enemies. The most important and growing alienated group, however, were urban youth (who were more aggressive and less fearful than their parents) who—aware of the expanding gap between the government's promises and dismal reality—demanded more and better goods and services. It was mainly this group who demonstrated in the streets and openly challenged the regime (not only in Eastern Europe but in China as well).

Since 1989 Castro has reiterated in several speeches that his regime did not forcibly collectivize land, but that, conversely, more than 200,000 peasants were given plots at the beginning of the revolution and they have benefited from many government services. Not surprisingly, he has failed to mention the bloody repression of the peasant insurrection in the Escambray mountains and in the southern Matanzas plains in the 1960s (although there were comparatively fewer deaths in these uprisings), the gradual elimination of private small farms in Cuba (which have declined from 30 to 8 percent of total agricultural land in 1963–88), and the stern passive resistance from the remaining small farmers. But it is true that land collectivization in Cuba was more gradual and relatively peaceful, hence generating less hostility than in the USSR and Eastern Europe.

The struggle against the church was also more subtle and considerably less violent in Cuba. Finally, socialism was established earlier in the USSR and Eastern Europe—hence the phenomenon of increasingly alienated youth is not as well developed in Cuba, although it is becoming serious. (To cope with the problem, the Union of Communist Youth has recently organized entertainment activities for young people.)

Economic Deterioration. The average annual growth rate in the GNP in Eastern Europe was 4.6 percent in 1971–75 and slowed down or declined in successive five-year periods to 2 percent, 1 percent, and −1 percent, respectively. (See chapter 2, table 2.1.) A similar deterioration occurred in living standards. Reasons for the socioeconomic decline were the oil shocks of 1973 and 1979 (combined with reduced subsidies for oil imported from the USSR), less available credit from the West, and worsening domestic productivity. East bloc leaders dealt with these problems by repressing opponents and controlling potential sources of opposition,

paying off key social groups (as well as introducing market-oriented re
forms in some countries), and, in some cases, relying on the threat of
Soviet intervention to keep them in power. Except for the last policy,
Cuba generally followed the East European pattern, although the timing
of economic decline has been different.

While East European economies stagnated in 1981–85, the Cuban
economy (at least officially) registered the highest growth rates under the
revolution: an annual average of 7.3 percent for that period, about seven
times the East European average. Soviet subsidies and aid to Cuba in that
quinquennium were the highest since the economic relationship between
the two countries began in the 1960s. Therefore Cuba enjoyed more and
longer protection under the Soviet economic umbrella against needed re-
adjustments than its East European counterparts, nor did it have to increase control and repressive measures until later. However, in 1986–90,
as a result of the Rectification Process and negative external factors, the
Cuban economy declined by 1.3 percent annually, slightly worse than the
East European average (a 1 percent decline).

Although we lack accurate comparable data for the early 1990s, Cuba's economic deterioration in 1990–91 was apparently worse than in
Eastern Europe (or about the same) despite the latter's difficult transition to the market system.[2] Because Cuba was less developed and much
more dependent on the USSR than its socialist allies, the disappearance
of both the CMEA and Soviet aid, combined with dramatically reduced
trade with those socialist nations, has had more severe effects in Cuba.
Reentry into the world capitalist market is also more difficult for Cuba
than for its former partners because of its limited trade with market economies and its excessive concentration on a single export, sugar (about 76
percent of total exports) which has poor prospects in world trade (see
chapter 5).

The rapid, sharp deterioration of the Cuban economy has provoked a
similar decline in living standards and significant popular discontent.
(Because of Cuba's tropical climate, however, the population has comparatively fewer needs than in East Europe: there is virtually no winter,
hence less necessity for fuel, warm clothing, and extra calories to withstand the cold). Government policies to cope with the economic problems
are mixed: egalitarian distribution and unemployment compensation are
balanced against increasing control and repression (discussed below).
The current economic strategy will be unable to improve conditions at

least in the medium term, so socioeconomic deterioration will probably continue and with it popular discontent (see chapter 6).

A Close and Successful Capitalist Countermodel. The success of the European Community offered an appealing countermodel to the USSR and its brand of socialism in Eastern Europe. Contacts with the West (particularly by the GDR, Poland, and Hungary) and information transmitted by Radio Free Europe exposed the East Europeans to a prosperous consumer society, fueling their desire to "return to Europe."

Over time, however, the positive effect of the countermodel turned perverse. The East bloc nations' difficult transition to a market economy—which included declining national production, price increases, the first appearance of unemployment, and the unrealized expectations of Western assistance and investment—were widely publicized in Cuba. They are discussed in Castro's speeches and by the local news media, although, as we have noted, Cuba's economic deterioration in the early 1990s appears to be equal or worse than in Eastern Europe. Cuban exiles have not helped either. In 1990, when a so-called real estate registrar was opened in Miami, hundreds of exiles whose properties had been nationalized under the revolution rushed to pay $150 each to enter a claim of ownership. Although this procedure lacked any legal base, the Cuban media quickly publicized it and Castro warned that the exiles would take away all the nation's housing and factories, should capitalism return to Cuba.

Furthermore, Cuba is not in Europe; it is more appropriate to compare it with its Latin American neighbors who in the 1980s suffered the worst crisis since the Great Depression. Official Cuban reports of booming growth rates in 1981–85 were reproduced uncritically by the Economic Commission for Latin America and the Caribbean (ECLAC) and contrasted with overall economic decline in virtually the entire region.[3] Cuban standards in health care, education, and social security are indeed better than those in virtually all Latin American countries. Castro often quotes these statistics in his speeches to prove that in spite of the crisis, Cuba has performed well in comparison with its neighbors. On the other hand (as can be expected), the strong economic performance of Chile, the steady achievement of Colombia, the recuperation of other countries such as Mexico and Argentina, and the comparable social gains of Costa Rica—which in 1960 ranked well below Cuba in social indicators and now matches Cuba's attainments—are not publicized in Cuba.[4] Finally,

Radio Martí, the equivalent for Cuba of Radio Free Europe, has been operating for only a relatively short time and has recently been disturbed by Cuban exile politics. The self-image of Cubans is: "We are in bad shape, but Latin America and Eastern Europe are worse"; hence any desire to move toward a market economy is mollified by fears of negative consequences.

Proximate Causes of the Fall of Socialism

According to Linden, the underlying factors just discussed might not have led to change in Eastern Europe, or the transformation would have taken much longer, without certain proximate factors.

Existence of a Domestic Political Alternative.   This factor was more critical in Poland than in the other European socialist countries. The Catholic church and the Solidarity Movement were instrumental in voicing the opposition's claims and eventually organizing it to overthrow the regime. In Czechoslovakia, Charter 77 and the personality of Vaclav Havel were important; however, there were only individual opponents in Hungary and Bulgaria, and there were no public opposition figures in Romania. The underground movement was vital in some of these countries; also mass demonstrations and the exodus to the West (in the case of the GDR) precipitated change. Ethnic and nationalistic movements played a role in eroding the regimes in Yugoslavia and the USSR. Economic reform (particularly in Hungary and Poland) also did more to undermine the regime than to improve and save it.

Previous popular rebellions (Hungary in 1956, Czechoslovakia in 1968, Poland in 1981) created symbols and heroes that served as catalysts and rallying points for the opposition. But, except for Poland, broad opposition fronts were actually organized in the midst of the rebellion rather than prior to it. Finally, military and paramilitary forces stood aside when the final confrontation came, except briefly in Czechoslovakia and in Romania, where the Securitate sided with the regime while the army joined the revolt. Splits in the leadership, the pressure of world opinion combined with wide news coverage, and the knowledge that the Soviet Union would not intervene and domestic repression might have been ineffective are fair explanations for the military's inertia. (On the other hand, similar circumstances did not prevent the Chinese from successfully smashing the student movement in Tiananmen Square in 1989. But the absence of Soviet support and the simultaneous crumbling of other regimes were nonissues in the case of China.)

Regarding domestic political alternatives, Cuba resembles Romania more than the other countries. The Catholic church in Cuba does not have the strength of the Polish church, and, until recently, Cuban bishops were extremely cautious about criticizing the regime. But the church has been gaining membership and, in recent pastoral letters, the bishops have mentioned the problem of youthful unemployment and condemned the repression of peaceful dissidents. The Cuban trade union movement has been tightly controlled by the government since 1961 and faithfully played the role of "transmission belts." There is no significant ethnic or nationalistic movement in Cuba—a point noted by Castro; the island is linguistically and culturally homogeneous, and there is no realistic possibility that blacks could organize themselves along racial lines against the overwhelmingly white leadership.

The great bulk of those who opposed the revolution have left the country (the number of Cubans in exile represents 10 percent of the current population). Castro wisely allowed them to leave and, on several occasions, opened Cuban ports for a massive exodus (125,000 left from Mariel in 1980). In contrast to Eastern Europe, the relatively open door policy served as a safety valve for discontent and tempered the urge to rebel. In the last two years, the virtual impossibility of legal emigration—mostly a decision by the U.S. government—has led to a sharp increase in Cubans illegally attempting to sail to Florida, risking their lives on primitive rafts and boats. The closing of the door at the time of worst deprivation under the revolution must have increased internal tension and the incentive for *desperados* to revolt. An intriguing question is why Castro has not opened a port for another massive exodus. Perhaps he is afraid that such an emigration could paralyze the regime and precipitate open rebellion, as happened in the GDR.

The Cuban opposition movement abroad is weak, fragmented, mostly conservative, and mostly represented by old figures from the past. (The powerful Cuban American National Foundation, however, has been very effective in lobbying against a U.S. rapprochement with Castro.) In recent years a few small dissident groups have emerged on the island and received wide publicity abroad, but, by the end of 1991, most activists were imprisoned by the regime. Although still very weak in numbers and organization, the domestic opposition is slowly gaining in profile, self-confidence, credibility, and strength. There is also a large silent segment—a majority?—of the population that does not actively oppose the regime because of fear but is dissatisfied and wants some type of change.

Since 1990 some political organizations in exile have established links with the domestic dissident movement and challenged the regime to hold a public dialogue, a plebiscite, and free elections. Cuba has lacked both popular rebellions and strong economic reform movements; the mild reform of 1976–85 was aborted by Castro in 1986, and its leader (Humberto Pérez, head of the Central Planning Board) was dismissed, expelled from the Central Committee, and subjected to a criminal trial as an example for other reform-minded bureaucrats.

The armed forces and the security apparatus were purged in 1989: a popular hero of many wars, Arnaldo Ochoa, and some of his colleagues were executed, and the chief of the Ministry of Interior (MININT) was jailed and died soon after, apparently of a heart attack. Raúl Castro has led the armed forces throughout most of the revolution and is loyal to his brother Fidel; after the purge of 1989, Raúl took control of MININT by appointing one of his men. The possibility of a split between the two forces is slight. The government has stepped up repression in recent months, launching rapid action brigades who attack dissidents and protesters, warning the Catholic church to stay away from counter-revolutionary behavior, unifying the "forces of order" to fight corruption, appointing tougher judges, and imposing more severe sanctions against economic crimes (see chapters 4 and 6). Finally, the Cuban people are kept busy struggling for survival, waiting in long lines to buy consumer goods, serving in "voluntary" work in agriculture, and participating in demonstrations and political activities for which they are periodically mobilized; hence, even if they were not deterred by powerful disincentives, they would have little time left to organize themselves and oppose the regime.

Simultaneous Crumbling of Regimes and Soviet Acquiescence. Before the late 1980s, isolated revolts or challenges to the East European communist regimes were effectively crushed by Soviet military force (in the GDR, Hungary, Czechoslovakia) or stopped domestically under Soviet pressure (Poland). The Brezhnev Doctrine was nevertheless theoretically laid to rest by Gorbachev in the 1988 Soviet-Yugoslav Statement of Principles, and he later gave signs to Eastern Europe that the USSR would not prevent market-oriented reforms and democratization.

Gorbachev's acceptance of a noncommunist government in Poland and his visit to the GDR, which helped to delegitimize Honecker, were added signs that the green light for change was for real. He also persuaded the old guard in Poland, the GDR, and Czechoslovakia to avoid repression and to yield power. In less than a year, the communist regimes of Poland, Hungary, the GDR, and Czechoslovakia fell. In Romania (the country most independent from Moscow), Ceausescu rejected Gorbachev's reforms and resorted to repression to maintain his regime, but he was violently overthrown. The fiercely orthodox Albanian regime was the last to disappear. Eventually, the Soviet communist regime and the USSR itself vanished. The contagion factor, or domino effect, largely prompted by Soviet acquiescence, was crucial in the simultaneous crumbling of communism in the region. The falling dominos stopped within the confines of Eastern Europe, although the repercussions for communist regimes and the Left elsewhere have been remarkable and are still unfolding.

And yet the Cuban regime (like that of North Korea) not only has resisted change, but also (unlike North Korea) has moved against the current for more than six years. An obvious explanation is that Gorbachev's green light for reform was irrelevant in Cuba (as it was in China and North Korea) because Cuban socialism was not imposed by Moscow. We have already noted that Cuba was the most politically independent country of the Soviet camp and had defied Moscow on several occasions.

The second, more subtle explanation is that Cuba was somehow protected from the contagion effect, or simultaneous collapse of regimes. (We assume that having survived more than two years after the last East European communist regime fell—a year and a half after the USSR—Cuba is not susceptible to such contagion.) Unlike Romania, where the leadership also opposed change and was relatively independent of Moscow, Cuba is not in the region and, being thousands of miles away from Eastern Europe, was relatively insulated from the virus. The fact that several of the underlying and proximate factors of change are absent or more subdued in Cuba is part of the explanation.

Last but not least, Castro's launching of the Rectification Process (RP) in 1986, just as Gorbachev was initiating glasnost and perestroika, might have functioned as a vaccine to protect Cuba against reform. In fact, Castro has given this as one of several explanations of why the domino effect did not touch Cuba: the RP, he says, turned the path of the revolution away from the wrong road (the mild market-oriented reform of 1976–85). But other features of the RP have undoubtedly played a role in at least temporarily avoiding change in Cuba: the recentralization of decision making, the expansion of Castro's powers after 1986 and by a constitutional amendment in mid-1992 (discussed below), the purges of reformists and military intelligence leaders, the closing of the small space for cautious discussion on socialist reform, and the increase in control, mobilization, and repression of the population (see chapter 4). We also have noted that publicity about the negative effects of the transitions in Eastern Europe has helped to sustain the Cuban regime.

If Castro has succeeded in avoiding the collapse of socialism in Cuba, at least for the time being, he has been unable to protect the island from the enormous impact of the communist downfall in Eastern Europe and the USSR. Politically, the "loss of community" or membership in the socialist camp means that Castro no longer counts on powerful allies and an international forum to publicize his views, praise his accomplishments, or attack his enemies. Not only are his staunchest colleagues who once supported communist orthodoxy gone, but virtually all Eastern Europe has turned critical of the Cuban regime because of its lack of democracy, inefficient management, and stubborn opposition to change. Cuba's military involvements abroad have been severely impaired by both the grave domestic economic crisis and the lack of logistical support and weapons from the USSR, the GDR, and Czechoslovakia.

The U.S. invasion of Grenada, the defeat of the Sandinistas in Nicaragua, the U.S. removal of Noriega from Panama (actions accomplished with the cooperation of, or at least no significant opposition from, Cuba's former socialist allies), the withdrawal of Cuban troops from Ethiopia and Angola, the agreement with South Africa over Namibia, as well as the peace agreement signed between the government and the guerrillas in El Salvador (all with the collaboration of the USSR and the United States), and the disarray of the Left in Latin America have eliminated sources of support for (and involvement of) Cuba and have increasingly isolated the island. Finally, although Cuban trade with China has improved, that country is in favor of market-oriented reform, which Castro abhors.

Economically, the loss for Cuba of these world-changing events is even more appalling than political loss: the CMEA has disappeared, all Soviet aid has been terminated and trade reduced to about one-half, the supply of oil to the island has been cut by 56 to 70 percent, while aid from Eastern Europe has also ended and trade with that region reduced to a trickle. Because Cuba was so economically dependent on the Soviet camp, this loss acquires even greater significance. The RP might have helped Cuba to avoid the collapse of socialism temporarily, but it lacks a cohesive economic model and viable strategy to bring Cuba out of the crisis, and its antimarket features are serious drawbacks.

In summary, several factors that led to change in Europe identified by Linden in chapter 2 are so far not present in Cuba. What distinguishes Cuba are a regime established by a popular revolution, not by Moscow (as well as relative political independence from the USSR); the lack of a successful capitalist countermodel (and the negative effects of the painful transition in Eastern Europe); the irrelevance of Soviet acquiescence in reform; the lack of a contagion effect; and the absence of domestic opposition institutions combined with a small but growing dissident movement (though this factor was insignificant in Eastern Europe except for Poland).

On the other hand, Cuba shares most of the politico-economic characteristics of the East European regimes, including economic deterioration—which took longer to arrive in Cuba, but is apparently worse than in Eastern Europe, as noted above. Furthermore, Cuba's links with the world capitalist market were few and weak; reintegration into that market will be more difficult because of the lack of export diversification, and the U.S. embargo. Last, the Rectification Process strategy cannot turn the Cuban economy around. As time passes and the economic crisis worsens, the regime's ability to satisfy the population's basic needs rapidly declines and its domestic sources of support erodes. Whether it can maintain the present course or change it to avoid collapse is the subject of the next section.

Politico-Economic Scenarios

Due to the lack of free surveys in Cuba, it is impossible to tap public opinion about issues of continuity and change. Nevertheless, from conversations in Cuba and with experts abroad, we have compiled a list of educated guesses about what most Cubans living in Cuba would like to see happen:

- resolution of the current politico-economic crisis by the Cubans themselves; some might accept an international negotiated solution (e.g., through Latin America, the European Community), but most would reject direct U.S. intervention;
- a peaceful transition rather than a bloody confrontation or a civil war;
- greater political freedom and participatory democracy, not a dictatorship;
- preservation of the positive gains of the revolution such as social services; while most understand that some of those gains would be lost in a process of restructuring, few want to return to the prerevolutionary status quo;
- better economic efficiency and production of goods and services; most would accept some type of economic reform to achieve that end.

This formulation of the emerging national consensus is nevertheless rather vague, particularly on four issues:

- what kind of economic reform should be introduced: a centrally planned, market socialism, mixed economy, or a predominantly market economy;
- how to resolve the crisis peacefully and increase political freedom and democratic participation;
- how to preserve the social gains of the revolution in the midst of a severe economic crisis;
- what should be Castro's role in this process, if any.

Fidel Castro is the most important single factor determining Cuba's political and economic future, but possible scenarios will be influenced by another set of interacting factors:

- how much popular support is be left to the regime, how fast and to what extent its legitimacy is be challenged, and the degree of influence of various forces within the regime: orthodox Communists, reformers, and Castro;
- the potential development of a domestic opposition—semiautonomous institutions and social groups such as the church, dissidents, youth—and opposition strategies in Cuba and abroad;
- the politics of major international actors: the United States, the European Community, the CIS, and Latin America;
- the evolution of other Latin American economies and the transition to a market economy in the former socialist states (serving as successful or failed countermodels);
- the magnitude and speed of Cuba's oncoming economic crisis.

We will briefly review five political and economic scenarios, the first four assuming a continuation of Castro's leadership, the last one without him. They are: (1) continuation of the status quo; (2) growing militarization and repression without economic change; (3) a shift to a Chinese-Vietnamese model of political authoritarianism and market socialism; (4)

democratization and market-oriented economic reform; and (5) a break-down of the regime by legitimate electoral means, a military coup, or mass insurrection. We will discuss the political and economic features, supporters, advantages and disadvantages (or conditions and obstacles), and the viability of each scenario.

Continuation of the Politico-Economic Status Quo

This scenario involves the extension of current policies, which combine an opening in the external sector, very limited political concessions (for example, the right to directly elect members of the National Assembly, accepting Christians into the Communist party), and limited repression. The basic framework remains unchanged: a command economy (lacking traditional central planning but with a state-of-emergency program), a one-party system, and Castro's hegemony. This model is favored by Castro to avoid further reform, and probably by the orthodox and radicals in the central bureaucracy and the party; it is opposed—although not openly—by reformers and the growing group of the silently discontented, and publicly by the small dissident opposition.

This model faces several obstacles: (1) it is not bold enough to turn the economy around, while opening up the external sector (with economic orthodoxy at home) probably will not get enough international financial support to promote vigorous growth; (2) the political reform is too timid to make a significant move toward democratization, reduce domestic pressure, and respond to international expectations; and (3) as the economy worsens, there will be increasing discontent and demands for change.

On the other hand, if joint ventures and decentralization in foreign trade become significant in Cuba, such market oases will generate tensions with the larger economy, which remains highly centralized. For instance, joint ventures will be pressured to acquire inputs from state-owned enterprises instead of cheaper imports; a two-tier system of prices, wages, and exchange rates will create complications, and so forth.[5] Managers of these enclaves will push to spread their economic practices and standards to other economic sectors and demand price reforms and other market-oriented changes. Workers will push for wages and working conditions similar to those in the privileged enclaves. Private farmers and potential entrepreneurs will call for applying the same practices to the domestic economy. The mass of the population, excluded from the tourist foreign enclaves, will demand access to these services.

Such pressures will strengthen the power of the economic reformers, temporarily defeated by Castro's antimarket rhetoric.

It is likely, therefore, that the current approach will be replaced by one of the following scenarios.

Growing Militarization and Repression without Economic Change

This scenario seems to have been unfolding since late 1991 (at least according to Mesa-Lago; for Fabian's view, see the fourth option, democratization and market-oriented reform, below). There is a tendency toward increased central control, closing the debate, militarization, and repression of all opposition (see chapter 4). An antecedent is found in the late 1960s, when the government realized that its political and economic strategy (moral stimulation, the ten million ton sugar harvest) was failing and a crisis was imminent. But the current crisis is more severe: the survival of the revolution is at stake (hence the slogan "Socialism or Death!") and measures are tougher than in the 1960s.

Some steps already noted are the purges in the army and internal security forces, organization of rapid action brigades to physically attack the regime's opponents, a narrowed space for human rights activists, imprisonment of dissidents, announcement of reinstitution of popular tribunals, warnings and threats to church leaders and opponents, unification in one single command of all law and order forces, appointment of tougher judges, and more severe sanctions for economic crimes. Indications of militarization were seen in recent congresses of the trade unions (where all delegates were dressed in green fatigues) and of the communist youth, where Castro announced the building of "hundreds of tunnels" for the island's defense and involving young people in such activity. The army now protects food storage centers in the countryside, and the "integral system of enterprise improvement," tested and applied in military enterprises, is presented as a model for the civilian economy.

There is also increased mobilization, in a militarized fashion, of workers, students, women, and the armed forces to work in agriculture. Recently, Castro publicly denounced the violation of production "norms" assigned to those groups and demanded a better performance.[6] In addition, he has called for an "all-out war" against those who "ignore facts," "people who do not understand" the government strategies, those who "think that [our] problems are the result of stupid acts committed by [our] cadres," "pseudo-revolutionaries," "fifth columnists," "traitors," "cowards," and "opportunists." Furthermore, he has criticized those who are "allergic to the repetition of the same arguments," maintaining that, as in the case of religion where "dogmas" are constantly reinforced, the revolutionary leadership "should not get tired of repeating arguments ten times, a hundred times . . . a million times."[7]

The centralization of power climaxed in July 1992, when the national assembly amended two-thirds of the articles of the 1976 constitution, without holding a previous referendum required by the constitution. The modifications added powers to those Castro already had (president of the Councils of State and Ministers, first secretary of the party, commander-in-chief of the armed forces): he was granted the power to declare a state of emergency and suspend the constitution in case of war, imminent attack, natural disaster, or events capable of affecting internal order and state security. He also took over the direction of the recently created National Defense Council, entrusted with managing the nation in a state of war or national mobilization or emergency.[8]

Possible causes for the growing repression in Cuba are the collapse of the USSR, which has left the United States as the only superpower and "world gendarme," combined with its tightened embargo against Cuba;[9] the growing assertiveness of the Catholic church and internal dissident groups (which have established links with exiled groups that share their views); the ideological and economic dangers implicit in opening Cuba up to foreign investment and reentering the capitalist world market; and the severe economic crisis and its pervasive social effects. These include increased theft of state property, declining labor discipline, growing unemployment, a booming black market, the resurgence of prostitution, and general delinquency.

The role of the United States requires special treatment. The Bush administration not only tightened the embargo in recent years, but also pressed the USSR to terminate economic aid to Cuba, pressured allies not to trade with Cuba, suspended or curtailed visits by Cubans to relatives in the United States, reduced the number of food packages that can be sent to the island, etcetera; furthermore, a law passed in 1992 prohibited U.S. subsidiaries abroad from doing business with Cuba (see chapter 6).

The U.S. government's view (supported by the Cuban American National Foundation) is that such measures will help to destabilize the Cuban regime and provoke its collapse. In addition to increased hardship for the Cuban people (many of whom oppose Castro), such U.S. measures reinforce the regime's siege mentality and help to rationalize increased repression. It should be pointed out that both Catholic bishops and well-known Cuban dissidents (such as Elizardo Sánchez) have called for an end to the U.S. embargo. Another approach, advocated by several Latin American and European leaders (as well as a minority of Cuban exiles), is to encourage internal democratization through a policy of detente, dialogue-bargaining, and openings in trade and communication. Noting that the hostile U.S. approach has failed to change Cuba for more than three decades, this group argues that detente helped to transform Eastern Europe and might be successful in Cuba as well.

The repressive option appears to be embraced by Castro as well as by the military and security forces. The army is the most powerful institution in Cuba (the biggest in soldier per capita in Latin America), and its successes in Africa brought prestige and privilege to its members. But in the late 1980s, the withdrawal of Cuban troops from Africa and the Ochoa affair diminished the military's role and prestige. The share of defense and security in the national budget increased from 5.4 to 10.7 percent in 1980–86, but declined to 9.6 percent in 1990. An increase in domestic militarization and security could restore the old status of these institutions and preserve at least some of their privileges in an environment of rapidly declining living standards. Furthermore, the East European experience has taught Cuban military and security personnel that they would be the big losers if the regime collapsed. There are rumors that former security personnel from Eastern Europe are now advising the Cuban government.

This option might succeed for a time, because the Castro brothers have a firm grip on the army and internal security, and these forces in turn have advantages in supporting their leaders. But defending the regime by repression would eliminate its remaining reservoir of political legitimacy and increase Cuba's isolation in the world. The European Community cut economic aid in the early 1990s because of Cuba's undemocratic ways, while Latin American and Spanish leaders have been pressuring Castro to allow multiple parties and free elections. Further hardening of the political situation on the island would close the few doors still open and discourage foreign investment. With a deteriorating economy and rising discontent, protests and opposition would grow, which in a chain reaction could provoke more repression. In the long run, therefore, this option does not appear to be viable.

A Shift to the Chinese-Vietnamese Model of
Market Socialism cum Political Authoritarianism

China's market-oriented economic reform is virtually a unique success story within the socialist world and is inspiring similar types of restructuring in other countries such as Vietnam. In 1978–90, real GNP in China grew at an annual average rate of 8.5 percent (11.2 percent in 1984–88), the real value of exports jumped fourfold, foreign capital utilized tripled, and savings deposits rose almost twenty-six times. This "socialist miracle" was achieved by expanding private village, group, and individual activities. Most agriculture is now done through contracts with villages and families. In industry the share of the village/group/private sector in gross output increased from 22.4 percent in 1978 to 53.7 percent in 1991.

Foreign direct investment expanded in three "special economic zones" surrounding Hong Kong (which has played a key role in the model), and a vigorous boom in those zones rapidly spread to other cities. Living standards have risen accordingly. Vietnam, which is more like Cuba than China (for example, having suffered a severe loss of trade with and aid from CMEA), has also applied a Chinese-style economic reform, with fair results: Vietnamese exports increased threefold in 1986–90, and Hanoi, a dead city before the reform, is now thriving.[10] Until 1989 economic reform induced a modest political opening in China, but the student demonstrations in that year ended in harsh repression in Tiananmen Square. Since then, the Chinese leadership has kept a tight grip on politics.

The Chinese and Vietnamese reform model has so far been rejected in Cuba. Some foreign observers as well as Cuban scholars and technocrats thought that the Fourth Party Congress would endorse a Chinese-style reform. There was wide support among the population for reinstating the free peasant markets and similar measures. The Congress did not even mention the Chinese model, and Castro has vigorously opposed market-oriented reforms in general and the peasant markets in particular. The congress ended by voting with the Maximum Leader: it supported an opening to foreign investment but maintained a command economy. Six months later, Castro admitted that some in Cuba still wanted the free peasant markets but again rejected them, together with any form of group or private contracts in agriculture, and insisted that the state sector would increase output—something that has not yet happened.[11]

As shown in chapter 6, Castro has resisted market-oriented reform (even of the Chinese variety, which controls against a potential collapse of socialism) due to both ideological and social concerns (inequality, corruption, erosion of revolutionary fervor) as well as the decentralization in decision making—and political delegation of power—which such reform entails.

Fabian argues that if Cuba's economic crisis persists or worsens (which is probable), pressure for economic reform will rise. Castro then might embrace Chinese-Vietnamese economic reform rather than democratization because its economic concessions would not immediately threaten his political control. But Mesa-Lago notes that a key element of the Chinese model (but apparently not as crucial in the Vietnamese variety) is not available to Cuba: Hong Kong. The analogy for Cuba is Miami, but it is not feasible under current conditions. More important, Mesa-Lago believes that even if Castro was forced to adopt the Chinese model, it would be jeopardized as soon as it threatened his political control. Mesa-Lago concludes that the chances of accepting this model in Cuba are low and, if implemented, it would not last long, unless Castro's power is significantly curtailed—an unlikely eventuality.

Democratization and Market-Oriented Economic Reform

This section analyzes these potential politico-economic changes in a regime controlled by Castro, and the next option considers them without Castro. These reforms can be combined in various ways; it is impossible to review them all here. Theoretically it is possible to combine democracy and a command economy, but in practice that combination has never materialized elsewhere. We assume therefore that a political opening would be accompanied by an opening to the market as well. The range of economic reforms is vast; it goes from Chinese market-socialism to the various styles of East European market economies. It is our feeling that the wider the process of democratization, the farther toward the market the economy will tend to move. Here we examine two kinds of political openings: a limited one under a one-party state and a more open variety of democratic pluralism.

Fabian believes that under the right blend of domestic and external conditions, Castro could accept and develop a strategy of "weak" (limited) democratization within a one-party state. There would be more institutional differentiation within the existing system (for example, between the party and the administration) as a substitute for the traditional separation of powers; more autonomy for some state and civil institutions (such as the National Assembly, unions, youth and women's groups); enforcing the rule of law and, especially, civil rights; allowing a semiloyal opposition within the party and in society; and asserting more government accountability and responsiveness.

This move would require a favorable environment: greater influence for reformers within the party and the government, strong civilian pressure, self-restraint on the part of the domestic opposition, and a U.S. disposition to engage in dialogue. Fabian argues that Cuban leaders are following an ambivalent, zigzag course rather than moving unswervingly toward repression. Castro is steering a ship in stormy weather; although he would like to follow a given route, he is forced to make corrections: for instance, he has made some political concessions, but they are minor and constrained by one-party rule; he has opened the economy to foreign investment, but has resisted full-fledged market reform. Within the party and the administration, too, there are diverse views on key issues.

The official politics, therefore—argues Fabian—are full of ambiguities and contradictions: between ideological fundamentalism and political pragmatism, between stimulating democratic participation and authoritarian centralism, between institutionalization and concentrating power in Castro, between tolerating a broader spectrum of political opinion and repressing critical voices, between nascent human and civil rights and arbitrary repression, and so on.

Fabian concludes that such weak steps toward democracy could help the regime in the short run, but the legitimacy of one-party rule and moving to a true pluralistic democracy would have to be addressed eventually. Castro could gain some time and political space under this option, but such an opening could unleash uncontrollable demands for further freedoms. Moreover, it is unlikely that the combination of favorable conditions would materialize. Hence the viability of this approach is low.

Fabian speculates that if Castro's other options do not work or threaten his power, he might, under an even more propitious set of circumstances, open the political system to include certain nationalistic reformist or social democratic parties. This scenario could follow the previous one, with the small, incremental changes (opening the external sector, weak democratization under one-party rule) setting in motion a process of true democratic reform. That option presupposes a growing political opposition as well as public protest and increasing strength among moderate reformers and the defeat of the hard-liners. This step could also be precipitated by the imminent danger of bloody popular rebellion or civil war.

International actors (the United States, the European Community, the CIS, Latin America) should support a peaceful transition and offer Castro incentives to move in that direction. Democratic reforms would have to be negotiated with him, and the price might be lifting the U.S. embargo and providing some economic aid. Most dissidents in Cuba endorse a strategy of public dialogue, negotiation, and national reconciliation, and some exile opposition groups are taking that stand as well. There are advantages for Castro in adopting this option: political stabilization of the regime, ending the international isolation of Cuba (and probably the embargo), and full reintegration of the island into the Latin American–Caribbean region; foreign investment, possibly including a group of Cuban-Americans who accept the negotiated solution; and control over the process of democratic transition and economic readjustment to prevent the elimination of the social assets of the revolution.

But there are risks for Castro as well. He could be defeated in free elections; the United States could use the opening to support the opposition and destabilize the regime; and Cuban-Americans might not invest in a mixed economy still dominated by Castro. In the short run this option is improbable. Up to now the political crisis has not reached the point where structural democratic reforms are inevitable—the leadership appears united, in firm control of the armed forces, and still benefiting from some political legitimacy. Furthermore, Castro has learned the lesson from Nicaragua, Eastern Europe, and the USSR (and the Latin American Southern Cone as well) that implementing a multiparty system and democratization usually leads to political defeat. If he takes that step, he should be certain that he can clearly win the elections (resorting to fraud would make things worse), yet his probability of winning declines with economic deterioration on the island. Furthermore, Castro fears the United States, and the latter is currently unwilling to lift the embargo.

Mesa-Lago disagrees with Fabian's view that Cuba currently follows a zigzag policy. Instead, since the end of 1991, there has been a clear trend of increasing concentration of power, militarization, and repression in the island. Furthermore, he has doubts that, even in a situation of extreme danger to the regime, Castro would be willing to accept pluralism and open his flank to pernicious U.S. influence. A constant of Castro's behavior throughout the revolution has been his struggle for political domination and his aversion to sharing power even with allies who disagreed on fundamental issues. Whenever the Maximum Leader perceived that his power was threatened or could be challenged, he promptly removed the obstacles in his path—for example, members of the 26th of July Movement and other groups in the revolutionary coalition in 1959 and the early 1960s, Guevara in the mid-1960s, the prerevolutionary communists in the mid- to late 1960s, the SDPE reformers in the first half of the 1980s, and possibly Ochoa and his group at the end of the 1980s.

It is thus difficult to conceive that Castro would risk his power in free elections or share it with an opposition whose ultimate goal would be to overthrow him. Castro has vehemently rejected a multiparty system and even minor concessions which—he says—would lead to more concessions and the ultimate collapse of the regime (see chapter 4). He also reiterates that he, the party, the government, and the entire nation are willing to die rather than to impair the system. In Mesa-Lago's view, therefore, Castro now has virtual total control and will rely on a combination of militarization, mobilization, and repression on the one hand, and the foreign economic enclaves, on the other, to save his regime. But that strategy will not work and the crisis will worsen.

Total Breakdown of the Regime

If forecasting the Cuban future under Castro is difficult, predicting the conditions of a downfall of his regime and its aftermath is almost impossible. This final section, therefore, only outlines a few possible prospects, particularly in the political realm. Cuban socialism may collapse after Castro's death or through elections (just discussed), a military coup, or mass action or insurrection. A U.S. invasion appears improbable, unless there is a civil war in Cuba.

In 1992 Castro was sixty-six years of age, aging but still fit and active; socialist leaders like Tito and Mao or fascists like Franco lived into their eighties and died from natural causes. And yet the Cuban crisis is so virulent that, without a dramatic change in policy, the regime is unlikely to last until he reaches that age.

If there is no peaceful transition to democracy, there will be a violent end to socialism in Cuba. Because the regime enjoys greater legitimacy than those of Eastern Europe and the population is more polarized (including a much more hostile exiled community), a civil war would take a heavy human, political, and economic toll. A massive exodus to the United States, resembling the flow of refugees into Europe escaping the civil war in the former Yugoslavia, would be likely. In case of war, Cuban exiles and other groups would pressure the United States to intervene—at a considerable cost in lives and property—and U.S. occupation would set the island back a century in its history. All this would make the process of reconstruction extremely difficult.[12]

A military coup is often cited as most likely to overthrow Castro. But the purge of Ochoa and his colleagues (as well as Castro's coup de grace, forcing all top military officials to publicly condemn Ochoa) has left no visible figure powerful enough to orchestrate a coup. And yet, Cuban military officers have had operative autonomy abroad and have been exposed to foreign ideas, including perestroika and glasnost. Still unknown leaders might possibly be capable of taking such action, particularly if the situation becomes intolerable, civil war (and potential U.S. intervention) is imminent, the standard of living of the military deteriorates, and the conspirators either believe that they can control the situation after the coup or receive assurances of protection in case of the regime's downfall.

A few experts on Cuba maintain that socioeconomic hardship is not enough to provoke a popular rebellion, particularly in a tightly controlled society such as Cuba's.[13] Another view is that with economic deterioration and desperation, mass demonstrations could erupt, triggered by innocuous events such as a riot in a food line aggravated by an attack from a rapid action brigade, a student rally, a religious procession, or a peaceful protest by a group of dissidents. It is symptomatic that after seriously considering welcoming a visit by the pope to Cuba, Castro decided against it: a gathering of hundreds of thousands of discontented Cubans to hear the charismatic pope could have easily turned into a massive demonstration against the regime.[14] Another indication of Castro's concern is the fact that he has not called for a new mass exodus, such as the previous ones in Camariocas and Mariel. In spite of its usefulness as a safety valve and food-saving device, such an exodus could light the spark of revolt. The constitutional amendment of 1992, which empowered Castro to declare a state of emergency and suspend the constitution, is still another sign that the Cuban leader fears mass rallies and prepares to confront them.

A crucial question is what the Cuban armed forces would do if ordered to fire against their fellow citizens. With few exceptions, the East European and Soviet armed forces refused to execute such an order, but the Chinese army did not and Castro hailed the action—although commenting that they lacked adequate riot control equipment (see chapter 6). If demonstrations cannot be controlled with nonlethal techniques and Cuban soldiers do fire on demonstrators, the isolation of Cuba would worsen and foreign investment and tourism would stop. In the case of China, the United States and other countries tried some minor sanctions after the Tiananmen massacre, but now relations are practically back to normal. But Cuba is not China, either politically or economically, and the U.S. and international reaction would probably be tougher and longer lasting. With ever worsening political and economic conditions, the probability of a military coup and/or revolt increases in Cuba.

Forecasting the type of political and economic system that might follow the downfall of socialism in Cuba is like "crystal ball gazing." If the ideal but improbable peaceful transition takes place through free elections, there are fair prospects for democracy in the long run. Eastern Europe has generally moved toward a more democratic system, and there are propitious features and influences that could encourage democracy in Cuba. The absence of ethnic or nationality divisions improves the probability of unity and stability. If Latin American nations retain democratic systems, their influence could extend to Cuba. And Cubans abroad could also be helpful if they support democracy, accept that the new leadership should come from inside, downplay their demands for restitution, control their urge for revenge, and lobby in the United States for economic aid to Cuba. But a military coup and a long civil war in Cuba could return the kind of dictatorship or strongman regime that has prevailed in Cuban history.

After socialism, Cuba would certainly move toward a market economy, but it is useless to speculate what exact mixture of market and the state would emerge. Svejnar and Pérez-López analyze in chapter 9 the economic differences between Cuba and Eastern Europe and outline a possible strategy for the transition. They also refer to similar exercises conducted by other scholars and groups.[15]

In summary, we agree that Cuba's current politico-economic model (*continuismo*) is not viable in the long run and will soon be replaced. Mesa-Lago sees a shift toward militarization and repression (without sig-

nificant economic change) since 1991. Fabian does not discard this option, but believes that democratization either within a one-party state is
possible (but unlikely), or under an opening that includes other parties
(although this is even less probable); Mesa-Lago virtually rejects that
possibility, particularly the second version. He and Fabian concur that
the Chinese model of limited market reform and political repression
would be more preferable to Castro than democratization, but Mesa-
Lago sees the chances of accepting the Chinese model to be low and, if
implemented, would not last long. Both agree that if there is no peaceful
transition to democracy, there will be a violent end to socialism in Cuba.

These outcomes would not only inflict grave hardship on Cuba but
also damage the prospects of democratization in that country and create
serious problems for the United States. A military coup appears (at least
to Mesa-Lago) as the most likely agent of change, while a popular rebellion appears a more remote possibility. In case of a socialist downfall
on the island, there probably would be a stronger move toward the market than if the Chinese model were adopted.

The prospects for democracy will vary depending on many factors
impossible to predict. We hope that whatever the new economic system
is, it is designed by taking into account the positive and negative experiences of adjustment and restructuring in Latin America and Eastern Europe. Above all, such a system should try to save, as much as possible,
the positive social accomplishments of the revolution while setting the
basis for a more efficient and productive economy. The stability and democracy of the new Cuba will largely rest on the success of an optimal
combination of growth and equity—a difficult but not impossible task
for the Cuban people, tested for more than a century in their struggle for
freedom and a better life.

NOTES

1. The first section of this chapter was written by Mesa-Lago, prompted by an anal-
ysis of chapter 2 and partly based on ideas from Mesa-Lago's paper, "Countdown in
Cuba?" *Hemisfile* 1, no. 2 (March 1990): 6–8, and Horst Fabian, "Will Cuba be the
Next Domino . . . ," unpublished, February 1992, Ivan T. Berend, "Remarks," Inter-
national Conference on "Cuba in the Post Cold War Era," University of Pittsburgh,
April 27–28, 1992, and other chapters in this book. The second section of the chapter is

essentially based on the organization and ideas of Fabian's unpublished paper cited above, with some additional data, interpretation and opinions from Mesa-Lago. We appreciate comments from Cole Blasier, Silvia Borzutzky, Jorge I. Domínguez, and Ronald H. Linden.

2. Estimates of 1990–91 annual GDP decline in Eastern Europe are about 10 percent; see Robert Holzman, "Adapting to Economic Change: Social Policy in Transition from Plan to Market," *Journal of Economic Policy,* forthcoming 1992, table A-2; and Andrés Solimano, "Diversity in Economic Reform: A Look at the Experience in Market and Socialist Economies," "Conference on Economic Reform: Recent Experiences in Market and Socialist Economies," El Escorial, July 6–8, 1992, table 6. Estimates of Cuban annual decline in GSP/NMP in 1990–91 range from 10 to 12 percent (see chapter 5). The average rate of open unemployment in Eastern Europe/USSR increased from virtually zero in 1989 to 5.4 percent in 1991 (Holzman, table A-4) while in Cuba it was 6 percent in 1988 *before* the crisis began (chapter 5). Cuba has avoided spiraling inflation but the scarcity of food is probably worse than in Eastern Europe.

3. See ECLAC, *Preliminary Overview of the Economy of Latin America and the Caribbean 1986 to 1991* (Santiago: ECLAC, 1986–1991).

4. See Carmelo Mesa-Lago, *Alternative Models of Economic Development and Performance in Latin America: Market, Command and Mixed Economies,* forthcoming.

5. Eliana Cardoso and Ann Helwege, *Cuba After Communism* (Cambridge: MIT Press, 1992), pp. 56–57.

6. Fidel Castro, "Discurso en la Clausura de la Cosecha de Papas en La Habana," *Granma,* May 1, 1992.

7. Fidel Castro, "Discurso en la Clausura de la Plenaria del Congreso de la UJC," Havana Radio, April 4, 1992.

8. *El Nuevo Herald,* July 13, 1992, p. 4A; ibid., July 14, 1992, p. 8-A. Domínguez makes a different point: Prior to the constitutional amendment, Castro could have performed de facto most or all of those functions; paradoxically, the new constitutional clause legally mandates him to consult with others before making those decisions (letter of August 18, 1992).

9. These reasons were given by the Cuban news media for the constitutional amendment of 1992.

10. Dwight H. Perkins, "China's Gradual Approach to Market Reforms," "Conference on Economic Reform: Recent Experiences in Market and Socialist Economies."

11. Castro, "Discurso en la Clausura de la Plenaria. . . ."

12. Some of these ideas came from Donald E. Shulz's and William LeoGrande's presentations at a conference on Cuba held at Dickinson College, 10 April 1992, and LeoGrande's presentation, "Scenarios for the Future," at the State Department, 27 September 1991. Other analyses of Cuba's political scenarios are by Manuel Ramón de Zayas, "Who's on First," *Apuntes Postmodernos* 1, no. 2 (Spring 1991): 8-26; and Edward Gonzalez and David Ronfeldt, *Cuba Adrift in a Postcommunist World* (Santa Monica: RAND R-4231-USDP, 1992).

13. Jaime Suchlicki, presentation at UCLA Seminar on Cuba, Los Angeles, February 28, 1992; and Shulz.

14. Castro may have been mindful of Pope John Paul's visit to Poland in June 1979. Certainly he was aware of its enormous impact. Of this visit, J. F. Brown commented: "The pope showed how many divisions he had! And apart from boosting the confidence of his compatriots, the pope's visit also helped make the situation in Poland the concern of the whole civilized West. It was over a year before the strikes began in Gdansk. They might well have begun without the pope's visit. But they would hardly have been carried through with the same determination and boldness of aim." *Eastern Europe and Communist Rule* (Durham and London: Duke University Press, 1988), p. 184.

15. A new strategy for a postcommunist Cuba is elaborated by Cardoso and Helwege, *Cuba After Communism*, pp. 53–114. A research project has just been launched by Florida International University's Cuban Research Institute to study future politico-economic changes and strategies in the island.

NOTES ON CONTRIBUTORS

HORST FABIAN was information manager in 1990–1992 for the Deutsche Gesellschaft für Technische Zusamenarbeit (GTZ) as information manager for Latin America and Eastern Europe. Since 1992 he has been a regional expert at the Centrum für Internationale Migration und Entwicklung (CIM) at Frankfurt-am-Main, responsible for Brazil, Peru, China, Malaysia, Philippines, Thailand, and Vietnam. His publications on Cuba include: *Der Kubanische Entwicklungsweg. Ein Breitrag zum Konzept Autozentrierter Entwicklung* (1981); *Ist Kuba der nächste Domino?* (1992); and *Wohin treibt Kuba? Szenarien der politicschen Entwicklung* (1992).

COLE BLASIER, now at the North-South Center at the University of Miami, served as chief of the Hispanic Division, Library of Congress. Until 1988 he was professor of political science at the University of Pittsburgh, where he founded the Center for Latin American Studies and organized the U.S./USSR Exchange in Latin American Studies (1980 – 1986). His special interests are the international relations of Latin American and post-1945 American foreign policy, with special attention to Germany, the USSR, and China. He is the author of *The Hovering Giant: U.S. Responses to Revolutionary Change in Latin America* (1976, 1985) and *The Giant's Rival: The USSR and Latin America* (1983, 1988) and is coauthor of *Cuba in the World* (1976).

SILVIA BORZUTZKY teaches political science at the University of Pittsburgh and Carnegie Mellon University. Her interests are South American politics and United States foreign policy. She is the author of several articles on Chilean politics and economic policies, and social security policies in the Southern Cone countries.

JORGE I. DOMÍNGUEZ is professor of government at Harvard University and chairman of the university's program in Latin American and Iberian Studies. He has served as president of the Latin American Studies Association and as chairman of the board of the Latin American Scholarship Program of American Universities. He is coeditor of the journal *Cuban Studies*. His most recent book is *To Make a World Safe for Revolution: Cuba's Foreign Policy*. He is at work on book projects concerning the Caribbean, Central America, and Mexico.

RONALD H. LINDEN is professor of political science and director of the Center for Russian and East European Studies at the University of Pittsburgh. He served as director of research for Radio Free Europe in Munich in 1989–1991. Linden has written numerous articles and chapters on Romania, East Europe, and international relations. He is the author of *Bear and Foxes: The International Relations of the East European States; Communist States and International Change: Romania and Yugoslavia in Comparative Perspective;* coauthor of *Politics and Government in Europe Today;* editor of *The Foreign Policies of East Europe: New Approaches;* and coeditor of *Elite Studies and Communist Politics.*

CARMELO MESA-LAGO is Distinguished Service Professor of Economics and Latin American Studies at the University of Pittsburgh and a former director of its Center for Latin American Studies. He has been president of the Latin American Studies Association, regional adviser at ECLAC, and a visiting professor or researcher at Oxford University, the Max-Planck-Institut, Instituto Universitario Ortega y Gasset, Instituto Torcuato Di Tella, University of Miami, and University of Madrid. He is the author of twenty-five books and more than one hundred articles or chapters in books, most of them on Cuba, and founded *Cuban Studies,* which he edited for twenty years. His work on Cuba has been awarded the Arthur Whitaker Prize, the Hoover Institution Prize, the Alexander von Humboldt Senior Prize, and the University of Pittsburgh President's Senior Research Award.

JORGE F. PÉREZ-LÓPEZ is an economist specializing on international trade matters and on the Cuban economy. His writings have appeared as chapters in several books and in professional journals such as *World Economy, Cambridge Journal of Economics, Energy Journal, Latin American Research Review, World Development, Journal of Inter-American Studies and World Affairs,* and *Cuban Studies.* He is the author of *Measuring Cuban Economic Performance* (1987) and *The Economics of Cuban Sugar* (1991) and the editor of volume 23 of *Cuban Studies.*

MITCHELL A. SELIGSON is professor of political science and research professor in the University Center for International Studies at the University of Pittsburgh. From 1986 to 1992 he served as the university's director of the Center for Latin American Studies. His research concentrates on Latin American development and democratization, and his most recent books include *Elections and Democracy in Central America* (1989) and *Development and Underdevelopment: The Political Economy of Inequality* (1993). He coedited *Authoritarians and Democrats: Regime Transition in Latin America* in 1987.

JAN SVEJNAR, professor of economics at the University of Pittsburgh, is the author of numerous articles and chapters in books on comparative economic systems and economic development, and labor market performance. He is a recognized expert on the economics of transition from planned to market economies and an adviser to the Czech and Slovak governments. He is also a consultant to the World Bank and PlanEcon and has served as consultant to the OECD Development Center, Paris, and the International Fund for Agricultural Development (IFAD), in Rome.

ALDO CÉSAR VACS is associate professor of government at Skidmore College, specializing in Latin America's foreign relations and political-economic issues. Vacs has published on Soviet – Latin American relations, including *Discreet Partners: Argentina and the USSR Since 1917* (1984) and many other studies. He has also published on Argentina's democratization process and the evolution of its political, economic, social, and foreign policies, South America's international diplomatic negotiations, and on the superpowers' role in the region. Vacs holds degrees in political science, sociology, planning and economic policy, and political science.

Pitt Latin American Series
James M. Malloy, *Editor*

ARGENTINA

Argentina Between the Great Powers, 1936–1946
Guido di Tella and Cameron Watt, Editors

Argentina in the Twentieth Century
David Rock, Editor

Argentina: Political Culture and Instability
Susan Calvert and Peter Calvert

Argentine Workers: Peronism and Contemporary Class Consciousness
Peter Ranis

Discreet Partners: Argentina and the USSR Since 1917
Aldo César Vacs

The Franco-Perón Alliance: Relations Between Spain and Argentina, 1946–1955
Raanan Rein

The Life, Music, and Times of Carlos Gardel
Simon Collier

The Political Economy of Argentina, 1946–1983
Guido di Tella and Rudiger Dornbusch, Editors

BRAZIL

Capital Markets in the Development Process: The Case of Brazil
John H. Welch

External Constraints on Economic Policy in Brazil, 1899–1930
Winston Fritsch

The Film Industry in Brazil: Culture and the State
Randal Johnson

Kingdoms Come: Religion and Politics in Brazil
Rowan Ireland

The Manipulation of Consent: The State and Working-Class Consciousness in Brazil
Youssef Cohen

The Politics of Social Security in Brazil
James M. Malloy

Politics Within the State: Elite Bureaucrats and Industrial Policy in Authoritarian Brazil
Ben Ross

Unequal Giants: Diplomatic Relations Between the United States and Brazil, 1889–1930
Joseph Smith

Urban Politics in Brazil: The Rise of Populism, 1925–1945
Michael L. Conniff

COLOMBIA

Economic Management and Economic Development in Peru and Colombia
Rosemary Thorp

Gaitán of Colombia: A Political Biography
Richard E. Sharpless

Roads to Reason: Transportation, Administration, and Rationality in Colombia
Richard E. Hartwig

CUBA

Cuba After the Cold War
Carmelo Mesa-Lago, Editor

Cuba Between Empires, 1878–1902
Louis A. Pérez, Jr.

Cuba in the World
Cole Blasier and Carmelo Mesa-Lago, Editors

Cuba Under the Platt Amendment, 1902–1934
Louis A. Pérez, Jr.

Cuban Studies, Vols. 16–21
Carmelo Mesa-Lago, Louis A. Pérez, Jr., Editors

Cuban Studies, Vol. 22
Jorge I. Domímguez, Editor

The Economics of Cuban Sugar
Jorge F. Pérez-López

Intervention, Revolution, and Politics in Cuba, 1913–1921
Louis A. Pérez, Jr.

Lords of the Mountain: Social Banditry and Peasant Protest in Cuba, 1878–1918
Louis A. Pérez, Jr.

MEXICO

The Expulsion of Mexico's Spaniards, 1821–1836
Harold Dana Sims

The Mexican Republic: The First Decade, 1823–1832
Stanley C. Green

Mexico Through Russian Eyes, 1806–1940
William Harrison Richardson

Oil and Mexican Foreign Policy
George W. Grayson

The Politics of Mexican Oil
George W. Grayson

Voices, Visions, and a New Reality: Mexican Fiction Since 1970
J. Ann Duncan

PERU

Domestic and Foreign Finance in Modern Peru, 1850–1950: Financing Visions of Development
Alfonso W. Quiroz

Economic Management and Economic Development in Peru and Colombia
Rosemary Thorp

The Origins of the Peruvian Labor Movement, 1883–1919
Peter Blanchard

Peru and the International monetary Fund
Thomas Scheetz

Peru Under García: An Opportunity Lost
John Crabtree

US POLICIES

The Hovering Giant: U.S. Responses to Revolutionary Change in Latin America
Cole Blasier

Restructuring Domination: Industrialists and the State in Ecuador
Catherine M. Conaghan

A Revolution Aborted: The Lessons of Grenada
Jorge Heine, Editor

SOCIAL SECURITY

Ascent to Bankruptcy: Financing Social Security in Latin America
Carmelo Mesa-Lago

The Politics of Social Security in Brazil
James M. Malloy

OTHER STUDIES

Adventures and Proletarians: The Story of Migrants in Latin America
Magnus Mörner, with the collaboration of Harold Sims

Authoritarianism and Corporatism in Latin America
James M. Malloy, Editor

Authoritarians and Democrats: Regime Transition in Latin America
James M. Malloy and Mitchell A. Seligson, Editors

The Catholic Church and Politics in Nicaragua and Costa Rica
Philip J. Williams

Chile: The Political Economy of Development and Democracy in the 1990s
David E. Hojman

Female and Male in Latin America: Essays
Ann Pescatello, Editor

Latin American Debt and the Adjustment Crisis
Rosemary Thorp and Laurence Whitehead, Editors

The Meaning of Freedom: Economics, Politics and Culture After Slavery
Frank McGlynn and Seymour Drescher, Editors

Perspectives on the Agro-Export Economy in Central America
Wim Pelupessy, Editor

Public Policy in Latin America: A Comparative Survey
John W. Sloan

Selected Latin American One-Act Plays
Francesca Colecchia and Julio Matas, Editors and Translators

The Social Documentary in Latin America
Julianne Burton, Editor

The State and Capital Accumulation in Latin America. Vol. 1: Brazil, Chile, Mexico. Vol. 2: Argentina, Bolivia, Colombia, Ecuador, Peru, Uruguay, Venezuela
Christian Anglade and Carlos Fortin, Editors

Transnational Corporations and the Latin American Automobile Industry
Rhys Jenkins